EDITING

**Recent Titles in
Bibliographies and Indexes in Mass Media and Communications**

American Journalism History
Wm. David Sloan, compiler

Guide to Sources in American Journalism History
Lucy Shelton Caswell, compiler

Better Said and Clearly Written: An Annotated Guide to Business Communication Sources, Skills, and Samples
Sandra E. Belanger, compiler

EDITING

AN ANNOTATED BIBLIOGRAPHY

BRUCE W. SPECK

Bibliographies and Indexes
in Mass Media and Communications, Number 4

GREENWOOD PRESS
New York • Westport, Connecticut • London

Library of Congress Cataloging-in-Publication Data

Speck, Bruce W.
  Editing : an annotated bibliography / Bruce W. Speck.
    p.   cm. — (Bibliographies and indexes in mass media and
  communications, ISSN 1041-8350 ; no. 4)
  Includes indexes.
  ISBN 0-313-26860-6 (alk. paper)
    1. Editing—Bibliography. 2. Manuscript preparation (Authorship)—
  Bibliography. 3. Publishers and publishing—Bibliography.
  I. Title. II. Series.
  Z5165.S67   1991
  [PN162]
  016.808′02—dc20   90-29290

British Library Cataloguing in Publication Data is available.

Copyright © 1991 by Bruce W. Speck

All rights reserved. No portion of this book may be
reproduced, by any process or technique, without the
express written consent of the publisher.

Library of Congress Catalog Card Number: 90-29290
ISBN: 0-313-26860-6
ISSN: 1041-8350

First published in 1991

Greenwood Press, 88 Post Road West, Westport, CT   06881
An imprint of Greenwood Publishing Group, Inc.

Printed in the United States of America

The paper used in this book complies with the
Permanent Paper Standard issued by the National
Information Standards Organization (Z39.48-1984).

10 9 8 7 6 5 4 3 2 1

Contents

Introduction	vii
Editing, General	1
Editing, Technical	101
Editing, Types of Publications	181
Abstracts	181
Advertisements	182
Anthologies	182
Booklets	182
Books	183
Computer-Based Education Lessons	194
Customer and Service Information	195
Direct Marketing Copy	195
Encyclopedias	195
Journals	196
Magazines	223
Manuals	237
Newsletters	241
Newspapers	248
Package Inserts	255
Patents	255
Presentations	256
Press Releases	256
Proceedings	257
Proposals	259
Reports	261

Teaching Materials	262
Translations	263
Author Index	265
Subject Index	273

Introduction

Editing as defined in this bibliography is the process of acquiring and preparing texts for publication. The bibliography says little about textual editing, the process of restoring a text produced by an author of historical or literary significance. The distinction between editing and textual editing is one of the few relatively clear-cut distinctions I have found in the literature on editing. However, even that distinction becomes a matter of degree when it is scrutinized.

For the most part, those who write about editing see it as a process that defies smooth, round categories. Is that the editor attending a lecture on biochemistry to become familiar with the work of a prospective author now lecturing on biochemical principles? Is that the editor eating lunch with a literary agent and learning that a best seller—for the right price—may be available? Is that the editor suggesting to a particular author that she might be just the person to produce a book on the Bolsheviks? Is that the editor answering the telephone, attending meetings, and writing letters to referees, but not putting a pencil to even one page of a manuscript throughout the whole work day? Is that the editor talking to a typesetter or a printer and discussing what grade of paper would be best for printing a particular job? Is that the editor writing advertising copy for a soon-to-be-released book? The answer to each question is yes, and we have yet to see the editor doing what editors are thought to do for a living: mark manuscripts.

Curiosity about the multifarious role of the editor, however, was not the genesis of this bibliography. Rather, this bibliography began with what I thought was a simple question: What is the difference between revising and editing? To answer that question, I searched the literature on editing and found only one book-length bibliography that listed materials on editing, *An Annotated Bibliography on Technical Writing, Editing, Graphics, and Publishing 1966-1980* published by the Society for Technical Communication (STC). Not finding an answer to my initial question and wanting to enlarge upon the editing component of the STC bibliography, I set out to produce an exhaustive list of annotated references on editing published from 1960 to 1988. My ambition to produce an exhaustive list was idealistic. I did not have the resources to acquire copies of *Blueline* or *The Editorial Eye,* two newsletters that publish articles on editing. (However, entry 12 in the bibliography points readers to one source that includes selections from *The Editorial Eye.*) I found out too late about the *CBE Style Manual,* so readers interested in a style manual for materials printed in the biological sciences will want to review a copy of that work. In fact, I did not adhere rigidly to the 28-year time frame, but included one entry published in 1959 and several published in 1989. In short, given human frailty (my own), the enormity of the task, the limited availability of resources, and time limits, I thought it wise to recognize that an exhaustive bibliography of the literature on editing is, perhaps, an impossible task.

To make manageable the more realistic task of providing readers with many of the sources on editing published during the last 28 to 30 years, I divided the literature on editing into three categories: editing, managing the editing process, and teaching editing. This bibliography covers the first category which includes materials that provide an overview of the literature on editing—general editing, technical editing, and editing particular

Introduction   ix

types of publications. I have reserved references in the second and third categories for future bibliographies on editing. The second category includes materials on the management of the editing process—hiring, training, and evaluating editors; preparing in-house style manuals; selecting referees and supervising the review process; determining the role of computer technology in the editorial process; and controlling editorial costs. The third category includes materials on teaching editing—methods of teaching editing, theories of editing, and textbooks on editing.

Although the present bibliography provides readers with sources under the first category, the categories are not mutually exclusive. It is not unusual for an article on editing to refer to a number of editorial tasks because editors, especially those in small organizations, perform various editorial functions. Rare is the editor who simply edits, especially since "simply edits" is difficult to define. Nevertheless, the sources in the first category provide a comprehensive view of what editing is and how editors edit.

This bibliography is the product of many colleagues' labors. I am particularly indebted to Richard Ramsey of Indiana-Purdue University at Fort Wayne (IPFW) for his valuable ideas about how to structure the bibliography. His significant advice about how to organize the literature on editing helped shape the final form of this work. Steve Hollander of IPFW not only rescued me from my ignorance about computer programming by setting up a database for the bibliography, but also prepared the camera-ready copy for the bibliography on his desktop publishing equipment. I called upon him often to employ his many talents in the service of the bibliography, and always he willingly and cheerfully helped. I owe him much. Since I began the bibliography while I was a faculty member at IPFW, I had the great opportunity to work with the librarians at Helmke Library—Marilyn Grush, Laura Neal, Cheryl Truesdell, Susan Skekloff, and Joyce Saltsman. Without their help I would not have been able to review the literature on editing, and I am deeply grateful for the professional assistance they faithfully rendered to me. My wife, Carmen, and children Heidi and Ryan have assisted with various administrative duties and have endured the humility of being next in importance to the developing manuscript that was to issue forth as the published bibliography. I appreciate their support and patience. Marilyn Brownstein, Senior Editor of Humanities at Greenwood Press, also has been extremely supportive and has graciously undertaken to tutor me on the preparation of bibliographies. Like the best editors, she would prefer to remain anonymous, but her professional advice should not go unmentioned.

Regardless of the lavish help an author receives in the preparation of his or her manuscript, a book—like its author—tends to harbor imperfections. As an imperfect author, I hope that my flaws have not unduly marred the presentation of the literature in this bibliography and that readers will be enticed to read and enjoy the literature on editing—the literature of a great and wonderful subject.

EDITING

Editing, General

1. Abshire, Gary M., and Dan Culberson. "'Editing Is Editing Is Editing' or, by Any Other Name, The Smell Is Sweet." *Journal of Technical Writing and Communication* 15, no. 3 (1985): 279-82.
   "An editor is a person who is trained in writing and language usage, who knows what correct grammar is, and who has a talent for not making a writer angry" (279). The trained editor does not use categories of editing, but uses a process whereby a writer's words are respected. The goal of editing is to please the writer and his or her audience. Thus the quality of the author-editor relationship is integral to the editing process. See 49.

2. Adams, Tom. "Be Your Own Editor." *Industrial Supervisor* 44 (1980): 6.
   Using three categories—usefulness, clarity, and accuracy—Adams lists questions authors can ask about their writing to improve it.

3. Arnold, Edmund. *Arnold's Ancient Axioms: Typography for Publications Editors*. Chicago: Ragan Report Press, 1978.
   Even though Arnold's first axiom is "take all axioms with a grain of salt" (1), he notes that if editors follow the axioms he teaches they "won't go wrong—at least not far wrong" (1). Arnold presents axioms for typographic procedures, body type, headlines, pictures, newspaper layout, and magazine layout. For instance, one axiom of typographic procedure is "type should be used to communicate, not ornament. The editor's basic job is always and only to communicate" (2). The two tools the editor can use to communicate are content and form. The alphabet is a primary form. "[T]hose 52 characters, the a-through-z's, and the A-

through-Z's, are the editor's main tools, irreplaceable ones" (4). To use the alphabet for typographic effectiveness, the editor should have a "smattering of ignorance" about the language typesetters and printers use when they produce a publication. Thus Arnold discusses the six type faces (and their families), emphasizing the need to keep type design simple. Editorial procedures also include preparation of copy for the printer, because in speccing "the editor must give the name of the type, the 'duplex', point size, leddin and line length or 'measure'" (11). According to one axiom, the editor should mark all editorial changes on the manuscript and keep a copy log, "a record of all material that the editor has prepared and sent to the typesetter or platemaker" (16). In reminding editors to correct galley proofs, Arnold says, "meticulous proofreading is the mark of an excellent editor" (20). Arnold discusses the book method and the guideline method of proofreading and three kinds of typographical errors. He advises editors not to ask for permission when circulating communal proofs, those approved by executives and other noneditors. In discussing body type, Arnold recommends using Roman type, saying sans serifs are not very readable, but are good for captions. Headlines, he says, should be written in the historical present tense and the larger the head, the more important the story. Axioms about heads include "avoid Shotgun heads. . . . Avoid bucket heads" (60), and "use cute heads sparingly" (61). In discussing pictures, Arnold recommends that editors make a list of old, stale poses and never "well, hardly ever" use them. To avoid pictorial cliches, "write out, in 25 words or less, just what you want the picture to say" (66). He discusses how to crop a picture and how to use catchlines and cutlines. He advises business editors to use names to identify executives and give unwieldy titles of executives "in a later paragraph of the cutlines" (79). One picture axiom advises editors to "use expo art generously" (81), and Arnold explains how to use screens to add interest to halftones. But "avoid montages. . . . Avoid collages! Avoid collages!" (84) two axioms warn. A discussion of mastheads and nameplates (flags) rounds out the section on pictures. The section on newspaper layout focuses on heads ("Every page must have a dominant head" [97]) and page design ("Every page must have folio lines" [98]). Arnold advises editors not to jump stories and to keep spacing consistent because "the convenience of the reader is always the prime criterion of good page layout" (105). In the final section, magazine layout, Arnold acknowledges the great variety "of page patterns that are possible in free-page magazines" (106), but notes that "the cover is the editor's most alluring bait" (107) and "Page 2 is a most important page" (108) because when readers open the magazine cover, they should be assured that the entire book will be "just as interesting as the cover" (108). To define the margins of a page, the editor can guarantee that "at least one element . . . touch each of the four margins of a spread" (113), and "nothing should encroach upon the margin" (113). Arnold also discusses headlines, scalloped pages, color, and paper. To test a layout, he recommends the finger-trace method. "Run your index finger down the column as the reader will consume the type," Arnold instructs. "Deliberately lift the finger off the page for the empty sweep, as the eye goes to the start of the next leg of type. Then lower the finger onto the paper again" (123). The finger-trace method helps the editor find "those sweeps which are too long or where the path has been interrupted by some non-verbal element" (123).

4   Bagby, Susan. "Editing as a Matter of Fact." In *The 577 Papers: Writing Processes, Editing Processes, Written Products,* vol. 1, edited by Roger E. Masse and Martha Delamater, 125-37. Las Cruces: New Mexico State University, Technical Communications Programs, 1983.
Editing by fiat is needlessly subjective, and unproductive. It damages relationships between authors and editors. Editing by fact is "coherent, concise, clear, objective, and factual" (128) and requires editors to treat authors and manuscripts with respect. For instance, editors can show respect for manuscripts by writing comments on the manuscript neatly and making major changes on separate sheets of paper. Editing by fact entails five steps: "Read the manuscript; outline the manuscript; edit for content, organization, and structure; edit for composition; and comment to the author" (129-130).

5   Baker, John F. "The Editor's Role." *Publishers Weekly,* June 7, 1985, 48-49.
Baker reports on the 1985 Jerusalem round-table forum, "The Editorial Vision in Today's Marketplace." General conclusions from the forum include: "the editorial process is very different in the Anglo-American publishing world and in Europe; that far too much is currently being written that is not worth publishing—and far too much is being *published* that is not worth publishing; that authors are skeptical of much of what editors do; that the pressure on editors, in these days of increasing commercialization, is intense and growing; that most editors do not feel close to the marketing process, accepting it, at best, reluctantly; that one of the biggest problems facing editors today is the quality of readers; and that there are as many answers to the question, what makes a good editor, as there are editors" (48).

6   Barzun, Jacques. *On Writing, Editing, and Publishing: Essays Explicative and Hortatory*. 2nd ed. Chicago: University of Chicago Press, 1986.

Divided into three parts, Barzun's collected essays cover a wide range of topics, including Lincoln's style, Poe's failure to proofread his French (and Poe's various editors' failure to correct Poe's French), a bibliographer's failure to write a useful bibliography, and editors' censorship of manuscripts by needless editorializing (all essays in section two entitled "Writers and Editors"). Section one is addressed to writers. Section three contains three essays. The first advocates the need for publishers to be business people. Good business practices would include better marketing (automatic vending machines for books, for example) and production techniques ("A modern book should be as light and handy and eye-gladdening as a package of perfume" [122]). The second essay disputes the need for the acknowledgement page in a book. The third is a series of playful letters between a fictional author and television promoters.

7   Bell, J. G. "On Being an Uncompromising Editor." *Scholarly Publishing* 14 (1983): 155-61.

An editor must compromise with authors to produce published works. Bell evaluates four categories of editorial work—acquisitions, substantive editing, language editing, and mechanical editing—to determine how much an editor can compromise. Under acquisitions, the editor should consider excellence, marketability, and politics when determining how much to compromise. Crucial to compromise in acquisitions is peer evaluation: "Only an author's peers, and preferably the most eminent of them, can make a reliable judgment of the book's excellence. . . . Get a report from the very best [reviewers] you can" (157), he advises editors. After acquiring a book, compromise in editing may be necessary; however, concerning substantive editing, the editor should defer to the author. "[T]here is no room here for being uncompromising, no matter how right one is. The editor's suggestions may make a good book more readable; but if it is a good book to begin with, it will be a good book no matter what happens" (158). However, if a book is too long for its content, the editor should be uncompromising in insisting that an author reduce the length to fit the content. If possible, an editor should compromise on the choice of a title, but should require one "that will not drain the blood from an honest sales manager's face" (159). In language editing—editing for clarity, grammar, syntax, consistency— "there can be no such thing as an uncompromising editor. . . . the editor proposes, the author disposes. . . . The process is strictly one of negotiation" (159). Mechanical editing also calls for compromise, unless an editor believes rules followed by copyeditors are inviolable. If authors resist suggested changes in mechanical editing, the editor "can make necessary changes without ever consulting the author" (160). In short, "there appear in the end to be only a few real-life transactions in which conscientious university press editors can be *relatively* uncompromising, and none at all in which we can let it all hang out" (161).

8   Berg, A. S. *Max Perkins: Editor of Genius*. New York: E. P. Dutton, 1978.

Berg's biography of Maxwell Evarts Perkins chronicles Perkins's editorial activity at Charles Scribner's Sons from 1910 to his death in 1947. The biography focuses on Perkins's professional relationship with F. Scott Fitzgerald, Tom Wolfe, and Ernest Hemingway, but Berg introduces a bevy of successful authors that Perkins edited. Of Perkins's relationship with authors, Berg notes that because Perkins was "more a friend to his authors than a taskmaster, he aided them in every way. He helped them structure books, if help was needed; thought up titles, invented plots; he served as psychoanalyst, lovelorn adviser, marriage counselor, career manager, moneylender. Few editors before him had done so much work on manuscripts, yet he was always faithful to his credo, 'The book belongs to the author'" (4). Because of his willingness to publish new writers, like Fitzgerald, "who spoke a new voice about new values of the postwar world" (41), Perkins consciously changed the standards of his age. Perkins caused this change by being an author's best friend, but he also had "two qualities that distinguish the professional editor: the vision to see beyond the faults of a good book, no matter how dismaying; and the tenacity to keep working, through all discouragements, toward the book's potential" (365). Yet, Perkins believed the editor ought to be unnoticed by the reading public: "'I think an editor ought to be anonymous. He should not be important, or known to be so, for the writers are the important ones in his life'" (420). Berg shows how Perkins practiced these editorial principles throughout his tenure at Scribner's.

9   Bessie, Simon M. "Small Publishing—Is It Beautiful?" In *The Art of Literary Publishing: Editors on Their Craft*, edited by Bill Henderson, 106-15. Yonkers: The Pushcart Press, 1980.

Bessie, a founder of Atheneum Publishers and executive and editor of Harper and Row, discusses the pros and cons of small and large publishing, saying both are needed. In recounting his experience at Atheneum, Bessie recalls, "to be small, independent and literary—which we were for years—is a rare and wonderful condition for the likes of me" (111). But during the 1970's, the publishing industry underwent changes that caused Bessie to return to a large publishing house, Harper and Row. At Harper and Row, he found that he could publish whatever he really wanted to publish, which was not often possible in a small house. A large house can do two things that a small house can't: very expensive projects and college or school text publishing. Yet, small houses continue to flourish because they focus on "two fundamentals of creative activity in a complex, industrialized society: Specialization and Doing Your Own Thing" (114). Both small and large houses are needed and "book publishing in our time. . . . can, indeed, be beautiful—large or small" (115).

10 Bestor, Dorothy. "Starting Out as a Freelance Editor." *Scholarly Publishing* 13 (1981): 55-69.

Citing the replies of 35 freelance editors to a questionnaire, Bestor outlines the job of a freelance editor. Generally a freelance editor begins working as a freelancer after being employed by a "commercial publisher, a university press, a newspaper, a printing company, or a periodical" (57), but having volunteer newspaper or newsletter experience, being a published writer, or taking courses in editing can also prepare a person to freelance. Freelancers acquire clients most often "through personal contacts, word-of-mouth recommendations, and repeat business from satisfied customers" (59); charge hourly fees, ranging from $5 to $25; and edit a wide range of documents. The biggest pitfall of freelancing is the feeling that "'you are never really your own boss'" (62), but most questionnaire respondents believe that freelance editing has "more satisfactions than frustrations" (62). For instance, a freelancer can find satisfactions from being part of the publishing industry and meeting other people involved in that industry. Bestor concludes by rebutting three misconceptions about freelance editing: it is (1) not just a moonlighting job, but "a serious and responsible exercise of trained judgement" (65), (2) not going to die out because of computers, and (3) not a diminishing market.

11 Bostian, Lloyd R. "Working with Writers." *Scholarly Publishing* 17 (1986): 119-26.

"Editors don't work in fortresses, wearing chain mail for protection, so they strive for effective compromises rather than unilateral decisions" (119). How do editors effectively compromise? They teach authors. But before teaching, editors analyze authors to understand an author's personality because "what writers think of their copy is far more important than its actual quality" (121). Editors must respect the writer's authority as a writer, but the editor also must teach the author how to improve his or her manuscript by querying the author. The best query is short and neutral. "A simple '?' may suffice, or an 'okay?' . . . Rather than writing 'You have an error on p. 2, line 18,' it may be enough to scribble a simple 'correct?' and underline the statement. Or to point out an apparent inconsistency: 'The number on p. 2, line 18 differs from the corresponding number in Table 2, column 1. Did you intend a difference?'" (122). The editor queries the author as a representative of the author's audience because editors are "advocates for the reader" (123). However, some author may not be capable of rewriting a manuscript according to an editor's specifications. Then the editor may need to edit a work substantively. However, sensitivity in copyediting is a trademark of good editors. Such sensitivity means an editor follows five guidelines, including working from a writer's strengths and being cheerful. However, even the most considerate editor may find situations, like editing material written by a superior, where status may interfere with the editing. In such cases, editors must make it clear that their editing and communication skills are professional skills on par with the writer's professional skills and that the editor can use his or her skills to help the writer. Women editors, in particular, may need to defend their editorial expertise against sexist treatment. "Above all, the editor must learn the fine lines between firmness and assertiveness, and between assertiveness and aggression" (126).

12 Boston, Bruce O., ed. *Stet!: Tricks of the Trade for Writers and Editors*. Alexandria: Editorial Experts, Inc., 1986.
The source for materials in *Stet!* is *The Editorial Eye,* a newsletter on publications standards and practices. *Stet!* is divided into seven sections: editing, writing, publications management, indexing, proofreading, lexicography, and the fine points (punctuation, spelling, usage). Most selections under each category run from one to three pages and range in topic from sexism (23-28) to levels of edit (69-79) to editing tests (178-180) to ellipsis (255-257). Throughout the anthology, Black Eyes, examples of incorrect grammar or usage, provide humorous mistakes ("From a book advertisement: SEXUAL HARASSMENT and other books that can make you a better manager" [189]).

13 Brett, Carlton E. "The Editor's Bootstraps." *Journal of Technical Writing and Communication* 1, no. 4 (1971): 307-16.
An editor should educate authors, and in preparing to educate authors, the editor "educates himself, and in so doing lifts his job by its own bootstraps" (308). Brett tells editors that when they train authors to pay attention to the details of preparing a manuscript, the editors elevate editing professionally. In particular, editors should create and use style

guides to teach authors about abbreviations, references, formats ("I preach flexibility," Brett says, "not a rigid format" [312]), and style. "Style is readability" (315), Brett notes, so simplicity is not improper when it helps an audience understand a document. But an editor may need to convince authors that simplicity is valuable because it can "prevent a slip of the mind from becoming a part of the permanent record" (316).

14 Bridgewater, William. "Copyediting." In *Editors on Editing: An Inside View of What Editors Really Do,* rev. ed., Gerald Gross, 69-88. New York: Harper & Row, 1985. (First published in *Editors on Editing,* edited by Gerald Gross, 52-70. New York: Grosset & Dunlap, 1962. Also published in *What Happens in Book Publishing,* 2nd ed., edited by Chandler B. Grannis, 54-79. New York: Columbia University Press, 1967.)

Although the rules of copyediting vary from publishing house to publishing house, ideally the copyeditor remains a professional who follows generally accepted rules of copyediting. For instance, the copyeditor should "aid the author . . . not judge him" (78) because a "book belongs primarily to the author, secondarily to the publisher, and not at all to the copy editor" (82). A copyeditor should have five qualities and interests: "he must love books. . . . he must respect authors. . . . he must have an eye for detail and a passion for accuracy in dealing with detail. . . . he must be truly familiar, even intimate, with the English language and current English usage. . . . [and] a copy editor must be curious" (87-88).

15 Briggs, Nelson A. "Editing by Dialogue." In *Technical Editing: Principles and Practices,* edited by Lola M. Zook, 56-61. Anthology Series, no. 4. Washington: Society for Technical Communication, 1975. ED 173 807. (First published in *Technical Communications* 16, no. 2 (1969): 10-13.)

Drawing upon Martin Buber's I-it and I-thou distinction, the author contrasts the I-it editor, one who views him or herself as an "ideal observer, audience-oriented critic, merciless examiner of the written word" (57), with the I-thou editor, one who respects authors by establishing a dialogue with them. An I-thou editor is concerned with "*a person* (not a piece of paper); with *subject matter* (the audience emerges only as a secondary consideration); with *improvements* (rather than corrections); and with the *mutuality* of editor and author (rather than the domination of one by the other)" (58). Dialogue, which preserves another's personhood, is not rapport, which does not allow for healthy opposition. Briggs discusses ten aids for practicing dialogue.

16 Brilliant, Alan. "The Decision to Publish." *Scholarly Publishing* 3 (1971): 55-57.

"The decision to publish . . . is an ethical problem" (55) because practical economy, pride, vanity, gluttony, and egotism are moral pitfalls that editors can fall into easily. How do editors/publishers escape these pitfalls? They must give a manuscript a fair reading. "It should take at least as long to read a thing as it took to write it. . . . if that manuscript isn't worth reading, really digesting, certainly you aren't going to spend the rest of the year producing it, are you?" (56) Brilliant asks editors. And editors/publishers should read the manuscript in an appropriate place. "The ideal place for reading a manuscript is the desert. And best leave your IBM Selectric behind. We can at least try to be fair to our authors" (57).

17 Broadbent, Margaret. "Productivity in Copy Editing." *Scholarly Publishing* 10 (1979): 170-74.

Because copyediting is a significant expense of manuscript preparation, redactorial offices may be able to increase efficiency and reduce costs by implementing certain copyediting practices. For instance, "journals should regularly publish specific Instructions to Authors, even though it may seem that authors never refer to them" (171), because authors that do comply with those instructions can produce manuscripts that will eliminate the need for some copyediting. In addition, the redactorial office should prepare a list of annual deadlines for printing manuscripts so that the editor can process manuscripts on a regular basis because "a crash program for handling late manuscripts is expensive" (171). Redactorial costs also can be reduced by training copyeditors using either a vertical or horizontal system. Under the horizontal system a trainee is trained to do one task. The drawback to the horizontal method is worker boredom, so personnel turnover is usually high, unless personnel advance rapidly. Under the vertical system, copyeditors learn the entire production process, so they are given greater responsibility for the entire manuscript's production. However, workers need a supervisor to train them and act as a quality controller. Of course the "judicious use of freelance copy editors" (174) reduces overhead costs. "There is no substitute, however, for copy editors that are full-time in the office" (174).

18 Broadhead, Glenn J., and Richard C. Freed. "Studying Revision in 'Real-World' Contexts." In *Proceedings A[merican] B[usiness] C[ommunication] A[ssociation] Midwest Regional Conference. Bridging the Gap: From Ivory to Corporate Tower,* edited by Patricia

Pearson, 16-26. Urbana-Champaign: American Business Communication Association, 1984.

Contains much of the information in the authors' "The Variables of Revision" (19). Please see the annotation for that article.

19 Broadhead, Glenn J., and Richard C. Freed. "The Variables of Revision." In *Proceedings 31st International Technical Communication Conference,* RET-8—RET-11. Washington: Society for Technical Communication, 1984.

A taxonomy of the revision process has six variables: (1) "What was changed?" (2) "What was done to make the change?" (3) "Was the change voluntary or involuntary?" (Involuntary changes are required because of a voluntary change), (4) "What was the orientation of the change?" (information, line of thought, cohesion, or usage/style), (5) "Did the change alter the reader/writer or reader/text relationship?" (Low affect addresses cognitive relationship; high affect addresses social relationships), and (6) "Why was the change made?" (What norms—cultural, generic, organizational, personal, and situational—guided the change?) The six-variable taxonomy yields a potential 2,640 ways to revise prose. An example shows how the variables operate.

20 Broer, Jan W. "Feedforward, an Old Strategy for Modern Editors." In *Proceedings FORUM '80, 2nd International Conference on Technical Communication (Lillehammer, Norway),* 17-23. 1980.

Feedforward is a creative process of writing and editing with two paths. Path I consists of determining who is the audience and matching publications to meet that audience's needs. To determine who the audience is, "the editor/writer must construct the type of readers he is after, the primordial feedforward in his work" (19). The editor uses a matrix that evaluates audience using size of audience and "reader's need to know, to feel, and to act—in that order" (19), to structure a publication for an intended audience. To evaluate a publication, an editor also can use feedforward because feedback from readers can help the editor determine "how realistically he has postulated reader types" (20). However, the form of a publication can be evaluated by formators, "the systemic elements in the text of the publication" (20), such as "titles, bylines, subtitles, introductory paragraphs, topic sentences, key words, outlines, abstracts" (20). Path II of feedforward pertains to the author-editor/writer relationship. "A creative editor/writer has original views and his author is to know it, for certain. He never hesitates to speak up to his author" (21). The communication cluster, a group of two to four workers which includes an editor/writer, is one way to foster feedforward because such groups "become sources of *innovation*" (21). See also 268.

21 Brogan, Marianne. "Scholarly Communication: Major Components of Cost—Redacting." In *1979 S[ociety for] S[scholarly] P[ublishing] Proceedings,* 22-24. Washington: Society for Scholarly Publishing, 1980. (Also published as "Costs in Copy Editing," *Scholarly Publishing* 11 (1979): 47-53.)

Within the American Chemical Society "redactory costs are $13-14 per printed page (220 X 280 mm, 8½ X 11 journal page) and approximately $2.50 per manuscript page. We account for from 3 to 9% of the various journal budgets and between 4 and 5% of the division budget" (24), Brogan notes. Redactor costs vary depending on the level of quality the publisher has established, the level of responsibility the journal editor has to control quality, and the level of responsibility the editor assigns to other staff members. Besides the judgment factors that determine quality, technological innovations also influence quality. However, technological innovations do not necessarily minimize redactory problems because complex hardware and software create their own problems. Borgan outlines four levels of editing, from none to technical editing, to explain the relationship between cost and effort, and although author-furnished copy reduces editorial costs, Brogan prefers to control the quality of the finished product. Even though a major duty of redactorial efforts is "attention to language: the written word, grammar, style, nomenclature, and presentation" (23), rising costs have a direct impact on the level of redactorial effort that can be expended on a particular publication.

22 Brookes, Martha H. "The Immutable System: Is It?" In *Scholarly Communication Around the World. Proceedings of a Joint Global Conference,* 127-28. Washington: Society for Scholarly Publishing, 1983.

Editorial policies should be reviewed at times "because the conditions that give rise to them change and those who interpret and implement them change" (127). Brookes describes the process used to review editorial policy at a government organization. An eight-member committee selected from 27 volunteers evaluated editorial policy by establishing evaluative procedures, constructing and administering a questionnaire, and recommending changes. Such reviews are valuable because a diversity of ideas in evaluating the editorial process are sought; future changes that may be perceived as too radical are introduced; the editorial system is scrutinized and more clearly understood; and a philosophy of corporate editorial responsibility is formulated.

23 Brooks, Paul. *Two Park Street: A Publishing Memoir*. Boston: Houghton Mifflin Company, 1986.

Brooks recounts incidents from his 25-year stint as an editor at Houghton Mifflin Company. Brooks's early employment with Houghton Mifflin included an apprenticeship at Riverside Press because the company believed "that an editor should have some feeling for the physical product he is dealing with" (13). As Brooks assumed more editorial responsibility, he sought authors. "An essential part of an editor's job is of course the discovery of new talent" (33). Roger Tory Peterson was a new talent in 1933 when he began his association with Houghton Mifflin, an association that resulted in a series of *Field Guide* books, which "have sold almost ten million copies" (71). Not all associations with authors are happy ones. When Ross Lockridge committed suicide, one magazine reported that Brooks had caused Lockridge's death by making him cut his manuscript. Brooks devotes much of his book to his editorial scouting trips and to books about nature, like the *Field Guide* series. While working on the Churchill memoirs on one trip to England, Brooks met Churchill. Brooks unfolds the dramatic story of getting the galleys of *The Gathering Storm*, volume one of Churchill's memoirs, to the press in time for publication. Brooks also gives a brief history of Rachael Carson's books, showing how in *The Edge of the Sea* "an editor's idea may evolve in the mind of a writer into something far more interesting than what was originally conceived" (152). Of *Silent Spring*, Brooks notes, "Rachael needed no editor, but I was involved in a minor way in making the introductory chapters on all these revolting poisons as readable as possible and also in supplying the title" (154).

24 Brouns, Virginia L., and Laurel K. Grove. "Comprehensive Editing—A Solution to Some Typical Editing Problems." In *Proceedings 35th International Technical Communication Conference*, WE-119—WE-121. Washington: Society for Technical Communication, 1988.

In mechanical editing, editors correct "grammar, punctuation, spelling, sentence structure, word usage, and document format" (WE-119). However, the effort to do a mechanic edit can be wasted when a document is later revised. Comprehensive editing, on the other hand, is audience-oriented, not rule oriented. In comprehensive editing, editors read and mark a document so that the author can make substantive changes and correct details. After an author has made revisions based on insights from a comprehensive edit, the editor can use a mechanical edit to refine the document. The authors also discuss the use of comprehensive editing for on-line documents.

25 Brown, David H. "A, B, C . . . And X, Y, Z of Editing and Writing." In *Proceedings 23rd International Technical Communication Conference,* 68-69. Washington: Society for Technical Communication, 1976.
    For each letter of the alphabet, Brown creates and explains a principle of editing and writing, i.e., accuracy, basics, clarity . . . xenophobia, zaniness.

26 Bryant, Mavis, and Stephen Cox. "The Editor and the Illustration." *Scholarly Publishing* 14 (1983): 213-30.
    Editors must train authors to be visually literate. Such training begins at the outset of a project when the editor helps the author determine the kinds and number of graphics appropriate for a project. The author is responsible for providing camera-ready graphics; however, editors will need to provide explicit instructions for the preparation of graphics. Bryant and Cox provide technical instructions for the preparation of photographs, maps, charts, and graphs.

27 Buehler, Mary F. "Creative Revision: From Rough Draft to Published Paper." *IEEE Transactions on Professional Communication* PC-19, no. 2 (1976): 26-32.
    The revision process is a continuum, "stretching from the rough draft to the published paper" (26). Seven types of revision—substantive, policy, language, mechanical style, format, integrity, and copy clarification—make-up the continuum. Buehler analyzes each type of revision and provides guidelines to show how one might revise using any one type. For example, language revision is divided into two parts: complete and screening. A complete revision is designed "to cover elements desirable for a top-quality publication" (30) while a screening revision "corrects a shorter list of faults that place a paper below the minimum level of quality considered appropriate to maintain the institutional image" (30) of the author's employing organization. When editors critique manuscripts using the seven levels of revision, the editors save publication time and money.

28 Buehler, Mary F. "Defining Quality: It Is Not the Same as Goodness." In *Proceedings 34th International Technical Communication Conference,* MPD-37—MPD-39. Washington: Society for Technical Communication, 1987.
    The Quality Control Committee at the Jet Propulsion Laboratory defined quality as conformance to standards, not goodness, because standards "can be specific and quantitative" (MPD-37), but goodness is "subjective

and ambiguous as applied to technical publications" (MPD-38). *The Levels of Edit*, for instance, define editing, another subjective and ambiguous term, in terms of standards. Thus editors do a good job when they edit a document according to the standards of a particular level of edit, even though the document is not given "the kind of edit that a conscientious editor has been trained to do" (MPD-38). Managers should define quality as conformance to standards to "protect writers and editors from the cross-currents of negative sanctions that can result from the uncertainty and ambiguity in defining standards that we [managers] will require and enforce" (MPD-38).

29 Burton, Lydia, Catherine Cragg, Barbara Czarnecki, Sonia Kuryliw Paine, Susan Pedwell, Iris Hosse Phillips, and Katharine Vanderlinden. *Editing Canadian English*. Vancouver, British Columbia: Douglas and McIntyre, Ltd., 1987.

"*Editing Canadian English* was written for editors," the authors note, "although it will also be useful to writers, teachers, and others who work with words" (1). The book is divided into two parts. "The first five chapters of *ECE*—Spelling, Compound Words and Hyphens, Capitalization, Abbreviations and Symbols, and Punctuation—are concerned with general issues of editing, where British and American practices not only vary but change over time. The last seven chapters—French in English Context, Canadianization [the process of changing the references of a work published in another country so that they conform to Canadian style], Avoiding Bias, Measurements: SI/Metric Usage, Documentation, Editors and the Law, and Glossary—discuss matters specific to Canadian editing" (1). One unique suggestion in Chapter 10 on documentations is that authors submit photocopies of "the title and copyright pages or comparable sources of information—mastheads, publications notices, album covers, etc.—of every source from which they copy a quotation" (143). Such a practice would save editors time in checking references and would help ensure the accuracy of citations.

30 Bush, Don. "Communication vs. Correctness." In *Proceedings 31st International Technical Communication Conference,* WE-15—WE-17. Washington: Society for Technical Communication, 1984.

"The English language in inconsistent. . . . Even grammar books are inconsistent" (WE-15), but rules about how to achieve consistency are necessary. Those rules can be evaluated using the criteria of history and idiom, with idiom being dominant. "[A]ccept violation of . . . these historic rules if the violations fit our idiom" (WE-15). Rules without foundation neither in history nor in idiom are the nonrules of pop grammarians like Simon, Safire, and Newman. Pop grammarians fail to recognize that flexibility "is one of the great strengths of English, not a weakness" (WE-16). Another class of rules does not have historic justification but is current today. The ultimate purpose of rules of correctness is to "tailor our speech or our writing to the audience" (WE-17).

31 Bush, Don. "How to Handle Grammatical Dogma." *Technical Communication* 27, no. 1 (1980): 14-15.

The first nine paragraphs of Bush's article "illustrate a point: Our revered rules of grammar can actually contribute to terrible writing" (14). For example, "four years of college don't seem to teach them much" (14), where the verb *don't* agrees with *years*. Bush asserts that "correctness is very subjective" (15) and suggests "the need for smooth, natural, communicative English, which does indeed observe the highest historical language standard but which is written to satisfy both the intelligent reader and the writer himself" (15).

32 Bush, Don. "The Trouble with Definitions." In *Proceedings 30th International Technical Communication Conference,* W&E-28—W&E-31. Washington: Society for Technical Communication, 1983.

Language is fluid, not static, so "words are defined by their context, not by the dictionary" (W&E-29). Five principles help a writer or editor define words: "Some things simply do not need defining. . . . The sentence is the smallest unit of thought, not the word. . . . Definitions . . . should not tell what things *are,* but what things *do*. . . . The word is not the thing. . . . Almost every word, except for proper names and technical terms, has at least two meanings" (W&E-29). In addition to using the five principles, one can define something by contrasting it to something else, "something that it is not" (W&E-30).

33 Butcher, Judith. *Copy-Editing: The Cambridge Handbook*. 2nd ed. Cambridge: Cambridge University Press, 1981.

The copyediting of books is the topic of Butcher's handbook. She divides the copyediting task into eleven chapters (1-11) that discuss illustrations, proofs, indexes, and bibliographical references, among other topics. Four chapters (12-15) discuss issues associated with specific types of books: symposia, science and mathematics books, special subject books (classical books, law books, music books), and reprints and new editions. Appendix 1 is a checklist of copy-editing that breaks down the copyediting task into specific steps, from checking to ensure that "no folios are missing" (270) to asking questions about new editions, like finding out "whether [the] book is to be reset" (283). Though detailed information is presented on a variety of copyediting tasks, Butcher notes, "as the copy-editing problems vary from book to book, it is impossible to list all the things you should do" (19). But the good copyeditor will seek perfection. "The good copy-editor. . . . cares enough about perfection of detail to spend his working hours checking small points of consistency in someone else's work." But Butcher adds, "he has the judgment not to waste his firm's time or antagonize the author by making unnecessary changes" (2).

34 *The Canadian Style: A Guide to Writing and Editing.* Toronto: Dundurn Press, Ltd., 1985.

The Foreword to *The Canadian Style* explains the purpose of the book by comparing it to the manual it replaces. "The new manual concentrates more heavily than did its predecessor on the specifically editorial aspects of writing, including abbreviations, hyphenation and compounding, spelling, capitalization, italics, numerical expressions, punctuation and quotations. Furthermore, the chapter on reference matter has been enlarged, sections on the preparation of letters, memorandums, reports and minutes have been included, and appendixes on geographical names and the elimination of sexual, racial and ethnic stereotyping in written communications have been added since these issues have been of increasing concern in recent years. However, unlike its predecessor, it does not treat graphics, tables and illustrations, which are properly the domain of the typographer" (20). The new manual also recognizes variations in publishers' standards. "[T]he standards and recommendations presented here should not be interpreted as categorical rejections of alternative forms which certain publishers may require" (20).

35 Carruth, Hayden. "Some Personal Notations." In *The Art of Literary Publishing,* edited by Bill Henderson, 49-56. Yonkers: The Pushcart Press, 1980.

"Can anyone argue that the popular press today, including book publishing, is not worse than it was a hundred years ago, worse and bigger?" (53). Carruth poses that rhetorical question because the subsidized presses, the emergence of a huge publishing bureaucracy, and the populace's lack of concern for serious writing, particularly the writing of poets, suggest that the published word as a medium for imaginative endeavor "has gone far toward obsolescence" (55). Though discouraged about the condition of the publishing industry, Carruth will continue to strive for better publishing practices in his own writing, and, he says, "in my work as publisher, author, editor, and reviewer" (56).

36 Carter, Edward P. "The Production Process—The Editing Function." In *Proceedings 25th International Technical Communication*

Conference, 216-17. Washington: Society for Technical Communication, 1978.

The Western Electric editor edits a manuscript, coordinates production of drafts for review, and coordinates production of the revised manuscript.

37 Charney, Patricia F. "Job Idea: Freelance Editing." *Writer's Digest,* January, 1969, 48-52, 84.

An aspiring writer can become a freelance editor to "see publishing from the inside . . . [and to] grow in experience [as] you grow in the use of your writing skills" (84). To become a freelance editor, a writer can begin as a typist or proofreader, but Charney says, "I'd never suggest that you give up proofreading; it is the backbone of the whole process" (50). To find jobs, the writer can consult want ads, trade publications such as *Publishers Weekly,* and the local telephone directory. When writers solicit employment by calling on a client, they should call themselves a writer/editor and leave a resume. Freelancers charge by the hour, but location, experience, and type of job have an impact on hourly rates. Freelance editing can become a lucrative job, so writers should consider writing, not editing, as the ultimate goal of freelance editing experience.

38 Cochran, Wendell. "Four Kinds of Style." In *Scientific Information Transfer: The Editor's Role,* edited by Miriam Balaban, 341-43. Dordrecht: D. Reidel Publishing Company, 1978.

Editors can communicate more effectively with authors about issues in style by distinguishing four types of style: "1. Editorial style (also called 'house style'). 2. Typographical style (or 'design style'). 3. Literary style (or 'writing style' or 'personal style'). 4. Usage style" (341). Editorial style includes spelling, abbreviation, and capitalization and punctuation. "Clearly, editorial style is the province of the editor" (341). Typographical style is within the editor's province, but the designer is a better candidate for evaluating "special characters or diacritical marks" (342) in the journal's content. Literary style is the author's domain, but many authors have no distinctive style. "If the author does have a distinctive and efficient style, the editor should not change it" (342). Authors who write "dull, turgid prose" should be told by the editor "how to make the necessary repairs" (342). Usage style, which "deals with grammar, syntax, idiom, and shades of meaning" (342), can be studied by consulting dictionaries and books on usage. Categorizing four kinds of style is important because editors and referees should not merely cite a problem in an author's style, "but should in each instance specify the kind at fault" (342).

39 Commins, Dorothy. *What Is an Editor?: Saxe Commins at Work.*
    Chicago: The University of Chicago Press, 1978.
    What Is an Editor? is a biography of Saxe Commins, an editor with Random House from 1933 until his death in 1957. During that time Commins edited the works of Eugene O'Neill, S. N. Behrman, Sinclair Lewis, W. H. Auden, Stephen Spender, Isak Dinesen, Irwin Shaw, and William Faulkner, among other noted authors. To answer the question posed by her title, Dorothy Commins portrays her husband as a person dedicated to his work. He reads and edits manuscripts continually; he writes reader reports; he travels to authors' homes or invites them to his home for 12- to 14-hour editing stints per day, two to four days in a row. At one point in his career, Commins even wrote a book for an incompetent author. But much of this biography is about authors and their often tragic lives: O'Neill's life with Carlotta and his son's suicide; Dreiser's vindictive attitude toward his publisher, Liverwright, when Dreiser had to repay—by court order—advances he never earned; John O'Hara's rage at Saxe for suggesting the deletion of obscenities in *A Rage to Live*; Faulkner's excessive use of alcohol to mitigate the trouble in his life. Still the biography is full of publishing successes, such as Faulkner's Nobel Prize. Dorothy Commins recounts her husband's relationships with authors, not only to show his keen eye as an editor, but to explain that "books are more a collaborative effort than the public realizes. Their quality, their impact on the reader, often depends on how well the writer's editor has done his job of 'cleaning and repairing'" (99).

40 Commins, Saxe. "The Fall of Liveright." In *The Art of Literary Publishing: Editors on Their Craft,* edited by Bill Henderson, 151-63. Yonkers: The Pushcart Press, 1980.
    The financial struggles of Liverwright publishing house during the 1930's caused Saxe Commins, an editor at Liverwright, to demand that Eugene O'Neill's royalties be paid in full. Commins not only edited O'Neill's plays but acted as his power of attorney. After Liverwright's dissolution, O'Neill signed a contract with Random House that included a guarantee that Commins along with O'Neill's works would be placed there. The fall of Liverwright also entailed legal action against Theodore Dreiser who had received $17,000 in advances over a period of years but had not produced the promised manuscript. The court ordered Dreiser to repay the advances, and his attitude toward his debt reflected his personality as an author. Commins notes, "working with him was not exactly rewarding. He was obstinate, truculent, and totally lacking in courtesy" (158). Commins acknowledges Dreiser's contribution to American literature but notes that Dreiser's behavior shattered Commins's

"romantic illusion that a writer must perforce be an able writer and a discriminating critic of his own or other's works" (159-60). Same material also found in 39.

41 Commins, Saxe. "Selected Correspondence." In *Editors on Editing: An Inside View of What Editors Really Do,* rev. ed., edited by Gerald Gross, 340-54. New York: Harper & Row, 1985.
Taken from *What Is an Editor: Saxe Commins at Work* (39), these selected letters are to S. N. Behrman and Robinson Jeffers. Commins's letters to Behrman give opinions about how Behrman can make his biography of Max Beerbohm more effective ("use anecdote as only you can" (342)). The letters to Jeffers ask him to rewrite *The Double Axe,* a book of poems, so as not to criticize Roosevelt about World War II. ("Manifestly he [Roosevelt] cannot defend himself, and on that score there arises the question of fairness and good taste" [348].) Commins and Jeffers had opposing political views, but through compromise, they were able to state their positions and publish Jeffers's book.

42 Corbett, William, and Susan Howe. "A Quarter Century of the Jargon Society: An Interview with Jonathan Williams." In *The Art of Literary Publishing: Editors on Their Craft,* edited by Bill Henderson, 116-33. Yonkers: The Pushcart Press, 1980.
Williams, founder and director of The Jargon Society, Inc., a small press, has produced 400 books in 25 years. He chooses to publish eccentric books. "The culls, perhaps, the ones that have the spots on them, the wrinkles. I'm not interested in the polished, packaged sort of supermarket poetry" (121). He wants, like Ezra Pound, "to *insist* that certain things be brought to people's attention" (124), and he chose books by "exercising what taste I had, what enthusiasm I had, and that was my responsibility" (124). Unfortunately, the modern preoccupation is with the present, so "we cannot ever achieve what is called Civilization in this country [the U. S.] as long as we wipe it out as quickly as we build it" (130).

43 Cord, Marian S. "Seeking 'Connectedness'." In *Proceedings 30th International Technical Communication Conference,* W&E-42—W&E-45. Washington: Society for Technical Communication, 1984.
Editors and writers can promote connectedness, the relationship of the parts to the whole, by analyzing manuscripts using three aids: inductive and deductive logic, the abstraction ladder, and parallel and subordinate structure. In addition, review of commas, titles and subtitles, graphs and charts, and a readability formula can aid connectedness.

44 Core, George. "Costs and Copy-editing." *Scholarly Publishing* 6 (1974): 59-65.

"[W]ell-edited books tend to sell better (at lower cost) and . . . they will make their publisher a greater reputation than the titles which are given superficial editorial attention" (59). However, good copyediting cannot make a poor manuscript a good one. Thus, the acquisition of good manuscripts is critical to the editing process. Referees and board members may not be an asset to the acquisition process if they do not understand that just because a manuscript has misspellings does not mean that it is unpublishable. Correcting minor problems is a relatively simple editing task. "The moral for the editor is this: treasure the referee and the board member who know . . . [that such faults can be corrected] and call upon them as often as possible" (62). After a manuscript has been acquired, the editor may work with an author to improve a manuscript, but the editor should reject a manuscript if the author cannot produce a publishable text after repeatedly revising it. Economics plays a part in determining how much to edit a manuscript. For instance, titles that receive little critical attention and do not produce much revenue should not be edited extensively. But decisions about who edits a manuscript and how it is edited are make by the sponsoring editor. Editors may choose to use a freelance copyeditor, and if they do, they should give the copyeditor "reader's reports, board minutes, staff commentaries, etc." (63) to promote efficient and cost-effective editing. Editors can also reduce costs by making judicious editorial decisions. For instance, some divisions and illustrations can be eliminated and notes can be combined. However, editing the manuscript is a cooperative effort among the author, the sponsoring editor, and the copyeditor. If the author does his or her work, "including, if necessary, having involved the help of a manuscript doctor with good credentials" (65), and the sponsoring editor has done his or her part in preparing the manuscript for the copyeditor, the copyeditor can complete the preparation of the manuscript for publication.

45 Cox, Alberta L. "Copy Editing—the Final Word." *Technical Communication* 26, no. 4 (1981): 18-20.
At the Naval Weapons Center, copyeditors review editors' work using the nine levels of edit developed at the Jet Propulsion Laboratory. Such copyediting has four benefits. One, publishers have high quality publications. Two, authors learn and use the company style. Three, editors get a second opinion on manuscripts. Four, the production process operates smoothly. Although copyeditors serve a useful function in publications departments, electronic text-editing programs may replace them.

46 Cox, Alberta L. "The Editor as Generalist as Well as Specialist." In *Technical Editing: Principles and Practices,* edited by Lola M. Zook, 7-11. Anthology Series, no. 4. Washington: Society for Technical Communication, 1975. ED 173 807. (First published in *Proceedings 14th International Technical Communications Conference. Technical Communications: Man's Record of Reality,* edited by Harold L. Mensch, paper #87, 1-10. Washington: Society of Technical Writers and Publishers, 1967.)

Editors need to know how to edit (be a specialist) but they also need to know how printed material is produced (be a generalist). To be a generalist, an editor should know about composition, illustration, layout, and printing. The editor can learn about the production process by admitting that he or she doesn't know certain things about production, spending time reading about production, looking at the actual production process, and asking questions of production technicians. When editors become familiar with the production process they can communicate instructions to production personnel who can prepare final copy according to specific directives.

47 Cox, Stephen. "An Editor's Chrestomathy." *Scholarly Publishing* 15 (1983): 17-37.

In his chrestomathy, a collection of literary passages, Cox discusses the variety of tasks an acquiring editor does and asserts "that acquiring manuscripts is the essential act of publishing" (19). Cox's chrestomathy is composed of 32 passages, each a simile. For instance, an acquiring editor is like sorting oranges. "Manuscripts all look very similar (black on white, linear, double spaced)—there are no apples, only oranges" (21). So the acquiring editor uses a decision-making process to determine whether to evaluated a manuscript. If "the proffered manuscript is on an identifiable subject, is addressed to an identifiable readership that your press can reach, seems as if it might be interesting—then you proceed to the next step. You open the manuscript box" (21-22). The editor constantly evaluates the quality of manuscripts, the growth or decline of an identifiable field of scholarship. The editor is "evaluating evaluations and evaluators—and then acting on hunches. Editing is only somewhat like analysing something" (32). An acquiring editor is like playing chess. "Bobby fisher teaches that the object of chess is checkmate. The object of editing is publishing good books. One concentrates upon the object" (36).

48 Crichton, Jennifer. "Dear Editor . . . Dear Author . . ." In *Editors on Editing: An Inside View of What Editors Really Do,* rev. ed., edited by Gerald Gross, 268-76. New York: Harper & Row, 1985.

The telephone has reduced the number and type of editorial letters that are written to authors. But the telephone conversation is not a permanent record that can be offered as evidence in court should a publisher reject a manuscript under contract. Legal issues aside, writing letters can help editors and authors focus an idea. In some situations letters are less expensive than long-distance telephone calls. What happens to editor-author correspondence publishers own? Many houses donate their files to universities. Others rent warehouses to store the correspondence.

49 Culberson, Dan. "'Editing Is Editing Is Editing' or, by Any Other Name, the Smell Is Sweet." In *Proceedings 33rd International Technical Communication Conference,* 357-58. Washington: Society of Technical Communication, 1986.

See 1 for same article.

50 Davin, Dan. "Editor and Author in a University Press." *Scholarly Publishing* 10 (1979), 121-27.

Unlike commercial presses, the university presses' "primary aim is to advance the purposes for which the university itself exists; to promote knowledge and learning by publishing good books" (122). Speaking primarily about publishing in the United Kingdom, Davin notes that the editor in a university press serves a different function than the editor in a commercial press, especially in relationship to authors. While some authors believe the editor in a commercial press "will act as arbiter of what should be the ultimate form of the book and impose his views without consulting the author or in spite of him" (121), the university press editor acts as a middleman between the author and the press. Acting as a middleman, the university press editor must solicit authors. "Publishing is one profession where it is not only legal but essential to solicit, even in the street" (123). The editor will probably live at the university and develop friendships with faculty members who may become potential authors; yet "once the friend is in fact his [the editor's] author he must be treated with the same porcelain solicitude as a stranger" (124). Indeed, scholars, since they are specialists, want expert opinion about their manuscripts. Thus a scholar is interested in how his or her peers respond to his or her book. Editors' criticisms of a scholarly manuscript are not held in high esteem by the scholar. The editor's job then is to ensure that a manuscript is given the best peer review possible so that the writer's work can be revised (or endorsed) and made into the best book it can be.

51 Delamater, Martha. "Editors: Trolls or Fairy Godpersons?" In *The 577 Papers: Writing Processes, Editing Processes, Written Products,* vol. 2,

edited by Roger E. Masse and Martha Delamater, 111-23. Las Cruces: New Mexico State University, Technical Communications Programs, 1983.

Trolls are egotistical editors and fairy godpersons are considerate editors. Only fairy godperson editors edit so that "both editors and authors feel positively toward each other and toward the message" (122). Readers suffer from trolls' editing. Considerate editors, however, are readers' allies because such editors "make choices to ensure the transfer of information from author to reader" (114). Delamater suggests that considerate editing requires three readings of a manuscript: once to mechanically edit, once "to analyze the structure and content of the paper" (116), once to "concentrate on the author's language and style" (117). Of the style edit, Delamater says, "while editing for style I am careful to respect the author's right to use any style desired as long as it does not become a barrier to the conveyance of meaning" (118). After editing a manuscript, the editor seeks the author's approval of suggested changes by using six components of editorial dialogue.

52 DeVivo, Anita. "Copy Editing Standards at the American Psychological Association." *IEEE Transactions on Professional Communication* PC-18, no. 3 (1975): 141-44.

Editorial practices at the American Psychological Association (APA) changed from 1950 to 1975 because editing has become more centralized to "publish 15,000 pages in its [APA's] 17 primary journals" (141). Manuscripts must conform to APA copyediting standards although quality control does suffer from high turnover among copyeditors. Premailing, mailing the copyedited manuscript to the author for review before the manuscript is typeset, has also enhanced quality and minimized authors' alterations in copyedited manuscripts. However, editors "can never do enough copy editing. . . . [because] whenever . . . standards are imposed, you accept a margin of error" (143). Ultimately, quality in copyediting depends upon good people. "If all you do is comma catching, good people won't work for you" (143).

53 Di Battista, Michael A. "Tape Proofreading: An Adaptation for Part-Time Staff." *Scholarly Publishing* 6 (1975): 147-50.

Following Jeanneret's method of proofreading using a tape recorder (117), Kent State University Press hired and trained students to record their readings of manuscripts. After a manuscript was copyedited, work-study students using basic symbols of editorial work would record their reading of a text. "When galley proofs were received, the copy editor acts as proofreader while the tape recorder acts as 'copyholder.' The original edited manuscript is, of course, kept close at hand to check on any discrepancies that might arise" (150). See also 117.

54 Dukes, Eva P. "The Art of Editing." *Technical Communication* 20, no. 3 (1973): 14-17. (Also published in *Technical Editing: Principles and Practices,* edited by Lola M. Zook, 62-66. Anthology Series, no. 4. Washington: Society for Technical Communication, 1975. ED 173 807.)

"Editing is a decision-making process that must take into account not only objective factors . . . but also subjective ones" (17); editing is both skill and art. The art of editing includes being courteous ("an essential lubricant against interpersonal friction" [14]), deciding whether to communicate with authors via telephone or letter, marking manuscripts (make editorial remarks on the original manuscript and treat it with respect), questioning ("Never be afraid to question a word or a passage that does not make sense to you. . . . do not fear to appear foolish" [16]), and admitting fault when one is wrong.

55 Dukes, Eva P. "Rules: To Bend or Not to Bend Them." *Technical Communication* 33, no. 3 (1986): 136-39.

The rules of English usage "should be applied situationally" (136). But editors do disagree on methods for applying the rules to specific situations. Should the consensus approach be used, where usage over time produces acceptance? or Should only those who have a command of language determine what changes should be made? Dukes affirms the need for language to change, but would like changes to earn their way into the language. She also believes that "Standard English will enable us to disseminate information more widely, or receive it from a far greater number of sources, than will any other form of language" (139).

56 Dukes, Eva P. "The Simple Joys of Editing." *Technical Communication* 19, no. 3 (1972): 7-8.

Citing Briggs's article "Editing by Dialogue" (15), Dukes confirms the need for editors to establish a bond between themselves and authors. Authors who will not tolerate such bonding (usually "extremely poor and sloppy" writers) should be avoided. Authors who allow bonding also allow the editor to experience the joy of editing: "in creating a relationship of trust with often, initially, perfect strangers; in overcoming the obstacles to understanding frequently present on both sides; and in the knowledge that the resulting manuscript will be better organized, more lucidly written, and more carefully documented than it had been in its raw, unedited state" (8).

57 Edmonds, Paul. "The Editor and the Merger." *Scholarly Publishing* 1 (1970): 389-94.
Although mergers of publishing houses create problems for editors, "the editor is, of course—and he knows it—the keystone of publishing: if there is any absolutely essential part of the process, it is that of negotiating the transformation of an author's knowledge and ideas into the script of a saleable book" (389). Yet during a merger, the editor may not be consider in the negotiations, even though "the personalities and potentialities of the editors, and the degree of cordiality subsisting between them and the authors, are powerful factors in the future of the company" (393). The value of a merger may be reduced if key editors leave the newly formed organization. Even when editors stay with a newly created organization they can be misused. For instance, editors can be offended when they have to report to a person whose expertise is in magazines, "for beyond the fact that both put print to paper and sell the result, the two industries could hardly be more different" (392). Even though a publishing merger can be a trial for editors, they can take comfort in the fact that they are the cornerstone of the publishing industry.

58 Edsall, John T. "Scientific Integrity and Responsibility of Authors and Editors." In *Scholarly Communication Around the World. Proceedings of a Joint Global Conference,* 62-63. Washington: Society for Scholarly Publishing, 1983.
Editors are responsible, in part, for maintaining ethical standards in the publication of articles, especially by detecting fraud in a submitted manuscript. Editors should select reviewers who will not impede the publishing process for personal gain because "attempts by a reviewer to block or delay the publication of a paper by a rival do occur" (62). The tendency to "count number of papers published rather than their significance" (62) also contributes to excess in publication that can lead to unethical practices. Once a journal has evidence that a paper is fraudulent, the editor can print a statement to that effect, but libel suits could result. Although editors are responsible for the integrity of printed research, "the core of the problem lies in what goes on before the manuscript reaches the editor's desk" (63).

59 Ellis, Rachael. "In-House Page Proofs." *Scholarly Publishing* 3 (1971): 70-76.
Substituting typed in-house page proofs for printer's galleys helped reduce the cost of author's alterations and gave the publisher greater control over manuscripts. "Typing of page proofs did not begin until the manuscript was as completely finished (e.g., all cross-references

completed, all queries answered) as a manuscript readied for a compositor" (71). Ellis provides two examples of books, including their indexes, that were producing using in-house page proofs, and in both instances, the books were produced on or ahead of schedule. Even the printer benefitted from in-house page proofs. "(One printer has found using our page proofs simplifies makeup in his plant; for one thing, his compositor no longer needs to guess how much space to allow for continued lines, which are normally supplied after page makeup)" (75). An example of an in-house page proof and its final printed page are included.

60 Evans, Nancy. "Line Editors: The Rigorous Pursuit of Perfection." In *Editors on Editing: An Inside View of What Editors Really Do,* rev. ed., edited by Gerald Gross, 102-15. New York: Harper & Row, 1985.

Interviews with five line editors emphasize that "the real skill in line editing . . . involves the subtle change, the small change that does not violate the author's style but results in a discernable improvement" (112). Thus, "a good line editor does not rewrite the [author's] manuscript; she provides answers to the question: What's wrong?" (110). "Editors raise the provocative, leading questions; writers go home to follow the leads where they will" (104).

61 Fargis, Paul. "The Editors Who Produce." In *Editors on Editing: An Inside View of What Editors Really Do,* rev. ed. edited by Gerald Gross, 156-62. New York: Harper & Row, 1985.

Book producers (also called packagers) can function in a number of capacities, but generally they "develop new ideas for books and take the responsibility and risk of delivering acceptable camera-ready mechanicals or bound books to a publisher" (157). As independent business people, book producers supply everything from the idea for a book to the jacket design. Fargis contrasts his experience as an in-house editor with his experience as a book publisher saying that as a book publisher he has "time to think an idea through, time to look things up, weigh alternatives, talk to others" (160). However, book producers generally operate one-person businesses, so they are busy: "one or two people will do the typing and filing; research an idea and write out the initial proposal; find an author; sell to a publisher; handle the accounting debits and credits; arrange for jackets, typesetting, paper, printing, binding, shipping; and pray" (160). And a book producer is an entrepreneur: "one's own mortgage money or grocery bill" (161) may be at stake.

62 Farkas, David K. "The Concept of Consistency in Writing and Editing." *Journal of Technical Writing and Communication* 15, no. 4 (1985): 353-64.
Consistency is "the orderly treatment of a set of *linked* elements in a document" (354). Major categories of consistency are semantic, syntactic (parallel structure, for example), stylistic, spatial, and mechanical (the category where most problems arise). Editors and writers should establish patterns of consistency—logical, evident, functional, resource efficient, and stable—to ensure manuscript consistency. However, consistency is reader based so unless a pattern is evident to the reader, it is inconsistent.

63 Farkas, David K. "Professional and Informal Editing in Complex Organizations." In *Communications: A Means of Exchange, Record of the Proceedings of the 1984 Canadian Regional Business and Technical Communication Conference,* edited by Robert C. Scott, 3-10.
Complex organizations should employ editors in the early stages of the document preparation process instead of expecting managers to edit staff members' writing. Managers should not serve as editors because their time is too valuable; the documents they edit may not be improved; and staff members tend to see managers' corrections as subjective. Staff members should not serve as editors because their time is also too valuable to be spent on editing; their editorial suggestions may be ignored by managers, thus causing interpersonal conflict; and staff members may refrain from making needed corrections "so as not to embarrass or annoy the manager" (5). Professional editors can help eliminate or reduce interpersonal friction, help produce quality documents, and save money for the organization by "freeing managers and staff members for the work they should be doing" (5). Editors, however, could cause distortion in a document's message because they don't have the knowledge needed to evaluate data about products. Also document turnaround time is increased when an editor is inserted in the document preparation process. Farkas provides four models of the editor-manager-staff member relationship to show how the editor can help an organization create quality documents.

64 Farkas, David K., and Nettie Farkas. "Manuscript Surprises: A Problem in Copy Editing." *Technical Communication* 28, no. 2 (1981): 16-18.
Discrete manuscript elements do not affect each other, but linked elements do. These linked elements are the source of manuscript surprises. The authors discuss three linked elements—mechanical

consistency, content, and organization. For instance, if an author uses time intervals in fraction form (1-1/2 yrs.) early in the manuscript and uses different fractional forms for time later in the manuscript (5/6 yr.) the editor may want to return to early portions of the manuscript and express all time intervals as years and months. To deal with manuscript surprises editors can train authors to use a style manual. Then editors can read the manuscript before editing it, "scout ahead" to see what problems may exist, and flag passages that may need to be changed.

65 Farrar, John. "Letter to an Unpublished Writer." In *The Art of Literary Publishing: Editors on Their Craft,* edited by Bill Henderson, 71-78. Yonkers: The Pushcart Press, 1980.

In his letter, Farrar, one of the founders of Farrar, Straus and Cudahy, rejects a writer's manuscript by explaining how to submit a manuscript to a publisher and how publishers review manuscripts. In particular, Farrar says of interviews with authors that "I prefer not to see an author until I have *something* he has written. It may be only a lively letter; but preferably a long enough piece of writing to prove that he has at least the ability to catch my interest, which is, after all, what *I* go by" (75). Of the rejection letter, he says, "in principle, I believe a letter of rejection should not give editorial advice" (75) because an author should not be given directions about reworking a manuscript unless the publisher intends to publish it.

66 Farrar, John. "Securing and Selecting the Manuscript." In *What Happens in Book Publishing,* 2nd ed., edited by Chandler B. Grannis, 27-53. New York: Columbia University Press, 1967. (First published in *Editors on Editing,* edited by Gerald Gross, 33-51. New York: Harper & Row, 1962.)

An editor's duties are varied, but encompass securing manuscripts, judging manuscripts, and working with authors and other publishing professionals to print a book. To secure manuscripts, "the editor searches for writing talent wherever he can find it, gets in touch with promising new writers, asks to read their work, nurtures them" (31). Finding talent includes working with literary scouts and literary agents. In fact, "the entire career of the author, the long view of his writing and publishing life, is the true duty of both agent and editor" (37). After receiving a manuscript, the editor judges it using instinct and training, but a publishable manuscript must excite an editor. "There are not rules [of manuscript selection] except that one must be excited. I do not believe in successful editors who maintain calm" (43). Once a manuscript is selected, the editor's first responsibility is to befriend the author so that the publishing experience will be cooperative. The editor will depend not only on a good editor-author relationship to see a book through its production, but the editor will need the good will of the sales force who will be the book's agents. Given all these tasks, "how does he [the editor] ever get any editing done, you ask? The answer is he usually does it nights and week-ends" (49). But in the end, the editor is handmaiden to the author. "Great editors do not discover nor produce great authors; great authors produce great publishers" (52).

67 Farrar, John. "Selected Correspondence." In *Editors on Editing: An Inside View of What Editors Really Do,* rev. ed., edited by Gerald Gross, 319-38. New York: Harper & Row, 1985. (First published in *Editors on Editing,* edited by Gerald Gorss, 157-74. New York: Grosset & Dunlap, 1962.)

A year's selection of letters to authors touches on many issues: revision, advice to authors about authors' attitudes ("you are loath to change the novel, or at any rate your arguments in support of your own point of view incline to be long and complex" [323]), religion ("You [Theodor Reik] will say that often, certain religious rigors produce the neurotic and the psychotic. I'd point out that Satan also plays his part here" [332]), and publishing ("When one sees more and more evidence of the account-minded upsurge in publicity, it is discouraging. . . . I've seen publishing house after publishing house succumb to dry rot as the business men got control" [337]).

68 Fensch, Thomas C. *"Between Author and Editor:* Selected Correspondence Between Pascal Covici and John Steinbeck." In *Editors on Editing: An Inside View of What Editors Really Do,* rev. ed., edited by Gerald Gross, 356-73. New York: Harper & Row, 1985.

Letters between John Steinbeck and his editor, Pascal Covici, show that Covici was more than Steinbeck's editor; he was Steinbeck's personal friend. The letters say little about detailed revision of Steinbeck's books, but focus on personal errands Covici ran for Steinbeck, their social meetings with each other, and Covici's encouraging Steinbeck to work on, especially to complete the last book of *East of Eden*.

69 Field, Leslie. *Thomas Wolfe and His Editors: Establishing a True Text for the Posthumous Publications*. Norman: University of Oklahoma Press, 1987.

Textual evidence that Field gleaned primarily from Houghton Library at Harvard University suggests that Thomas Wolfe wrote his posthumously published works and the editors edited. Controversy about the part Maxwell Perkins, Elizabeth Nowell, and Edward Aswell played in the posthumous publication of Wolfe's works centered on a belief among some scholars that Wolfe's editors overstepped their editorial duties to write parts of Wolfe's novels. To resolve that controversy Field analyzed Wolfe's manuscripts at Houghton Library and prepared four Cameo Test Cases that indicate Wolfe is the author of his posthumous works. Of *The Web and the Rock*, Field says, "an examination of the various drafts, both manuscript and typescript, provides sufficient evidence, I believe, to show that Thomas Wolfe was the author, although the book was edited meticulously be Edward Aswell" (117). Field draws the same conclusion about Wolfe's other posthumous works. (See pages 134, 150, and 165.) In evaluating the larger problem of editing any work, Field notes, "editors, like teachers, tread a fine line between redoing what has been done and making suggestions and guiding the writer as they alter the text" (180). In treading that fine line, Wolfe's editors "always kept one thought in mind: how least to edit Wolfe to capture exactly what he had wanted to write" (180).

70 Fischer, John. "The Editor's Trade." *Harper's Magazine,* July 1965, 20-22, 24.

"[M]ost editors are utterly incapable of explaining what they do, or why. . . . [because] the primary piece of equipment for a good editor probably is an instinct, or hunch, which tells him what people will want to read a month, a year, or a decade from now" (20). Besides possessing "curiosity, in abnormal quantity" (21), a good editor identifies with his or her readers, has "an intellectual companionship with his constituents" (21), "has the enthusiasm of an adolescent in the spasms of first love" (21); and is ruthless because he or she must reject a great deal of poor writing submitted by friends, relatives, and associates. "Yet somehow the indispensable ruthlessness must be combined with a genuine liking for writers, a wide acquaintanceship among them and their agents, a sympathy for their problems and respect for their work" (24). Like a Japanese gardener, the good editor wants "to guide and encourage natural growth" (24), to help writers make the most of their own essential natures.

71 Fletcher, Marjorie. "On Spaghetti and the Alice James Cooperative." In *The Art of Literary Publishing: Editors on Their Craft,* edited by Bill Henderson, 254-58. Yonkers: The Pushcart Press, 1980.

Historically, publishers and editors decided to print a book because they believed it had literary value. Today publishing conglomerates determine what should be published based on a profit motive, not literary quality. "[W]hen the businessmen who run our large houses display a frightening inability to distinguish literature from spaghetti, one way to insure that quality poetry and fiction will be issued in the future is to form publishing ventures that are owned and run by authors" (256). The Alice James Poetry Cooperative is one such venture. At Alice James, "although the cooperative has final approval ... all authors select the art for their covers, design a format for their interiors, choose a typeface, consult with our printer" (256). In short, authors perform many editorial functions. The success of Alice James suggests that authors should form their own publishing ventures.

72 Fruge, August. "Editing, Production, and Survival." *Scholarly Publishing* 4 (1973): 113-20.

Speaking as a university press editor, Fruge says, "our System of turning manuscripts into books ... is almost totally unsuited to the kind of business we are in" (117). A major problem with the system is that editing and production are confused. Authors are allowed to change their manuscripts during the production process and copyeditors rewrite authors' works because "one of the underlying assumptions, not stated but nearly always there, is that authors cannot write books" (115). Yet authors should be responsible for their words, a responsibility shared by the sponsoring editor whose work is "the intellectual heart of the enterprise. Quality control begins, and except for accuracy of detail ends, here. It will be clear to those editors that they must take full responsibility; there will be no other set of editors to second-guess their judgement or patch up their mistakes" (119). Thus editing should be completed prior to production. The linear model of editing and production, not the recursive model, will change the nature of publishing.

73 Fruge, August. "Editing, Production, and Survival—Progress and Anti-Progress." *Scholarly Publishing* 7 (1975): 31-35.

As a follow-up to an earlier article (72), Fruge reiterates that those in the publishing business "have allowed editing and composition to become almost unbelievably confused, with the flow of work doubling back on itself like a sluggish river snaking its way across a meadow, or a troopship zigging and zagging to avoid torpedoes" (31). At his press, the University of California Press, a streamlined method of producing books has reduced publication time because "composition is becoming an office operation, rather than a plant operation" (33) and design is combined with editing and composition when the "manuscript and proof go back and forth between only two parties (editor and author) instead of three (production, editor, author)" (34). Authors are reminded that they will be able to make changes in their edited manuscript only once. When they send the manuscripts back to the publisher, it is no longer possible to edit the work. That practice is defensible because "10 percent of composition (the traditional allowance for author's alterations) has never been clear to anyone that I know of," Fruge notes, "whereas zero is a figure of unmistakable clarity" (35).

74 Fulton, Len, and Ellen Ferber. "Piecework." In *The Art of Literary Publishing: Editors on Their Craft,* edited by Bill Henderson, 163-78. Yonkers: The Pushcart Press, 1980.

As editors of Dustbooks, a small literary publishing company, Fulton and Ferber discuss a pieced-together operation with "four identifiable phases: editorial, production, promotion and distribution" (165). The editorial phase consists of two processes. "In the first we accumulate, attract, gather; in the second we select, discard, polish, hone" (170). All the manuscripts Dustbooks publishes are unsolicited, and an editor edits an author's work without any personal contact with the author. Selecting manuscripts is based on editorial taste. "Once we have accepted a manuscript the major editorial work is done, largely because we accept what we like. . . . what pleases and excites our ears" (171).

75 Galassi, Jonathan. "Double Agent: The Role of the Literary Editor in the Commercial Publishing House." In *Editors on Editing: An Inside View of What Editors Really Do,* rev. ed., edited by Gerald Gross, 248-56. New York: Harper & Row, 1985. (First published in *The Art of Literary Publishing: Editors on Their Craft,* edited by Bill Henderson, 78-87. Yonkers: The Pushcart Press, 1980.)

Modern publishing is increasingly concerned with books that sell and make money. The literary editor, therefore, typically is seen as an anomaly because in general, literary works, serious works, are not big money makers. Yet, "if the publishing industry cannot find room for new writers, eventually it will have nothing to publish" (254). So the successful literary editor must play two roles. "With the writer the editor is collaborator, psychiatrist, confessor, and amanuensis; in the publishing house he must be politician, diplomat, and mediator. He is a double agent" (252). To work effectively in the publishing house the literary editor must gain colleagues' respect and confidence, and work tirelessly to promote his or her authors. Though underrated by colleagues, the literary editor can comfort him or herself by recognizing that "if the publisher is intelligent he recognizes that the serious writer's work is the heart and soul of his undertaking" (256).

76 Gardener, Christina. "Eliminate Errors by Checking Copy before Typesetting." *Business Graphics,* October 1967, 32.

Typesetters should mark copy "for inconsistencies of style, misspellings, etc." before setting it into type. "This gives the customer a chance to insist on the misspelling if he wants it that way." Compositors also should mark and count heads and the number of spaces used for indentation.

77 Geiser, Elizabeth A., Arnold Dolin, and Gladys S. Topkis, eds. *The Business of Book Publishing: Papers by Practitioners*. Boulder: Westview Press (1985).
See "The Editorial Process: An Overview" (174), "The Editor's Job In Trade Publishing" (477), and "The Editor's Job in Professional/Scholarly Publishing" (481).

78 Genin, Michael S. "Editing Report Art Differs from Editing Presentation Art." In *Proceedings 31st International Technical Communication Conference,* VC-53—VC-55. Washington: Society for Technical Communication, 1984.
Report art is used for printed documents while presentation art is used for oral presentations. The editor can help authors prepare presentation art by selecting appropriate visuals ("[H]ighly technical materials such as periodic tables or multi-level equations are inappropriate as visuals" [VC-54]), by being "aware of the font, leading, point size, and legibility of any written material that appears in the visual" (VC-54), and by coaching the author. Coaching can consist of videotaping a speaker's presentation and reviewing it with him or her and advising speakers how to best use media equipment. The editor must foster good interpersonal relationships when suggesting that authors improve their public speaking skills.

79 Giamatti, A. Bartlett. "Safeguard of Process: The Editorial Committee." *Scholarly Publishing* 7 (1976): 129-33.
At academic presses, the editorial committee and the process of reviewing manuscripts are "crucial to university publishing" (130). The faculty editorial committee is responsible for the quality of a press's list and for the process that produces that list. To ensure quality, the committee should see itself as a counterbalance to editors. Giamatti says, "I believe a university press is intellectually healthy when a spirit of affectionate antagonism exists between the editorial committee and the house editors" (130). "To oversimplify, an editor is obligated to create a product, a committee member is obligated to safeguard a process" (131). That process should be based on policy. For instance, the committee should know when and how to encourage authors to rework a manuscript that is potentially publishable. The editor should communicate to the authors the committee's decisions, but the process of evaluating manuscripts belongs to the board because the process, "itself an adversary one, is designed to identify and reward genuine quality" (131). See also 225.

80 Gibbs, Wolcott. "Theory and Practice of Editing *New Yorker* Articles."
In *Editors on Editing,* edited by Gerald Gross, 241-45. New York: Grosset & Dunlap, 1962.
Gibbs lists 31 general rules to authors of *New Yorker* articles, including "our writers are full of cliches, just as old barns are full of bats. There is obviously no rule about this, except that anything that you suspect of being a cliche undoubtedly is one and had better be removed" (242); "editing on manuscript should be done with a black pencil, decisively" (243); "how many of these changes can be made in copy depends, of course, to a large extent on the writer being edited. By going over the list, I can give a general idea of how much nonsense each artist will stand for" (244); and "try to preserve an author's style if he is an author and has a style. Try to make a dialogue sound like talk, not writing" (245).

81 Girodias, Maurice, William Burroughs, Allen Ginsberg, Carl Solomon, and James Grauerholz. "The Struggle Against Censorship."
In *The Art of Literary Publishing: Editors on Their Craft,* edited by Bill Henderson, 212-29. Yonkers: The Pushcart Press, 1980.
The roundtable discussion recounts the struggles of Girodias and others to publish books like *Naked Lunch* and *Lady Chatterley's Lover* in the 1950's and 1960's. Grauerholz notes that "'most of the American literary establishment, the publishers and editors,'" promoted censorship because they "'adopted a party line which said that the reason "obscene" books were not published in America was that there were not very many of literary merit anyway'" (217). However, as Girodias notes, censorship was an international political effort to suppress writing and thinking. "'To force the people to follow moral rules in their sex life was the only way to impose the same old rules in terms of politics and social conduct'" (225). Burroughs agrees "'that all censorship is political,'" but the roundtable participants see the dissemination of pornographic works as a way to fight censorship because the works are in private hands and younger generations would be able to read these "'secret artifacts . . . secretly within the family'" (228).

82 Goffstein, M. B. *My Editor.* New York: Farrar, Straus & Giroux, 1985.
Goffstein's poem is written from an author's perspective as she works with an editor to revise a manuscript. The author is compared to an archaeologist reconstructing a site. Each page of the poem is headed with a geometric figure/figures that symbolize the construction of her manuscript as it goes though successive revisions.

83 Golbitz, Pat. "On Being a Senior Acquisitions Editor." In *Editors on Editing: An Inside View of What Editors Really Do,* rev. ed., edited by Gerald Gross, 129-42. New York: Harper & Row, 1985.

As an acquisitions editor, Golbitz categorizes her job into three major parts: "getting the book, working with the author, and marketing the book" (129). To get a book an acquisitions editor maintains contacts with agents, participates in auctions, and negotiates contracts. Working with the author ("For me, the heart and soul of my profession is working with the author" [133]) includes editing the manuscript by structuring, cutting, and line editing and copyediting. Authors do not create text according to carefully predefined systems and Golbitz notes, "I've learned that most authors are very uncomfortable with outlines, hate them, in fact. They think of them as boundaries to hem them in" (136). Marketing the book includes attending the marketing meeting where for "the very first time a book comes to the attention of the house since its purchase" (138), designing the cover, writing copy for the catalogue and flap, coordinating advertising and publicity, and promoting the book at the sales conference.

84 Goodman, William B. "Editing: Inside the Enigma." *Library Trends* 33, no. 2 (1984): 153-64.

Goodman quotes Sifton's law to explain the enigma of editing: "'there is a natural limit to the readership for [new] serious fiction, poetry and nonfiction in America that ranges, I would say, between 500 and 5000 people—roughly a hundred times the number of the publisher's and author's immediate friends" (154). Sifton's law, followed assiduously by trade publishers, means that new serious works are becoming more difficult to publish, in part, because of rising printing costs. Goodman notes, however, "the logic of practical economics . . . has never ruled publishing" (157). Based on Sifton's law, Goodman makes several predictions: that new serious works will emerge, but perhaps academicians who are financially secure because of their teaching positions may be the major group of writers of such books; that the short story "is back as a publishing staple" (163); that "the literary and academic respectability of detective fiction" (163) should increase.

85 Grant, Jane. *Ross, The New Yorker, and Me*. New York: Reynal and Company, 1968.

Much of Grant's book is about her and her marriage to Harold Ross, founder and editor of *The New Yorker*. However, chapter 2 provides background on Ross's upbringing in Colorado and Utah and his numerous jobs as a newspaper reporter throughout the United States. Chapter 12 through chapter 14 recount the beginnings of *The New*

Yorker until Grant and Ross's divorce. In those last three chapters, Ross is portrayed as a perfectionist who "would have worked night and day if I had permitted it" (237), Grant says. She also notes that Ross was a well-educated, though self-educated, man. Between chapter 2 and chapter 12, Grant focuses on their lives at 412 West Forty-seventh Street, named Fountain House. Grant names a host of famous people who visited Fountain House. The other major character in the book, Alexander Woollcott, the critic who also lived at Fountain House, "played a big part in making our marriage impossible" (242), Grant says. Ross's dislike for Woollcott manifested itself by Ross's purposefully misspelling Woollcott's name whenever possible. For another biography of Ross see 223.

86 Griffin, George D. "Meet The Manuscript Editor." *Writer's Digest,* July 1968, 42-47, 94.
Griffin explains how a manuscript editor processes a manuscript: "It is recorded as a submission, it is examined, it is read, a decision is reached. And it all takes time" (46). He also gives suggestions on how to submit manuscripts, and when manuscripts are rejected, Griffin notes, "in the final analysis editorial opinion about any manuscript is a matter of personal judgment" (94).

87 Gross, Gerald, ed. *Editors on Editing.* New York: Grosset & Dunlap, 1962.
Of his book, Gross says, "*Editors on Editing* attempts to give a rounded, clearcut portrait of the editor as a man and as a skilled professional. I have tried to reveal the particular types of personality and temperament of the editor: his attitude toward literature, his educational background, his involvement and/or detachment with the author he works with, ways of approaching the manuscript he edits, etc. And, in addition, I have tried to show many of the areas in which an editor functions: obtaining and selecting manuscripts, criteria used in ascertaining the quality of a manuscript, dealing with authors, agents, revising the manuscript, 'packaging' the manuscript, etc." (xiii). See "What Is an Editor" (219), "An Open Letter to a Would-be Editor" (191), "Editors Today" (132), "Securing and Selecting the Manuscript" (66), "Copyediting" (14), "Editing Quality Paperbacks" (469), "Editing the Mass-Market Paperback" (482), "Textbook Editing" (470), "The Editorial Function" (91), "Editing Children's Books" (467), "Confessions of an Author-Editor" (131), "Editing for Sense and Effect" (214), "The Objective View" (143), Perkins "Selected Correspondence" (165), Farrar "Selected Correspondence" (67), Simon "No Title" (196), "No Title" (153), Strauss "Selected Correspondence" (216), "Editing: Or Arguing, Procuring,

Tinkering, and Sending Things Back" (105), "The Constant Function" (555), Weeks "No Title" (233), Sedgwick "No Title" (193), "Theory and Practice of Editing *New Yorker* Articles" (80), "Harold Ross" (222), and "The Fruit of the Bittersweet" (575).

88 Gross, Gerald, ed. *Editors on Editing: An Inside View of What Editors Really Do*. Rev. ed. New York: Harper & Row, 1985.

Editors on Editing is a collection of essays on the multifaceted role editors play in book publishing. The book is divided into three parts: theory, practice, and editor-author correspondence. Under theory see "What Is an Editor" (219), "An Open Letter to a Would-be Editor" (191), "Letter from the Editor" (229), "The Author as Editor" (213), and "The Manuscript" (145). Under practice see "Copyediting" (14), "Negotiating a Publishing Contract" (159), "Line Editors: The Rigorous Pursuit of Perfection" (60), "Slush" (197), "The Editorial Assistant" (189), "On Being a Senior Acquisitions Editor" (83), "A Life in the Day of an Editor in Chief" (171), "The Editors Who Produce" (61), "The Truth About Trade Paperbacks" (478), "Born to Be a Paperback" (476), "Editing Fiction" (188), "Editing Nonfiction: In the Service of One Book and Many Readers" (231), "Editing the Mystery Novel" (468), "Editing the Science Fiction Novel" (471), "Editing the Illustrated Book" (463), "Editing Scholars and Scholarship" (112), "Double Agent: The Role of the Literary Editor in the Commercial Publishing House" (75), and "Planting Inflammatory Ideas in the Garden of Delight: Reflections on Editing Children's Books" (465). Under editor-author correspondence see "Dear Editor . . . Dear Author . . ." (48), Perkins "Selected Correspondence" (164), Strauss "Selected Correspondence" (216), Farrar "Selected Correspondence" (67), Commins "Selected Correspondence" (41), and *"Between Author and Editor:* Selected Correspondence Between Pascal Covici and John Steinbeck" (68).

89 Hallinan, Edward J. "Practical Writing and Editing Techniques." In *Proceedings 31st International Technical Communication Conference,* WE-34—WE-36. Washington: Society for Technical Communication, 1984.

The writer/editor can use four techniques—exposure, research, participation, and review—to produce "a reasonably accurate, politically acceptable document with a minimum of supervision" (WE-34). Research means "extracting information from both source documents and legal documents" (WE-35), especially the "bibles" of a particular discipline. Participation means that editors involve themselves in the process used to produce a document, including project and scheduling meetings. Early participation in the process gives the editor "a clear idea of what the author and approvers want out of the document" (WE-35). The reviewer's techniques include revising documents for inconsistencies and asking selected questions, for instance, about calculations or support for results. When an editor has not been able to use all five techniques, "the best approach under tight deadlines is to scan source and legal documents for useful information written in acceptable wording" (WE-36).

90 Halpenny, Francess. "The Editor on His Campus." *Scholarly Publishing* 2 (1971): 369-76.

The editor of a university press has a responsibility to promote scholarly publishing by active involvement in campus affairs. For instance, editors can attend special campus lectures that pertain to topics on which they want to publish. Attendance at a conference not only allows editors to become more knowledgeable about academic topics but also puts them in touch with potential authors. The editor should also cultivate professional relationships with librarians and explain the publishing business to them. In all these endeavors, the editor should "maintain a disinterested position where academic controversies over schools of thought or approaches in a discipline ebb and flow, and sometimes swirl, about him" (374). The editor is seeking scholarly manuscripts that appeal to a variety of viewpoints because "the editor's loyalties are in the first and last analysis to manuscripts and their possible addition to knowledge" (374).

91 Halpenny, Francess. "The Editorial Function." In *The University as Publisher,* edited by Eleanor Harman, 67-71. Toronto: University of Toronto Press, 1961. (Also published in *Editors on Editing,* edited by Gerald Gross, 93-97. New York: Grosset & Dunlap, 1962.)

At a university press, the editorial function begins with an evaluation of a manuscript and ends with a printed book or journal. The evaluation phase may be time consuming, but "a manuscript which has taken years of devoted labour to prepare deserves the compliment of a report by the person best qualified, and that person should be given time for reading and reflection" (68). After a manuscript has been accepted, the editor confers with the author about revisions, making suggestions on ways to improve the manuscript without altering the author's style. When editors are successful in their function, their work is least noticed. Editing "has been well performed when the hovering pencil is least evident in the final result, and the book is clear, valid, and convincing in the procession of its words and sentences. Then author and reader are communicating to the best advantage" (71). The editorial skill needed for an editor to be invisible—the development of judgment in technical matters and the honing of interpersonal skills to query authors successfully—takes time. The editor takes his or her job seriously because publishing is important, and "the editor or publisher has such respect for the difficult art of writing that he frets so much about what it is that he is publishing'" (71).

92 Halpenny, Francess. "Of Time and the Editor." *Scholarly Publishing* 1 (1970): 159-69.

Why does the processing of a scholarly book manuscript for publication take so much time? Step-by-step, Halpenny explains how a manuscript is processed, showing that the evaluation and production process is time consuming. For instance, editors must enlist competent readers to appraise a manuscript. Editorial boards must convene and decide whether to publish a work. Editing is time consuming. But the expense of time can also be accounted for by the large number of poorly prepared manuscripts. "The sad truth is, of course, that manuscripts of 'solid authors' are rare in scholarly writing, and appear much too seldom on the desks of procurement or manuscript editors" (163). Thus editors spend time helping authors reach publication standards by encouraging authors to rewrite a work. Even then, "an editor may make suggestions . . . but these can only be suggestions" (164). Guidance alone, however, does not produce a quality manuscript. Editors "can never compensate for lack of the power of insight or of words. . . . they cannot impose clarification unilaterally since only an author responding to a theme of his own free will and with enthusiasm can make it his own" (166). That enthusiasm may be missing because academic authors feel that they should write a book. Could they not be encouraged to write quality journal articles instead? Academic authors who really desire to write a book should be given the appropriate support— adequate time—to prepare a quality manuscript. However, the publication process begins years before a manuscript is ever written. The process "starts, I submit, with students in the lecture and seminar rooms" (169) where they learn how to do research and to write about their ideas.

93 Halpenny, Francess G., Wayland W. Schmitt, Eleanor D. Kewer, Weldon Kefauver, and R. J. Schoeck. "Press Editors and Project Editors." In *Editor, Author, and Publisher,* edited by Wm. J. Howard, 47-87. Toronto: University of Toronto Press, 1969.

Each author comments on the role of university presses in the development of large-scale critical editions. Halpenny provides an overview of the university press's role in preparing critical editions. Schmitt, representing Yale Press, discusses the editor's role as a representative of potential audiences for the proposed edition. Kewer, representing Harvard University Press, discusses organizing a work such as the Theodore Roosevelt letters, indexing, and using symbols to give an author's complete text (hesitations, second thoughts, misspellings). Kefauver, representing the Ohio State University Press, discusses the Centenary Edition of the works of Nathaniel Hawthorne with particular attention on teaching compositors to "violate" their rules to produce page proofs with an author's original "mistakes." Schoeck discusses group scholarship and makes distinctions among communal, co-operative, and team scholarship.

94 Harman, Eleanor. "Hints on Proofreading." *Scholarly Publishing* 6 (1975): 151-57.

Authors are responsible for proofreading their manuscripts before they are published. To proofread proofs effectively, an author should use appropriate symbols. For instance, "it is pleasanter to call for '12-pt' type for the text, '10-pt' for the quotations, and '8-pt' for the footnotes, than to maunder about 'big', 'small,' and 'extra small' type" (152). Authors should also recognize the difference between correcting a manuscript by writing missing letters or words above a line and proofing a manuscript by making marking corrections in the column next to the line that needs changing. An author should write proofing changes in a readable hand rather than print them because "most compositors become rather expert at reading handwriting" (155). Advice on author's alterations is quite clear: "on the subject of Author's Alterations, that is, author's late inspirations, an entire article might be written, and then summed up in one word, 'don't'" (153). Harman reviews two methods of proofreading—using a copyholder and using a tape recorder—and notes, "the eye can be treacherous; it has a tendency to supply what should be there but may not be" so the best preparation for proofreading is "a humble and prayerful state of mind" (157).

95 Harman, Eleanor. "A Reconsideration of Manuscript Editing." *Scholarly Publishing* 7 (1976): 146-56.

Today's editors have evolved from the printer's redaction activities. That evolution is not complete because printing technology has changed to include computers and attendant technology. As a developing profession, editing can become two self-conscious and editors can face the danger of "creating artificial functions and developing an artificial mystique of editing" (151). This danger easily leads to "the development of personal whims, and the injection of these into the material he [the editor] handles" (152), resulting in perfectionism that is costly in terms of time and labor. The seasoned editor "is willing to let the author pretty well say his own thing, as long as the latter actually says what he apparently means" (152). Ethics also is an issue when editors extensively revise an author's manuscript and "he reaps the credit" (153). Unfortunately, that credit may be counted toward tenure and promotion.

96 Harman, Eleanor. "On Seeking Permission." *Scholarly Publishing* 1 (1970): 188-93.

Although the author is responsible for securing permissions to quote copyrighted materials, often a publishing house will help the author, but "the job of securing permissions being a thankless one, it is frequently given to a junior, less experienced editor" (188). Seeking permission should begin when a book contract is signed. Then the author should carefully review the doctrine of fair use, which is ambiguous. In addition, "it cannot be assumed that no copyright exists anywhere because the material was published in the nineteenth century. The duration of copyright varies from one country to another" (190). In fact a writer's descendants, if they can be located, own the rights of a deceased writer's unpublished work. Once permissions are agreed upon, they should be in writing. When requesting a reduction in standard fees, the author should avoid approaches that seem to disregard sound reasoning and when acknowledgements are printed, the publisher should "follow all instructions about the wording and placing of acknowledgements *to the letter*, despite the importuning of editors and book designers who think that euphony or aesthetic considerations justify a different handling" (192).

97 Harman, Eleanor. "Selecting a Title." In *The University as Publisher*, edited by Eleanor Harman, 93-96. Toronto: University of Toronto Press, 1961.

"The ideal title, besides being short and memorable, is precisely descriptive of the book, and normally requires no sub-title for clarification or amplification" (93). If the author or editor cannot create a descriptive title, "the allusive or provocative title is the next best solution" (94). When are books christened? At the University of Toronto Press approximately half of the titles that are published are the original titles. The others are created by the author and editor together.

98 Harman, Eleanor, ed. *The University as Publisher*. Toronto: University of Toronto Press, 1961.

Published to commemorate the diamond anniversary of the University of Toronto Press, *The University as Publisher* makes "a modest contribution to the economic and cultural history of the last sixty years in Canada" (v). As a history of The University of Toronto Press, "this volume may, therefore, be of interest to those institutions contemplating the founding of such scholarly publishing departments, whether to profit by the account of Toronto's mistakes, or to be cheered by knowledge of such success as Toronto has enjoyed" (v). For selected annotated articles, see "The Editorial Function" (91), "Selecting a Title" (97), "Publishing the Proceedings" (626), and "A New Technique in Proofreading" (117).

99 Hartley, Herbert L. "Should an Editor Edit or Rewrite Submitted Articles?" *Medical Communications* 3 (1974): 8-10.

Editors should take an eclectic approach in answering the question about whether to rewrite an author's manuscript. If an author's manuscript needs "little more than marking for type" (10), the editor need not rewrite, "but, if the paper is poorly written, or poorly organized, or both, don't be *afraid* to rewrite," Hartley advises editors. "Reorganize and rewrite, even if you have to cut the paper into pieces and paste them up in logical order" (10). The eclectic approach is midway between two extremes. At one pole, editors do not do any rewriting; at the other pole, the "editor rewrites everything and this means material from authors of all degrees of eminence" (9). The one extreme of rewriting everything is represented by the editor of the *New England Journal of Medicine* and the other extreme of not rewriting at all is represented by the editor of *Nutrition Today*, two successful journals.

100 Hays, Robert. "Rapid 'Debugging' Technique." *Technical Communication* 26 (1979): 12-15.

Rapid debugging is editing "for content—accuracy, completeness and logical order" (12) by going through a manuscript twice and applying nine reviews. The nine reviews are: 1. Making sure the report complies with requirements, 2. Testing complex procedures, 3. Deleting or harmonizing incongruities, 4. Checking computations, 5. Investigating seemingly spurious sources, 6. Ensuring needed ideas are included, 7. Including all the data the text says is included, 8. Being a critic, and 9. Ensuring that conclusions and recommendations are complete. Hays explains each review and notes that rapid debugging should not take the place of "careful, creative editing" when time permits and that rapid debugging will not "produce a consistent style in a report written by several people. . . . [or] atone for writers' lack of competence and knowledge" (15).

101 Heatley, Kenneth R. "The Making of an Editor: A New Approach." In *Proceedings Sixteenth International Technical Communications Conference,* S-67—S-72, Washington: Society for Technical Writers and Publishers, 1969.

Heatley recounts his experience of acquiring and training editors in an organization that had "a major upheaval in both type and volume of work load" (S-67). That upheaval required the use of more editors but local freelance editors were not available. To cope with sudden changes and lack of personnel, Heatley reorganized his department by establishing ground rules in the form of a style manual and by assigning specific responsibilities to writers and editors. New editors were selected from the typing pool after they passed an editing test composed of three extremely "complex and poorly written, although nontechnical, paragraphs" (S-70). Three former typists became "student editors," apprenticed to an experienced technical editor. Initially, they checked page numbers, compiled lists of illustrations, and assigned control numbers to art. Over time, the student editors were given more editing responsibilities under the supervision of experienced editors. After having worked with student editors, Heatley believes that they are valuable because they increase the amount of work a department can process at a lower cost; "backstop" writers so that they can concentrate on presenting technical data, not concentrating on format and style; and "provide the final 'touch' . . . that reflects the quality a professional organization imparts to all its delivered products" (S-72).

102 Heffner, Maxine. "Stalking the Trouble-Some Hyphen." In *Technical Editing: Principles and Practices,* edited by Lola M. Zook, 53-55. Anthology Series, no. 4. Washington: Society for Technical Communication, 1975. ED 173 807. (First published in *Proceedings 14th International Technical Communication Conference. Technical Communications: Man's Record of Reality,* edited by Harold L. Mensch, paper #97, 1-28. Washington: Society for Technical Writers and Publishers, 1967.)
"[T]he hyphen is not merely an ornament; nor is it just a short dash. The dash is a separator; the hyphen is a joiner!" (53). Twenty-nine do's and don't's explain when and when not to use a hyphen. The article in the *Proceedings* includes an alphabetical list of over 1,500 troublesome compound words.

103 Henderson, Bill, ed. *The Art of Literary Publishing: Editors on Their Craft*. Yonkers: The Pushcart Press, 1980.
In the Introduction to *The Art of Literary Publishing*, Henderson writes, "in assembling this collection over the past few years, I invited a variety of views—personal, practical, and philosophical. While this volume is in no way meant as a complete survey of all outstanding editors, it is intended to be a thorough sampling of prevailing—and usually very different—editorial opinion" (x) with emphasis on *prevailing*. "[T]his is not a book of yesterdays. Most of our editors [who wrote essays for this book] thrive today in New York publishing corporations or in small

presses across the country" (xi). See "Publishers, Booksellers, Readers, and Writers: Some Straws in a Whirlwind" (205), "New Directions: An Interview with James Laughlin" (111), "Some Personal Notations" (35), "Letter to an Unpublished Writer" (65), "The Double Agent: The Role of the Literary Editor in the Commercial Publishing House" (75), "The Life and Death of an Academic Journal" (501), "The American Literary Scene as a White Settler's Fortress" (176), "Small Publishing—Is It Beautiful?" (9), "A Quarter Century of the Jargon Society: An Interview with Jonathan Williams" (42), "The Editor as Undertaker or This Way to Temporary Immortality" (123), "On Editing *The Ontario Review*" (526), "The Fall of Liveright" (40), "Piecework" (74), "Poor and Pure" (167), "A Revolution of Twerps" (579), "Cheek by Jowl: On Reading, Angels, and the Threat from Within" (550), "The Struggle against Censorship" (81), "True Confessions of a Failed Reader" (127), "The Story of My Printing Press" (152), "Publishing Thomas Wolfe" (164), "On Spaghetti and the Alice James Cooperative" (71), and "Dealing with Mambrino's Helmet" (175).

104 Hill, Iris T. "An Editorial Perspective on Institutional Relations." *Scholarly Publishing* 9 (1977): 80-85.

The editor of a university press has a responsibility to cultivate good institutional relations, which "from the editorial perspective require a willingness to communicate with local faculty and administrators, to listen and respond seriously, to care deeply about scholarship and teaching, and to act fairly and coherently in the review of manuscripts" (85). Communicating with local faculty and administrators means the editor finds out who the productive campus scholars are because they are potential contributors to the press. Editors also should build their lists by asking chairs and deans what topics are emerging in a particular field. The editor must educate the campus community about the press's role by explaining the review process to authors and administrators, citing the need for exceptional members for the faculty advisory committee, and coordinating marketing activities to keep the press and its authors before the academic community. Press personnel can also "play an active role in any publishing course offered on the campus" (84).

105 Hills, L. Rust. *Editing: Or Arguing, Procuring, Tinkering and Sending Things Back.* In *Editors on Editing,* edited by Gerald Gross, 201-08. New York: Grosset & Dunlap, 1962.

The word *editing* means either (1) choosing the contents for a magazine or being an editor for a company that publishes books or (2) actually editing a manuscript, "working over it with a pencil and various perceptions" (201). The magazine editor spends time arguing with other editors, advertising salespeople, circulation and promotion people, and management to promote his or her view of what the magazine should be. The magazine editor at the highest level of the magazine hierarchy hires a staff to get material for the magazine. At the lower levels, the editor procures authors. This can be done by reading little magazines to look for new talent. Editing a manuscript, the second type of editing, consists of the skill in understanding a work's purpose and showing the author that he or she can fulfill that purpose in better ways than he or she has already used. Both types of editors (and one person may perform both functions) should use constructive sending back, which means corresponding with authors to encourage them to write more or to discourage them from writing at all.

106 Hmnnn, H. O. "Appropriate Typos Revis(it)ed." *Scholarly Publishing* 13 (1982): 340-46.

Hmnnn provides numerous examples of typos, including "'Wh lesome Bakery'" (340), a business example, and an example from an author: "In arguing that his point had been sufficiently made, and the manuscript needed no revision, one author typoed: 'I'm not sure a sludge hammer is required.' On the same page, he referred to his 'convincing case for preserving the contirved theoretical ambiguity'" (342). The use of quotation marks also can raise questions of meaning. "Our favourite Toronto meat market constantly features signs that say 'Special "now" only $2.95 lb.' Oddly enough, when I ask for the item, it is always 'now'" (344), and "a rural Ontario shop displays a sign reading '"Antiques"'" (345).

107 Holder, Laurel N., and Stephen O'Neill. "Editorial Authority and the Author: Who's in Control?" *Technical Communication* 34, no. 1 (1987): 19-21.

Editors should exercise control over the editorial function in an organization. Selective editing, editing a document to suit an author's tastes or editing according to management's arbitrary editorial policy, erodes an editor's authority. To improve editorial control, editors can follow twelve suggestions, including involvement in professional activities that enhance an editor's credentials, using interpersonal skills with authors (rapport and respect), demonstrating the need for editorial services, sending a proposal to management explaining how editorial services benefit the company, and preparing a "a group-compiled style guide" (21). If editors are to function with authority, they must have support from management in the form of policies and procedures.

Once they have that support, editors should exercise their authority "sensibly and accurately" (21).

108 Holmes, Olive. "Editing East Asian Publications." *Scholarly Publishing* 10 (1979): 155-60.

Western "publishers' editors of East Asian books do not even try to learn an Asian language. They know which problems they can handle and which they must turn over to others" (156). The problems that must be handled include printing Chinese characters, finding a competent calligrapher, and citing names. For instance, Chinese surnames number about 600. "Therefore, one is apt to find in the course of a single manuscript several Wus or Lius. . . . Obviously, one cannot write a second citation by surname alone or great confusion results. So a handy little house rule is always, but *always*, use the full Chinese name. Ah, but—which is the surname? . . . To save a lot of time and trouble, we have another house dictum: always use the Asian order, surname first, even in notes" (158). If editors need to correct a calligraphy error by calling an author, Holmes suggests using the *Matthews Chinese Dictionary* where "each character has a number" (159). Because of the many pitfalls, "the making of an East Asian book is still part puzzlesolving, part craft, and, in some respects, an art" (160).

109 Horne, David. "Take an Editor to Lunch." *Scholarly Publishing* 9 (1978): 99-106.

Editors and business managers can be at odds with each other, but they can—and should—be allies. The keys to a successful relationship are objectivity and a free exchange of information. Horne notes, "By 'objectivity' I mean less ego, more interest in common goals" (101). Business and Editorial must work together to achieve common goals. Editorial, for instance, can keep Business informed about what books are being planned for future production. "Business . . . must keep the director informed, from a financial point of view, on Editorial's list-building, both actual and prospective" (103). Business can also help Editing by compiling reports on title accounting and print runs. Reporting in itself, however, will not establish positive relationships. Editing and Business must communicate with each other informally "towards the end of the day every so often, for tea or sherry—and to mingle on equal terms, to listen to each other, to hear how each department works, to discover what they have in common" (101).

110 Howard, William J., ed. *Editor, Author, and Publisher*. Toronto: University of Toronto Press, 1969.

Editor, Author, and Publisher contains five papers presented at the "fourth Editorial Problems Conferences held at St. Michael's College in the University of Toronto, 8 and 9 November 1968" (4). For annotations of individual papers see "Authors, Editors, and Publishers" (154), "Press Editors and Project Editors" (93), and "Maxwell Perkins: The Editor as Critic" (128).

111 Howe, Susan, and Charles Ruas. "New Directions: An Interview with James Laughlin." In *The Art of Literary Publishing: Editors on Their Craft,* edited by Bill Henderson, 13-48. Yonkers: The Pushcart Press, 1980.

James Laughlin, President and publisher of New Directions Publishing Corporation, discusses his publishing career in an interview with Howe. Laughlin started publishing books at Ezra Pound's behest because none of Pound's friends had publishers. The tradition of publishing friends' friends' works is the basis of New Directions's growth. Once a work is acquired, Laughlin relies upon editors to do much of the mechanical manuscript preparation. However, he attempts to read whatever a friend or an editor recommends. In determining what to publish, Laughlin notes, "I have tried to publish the things that for me rang the bell. . . . I did what pleased me or what pleased my friends and what my friends could convince me was worth doing" (38-9). When what rang a bell also had potential for being censored, Laughlin used a test: frankness or outspokenness is necessary to the art form if the author does not use sex for sex's sake, for sensational purposes. Much of the article is devoted to Laughlin's remembrances of Pound, Tennessee Williams, Dylan Thomas, Herman Hesse, Merton, and William Carlos Williams, all writers Laughlin has published.

112 Isay, Jane. "Editing Scholars and Scholarship." In *Editors on Editing: An Inside View of What Editors Really Do,* rev. ed., edited by Gerald Gross, 240-46. New York: Harper & Row, 1985.

An editor of scholarly works should follow two rules: understand what the author is saying and respect it. Once an editor understands and respects the research, he or she should follow some tricks of the trade: organize a book so that what is of most general interest comes first; find subheads to help the author look at the order of an argument; place reference notes at the foot of the page (however, "when some juicy notes are interspersed with reference notes . . . I'd rather segregate the reference notes at the end and leave the interesting ones on the page" [244]).

113 James, Rowena G. "Et Alia." *Scholarly Publishing* 2 (1970): 59-65.

More multiauthor volumes are likely to be published because of the need for specialists to work and teach together. The cost of multiauthor volumes is high, so publishers should use volume editors and give them precise instructions about how to prepare a multiauthor work. Part of that preparation should be the preparation of "a set of author instructions [by the volume editor] under the guidance and approval of the publisher's editor" (62) because each multiauthor volume presents unique problems. Early planning is the key to producing a successful multiauthor volume, so author instructions and other pertinent documents should be developed at the beginning of the project so that the job of styling all the papers is not relegated to the final stages of preparing the multiauthor work for publication. Besides preparing author instructions, the volume editor's duties are broad, including "establishing deadlines for first and second drafts; settling disagreement of whatever kind; editing first and second drafts" (62); and working with an indexer. James summarizes the volume editor's duties in an eleven-point list and notes that volume editors can function properly to the extent that they are informed and educated by the publisher about house procedures for producing a multiauthor volume.

114 Jarman, Brian. "Advice on Crash Editing." *Journal of Research Communication Studies* 3, nos. 1-2 (1981): 217-20.

Essentially the same data presented in "Coping with Crash Editing" (115).

115 Jarman, Brian. "Coping with Crash Editing." In *Proceedings 27th International Technical Communication Conference,* W-9—W-12. Washington: Society for Technical Communication, 1980.

Crash editing is required when an editor has no more than eight hours to edit a manuscript. Jarman recommends preparing for a crash edit by "psyching up, attacking the manuscript, and trading off quality with time in order to meet a deadline" (W-9). Psyching up means gaining control of the manuscript by assuming a totally positive self image, which conveys a calm, confident editor. When receiving the manuscript from the author, the editor asks questions to determine the time available to edit the manuscript. To calculate how to use that time, Jarman thoroughly edits the first two pages of the manuscript, attacking it and timing that attack. Based on that timing and the type of corrections made (Jarman lists five levels of editing), he consults a matrix developed from an analysis of how much time it takes him to complete each level of edit. Jarman provides time calculations for each level of edit and the matrix for estimating editing time.

116 Jarrett, Beverly. "Secrets of an Acquisitions Editor." *Scholarly Publishing* 15 (1984): 147-53.

A successful acquisitions editor has the ability to listen, to read, and to respond. "A good editor unceasingly listens creatively" (148) by analyzing what authors say and helping them to piece together ideas. Reading is usually slow "because it is reading that permits the editor to become involved, entangled even, with the manuscript's content, its ideas, its methods, its mood or tone, its contribution to the larger field" (150). Such reading results in an evaluation of a manuscript. The editor also reads readers' reports to interpret "what a reader means by a cool affirmation or a vehement negation" (151). Responding entails saying yes and no to authors and acting as a midwife to help authors bring to birth their ideas. Essentially, all three abilities are one. "Responding, after all, is listening; it is even reading sometimes. The small difference is that in listening and reading the editor generally is reacting to the spoken and written word; in responding—in the kind of nurturing response I have referred to—the editor is reacting to something more, to the unspoken and unwritten word" (153).

117 Jeanneret, Marsh. "A New Technique in Proofreading." In *The University as Publisher,* edited by Eleanor Harman, 135-38. Toronto: University of Toronto Press, 1961.

Jeanneret describes a new method of proofreading—electronic copy-holding. After explaining two tradition methods—the comparative method and the read-in-pairs method—he explains that proofreaders can become their own copy-holders by recording their reading of a manuscript using a Philips Dictating machine and then proofreading the manuscript by replaying the recording. The new method "possesses advantages ranging from increased accuracy to increased output and lessening of an operator's fatigue" (138). See also 53.

118 Judd, Karen. *Copyediting: A Practical Guide.* Los Altos: Crisp Publications, Inc., 1988.

Copyediting is designed to teach a person how to copyedit. Thus, Judd repeatedly emphasizes that writing and copyediting are distinct activities. The copyeditor's job is to ensure that a manuscript conforms to a publisher's style guidelines, not to rewrite an author's work. A copyeditor must (a) *"have a good sense of grammar and punctuation"* (14), (b) be observant, and (c) be curious. In addition, a copyeditor needs to understand the practical aspects of copyediting, including using proofreading and typemaking symbols, preparing a style sheet, and interacting with publishers, editors, and authors. Specific chapters are devoted to copyediting different types of manuscripts and to freelance copyediting.

119 Kador, John. "Editor's Guide to Periphrasis." *Technical Communication* 25, no. 3 (1978): 10-11.

In his "lexicon of periphrastic editorial terms," Kador gives examples of 14 common editorial problems and explains that instead of using overblown, wordy, or oblique language to describe an author's prose, "give the author with an aversion to direct and common wording a taste of his own syntax. Note periphrasis and be done with it" (10). Besides periphrasis, Kador discusses amphibologia (vague), pleonasm (redundant), asyndeton (too turgid), polysyndeton (babytalk), anaphora (monotonous), euphemism (weaseling), ambage (deceptive circumlocution), hyperbole (overstated), meiosis (understatement), perissologia (long-winded), prosopoeia (personification), cacozelia (bookish), and solecism (nonstandard usage or grammatical construction). Kador, a bit tongue in cheek, claims, "the device of periphrasis allows us to label our reasons for making changes without offending the writer. For how many writers will be offended by a charge of periphrastic writing? By the time they look it up, all offense is gone" (10).

120 Kasher, Asa. "Style! Why bother?" In *Scientific Information Transfer: The Editor's Role,* edited by Miriam Balaban, 299-301. Dordrecht: D. Reidel Publishing Co., 1978.

Editors who insist on stylistic uniformity among the articles in a journal make the readers' interests prevail over the authors', which is a wrongheaded approach to style. Rather, "stylistic instructions [are] of two kinds: those that should be followed in order to enable a professional reader to put under scrutiny every detail of the content of the paper, and all the rest" (300). Thus, "beyond a small cluster of necessities authors should be exempted from any requirement which is not directly related to the process of getting down on paper their thoughts, and furbishing it for the sake of clarifying the content" (300). However, authors should be consistent throughout a work. Aesthetic qualities, though, are not enhanced "by uniformity of trivialities such as indentations of first lines of first paragraphs of first chapters. Diversity is beautiful, isn't it? (Ask you wife about her dresses, if you fail to grasp the point easily)" (301).

121 Koski, Raymond J., and Gerald A. Mann. "The Editor's Role in Reducing Future Shock." *Technical Communication* 21, no. 2 (1974): 2-5.

Drawing upon Alvin Toffler's *Future Shock*, Koski and Mann cite three kinds of changes that will affect editors. First, transient teams, which will be organized to perform a specific task and then be disbanded, will require editors to adapt to new situations. Second, technological development, which provides more topics for writers and more ways to prepare publications, also allows "faster, higher volume production, with resulting pressures to lower quality standards" (4). Editors must find ways to maintain accuracy and clarity under such pressures. Editors also must learn to coordinate team efforts "of illustrators, technicians of all sorts, typists, printers, and all the peripheral personnel concerned with production, budgets, and scheduling" (4). Third, informational content and publication forms, which include microfiche and videotape packaging, will require "engineered messages" that are carefully constructed. Editors will work in new mediums. The effective editor of the future will help reduce the effects of those three changes by structuring and clarifying information.

122 Kubeck, James E. "The Freelance System Works for Us." *Scholarly Publishing* 3 (1972): 268-72.

Freelance editors can be cost effective, if they are properly chosen and trained. Potential freelance editors should be given "an editorial test that reveals aptitude and experience" (269). However, Kubeck warns employers to be leery about hiring professor's wives and rewrite types. Once freelance editors are hired, they should be given guidance by an in-house editor. "'[O]utside' books can be spread around the staff so that they don't become a burden on any one individual" (271). Freelance fees can be negotiated given the condition of a manuscript, and the publishing house can "always leave the fee open in the event that there are unforeseen problems" (271). Both the quality and cost of freelance editorial work justifies using freelance editors. See also 215.

123 Landis, James. "The Editor as Undertaker or This Way to Temporary Immortality." In *The Art of Literary Publishing: Editors on Their Craft*, edited by Bill Henderson, 134-41. Yonkers: The Pushcart Press, 1980.

Editors cannot evaluate their success by the success of the books they publish because literature may not sell well. Yet editors tend to equate sales with success; "even the most literary of editors tend to mention only those books of theirs that sell, and this leads further to the emphasis on sales in the publishing business" (139). Even positive critical reviews of an author's work are not adequate indication of an author's literary merit. In fact, "it's just such exuberant encomia . . . that often drive away prospective readers, who confuse good writing with difficult writing" (140). In short, "there are no standards" (140) by which to judge literature from a publisher's perspective.

124 Lane, Michael. "Shapers of Culture: The Editor in Book Publishing." In *Perspectives in Publishing,* edited by Philip G. Altbach and Sheila McVey, 27-35. Lexington: Lexington Books, 1976.

Historically, "the editor as he is known today is essentially a postwar figure" (30) whose role is to shape his or her culture by the books he or she publishes. Speaking specifically of British editors, Lane says that they apply standards of judgment and are active creators of culture, at least this is so for those who see themselves as creating standards of judgment. The editorial function, however, has evolved so that editors are central to the entire publishing endeavor. "By virtue of their responsibility for the content of the text and contact with the author, editors inevitably tend to become middlemen around which all other skills necessary to a book's production revolve" (33). Thus editors shape culture by the books they choose to publish. "The twentieth century has witnessed the rise of editors whose task has been to choose what books will be made publicly available" (35). However, literary agents are beginning to exert influence on book publishing and through that influence, they may replace editors as the shapers of culture.

125 Leavitt, William D. "The Proof of Your Editorial Pudding Is in Its Tasters." In *Proceedings 30th International Technical Communication Conference,* MPD-16—MPD-18. Washington: Society for Technical Communication, 1983.

Editors can use an editorial survey to determine the effectiveness of their publications. If the results of the survey are positive, management can have "'absolute' proof" of a publication's success (MPD-17). Leavitt helped develop a survey that was administered by an independent marketing research company. He did not administer the survey himself because "even the most honest and objective survey falls under question if it is conducted by the editor" (MPD-17). He explains how the survey was administered, including how readers were selected for participation in the survey. Leavitt used the survey results to prove that his publications were helping the company to be profitable. The survey results also helped convince many people in the company "that we [in publications] knew what we were doing and should be permitted more freedom in running the program" (MPD-18).

126 Lindberg, Helen A. "Hello Out There! Are You Reading Me?" In *Proceedings 29th International Technical Communication Conference. Technical Communication—Charting the Course of Technology,* C-57—C-60. Washington: Society for Technical Communication, 1982.

Audiences can be analyzed based on the types of information they need. Following Stroud, Lindberg lists three types of information: information which "enhances decision making, identifies relative priorities, and records accomplishments" (C-57). However, "all publication may have one audience in common—management" (C-57). Audiences can also be identified by the type of publication: manuals, press releases ("Editors make up the primary audience for press releases" [C-58]), public relations publications, in-house publications (magazines and house organs), journal articles, and technical reports. Five questions, for instance, "How complete must information be to meet reader needs?" (C-59), help identify an audience's needs.

127 Lish, Gordon. "The Confessions of a Failed Reader." In *The Art of Literary Publishing: Editors on Their Craft*, edited by Bill Henderson, 230-38. Yonkers: The Pushcart Press, 1980.

Lish chronicles his editorial work beginning with his memories of staring at "stuff in the gutter—which on a good day was twigs, gum wrappers, maybe something unknowable and all glinty with mystery" (231) when he was about six years old. (Later, Lish glosses his early memories by noting, "of course, the glinty, unknowable thing" [237] became a book.) By "shoveling sand," Lish progressed from being a co-editor of *Chrysalis Review* to editor of *Genesis West* to the fiction editor of *Esquire* to editor at Knopf.

128 Litz, A. W. "Maxwell Perkins: The Editor as Critic." In *Editor, Author, and Publisher*, edited by Wm. J. Howard, 96-112. Toronto: University of Toronto Press, 1969.

Litz discusses Maxwell Perkins's relationship with Hemingway, Fitzgerald, and Wolfe "to suggest the ways in which his work was symptomatic of a general departure from the traditional relationship of author, editor, and publisher" (97). Perkins helped change the publishing policy at Scribner's from a quite conservative to a more liberal policy. Perkins believed that "'a publisher should not be, as such, a partisan, however strongly, he may be as an individual. If he allows his partisanship to govern him in his choice of books, he is a traitor to the public. He is supposed to furnish a forum for the free play of the intellect, in so far as he possibly can'" (99). Perkins's work with Wolfe, in particular, has been the source of debate about Perkins's reputation as a "creative" editor, "a reputation he never sought and firmly rejected" (105). Litz classifies Perkins "as one of those catalytic figures who emerged with the great generation of twentieth-century writers and, by combining personal and financial support with perceptive criticism, became an essential part of the literary history of their age" (109).

129 Lockwood, Willard A. "The Decision to Publish: Scholarly Standards." In *Scholars and Their Publishers*, edited by Weldon A. Kefauver, 6-17. New York: The Modern Language Association of America, 1977.

To make a decision to publish a book, publishers of scholarly works enlist readers and judge readers' reports. However, selecting and judging readers' reports are not simple issues. First, time is a problem, especially when readers' reports do not recommend publication of a manuscript after considerable time has elapsed since the manuscript was submitted. Second, the selection of readers is problematic, although "perhaps more important than any other single element in the evaluation process" (11). To select readers, "the editor tries to avoid readers who might bring to the manuscript considerations that are irrelevant, such as friendship, animosity, competition, political bias, and so forth" (12). Third, reading readers' reports is critical because it entails "making judgment of judgments" (13). Should the editor pass on readers' comments to authors? Lockwood says, "reports should be divulged to the extent that the information they contain will actually help the author" (14), even if a manuscript is rejected. However, readers should maintain anonymity to be protected from "abuse and subtle or not-so-subtle reprisals" (16) from rejected authors. Without the protection of anonymity, "many readers would, I fear, refuse the pleasure" (16) of reading manuscripts.

130 Lutz, Jean A. "Attitude Toward the Editing Process—Theory, Research and Pedagogy." *Journal of Technical Writing and Communication* 16, nos. 1-2 (1986): 157-165.

Though editing is often characterized as "no brains" work, a matter of simply following a prescribed set of rules, Lutz's research suggests that editing is a complex task involving knowledge of the writing context and an ability to negotiate a consensus about truth and reality with authors. Editors acquire knowledge "through organizational or contextual indoctrination that enables an editor to relate context to text" (160), and since the editor is a reader's advocate, the editor represents the reader to the author so that editor and author can negotiate "a shared contract about reality" (163). Using protocol analysis, Lutz evaluated the editing and revising traits of seven writers and found "that revising and editing may be equally demanding tasks" (162). To translate theory about editing into classroom practice, Lutz recommends a case study method or dyadic simulation to help students recognize that editing is a "negotiation for meaning in their texts" (164).

131 Lynes, Russell. "Confessions of an Author-Editor." In *Editors on Editing,* edited by Gerald Gross, 105-10. New York: Grosset & Dunlap, 1962.

Lynes humorously discusses the plight of "an author who is also an employee of the publisher who publishes his book" (105).

132 McCormick, Ken. "Editors Today." In *Editors on Editing,* edited by Gerald Gross, 13-32. New York: Grosset & Dunlap, 1962.

McCormick outlines editorial responsibilities, including the need to consider the legal ramifications of libel and plagiarism, the need to promote good translations of foreign works, and the need to resist censorship. He also discusses the need to discover potential writers, even the editor's duty to identify writers who can become collaborators because ghostwriting and collaborative writing have produced many good books. "The editor who brings the right man of ideas in contact with the right man of expression has effected something of a creative process in so doing" (17). Editors, however, should select books that will "protect the reader from boredom and the market from saturation" (18). The editor should also find writers who have the ability to explain scientific ideas to a lay readership. In doing editorial work, the editor should recognize that he or she is a steward. The publishing house, not the editor, owns the writer. In other words, "the entire [publishing] business is founded on one man: the author. The editor who for an instant loses track of this fact is not doing his job" (28-29).

133 McEldowney, Dennis. "An Editor's Reading." *Scholarly Publishing* 7 (1976): 315-20.

Editors can reduce their editorial acumen if they read only unedited manuscripts because the editor might begin to judge unpublished manuscripts against other unpublished manuscripts or against books he or she has published. Therefore, the editor should "inoculate himself from time to time with wider reading" (319). Wider reading will allow the editor to discern jargon, needless verbiage, and poor organization. The ultimate purpose of an editor's reading is to prepare him or her to help authors recognize prose that does not address an audience's needs.

134 McNaughton, Harry H. *Proofreading and Copyediting: A Practical Guide to Style for the 1970's.* New York: Hastings House Publishers, 1973.

Beginning with proofreading marks, McNaughton explains how to proofread, how to check for capitalization, spelling, and plurals, among other mechanics. Throughout, McNaughton explains how to mark copy for the compositor. Of copy specifications, for instance, McNaughton notes that "there are four basic instructions that must appear on copy to tell how it is to be set. They are: the name of the typeface, the point size, the leading, and the measure (width of the line)" (28). When reading copy, the copyholder must recognize that "there are many ways to put a thing down in print and that he must read exactly what he sees—not what he associates with it" (44). Thus when reading, the copyholder uses "code words to be substituted for most symbols and signs" (44). For instance, "for a question mark, the hillbilly 'huh?' is good" (44). Besides advice on how to proof figures, how to use bullets, how to use italics (versus quotes), McNaughton explains when to query an author or editor. He also discusses printing terminology and technology (chapters 13-17) and conditions of employment for proofreaders (chapter 18).

135 Maggiore, James G. "Who Needs Editors Anyway?" In *Proceedings 34th International Technical Communication Conference,* WE-31—WE-34. Washington: Society for Technical Communication, 1987.

We all need editors, Maggiore affirms, because electronic text-processing tools cannot make critical judgments about quality, style, and medium. "Text-processing tools provide us with data; the editor must collect and analyze this data to help improve the quality of writing" (WE-31). Editors should also develop a quality plan by critiquing all the books that will comprise a data-base library. Determining which medium is best for a particular product is another editorial responsibility. Because the editor can be "a true buffer between writer and audience," (WE-33), all writers need an editor.

136 Malcolm, Andrew. "Do Editorial Changes for Clarity Really Improve Readability?: A Look at a Personal File of Original and Edited Copy." In *Proceedings Canadian Regional Business and Technical Communication Conference. Your Brand of Communication,* edited by David Pilfold, 63-69, 1982.

Malcolm conducted a study to determine if edited text is preferable to unedited text and found that he should use an editor. He reached this conclusion because the study was based on three passages he had written that were "edited by three persons acting as editors" (63). When 69 attendees of a Society for Technical Communication seminar evaluated eight pairs of Malcolm's edited and nonedited text, they "preferred five edited versions, one original version, and saw no difference on two of the passages. Overall preference for the edited version of the eight passages was statistically significant (p <0.005)" (65).

137 Mann, Gerald A. "Minimal Editing: How Much Is Too Much?" In *Proceedings 27th International Technical Communication Conference,* vol. 2, W-5—W-7. Washington: Society for Technical Communication, 1980.

Minimal editing involves making necessary changes or corrections to a manuscript so that it communicates the intended meaning to the intended audience. The reader is the focus of minimal editing, so "the basic justification for the changes is to avoid unanswered questions in the reader's mind" (W-6). Minimal editing requires (1) correcting mechanical errors without changing an author's style, (2) reviewing the manuscript to ensure that it has an appropriate "framing" for the reader, (3) checking organization, including transitions, (4) making sure "there will be no unanswered questions in the reader's mind" (W-7), and (5) making only "those changes that can be justified in terms of the reader's needs" (W-7).

138 Mann, Michele H. "How to Edit the Passive Writer's Work." *Technical Communication* 32, no. 3 (1985): 14-15.

The passive writer "does not question any editorial comments" (14) about his or her writing because he or she is not sufficiently involved in the creation of a document. An editor can use a four-step process to help passive writers become involved. Step one is to stress the ability to improve by explaining that writing is a craft. Showing the writer "a page that you yourself wrote that has drawn editorial comment" (14) will help demonstrate that writers can learn about writing. Step two is motivation. Explaining that "good writing is part of technical accuracy" (14) and that an editor can only "be expected to push a draft one or two rungs" (15) up the Ladder of Quality are ways to motivate a passive writer. The third step is to encourage the writer to use reference books on style and grammar. The fourth step is instruction, individual and group. During the editorial conference, individual instruction, an editor can teach the passive writer basic skills that will raise questions about organization and clarity. Group instruction can consist of a skills workshop where passive writers learn how to critique writing by actively participating in the workshop.

139 Marcus, Judith H. "The Editorial Purview—or This Is a Pencil, Not a Wand." In *Proceedings 32nd International Technical Communication Conference,* MPD-14—MPD-16. Washington: Society for Technical Communication, 1985.

As the editor of an in-house editorial service, Marcus received drafts from authors who submitted manuscripts for editing before the documents had been approved, which was a violation of standard procedures. After editors revised an unapproved manuscript, authors incorporated editorial comments into a co-author's draft of the manuscript to produce a final copy. The result was a manuscript with "errors in grammar, spelling, and syntax, as well as inappropriate language" (MPD-14). By enlisting the aid of a manager whose department seemed to produce most of the offending authors, Marcus initiated a 13-step procedure that clearly differentiated between the responsibility of editors and that of writers.

140 Markland, Murray F. "To the Editor: On Rejecting." *Scholarly Publishing* 18 (1987): 163-69.

In an open letter to editors, Markland discusses the editor's dilemma when writing a letter of rejection to authors and explains the ways authors read rejection letters. When writing rejection letters, editors take one or a combination of three approaches: the messenger approach, the explainer approach, and the mentor approach. The straight forward rejection letter is the best way not to foster further involvement with an author, but most editors want to justify their decision to reject. The conflicting roles an editor may assume when writing a rejection letter suggest that "editors must act out a paradox" (166). On the one hand, they seek contributions. On the other hand, they hope to receive enough contributions so that they can reject those that do not meet the journal's needs. Without this paradox a journal would have difficulty achieving quality. Authors generally want significant response to their work, but they can read an editor's rejection negatively, particularly when editors don't seem sincere. Editors can satisfy an author's desire for genuine criticism of his or her work by editing referees' comments and sending them to the author. As an editorial principle, "when what is said causes embarrassment, discouragement, resentment, and defensiveness, the whole act of criticism becomes unconstructive and futile.... Like good huntsmen, editors must control their hounds so that the hounds do not destroy the prey" (168).

141 Masse, Roger E., and Martha Delamater, eds. *The 577 Papers: Writing Processes, Editing Processes, Written Products.* 2 vols. Las Cruces: New Mexico State University, Technical Communications Programs, 1983.

For volume I, edited by Masse, see "Overcoming the Manuscript: An Editing Process" (230) and "The Editor Won't Let You" (179). For volume II, edited by Masse and Delamater, see "Editors: Trolls or Fairy Godpersons?" (51), "Editing as a Matter of Fact" (4), and "Attitudes and Method: Complements of an Editing Process" (224).

142 Mathes, J. C. "Contextual Editing: The First Step in Editing Sentences." In *Proceedings 23rd International Technical Communication Conference,* 21-25. Washington: Society for Technical Communication, 1976. (Also published in *A Guide for Writing Better Technical Papers,* edited by Craig Harkins and Daniel L. Plung, 99-103. New York: IEEE Press, 1982.)

Determining the structure of a paragraph's core sentence is the key to editing sentences in the paragraph because the core sentence signals "the pattern or structure of the paragraph" (23). Three steps are needed to edit contextually, within the context of a paragraph: (1) Locate the core sentence and determine the paragraph's pattern; (2) Decide whether the pattern fits the paragraph's purpose and content; and (3) Determine whether each sentence unmistakably follows the established pattern. Contextual editing also requires vertical thinking, "thinking holistically, grasping all the parts simultaneously" (25). "For instance, you take a unit of prose . . . and place sentences one below another so that subjects, verbs, and objects fall into vertical columns" (25). Contextual editing is thinking in terms of relationships.

143 Maule, Harry E. "The Objective View." In *Editors on Editing*, edited by Gerald Gross, 119-26. New York: Grosset & Dunlap, 1962.

"The function of the editor is to bring a sensitive understanding to the [author's] work and, with it, the objective view that the author may have lost in the writing process" (120). This is particularly true in editing far-out or experimental writers who disregard conventional writing techniques. "The job of the editor, then, is to bring to the manuscript the objective view, to understand what the author is driving at, and, in consultation, to help him to achieve as nearly perfect a work of art as he can" (123).

144 Mitchell, Burroughs. *The Education of an Editor*. Garden City: Doubleday, 1980.

Mitchell introduces his autobiography by saying it "consists of patches of reminiscence, literary appreciation, portraiture, and reflection" (ix). Much of the book is devoted to recounting his professional relationship with and knowledge of authors he worked with at Scribner's, including Zora Neale Hurston, Josephine Herbst, Jim Jones, Maeve Brennan, Dorothy Davis, Morton Thompson, Bill Swanberg, C.P. Snow, May Swenson, and Thomas Bergu. Chapter 3 recounts Mitchell's reminiscence of Max Perkins. Such reminiscences lead to editorial advice. "It isn't uncommon for a bright editor to think of a way to improve a book; but if the 'improvement' distorts the writer's views or alters his tone of voice, then the editor has reached the biggest peril there is for him" (35). "[B]y allowing a professional relationship to grow into a friendship, an editor makes himself vulnerable to troubling experience—to outrage and disillusionment and sometimes to great sadness" (90). "It may be that the biggest accomplishment he [an editor] can expect will consist in persuading the writer that there is somebody who actually appears to understand what his book is about" (159).

145 Mitchell, Burroughs. "The Manuscript." In *Editors on Editing: An Inside View of What Editors Really Do*, rev. ed., edited by Gerald Gross, 63-67. New York: Harper & Row, 1985.

"The Manuscript," an excerpt from *The Education of an Editor*, focuses on three moments in an editor's life: "finding a manuscript that is animated with a life particularly its own" (63), the first meeting between editor and writer, and the publication of a book.

146 Montgomery, Tracy T., Susan R. Glasstetter, and Daniel L. Plung. "The Professional Imperative: Redefining the Boundaries of Editorial Responsibility." In *Proceedings 34th International Technical Communication Conference,* WE-96—WE-99. Washington: Society for Technical Communication, 1987.

Editors should initiate editorial policy in an organization by preparing a documentation plan, "a comprehensive strategy for classifying, organizing, and standardizing both the individual documents in a project and the actual flow of those documents through the project hierarchy" (WE-96). Existing documents may also need to be converted to new formats and "the onus of the conversion rests with the editorial staff" (WE-97) just as the onus for convincing management that a documentation plan is necessary rests with the editor. However, the responsibility for ensuring appropriate document review is the author's. At the same time, editors "should keep some sort of auditable system documenting that reviewers' comments were resolved" (WE-98).

147 Moore, Charles B., and William F. Blue, Jr. *Editing and Layout Techniques for the Company Editor.* Indianapolis: Ink Arts Publications, 1979.

The Company Editor "—all 185 pages of it—is crammed with *useful, usable* information for the novice editor of *any* organization publication— and considerable information for the more experienced" (i). However, "the bulk of the text is oriented to publication design techniques" (iv). Chapter 1 discusses audience. Chapter 2 reviews readability techniques and offers two ways to make text more readable. Chapter 3 outlines a copyeditor's eight duties. Chapter 4 explains how to design a publication using body type. The authors note that "packaging, of course, is design" (25). They provide a formula for ideal line length; examine subheads, overprints and screens; and discuss bylines. Chapter 5 explains guidelining. Chapter 6 discusses copy fitting. Chapter 7 reviews headlines (news, feature, and editorial) by explaining kicker, hammer, sidehead, and tripod heads; and gives instruction on punctuating and creating heads. Chapter 8 focuses on photography, how to scale and crop photographs using a proportional scale method or diagonal line method. Tongue-in-cheek advice to photographers is included. Chapter 9 explains how to write cutlines ("As a rule-of-thumb, photos, whether they have an accompanying story or not, need some form of cutline" [64]) and how to cite credits. Chapter 10 explains proofreading using the guideline system. Chapter 11 discusses basic design. The authors note that "the combination of good design and good content will give you a constant readership" (72). However, "a major problem with most editors and advertisers is their overwhelming desire to clutter design" (73). The authors recommend the Golden Triangle, the 3:5 ration, as one way to produce "pleasing graphic shape" (75). Chapter 12 explains how to design photo features using five principles. Chapters 13 (newsletters), 14 (tabloids) and 15 (magazines) discuss similar issues for each type of publication, including page and column formats, nameplates, mastheads, headlines, photographs ("grip and grins" and morticing) and line art, cutlines and captions, body type, logos, design (horizontal, vertical, modular and megapaper design), editorial pages, doubletrucks, sectioning, dummying ("Good editors dummy; poor editors do not" [142]), magazine covers, table of contents, and "magic line" format.

148 Mount, Robert L., Sanford R. Smith, and Victor Valderrama. "Roof Bolts—For Editters and Riters." In *Proceedings 26th International Technical Communication Conference,* W-122—W-127. Washington: Society for Technical Communication, 1979.

"Hard rock miners in the gold-rush era of California used roof bolts to shore up the sagging overhead in a weakened tunnel" (W123). The authors discuss nine "roof bolts" for editors and writers: (1) "Consider adding to your production checklist a final cycle to proofread all headings, subheadings, titles, and captions" (W-123). (2) When using conventional typing equipment, consider not proofreading certain documents if you are a "very small fast-response operation" (W-123). (3) Use adhesive-backed materials for typing corrections. (4) Use copying equipment to eliminate undesired text, restore faded, low-contrast text, and revise drawings. (5) Do not misrepresent your deadlines to your printer. (6) Resist the urge to use technical graffiti instead of professional art. (7) Help authors who are behind schedule by gathering data they need to write a document. (8) Keep work logs and task lists to plan your work. (9) Take time to relax, even when work pressure is continuous.

149 Mullins, Carolyn J. "Mechanics and Substance in Manuscript Editing." *The Sociological Quarterly* 19, no. 1 (1978): 3-6.

Although some scholars object to editors' making changes in scholars' manuscripts, changes are often warranted. Many scholars have a clear idea of what to say, but they do not know how to express their ideas or how to frame a concept for a particular audience. Editing the manuscripts of such writers requires the editor to make substantive changes, but editors do not have to have specialized knowledge to make those changes. Rather, editors should know how to apply the rules of writing, rules about grammar and correctness, for instance, to produce a well-written manuscript. In particular, Mullins discusses the organization of manuscripts, giving examples of reorganized papers.

150 Nelson, Roy P. *Humorous Illustrations and Cartooning: A Guide for Editors, Advertisers, and Artists.* Englewood Cliffs: Prentice-Hall, 1984.

Chapter 11, "The Role of the Editor," is a discussion of the part the editor plays in selecting humorous art for a publication, particularly a magazine and newspaper. One role of the editor is to decide whether to use a caption with art. If artists provide copy, "an editor watches over all the wording in the illustration, for cartoonists are not noted for their ability to spell" (199). Editors of organizational publications may find illustrators among company employees, and may need to give those illustrators detailed directions about what art to produce. As a rule, however, "an editor should be willing to let an illustrator take a few liberties with the text" (204) when preparing art for a particular piece of prose. Editors should also recognize artists by supplying credit lines when art is published and by using typefaces that complement art. "Sometimes an editor can remove a single letter from an ordinary typeset title—especially the title of a book on a cover or jacket—and substitute a piece of art. A capital 'I' especially lends itself to this treatment" (207). Nelson concludes chapter 11 by reviewing design principles and noting that the way a piece of art is cropped determines what the art says to the reader.

151 Nestor, Margaret B. "The Eternal Triangle: Author, Editor, Reader." In *Proceedings 34th International Technical Communication Conference,* WE-81—WE-82. Washington: Society for Technical Communication, 1987.

Editors are the Tertium Quid in the author-reader relationship. As such, an editor acts as an epigrapher, "one who deciphers inscriptions," and a protolector, the "earliest or first reader" (WE-81). "The task of the editor as epigrapher is to do what the author would have done, given the time, temperament, and skills to do it, and to do it quickly, unobtrusively, and well" (WE-81). As a protolector, the editor's work should be unnoticed. Poor editing can be noticed; "good editing is like tact: no one notices it unless you don't have it" (WE-81). Editors can develop skills as epigraphers and protolectors by writing something and then having that writing edited to learn more sympathy for authors. Reading thoughtfully the efforts of other editors and "noticing what the editor did (and didn't do) to help you [as a reader] can help you understand and meet the needs of your own readers" (WE-82), Nestor tells editors.

152 Nin, Anais. "The Story of My Printing Press." In *The Art of Literary Publishing: Editors on Their Craft*, edited by Bill Henderson, 239-43. Yonkers: The Pushcart Press, 1980.

Because commercial publishers would not print her early works, Nin produced her own books. The experience of "setting each letter [of type] by hand taught me economy of style," (240) she says. When commercial publishers were attracted to her books, she stopped printing her own work. However, she would prefer to publisher her works because she believes commercial publishers equate sales with literary judgment, a wrong equation in Nin's view. In fact, commercial publishers "should sustain explorative and experimental writers, just as business sustains researchers, and not expect huge immediate gains from them. They herald new attitudes, new consciousness, new evolutions in the taste and minds of people. They are the researchers who sustain the industry" (242-43).

153 No Title. In *Editors on Editing*, edited by Gerald Gross, 181-87. New York: Grosset & Dunlap, 1962.

In correspondence between an editor and author about the author's novel that is in progress, the editor says, "'good editors are made by good writers. . . . I am like an echo chamber or a camera eye in that I can record and see and feel only what you yourself have put on paper'" (184). In fact, "my absolute conviction [is] that editors can only affect and never direct'" (186). The author, however, says, "'as an editor, you are plain genius. . . . I also think you wear a bandanna and hoop earrings, for forecasting so completely what I have been trying to say in the book'" (183). The writer also compares the editor to a witch who casts a spell that makes the writer "'work so damn hard'" (183). Then the writer thinks of the editor as "'a third grade schoolteacher, because when I think I can sneak by with something because I haven't quite understood it myself, you grab me by the seat of my pants and make me go back to my desk and open my answer book. It wouldn't surprise me in the least if you practised facelifting without a license. I love you'" (183).

154 Nowell-Smith, Simon. "Authors, Editors, and Publishers." In *Editor, Author, and Publisher,* edited by Wm. J. Howard, 8-27. Toronto: University of Toronto Press, 1969.

Nowell-Smith discusses two aspects of publishing: censoring authors and editing the letters of literary authors. Remarks about censorship are punctuated by examples of conflicts between authors and publisher-editors in the nineteenth century. In particular, editors invited problems when they accepted books they had not read, including the serialization of yet to be written books. About the twentieth century Nowell-Smith comments "that much modern research and criticism and editing is antipathetic to literature" (18) because some textual editors focus on the apparatus used to edit letters instead of considering their audience, an audience they believe to be uneducated. To produce edited letters for a general audience, publishers should construct a code of guidance to editors. Such a code might include instructions on how to deal with an author's idiosyncrasies in his or her letters. For instance, "unless it can be persuasively argued that a writer's idiosyncrasies are integral to the personality of his letters, then his idiosyncrasies, as well as his inconsistencies and slips of the pen, should be ironed out by the editor" (23), a proposal that is contrary to the practice of some editors.

155 O'Connor, Maeve. "Copy-Editing and the Future." In *Scholarly Communication Around the World. Proceedings of a Joint Global Conference,* 64-65. Washington: Society for Scholarly Publishing, 1983.

"[C]opy editors are responsible for checking for correctness and completeness, for removing ambiguities and for ensuring consistency" (64). In doing their job, copyeditors deal with questions of balance or compromise. For instance, the styling of references is not uniform, and although a uniform style would allow authors to prepare correct reference lists, a uniform style does not exist.

156 O'Neill, Carol L., and Avima Ruder. *The Complete Guide to Editorial Freelancing.* New York: Dodd, Mead and Company, 1974.

O'Neill and Ruder devote much of their book to the big three editorial skills—copyediting, proofreading, and indexing—explaining how to get started as a freelancer and how to be successful once a person is employed as a freelancer. To get started as a freelancer, a person can accept "any kind of work that uses editorial skills, whether or not it has anything to do with publishing" (24), because many publishers subcontract not only editorial work, but typing. Appendix III lists courses that teach skills a person can use in editorial freelancing and appendix IV lists publishers who hire freelancers. Once a person has a freelance job, professional performance is imperative. For instance, a copyeditor is "not expected to research every fact, but she is supposed to look up or query everything that seems wrong" (36). To make such queries, the freelancer must be informed. Should the text say whiskey or whisky? "General knowledge is all that can help identify questionable statements or spellings" (37). The authors examine copyediting problems using the "six major elements involved in the all-inclusive term 'style': punctuation; capitalization; abbreviations; spelling; numbers; and special display matter (footnotes, tables, lists, extracts, bibliography)" (47). Proofreading, like copyediting, requires an understanding of style, because the proofreader must correct errors, but "this is the proofreader's dilemma: She must read slowly enough to let her mind become cognizant of every detail caught by the eye, but not so slowly that the grouped letters do not convey meaning" (91). Use of proofreading symbols and an understanding of typography help proofreaders communicate their findings to editors. Indexing requires a kind of reading that focuses on the reader because "the function of an indexer is to enable the reader to find what he is looking for" (129). The authors discuss indexing, including cross references and two methods of alphabetical entries (letter-for-letter and word-for-word), with the admonition, "do not index according to adjectives and adverbs" (154). They note that "even a basic index of names cannot be done mechanically" (131) because indexers must make judgments about what should be indexed. Other facets of freelancing the authors mention are doing research, writing reader reports, editing pictures, and translating texts. A final chapter explains the importance of keeping records for tax purposes.

157 Osborne, Harold F. "Deliberate Editing." *Technical Communication* 26, no. 1 (1979): 10-11+.

Editing is "concerned with *improving the quality* of some communication, usually prepared by others, by a decisive judgmental action" (10). Editing, then, is akin to literary criticism, which results in judgments about the quality of what is written and read. Deliberate editing is the art of making unrushed judgments by allowing "time for considered judgments" (10). Editors should also have humility. "You must be able to make a professional appraisal of your own skills and accept the fact that you, too, are fallible" (11). How then should one edit? "You do it ver-r-r-y carefully. You do nothing that is not absolutely necessary. You edit *deliberately*, in other words" (11).

158 Osborne, Harold F. "Intuition, Integrity, and the Decline of Editing." *Technical Communication* 26, no. 4 (1981): 21-26.

The decline of editing standards that is seen in popular books, even best sellers, is also seen in technical documents. Widespread deterioration in editorial standards can be attributed to social forces that devalue language: "the pressure of quantification; the changing technology; the shift in what our schools teach . . . the changes in this generation's attitudes" (22). These changes point to "the dispensability of human mindpower" (23) and the elevation of technology as the answer to the intellectual demise. Technical editors participate in this demise by excessive conformity to uniformity. "Our uniformity hangs around many an ancient redactor's neck" (24). To remedy the decline in editing, editors should emulate the great editors of the past who "were preceptors, counselors, mentors, guides, teachers, not copy-fixers" (25). The Society for Technical Communication can also help by establishing a Language Council and developing programs to encourage and reward editing.

159 Oskam, Bob. "Negotiating a Publishing Contract." In *Editors on Editing: An Inside View of What Editors Really Do*, rev. ed., edited by Gerald Gross, 90-100. New York: Harper & Row, 1985.

Although three people can negotiate a contract—the writer, the editor, and the writer's agent—authors can negotiate directly with editors. Oskam uses a hypothetical situation to discuss how a first-time author can negotiate directly with an editor. In particular, Oskam discusses how to negotiate an advance from both author's and editor's viewpoints. However, Oskam says an author is probably "more secure if she [works] through a conscientious editor" (100).

160 Parsons, Paul F. "The Editorial Committee: Controller of the Imprint." *Scholarly Publishing* 20 (1989): 238-44.

Faculty members of a university press's editorial committee only evaluate a manuscript based on its contribution to scholarship because their goal is to approve works that the university will publish. In most cases, committee members confirm the editor's recommendation to publish a particular manuscript, but "editorial committees have the power—and they occasionally use it—to reject a work after an editor may have spent months acquiring the manuscript, obtaining positive outside reviews, and working with the author to make the necessary revisions" (240). Members of editorial committees number from seven to fifteen and serve from two- to five-year terms. Members are generally tenured, but are not paid for their committee appointment.

161 Pascal, Naomi B. "Freedom, Responsibility, and the Agile Editor." *Scholarly Publishing* 16 (1985): 255-61.

University press editors may have to resist pressures to publish books that are not appropriate for a university press. Pascal provides anecdotal evidence to explain that "an editor must be not only intelligent and responsive, but flexible and agile as well" (260). For instance, what if a wealthy patron of the university wants the university press to publish his or her book? The editor must decide the best way to reject the book while maintaining the author's goodwill toward the Director of Deferred Giving. Pascal takes special care in those cases to tell the author that the faculty editorial committee ultimately accepts manuscripts based upon the evaluations of outside readers. The editor does not control either the committee or the readers. Sometimes she is able to give advice that will help authors get their book published. Books that treat controversial topics present another opportunity for practicing editorial agility. In evaluating such books, the editor can appeal to a rule: "what the university press imprint means—or ought to mean—is that the book will be not an unsubstantiated polemic but a carefully reasoned and meticulously documented presentation" (258), so the quality of the book's argument is important in making a publishing decision.

162 Pascal, Naomi B. "How Much Editing Is Enough?" *Scholarly Publishing* 13 (1982): 263-68.

Although the question in the title is difficult to answer, the editor's role in the production of a manuscript remains one of "a patient, invisible gardener, wielding a blue pencil instead of a green thumb to coax into full bloom the sometimes deeply hidden beauty of the author's original conception" (263). To do that, editors must learn how to be "solicitous or stern [to authors] as the circumstances require" (265); must be realistic about constraints, especially economic constraints, and "mindful of those shadowy characters who wait at the other end of the publishing process—the potential readers of the published book" (265). Financial contracts are causing publishers to shift editorial responsibility to authors who are asked to bear the expense of extensive revisions by hiring a freelance editor, by producing camera-ready copy, and by acquiring a personal word processor so that authors can incorporate editorial changes into final copy.

163 Paxson, William C. "A Survival Kit for Editors." *Technical Communication* 28, no. 4 (1981): 3.

For editors to survive their editing of "some of the worst prose ever written," a survival kit is needed. The kit would include "deaf ears and a blank look: Useful when editing works by writers who glare at you and grumble, 'I like it better my way' or 'What's the difference as long as the reader gets the point?'" and "A dictionary: For throwing at the more belligerent writers." Paxson recommends eleven survival items.

164 Perkins, Maxwell. "Publishing Thomas Wolfe." In *The Art of Literary Publishing: Editors on Their Craft,* edited by Bill Henderson, 244-53. Yonkers: The Pushcart Press, 1980.

Perkins, the editor of *Look Homeward, Angel* and *Of Time and the River,* recounts his association with Thomas Wolfe. Even before Perkins met Wolfe, he realized "that Wolfe was a turbulent spirit, and that we were in for turbulence" (246). Turbulence came, in part, because of misperceptions about Perkins's role in the editing of Wolfe's books. Perkins notes that Wolfe approved of whatever changes Perkins made. For instance, about *Of Time and the River* Perkins says, "there never was any cutting that Tom did not agree to. He knew that cutting was necessary. His whole impulse was to utter what he felt and he had no time to revise and compress" (248). However, Wolfe's dedication to Perkins in *Of Time and the River* "gave shallow people the impression that Wolfe could not function as a writer without collaboration" (249), and to prove that he could, Wolfe changed publishers. Such criticism of Wolfe's abilities caused him to change his artistic purpose by "distorting Eugene Gant into George Webber" (249).

165 Perkins, Maxwell E. "Selected Correspondence." In *Editors on Editing: An Inside View of What Editors Really Do,* rev. ed., edited by Gerald Gross, 278-306. New York: Harper & Row, 1985. (First published in *Editors on Editing,* edited by Gerald Gross, 129-56. New York:Grosset and Dunlap, 1962.

Letters from John Hall Wheelock's *Editor-to-Author: The Letters of Maxwell E. Perkins* (234) are excerpted for "Selected Correspondence." Letters to F. Scott Fitzgerald, Ring W. Lardner, Allen Tate, Ernest Hemingway, and Thomas Wolfe, among others, emphasize the authority of the author over a manuscript. Writing to Wolfe, Perkins affirms, "I believe the writer, anyway, should always be the final judge, and I meant you to be so" (287). Throughout this selection of correspondence Perkins upholds the freedom of the press and "that one relatively free realm left, the republic of letters" (306).

166 Petersen, Judy. "Editing Out Your Blind Spots." In *Proceedings 35th International Technical Communication Conference,* WE-31—WE-33. Washington: Society for Technical Communication, 1988.

Blind spots, which can be traced to discipline-specific and regional language, develop when a person becomes accustomed to hearing and reading nonstandard language. Examples of discipline-specific language include variant spellings and punctuation. It is Re-entry or Re-Entry? The preferred spelling, according to the *IBM Dictionary of Computing*, is reentry. Regional-specific blind spots include transliterations that are an acceptable use of words, but not accurate in meaning. To heal blind spots, ask people who are new to a particular region to tell you if you use phrases that seem unusual to them; make a list of unusual phrases and use it to edit documents; ask your peers for help when editing a document; use terms that have a generally understood meaning; and memorize the company's standards.

167 Phillips, William. "Poor and Pure." In *The Art of Literary Publishing: Editors on Their Craft,* edited by Bill Henderson, 179-85. Yonkers: The Pushcart Press, 1980.

Noncommercial literary magazines, like *Partisan Review*, are based on a mixed economy whereby editorial activities become enmeshed with business matters. This mixing became particularly evident to Phillips when *Partisan Review* changed from a quarterly to a monthly publication. Comparing the monthly with the quarterly publication, Phillips says that the monthly schedule requires the editor to focus on publishing topics that will please a wide readership. The quarterly, with its slower pace, allows the editor to focus on topics that may not be popular but please a "smaller devoted audience of writers, teachers, and sophisticated professionals who identify with the aims of the magazine" (183).

168 Plotnik, Arthur. *The Elements of Editing: A Modern Guide for Editors and Journalists*. New York: MacMillan, 1982.

In ten chapters, Plotnik surveys the editor's job. Chapter 1 discusses compulsions that editors should and should not possess and introduces Plotnik's mantra: "NOTHING HAPPENS WHEN IT IS SUPPOSED TO HAPPEN WITHOUT WELL-TIMED REMINDERS" (6). Chapter 2 lists ten steps for processing a manuscript. Chapter 3 investigates the editor-writer relationship, affirming that "an editor's job is to shape the *expression* of an author's thoughts, not the thoughts themselves" (32). Chapter 4 describes line editing as "an excruciating act of self-discipline, mind-reading, and stable-cleaning" (34). Chapter 5 explains troubleshooting, ways to "sniff out trouble before it gets into print" (50), including a glossary of libel and remarks about obscenity and pornography. Chapter 6 discusses how the editor can garner information from libraries and includes an annotated list of desk references for editors. Chapter 7 answers 15 questions about copyright. Chapter 8 describes the working life of a book editor. Chapter 9 defines printing (halftone, moire, stripper). Chapter 10 explains the fundamentals of photography to the novice photographer and tells how to edit pictures for publication. An afterword welcomes computers to the world of editing.

169 Podhoretz, Norman. "In Defense of Editing." *Harper's Magazine,* October 1965, 142-47.

Editing is necessary to combat a "further debasement of our language and a further loosening of our already tenuous hold on the traditions of civilized public discourse" (146). But editing is time consuming, often requiring editors to pass through the shadows of doubt, deliberation, labor, and negotiation. Doubt because at times even a commissioned article "only faintly approximates the editor's ideal conception, or else differs radically from it" (144). Deliberation because the editor struggles with questions of appropriateness and questions of effectiveness of the editing process—Can a manuscript be revised? Should it be revised? Labor because "under the editorial microscope things that were not visible to the naked eye—neither the editor's nor the author's—suddenly make an unexpected appearance" (145). Negotiation because an author may resist editorial changes.

170 Portugal, Franklin H., and Bernard K. Forscher. "Can Editing Be Quantitated?" In *Scientific Information Transfer: The Editor's Role,* edited by Miriam Balaban, 265-70. Dordrecht: D. Reidel Publishing Company, 1978.

To study the editing of 83 manuscripts printed in the *Proceedings of The National Academy of Sciences of the United States of America,* the authors evaluated the manuscripts using four defect areas: nomenclature, punctuation, spelling, and construction. "A 'defect' was defined as an entity that was corrected by the manuscript editors" (266). Of the four areas, punctuation and construction ("agreement between subject and verb, use of the correct verb tense, and sentence rearrangement by repositioning, adding, substituting, or deleting individual words or groups of words" [266]) required the most changes. The authors conclude that editors who have similar training but different degrees of experience treated the manuscripts in remarkably similar ways. The authors further conclude that authors do not always pay attention, for instance, to the correct use or spelling of scientific abbreviations or terms.

171 Prashker, Betty A. "A Life in the Day of an Editor in Chief." In *Editors on Editing: An Inside View of What Editors Really Do,* rev. ed., edited by Gerald Gross, 144-54. New York: Harper & Row, 1985.

As an editor in chief, Prashker recounts a typical "life in her day," which includes attending an editorial meeting (9:30-11:30), considering personnel problems (12:15-?), lunching with an agent (late, 12:45-2:30), attending a marketing meeting (3:00-5:15) and a cocktail party (6:00-?). After the party, Prashker, like most editors, will "at least dip into" a manuscript or two before going to bed. Because the editor-in-chief's life is so diverse, "a good editor in chief needs to be warm and cool; creative and businesslike; a leader and a follower. On reflection, there is one quality that I think indispensable: the ability to deal with paradox" (154).

172 Putnam, Constance E. "Myths about Editing." *Technical Communication* 32 (1985): 17-20.

Misinformation about editing is formulated into nine myths, from "every English major is qualified to be an editor" (17) to "only those trained in technical and scientific fields can be technical editors" (20). Putnam refutes these myths by emphasizing the editor's need to possess language aptitude, to think clearly, and to respect the power of words. Those are "essential characteristics of a good editor" (12). The editor should also be positive. "The ability to find merit in every piece of writing, however flawed, is the mark of a mature and creative editor" (19). Editors should also be good writers. Eight rules for hiring and training editors conclude the article.

173 Raphael, Phyllis. "On Being Edited." *Teachers and Writers* 17 (1986): 4.

Raphael recounts her experiences of being edited by three editors from different organizations, concluding that (1) from the writer's perspective, faith in the editor is essential and that (2) teaching and editing are quite similar because the teacher and the editor "create assignments, impart tricks of technique, cut, revise, and inspire."

174 Rawson, Hugh, and Arnold Dolin. "The Editorial Process: An Overview." In *The Business of Book Publishing: Papers by Practitioners,* edited by Elizabeth A. Geiser, Arnold Dolin, and Gladys S. Topkis, 21-42. Boulder: Westview Press, 1985.

The editor can be characterized as a one-person publisher who is the advocate for both the author and the publishing house, the manager moving the author's book through the publication process, and the marketer ensuring that the book receives the attention it deserves—both inside and outside the publishing house. Those editorial roles are predicated upon the actual or potential existence of manuscripts. To procure manuscripts, the editor may give the right idea to the right author and work with the author to develop that idea. Once a manuscript is in hand, the typical editor spends the working day on administrative details—writing letters, answering telephone calls from authors and agents, attending meetings—and takes a bulging briefcase home to edit manuscripts. If the manuscript needs little editing, the editing task will progress at the rate of approximately ten pages per hour. The editor should communicate all comments about the manuscript in writing to the author for legal and professional reasons. Legally, an editor may need to reject a manuscript and written comments serve as evidence that the editor has given the author the opportunity to make the manuscript publishable. Practically, written comments should explain concisely an editor's reasoning for suggested changes so that the author can make an informed decision about whether to accept those suggestions. However, the editor should not tamper with an author's style, in part, because "it is all too easy to recast a cloudy sentence and in doing so distort the author's meaning or introduce a factual error" (34). To design and produce the book, the editor provides copy for the jacket or cover and explains to the art director what special elements in the book deserve his or her attention. In marketing the book, the editor will want to undersell rather than oversell it to the house and make sure, among other marketing details, that subsidiary rights and British rights are investigated. Galleys should be sent to influential review journals. Throughout the publication process, the editor acts "as general coordinator, universal backstop, and constant nudge—all in the interest of ensuring that the book is published in the best possible manner" (42).

175 Ray, David. "Dealing with Mambrino's Helmet." In *The Art of Literary Publishing: Editors on Their Craft,* edited by Bill Henderson, 259-68. Yonkers: The Pushcart Press, 1980.

Editors are faced with polarities: accepting writers and rejecting them. Ray sees the rejection end of that polarity as problematic, and asks how an editor can "accept his function as the hated Naysayer for so many, the person who dishes out to others what he himself most dreads? It is a sadomasochistic situation" (261). Although little magazine editors are not immune to the accept-reject polarities, such editors can develop relationships with authors based on appreciation, not the economic relationship based on name recognition that is typical of our culture. In this regard, "the little magazines offer a counter-culture" (266), but that culture erodes "if, as is occasionally the case, an editor merely imitates more popular fashions" (266). Speaking of his relationships with authors, Ray says, "as an editor I can only pray that I myself have not been too rejecting, too deadly an influence, in any artist's life" (268).

176 Reed, Ishmael. "The American Literary Scene as a White Settler's Fortress." In *The Art of Literary Publishing: Editors on Their Craft,*

edited by Bill Henderson, 100-05. Yonkers: The Pushcart Press, 1980.

Because white males have used their power to control what is published in America, most people, including the international community, have not had the opportunity to read nonwhite American literature. Reed discusses his and others' efforts to break the white monopoly by publishing both white and nonwhite American authors.

177 Reimold, Cheryl. "Writing and Editing—The Two Halves of Language. Part 2: Editing—The Shaping of a Manuscript." *Tappi Journal* 65 (1982): 134-35.

Instead of writers editing their work, they should *shape* it. "The red pencil becomes an instrument of creation, not amputation" (134). To shape a document, find its unifying force by formulating "a one-sentence answer to the question: What do I want to convey?" (134). Then evaluate each sentence of the document to determine if it "makes a relevant point, illustrates or explains a point already made, or connects one point or thought to another" (135). Sentences that do not fulfill one of these conditions probably should be excised. The final phase of shaping includes evaluating the document using a ten-point checklist, which includes the categories of cliches, punctuation, and coherence.

178 Reuter, Madalynne. "Curtis-Doubleday Decision Discusses Duty to Edit." *Publishers Weekly,* June 7, 1985, 25.

In a court case in which actor Tony Curtis claimed that Doubleday publishers had unfairly rejected his second novel because the publisher had not edited it to make it satisfactory to publish, the court ruled in favor of Doubleday. In part, the court's ruling said, "'although we hold that publishers must perform honestly, we decline to extend that requirement to include a duty to perform skillfully. The possibility that a publisher or an editor—either through inferior editing or inadvertence— may prejudice an author's efforts is a risk attendant to the selection of a publishing house by a writer, and is properly borne by that party. To imply a duty to perform adequate editorial services in the absence of express contractual language would, in our view, represent an unwarranted intrusion into the editorial process.'"

179 Richardson, Marie. "The Editor Won't Let You." In *The 577 Papers: Writing Processes, Editing Processes, Written Products,* vol. 1, edited by Roger E. Masse, 75-91. Las Cruces: New Mexico State University, Technical Communications Programs, 1982.

Richardson cites four stages in the editing process—"reviewing (determining the level of edit), repairing (making the necessary changes in each level of edit), conferring (discussing the project with the author), and evaluating (reviewing the edited product)" (77)—based on a review of the literature on editing.

180 "The Rising Cost of Editing." *Scholarly Publishing* 1 (1970): 347-61.

In general ten publishing professionals agree that editorial costs are high for a variety of reasons. One, the trend to publish more technical books will increase costs. As Bauer (Cornell University Press) notes, "science manuscripts are generally more costly to edit because of the shortage of scientifically trained editors" (347). Two, because copyeditors do not participate in the selection of texts, their judgment about changes that are needed to publish a manuscript can increase projected production costs. Kefauver (Ohio State University Press), says, "editorial departments are asked to play a central role in the publication of a book only *after* others have decided that the manuscript, of which the editorial department is often little more than a passive recipient, is indeed publishable" (353). Three, the best copyeditors tend to overedit, which increases costs. As Unwin (George Allen and Unwin, Ltd.) remarks, "this seems to me the paradox of the manuscript editor's job: he can get true job-satisfaction only by spending twice as long as is strictly necessary in order to make his own contribution creative, and thus, almost inevitably, he over-edits" (358). Four, authors often do not adequately prepare their manuscripts for publication. To combat these problems, managers can ensure that editors work with authors during the early stages of manuscript preparation, even becoming involved in the selection process; can hire freelance editors; and can require authors to meet certain editorial standards or be charged out of their royalties for their disregard of house rules.

181 Roberts, William C. "Writing Versus Editing." *American Journal of Cardiology* 54, no. 7 (1984): 934.

As a writer turned editor, Roberts compares writing and editing, saying, "writing is relatively lonely and selfish. . . . Editing, in contrast, is relatively social and unselfish in that it requires much communication with authors, publishers and readers. . . . of the two, however, editing is much easier than writing; judging is much easier than creating."

182 Rogers, Geoffrey. *Editing for Print*. Cincinnati: Writer's Digest Books, 1985.

Rogers explains the editor's role in the production of a book or magazine issue by beginning with print production and the role of budgets and schedules in that process. The editor is portrayed as the manager of the entire production process that includes editing a text by making arrangements for content editing and copyediting of the text.

One approach the editing task is to have a freelance or in-house content editor make any major revisions and then have a copyeditor make any final changes to prepare a manuscript for the typesetter. However, Rogers includes advice on copyediting—how to use style sheets, how to mark copy, how to compile a master proof. The editor also should participate actively in the design process. "Broadly speaking," Rogers informs editors, "it is your task as the editor to amass the reference materials and the designer's task to visualize the illustrations" (83). Thus, Rogers explains how to commission artwork and photographs, how to do picture research (or how to have it done for you), and how to write captions. The printing process is described as the next step in producing a book or magazine, including definitions and examples of halftones; types of printing processes (letterpress, offset lithography, and gravure); and types of bindings. Once a book or magazine is printed, the editor must help sell the finished product. "As an editor, you will be involved throughout the year in helping to prepare publicity and promotional material of all kinds" (124), including copy for book jackets, magazine covers, blads, and catalogue copy. An editor may decide to repackage a book or magazine, so Rogers explains the legal and technical aspects of repackaging. Throughout the book, Rogers discusses the impact of computer technology on the editor.

183 Rogers, Trumbull. "On the Road to Mediocrity." *Publishers Weekly,* December 4, 1987, 42.

"Years ago, you rarely saw a typo in a book; now you rarely pick up *any* book that isn't riddled with every imaginable kind of error." Rogers attributes the decline in copyediting to six factors: attitude (quality is not that important anymore), pay (low for copyeditors), time (publishers want more in less time), computerization (often English is not the keyboarder's first language), and skill (freelancers are required to be jacks-of-all-trades.) Rogers predicts that quality will continue to decline if publishers "eliminate the copyediting and perhaps even the proofreading phases of book production, leaving full responsibility for these functions with the author."

184 Ross, Peter B. "Slash for Quick Editing." *Technical Communication* 24, no. 3 (1977): 11-14.

Slashing, "marking off ideas with slash lines" (11), allows the editor to separate concepts to evaluate them. Slashing has four steps: "(1) *Draw* a line at the end of each idea. (2) *Number* each idea as it appears in the sentence. (3) *Write out* each ideas separately, one idea to a line. (4) *Edit* for sequence, completeness, clarity, and relevance" (11). Ross identifies five types of sentences that need slashing—overloaded, slow-takeoff, cause-and-effect sequences, long-tailed standstill, and long passive-voice. Slashing can be time consuming, so Ross provides eight guidelines for determining when to slash.

185 Ross-Larson, Bruce. *Edit Yourself: A Manual for Everyone Who Works with Words.* New York: W.W. Norton & Company, 1982.

Edit Yourself, a manual on style, is divided into two parts. Part I, "What Editors Look For," consists of eleven chapters on such issues as pronoun reference, dangling constructions, and parallel constructions. Chapter eleven discusses style sheets and a checklist for editing a document. Part II, "What Editors Cut, Change, and Compare," is an alphabetical arrangement of "more than fifteen hundred common cuts, changes, and comparisons that editors make to produce clear, concise writing" (ix). For example, *erstwhile* should be changed to *former* (63).

186 Rubin, Harriet. "Working Both Sides of the Desk: Editors Who Write, Writers Who Edit." *Publishers Weekly,* November 7, 1980, 28-31.

Five author-editors give their views about the relationship between writing and editing. Sol Stein says, "'editing exists only because writers don't have the patience to take a first- or second-draft manuscript and put it into a drawer and not look at it for a year'" (29). Toni Morrison notes, "'as a writer I know all the time . . . all the things I threw away to get that paragraph. The editor doesn't know and shouldn't care. Editors just know what they see; and it works or it doesn't'" (29). Carol Hill believes, "'writing and editing are so totally opposite . . . . an editor's impulse has to be to take apart, to analyze, to critique, to see why it doesn't come together. A writer's impulse is never to stand that far outside the material'" (30). Michael Korda agrees with Hill. "'Other people's prose I can work on,'" Korda notes. "'My prose is mine; I can't see it objectively'" (31). Joyce Engelson suggests, "'publishing wouldn't collapse without editors; it *would* collapse without the person sitting at the typewriter, writing. It's all the author'" (31).

187 Rude, Carolyn D. "The Rhetorical Basis of Substantive Editing." In *Proceedings 34th International Technical Communication Conference,* RET-143—RET-145. Washington: Society for Technical Communication, 1987.

When editors are responsible for ensuring that a document is not only correct, but usable, they should use a rhetorical approach to editing. Rhetorical editing focuses on audience and purpose and like the writing process, it progresses from discovery to considering how to arrange and style a document. Discovery includes analyzing, evaluating, establishing editorial objectives, and revising the manuscript with the author. Five guidelines for editing arrangement "help assure systematic, objective editing. . . . Thus, they increase the chances that the editing will be purposeful rather than reactive and thoughtful rather than arbitrary" (RET-144). The purpose of using the discovery process is to establish a partnership with authors and to avoid adversarial relationships. The discovery process also should produce quality editing.

188 Sale, Faith. "Editing Fiction." In *Editors on Editing: An Inside View of What Editors Really Do,* rev. ed., edited by Gerald Gross, 187-99. New York: Harper & Row, 1985.

After recounting a day in her life as an editor, Sale notes, "this absolutely typical day in the life of an editor included absolutely no editing. In fact, it included nothing that would suggest where a book comes from" (192). Much of an editor's time is spent attending to all the details of publishing: checking with production personnel about a book's binding and the stamping for the spine, meeting with in-house lawyers, and reading book reviews. The actual editing is "an organic process" in which the editor helps authors achieve their writing purposes. Sale shows how that organic process works when she recounts the production of a novel she edited.

189 Santino, Charles. "The Editorial Assistant." In *Editors on Editing: An Inside View of What Editors Really Do,* rev. ed., edited by Gerald Gross, 123-27. New York: Harper & Row, 1985.

As an editorial assistant, an understudy to editors, Santino did a variety of secretarial duties and quickly learned that "a staggering work load requires rapid decision-making" (123) about whether to publish a manuscript. Because Santino worked concurrently for four editors, he notes that "being a good editorial assistant has more to do with a person's skills of organization and diplomacy than it does with being able to spot a masterpiece" (126).

190 Schlosberg, Jeremy. "Ten Ways to Trim Your Manuscript Down to Size." *Writer's Digest,* March 1989, 37-39.

Self-editing one's manuscript is not revising, which "concerns structure, flow, logic, coherence; revising turns a first draft into a second, a second draft into a third, a third into a final" (37). Self-editing entails shortening a final draft by applying "the self-editor's one guiding principle: NOTHING IS SACRED" (38). To self-edit, make an outline; know your central thesis ("sum up the entire premise in one sentence" [38]); examine your lead; spare those summaries; check your conclusion; watch for multiple quotations; curb the extra anecdotes; beware of backgrounds; attack all extra words, sentence by sentence; and steel yourself, good stuff goes too. "If you are now within 10% of your goal [to reduce the manuscript's length], stop. . . . Editors do like to have *some* things to edit" (39).

191 Schuster, M. L. "An Open Letter to a Would-be Editor." In *Editors on Editing: An Inside View of What Editors Really Do,* rev. ed., edited by Gerald Gross, 33-37. New York: Harper & Row, 1985. (First published in *Editors on Editing,* edited by Gerald Gross, 7-12. New York: Grosset and Dunlap, 1962.)

Schuster lists twenty-four statements, sometimes almost aphorisms: "Start trends, don't follow them" (35). Others include, "You ask for the distinction between the terms 'Editor' and 'Publisher': An editor selects manuscripts; a publisher selects editors" (33). "There are times when you must finally say: 'Although this is a bad idea, it is also badly written'" (34).

192 Schwartz, Laurens R. *What You Aren't Supposed to Know about Writing and Publishing: An Expose of Agents, Editors, Publishing Houses and More . . . An Insider's Report.* New York: Shapolsky Publishers, Inc., 1988.

Two chapters—chapter 4 and chapter 7—explicitly discuss editing, or rather, expose editing practices. Chapter 4 is devoted to freelancing, including freelance editing. Schwartz's advice on how to get a freelance job applies to writers and editors. Freelance editing "is an extremely lucrative field. Depending upon the names of editors still employed at houses that the freelancer can drop—suggesting that he has strong contacts for eventual publication of the work—these people charge from $500 to $15,000 per manuscript. What they do is read it, synopsize it (just in case you forgot what you had written about), and add up to a ten page critique of your literary failings. They do not rewrite" (35). Like chapter 4, chapter 7 is written for authors and explains what editors do for authors. Today's editors don't edit because they are marketers. Normally, a manuscript will be processed by moving it from "editor to marketing/production, back to editor. If that report [from marketing/production] is positive, the editor will circulate the work to editors who owe him favors or seem predisposed toward the promoted project. Enough support at the first editorial conference will lead the editor to stick his neck out even further" (78). If an editor accepts a manuscript, yet after considerable time it is not published, "what has happened here is that an editor might have decided that the book fits his list, but the book was nixed at the final conference. He nonetheless continues fighting for the book. Or the editor is considering leaving the house and wants a backlog of acceptable books to take to a new house. Or the editor at the end of each season keeps coming across a book which is, to him, even more suitable to his lists than yours—which he hangs onto anyway" (80). In fact, editors select books that will not be successful, yet "editors always forget that some books are chosen to be loss leaders, and that tax loss carryovers have been found beneficial to large companies" (84). Authors should also be concerned about editors who have just taken a position with a house. In particular, "the editor who has just come to a house from a magazine is the one to worry about most. He or she will feverishly rewrite everything so that it follows the style of the magazine" (86).

193 Sedgwick, Ellery. No Title. In *Editors on Editing,* edited by Gerald Gross, 232-40. New York: Grosset & Dunlap, 1962.

In a selection from his *The Happy Profession,* Sedgwick argues that the editor should possess prejudice based on good taste. This prejudice should be focused on words, "and against the misuse of words every editorial prejudice should be fixed in concrete" (232). Thus Sedgwick advises beginning editors "not to neglect prejudice but not to bear down upon it in too many directions at once" (233). At the same time, "to an editor open-mindedness is of the first importance. There is a point just below credulity and very far above skepticism where his mind should stick and open not one jot further" (234). Editors, therefore, don't prejudge, but do judge based on their taste, their values. "Taste underlies judgment. . . . In this world, it is quite as important to hate as to love. If you hate insincerity, if vulgarity has an instant effect upon the balance of your diaphragm, you won't go far astray" (236-37). In other words, "vulgarity is a total misconception of the values of life. Real values have not a touch of it, and these are the editor's everlasting lure" (238-39).

194 Sheppard, R. Z. "The Decline of Editing." *Time,* September 1, 1980, 70-72.

Egregious grammatical errors of best-selling novels suggest that "the anything-goes school of writing" (70) is firmly entrenched. Why? "The most frequently mentioned culprit is financial pressure" (70), the bottom line. "Inflation pushes up the cost of paper, printing and distribution; recession makes buyers think twice about purchasing a book for $12.95, almost three times the cost ten years ago" (71). The way books are acquired has turned editing into a "harrowing vision of a rat race on a roulette table" (71) where editors bet on books, sometimes with million-dollar bids. Also, editors may be reluctant to edit the works of authors who are successful. Some newly successful authors "who view their own crudities as an inviolate form of personal expression"

(71) do not want an editor's assistance. However, Sheppard cites two author-editor relationships that produced well-written books.

195 Shimberg, H. Lee. "Editing Authors' Style—A Few Guidelines." *Technical Communication* 28, no. 4 (1981): 31-35.

"[F]or those editors who are senior and adept enough to be authorized to edit authors' styles: do not do so unless absolutely necessary" (31). However, an editor should discern which styles need to be edited. "A style that includes vicious sarcasm—as opposed perhaps to gentle understatement—or a style characterized by elegant phrases and complex thoughts should be edited even though the authors will almost certainly be reluctant to accept the suggested changes" (32). Editing for style can be divided into two parts: determining whether a particular style hinders communication with the intended audience and convincing authors to accept editorial changes that will improve the manuscript. Shimberg discusses editing for readability by explaining how to edit poor organization, verbosity, indirect and imprecise language, and poor diction. He also says that the works of nonnative writers should be edited without much conversation between editor and author and without much intrusion into the text. "Remember, a friendly editor is an effective editor" (35).

196 Simon, Henry W. No Title. In *Editors on Editing,* edited by Gerald Gross, 175-80. New York: Grosset & Dunlap, 1962.

Five pieces of correspondence between Henry Simon, Vice President of Simon and Schuster, and Niven Busch, a novelist, explore the best way to prepare a blurb and dust jacket to sell a book. Both Simon and Busch agree that "there *is* no legitimate distinction" (178) between a commercial and a literary book, and Simon adds, "I always think it is a very bad idea to tell very much of the story on the jacket" (178). The occasion of these letters is the preparation of a book by Busch. Author and editor disagree about what that book's dust jacket should look like, but the author's wishes win out.

197 Simons, Rayanna. "Slush." In *Editors on Editing: An Inside View of What Editors Really Do,* rev. ed., edited by Gerald Gross, 117-21. New York: Harper & Row, 1985.

Slush refers to unsolicited manuscripts sent to publishers. Traditionally, the first reader makes decisions about the publishable quality of slush. On occasion, a slush manuscript can be a profitable publishing endeavor. Simons, who spent four years as a first reader for Macmillan, laments the change in publishing practices that has eliminated the first reader and thus reduced the opportunity for writers without agents to receive a publisher's appraisal of their work.

198 Skidmore, Bill. "Editorial Compromise." *Technical Communication* 30, no. 3 (1983): 35.

Crash deadlines may require editorial compromise of what to improve in a document and what to leave unchanged. Five key editing functions and the estimated time needed to complete each function (in minutes/page) can help an editor determine what to compromise, given strict time constraints.

199 Smith, Howard. "Author's Editors: Responsibilities and Professional Standards." *Journal of the American Podiatry Association* 72, no. 9 (1982): 473-75.

The author's editor helps the author express ideas "in the way the author desires and, at the same time, make[s] the content clear to the reader and acceptable to the publisher" (473). To accomplish that three-pronged goal, editors can perform three types of edit (technical, substantive, and creative), facilitate production of the manuscript, and teach the author how to improve his or her writing skills. Smith also discusses remuneration for editors and professional standards for the editor-author relationship.

200 Smith, Patricia N. "Here, Edit This!" In *Proceedings 28th International Technical Communication Conference*, W-92—W-94. Washington: Society for Technical Communication, 1981. ED 227 479.

"Respected editors deliver good work on time. You should try to follow their example" (W-92), Smith advises editors. To deliver good work, an editor should understand the task before starting it, including knowing a document's audience and purpose and any restrictions pertaining to audience and purpose; pinpointing problems in organization, diction, style, content, and layout and design; and resolving difficulties by choosing either light or heavy editing to revise the document. To deliver work on time, an editor "should know how long you have to complete the task" (W-93). Then the editor can evaluate a manuscript. "Your answers to the questions of 'how much' and 'what kind' will largely determine the amount of time demanded by the task" (W-93), Smith counsels editors.

201 Smith, Peggy. *The Proof Is in the Reading*. Washington: Typographers International Association, 1986.

The Proof Is in the Reading is addressed to prospective proofreaders and to managers of proofreaders. Both need to know that "for good proofreading, you need *the right people* with *the right training* working in *the right environment*" (1). The right people have a natural aptitude, the "Eye," for detecting broken patterns, whether for solo or team proofreading. To hire good proofreaders, managers should test applicants. "Never hire a proofreader without testing for spelling and comparative reading" (7). (Sample tests are provided in the appendices.) Good proofreaders can improve through proper training. Learning the level of proofreading and how to query are part of that training, culminating in perfection, which "is a proofreader's duty" (20). Smith also discusses proofreading pitfalls on the road to perfection. Proofreaders will work best in the right environment, an environment where they are treated with respect. In such an environment and, often under the tutelage of a master proofreader, they can be taught how to increase their speed and accuracy in proofreading. Smith says, "I believe in fast team proofreading. Slow puts people to sleep; fast keeps them alert. But the key to speed is steadiness" (31).

202 Smith, Peggy. "Typos Yesterday, Today, and Tomorrow." *Scholarly Publishing* 16 (1985): 175-89.

Drawing upon an 1883 article by Alfred Watts, Smith presents Watts's classification of typographic errors to demonstrate that errors in copy have remained consistent over time. Thus Watts's classification of errors "provides a map of the enduring pit-falls in copying a document of any kind by any human means" (176). Watts divides copying errors into five major categories: omissions, substitutions, doubling, insertions, and transposition. One type of omission is homeotel where "the copyist's eye skips from one word to another that is the same word, has the same ending, or appears in the same position on the page" (176). Another type of error, a subcategory of substitution, is replacing a word with a like-sounding word. For example, "'from the Printers' Bible (1702): Printers' [princes] has persecuted me without cause—Psalms 119:161. . . . From the Large Family Bible (1820): Shall I bring thee to the birth and not cease [cause] to bring forth?—Isaiah 66:93'" (183). Watts's study was based on text "'set by twelve compositors all thoroughly up to their work'" (187). Summarizing Watts's results, Smith notes, "Watts found 223 errors in sixty pages, an average of 3¾ per page (affecting 6½ words per page). . . . we can guess that each page had roughly 6500 characters, which puts the rate at about one error every 1750 characters" (188). Smith equates Watts's results to modern units. "Watts's error rate for good compositors equates to an average of one typo in copy set from each page of double-spaced typewritten manuscript" (189). The moral of Watts' study for present-day proofreaders? "Although new technology presents new pitfalls for compositors and proofreaders, the old ones—the ones caused by human imperfection—remain to humble us. And proofreading a copyist's work by comparing the manuscript with the copy continues to be necessary, because, as Watts said, 'unless we can feel assured of a strict and continuous comparison with the copy having been made, no evidence of general carefulness in the copyist can be assumed as a security against even gross mistakes'" (189).

203 Smylie, Patricia O. "The Care and Feeding of Freelance Editors." *Scholarly Publishing* 5 (1973): 41-52.

How can university presses find freelance editors? A press editor can take several press personnel who have worked for other university presses out for coffee and engage them in reminiscences about "Editors I Have Known." The list of names that the editor constructs because of those reminiscences is the beginning of the search for freelance editors. The editor will need to contact prospective freelancers, and test them using "a straightforward job of mechanical editing" (45). Once editors hire a freelance editor, they must supervise the freelance, especially using correspondence. Smylie notes, "some of the notes and memos might seem too casual to be classed as 'supervision,' but they are clearly directions to me and reports from me, and this is what I understand supervision to mean" (46). She also explain how a series of letters between editor and freelancer establish what is expected of whom. However, "if freelancers are seriously interested in a career, they must be cheaper, or faster, or better, than the house editors—and preferably, all three" (50), and freelance pay must not be counted only in dollars and cents, else the job is low paying. Rather, freelancers should consider the personal educational benefits their work provides them.

204 Soderston, Candace. "The Usability Edit: A New Level." *Technical Communication* 32, no. 1 (1985): 16-18.

During usability edit, readers "flag usability problems in the material" (17) by using the material to perform a task. The usability edit is based on the assumption that writing is a way to get people to do something; the audience uses information to perform certain tasks. The usability edit is conducted in a room with a one-way glass, microphone, telescreen monitor, videotape, and display screen so observers can monitor a volunteer's use of a document. The usability edit should be used early and repeatedly in preparing various drafts of a document. Usability edits are important because usability "is a function of the interaction between the text and the reader, rather than solely an attribute of the text" (18).

205 Solotaroff, Ted. "Publishers, Booksellers, Readers, and Writers: Some Straws in a Whirlwind." In *The Art of Literary Publishing: Editors on*

Their Craft, edited by Bill Henderson, 3-12. Yonkers: The Pushcart Press, 1980

Editorial publishing decisions are often based on economics. "The initiatives and risks of the editor give way to the prerogatives and assurances of the money managers—even to the money manager inside the editor" (4). This preoccupation with economics is rooted in the late 1960s when "the expanding educational market" provided great financial rewards, but a new audience also emerged, one that is "fragmented, diffuse, and dispersed, composed as it is of diverse and contending interests, values, and tastes" (10). Once in awhile an author's work will draw together a large part of this audience, but the audience remains volatile. This audience has helped promote small presses and small literary magazines, but those publishing endeavors generally have small circulations. In the volatile, fragmented market, Solotaroff advises writers to learn how to endure, saying, "I think that perhaps the most appropriate workshop [for writers] that could be given is one in how to deal with rejection for years to come, and how to support yourself if a teaching job doesn't materialize" (12).

206 Spencer, John D. "Instant Tips for Authors." *S[ociety of] T[echnical] W[riters and] P[ublishers] Review* 13, no. 3 (1966): 18.

Editors can educate authors about writing by preparing and circulating a series of tips. "Sent out monthly with copies of our progress reports, these aids cover text, tables, and illustrations." The result of these monthly tips "has been a painless, if limited, technical writing education and a more relaxed and human approach to the subject."

207 Stainton, Elsie M. "Another Mixed Bag." *Scholarly Publishing* 9 (1978): 219-30.

In giving more advice to editors (see 208), Stainton addresses questions about punctuation, grammar, footnotes, subheads, indexes, foreign terms, and lectures. For instance, she says that punctuation, especially the use of commas, changes. When, however, two different but correct ways of punctuating a passage are in question, "the author, not the editor, should decide" (223) which way will be used. While rules of punctuation may change, certain rules like antecedent references do not change. Stainton also notes that indexes should be prepared by the author with help, if needed, from an editor or indexer. Authors should produce concise indexes. Because of her experience in preparing lectures as book chapters, Stainton advises, "when an editor is scheduled to work on a manuscript derived from lectures, attending one or more of the lectures is sure to be useful in the editing" (229). About the state of editing, Stainton notes, "this generation of editors has much work to do, because many of the present crop of authors were not taught the basic skills of writing" (230).

208 Stainton, Elsie M. "A Bag for Editors." *Scholarly Publishing* 8 (1977): 111-19.

Stainton's bag is filled with advice to editors on a number of subjects. Examples include: "good judgment and discretion are constantly required of an editor" (112); "the poetic main title that requires a subtitle is bad" (112). The editor can evaluate a title by asking if it describes what the book is about and if the title will help sell the book. "Caution: do not press an author to hurry over changing a title that he has lived with for a long time" (113). Stainton advises editors to query authors about using certain adverbs (really, undoubtedly, manifestly) and encourages authors to delete them "or at least some of them. (Often the editor must settle for less than perfection)" (115). Without sales, the editor should recall, "then no publishing house, and no editors" (117). "An editor without an author is like a mechanic without a car to work on, a doctor with no patients, a teacher without students, like electricity with nothing to light up. We should praise bad authors for providing our livelihood" (118).

209 Stainton, Elsie M. "The Copy Editor." *Scholarly Publishing* 17 (1985): 55-63.

Using five W's and one H, Stainton surveys the copyeditor's job. What do copyeditors do? "A copy editor takes someone else's words, which the editor may have no particular interest in, and works hard and long to make them right (or better)" (55). What kind of person is an editor? The editor is committed to language. "The editor's credo, then, is 'I care'—about the words, sentences, and paragraphs in the articles, pamphlets, and books that are helped along towards publication" (57). Why bother with editing? Editing pays its way. Who gains by professional editing? The publisher, the author, and the readers gain. Because the editor is so intimately involved in a book's production, whose book is it? "The author is boss about it except in a few matters—in some important legal areas and in most production decisions, in which the publisher is seriously concerned" (58). For instance, libel could cause an editor not to publish a book, if the author will not rewrite the offending passages. Indiscretions and male chauvinism, though not as serious as libel, could "discourage or offend readers needlessly" (60). How can an editor do a good job? "Much of an editor's success depends on personal relations" (61). The editor can develop positive relationships with authors by using praise, even when a manuscript seems unpraiseworthy. "Suppose a manuscript seems to make perfectly obvious points, hashes over arguments that go without saying. What to praise? The editor can comment: 'Many readers will agree with you.' And then add: 'Would you try to give your argument a new twist?'" (62). In short, "a little honest praise may help to regularize spellings, to enforce rules of punctuation, and generally to improve a writer's style" (63).

210 Stainton, Elsie M. "A Mixed Bag: Getting Along Together." *Scholarly Publishing* 9 (1978): 149-58.

Stainton gives advice about how authors and editors can work together. She advises editors to praise authors, even when an author's work requires significant editing. Genuine praise helps establish trust and the most direct way to establish trust is to show appreciation for a manuscript's good points. Editors should not change an author's work unless they "have a specific, very specific, reason for every change—a matter of grammar, syntax, clarity, or recognized points of style: the editor should not change wording because other phrasing 'sounds better'" (154). However, editors should not be so permissive that any word the author coins is acceptable. To both authors and editors she says, "to unpleasantness, prefer pleasantness; to shouting, soft words; to self-aggrandizement, sincerity. Before confrontation, try communication" (158).

211 Stainton, Elsie M. "Writing and Rewriting." *Scholarly Publishing* 10 (1978): 75-83.

Substantial part of "Writing and Rewriting" is incorporated into chapter 2 of Stainton's *Author and Editor at Work: Making a Better Book* (478).

212 Stearns, Laurie. "The Importance of Copy Editing." *Publishers Weekly,* July 10, 1987, 48.

Copyeditors do not receive adequate remuneration for their work; yet they are a vital part of publishing. Copyeditors may be undervalued because they work with words, not numbers. But for publishers, "words are our business. If we don't treat them with respect, no one else will." Stearns recognizes that publishing is not a high-paying profession, but she would like to see "the revenues divided fairly among publishing professionals."

213 Stein, Sol. "The Author as Editor." In *Editors on Editing: An Inside View of What Editors Really Do,* rev. ed., edited by Gerald Gross, 54-61. New York: Harper & Row, 1985.

To help authors achieve their purposes, whether commercial success or a sense of personal satisfaction, an editor must often help "the writer understand that the proper intention of his work is to create something that will move an audience" (55). To do this, an editor needs to be candid with authors about ways to improve their work, to improve their craft and touch their audience. Thus, "an editor's primary function is to help the writer realize that he must keep his audience in mind while writing; in fiction, with a view toward moving that audience as often as possible; in nonfiction, toward getting that audience to accept what the writer has written as accurate, true, and, if possible, wise" (60).

214 Stevens, George. "Editing for Sense and Effect." In *Editors on Editing,* edited by Gerald Gross, 111-18. New York: Grosset & Dunlap, 1962.

"One may say that there are two kinds of editing; editing for correctness and consistency, and editing for sense and effect" (112). To edit for sense and effect, an editor must go beyond mechanical styling and ask substantive questions about an author's work. For instance, in editing nonfiction works, the editor must ensure that authors say what they mean in terms that the intended audience can understand. In fictional works, the editor focuses on clarity, "making convincing the action and the motives of the characters" (16), and interest. In editing for sense and effect, "an editor's function is to make the author work harder and longer than the author originally intended" (115). In doing their work, editors find that experienced authors do not take editorial suggestions personally, but inexperienced authors do take editorial suggestions personally.

215 Stith, Mary E., Naomi B. Pascal, Iris M. Wiley, and James E. Kubeck. "The Out-of-House-Editor." *Scholarly Publishing* 3 (1972): 259-72.

"The Out-of-House Editor" is a four-part article on freelance editing. Each part is written by one of the four authors. Stith summarizes a questionnaire returned by 19 presses of different sizes. The questionnaire asked how much freelance editing is being done (about 25 to 50% for the titles in a publisher's total list), how the editors are paid (by the hour, by the job, or by the page), how much direction freelancers get from the publisher (The presses that responded to the questionnaire endorsed training or standardizing instructions for freelance editors), how the edited manuscript is processed after it is returned by the freelancer, and what happens if the work is unsatisfactory (Screening and training of freelance editors is the key to reducing unsatisfactory work). Stith notes that "perhaps the most important conclusion to be drawn from the questionnaire and subsequent discussions is the importance of training" (261). Pascal cites positive and negative experiences to support her assertion that "only under exceptional circumstances is freelance editing a satisfactory arrangement" (262). However, the best freelancer to hire is one who has experience working at a press and knows press style. Even then, freelancers must be supervised. "[N]o matter who else is editing a manuscript, an in-house editor must always, always, be responsible for checking the accuracy and completeness of front matter" (265). Wiley also expresses doubt about using freelance editors because finding a good one is difficult, and developing procedures for processing the freelance-edited manuscript is also a problem. But by using freelancers a press has access to specialized talent, particularly when scientific manuscripts need to be edited. Wiley advises employers to try out freelance editors on short manuscripts like a book chapter because the in-house editor can scrap a chapter or two more easily than mend a poorly edited book-length manuscript. For Kubeck's part of the article see "The Freelance System Works for Us" (122).

216 Strauss, Harold. "Selected Correspondence." In *Editors on Editing: An Inside View of What Editors Really Do,* rev. ed., edited by Gerald Gross, 308-18. New York: Harper & Row, 1985. (First published in *Editors on Editing,* edited by Gerald Gross, 188-200. New York: Grosset and Dunlap, 1962.)

Selected letters by Strauss give unnamed authors explicit details about how to revise their works, mostly scientific works or works based on science. Because two letters are addressed to non-American authors, Strauss goes into detail about stylistic issues for nonnative speakers. He insists that writers evoke clear images for the nonspecialist.

217 Swaney, Joyce H., Carol J. Janik, Sandra J. Bond, and John R. Hayes. *Editing for Comprehension: Improving the Process Through Protocols.* Technical Report No. 14. Pittsburg: Document Design Project, Carnegie-Mellon/American Institute for Research, June 1981. ED 209 642.

In an experiment to determine how to edit a document, four skilled editors reviewed four one-page documents (a guarantee, a selection from an employee handbook, a medical form, and a page from an insurance policy) with the goal of presenting information "that could be easily accessed and understood but not necessarily remembered" (4). Twenty-four members of the general population were recruited to read and answer questions about the documents. The car insurance policy was not any easier to read even after being reviewed by seasoned editors. Reading protocols were used to determine what made the policy hard to read. Using the result of reading protocols, the editors found that "subjects were having [difficulty] with instantiation, context, inferencing, and attention management" (19). Editors redesigned the policy based on protocol results, and produced a document which was four times as long as the original document. However, "it took subjects an average of two and one-half times as long to read the revision as it had the original" (19). Even though the revision was longer than the original, "readers had no major problems with the final revision [which] indicates that our experts [editors] were successful" (21) in providing a readable document. The authors conclude that "protocols can increase an editor's awareness of readers' problems" (21).

218 Tacker, Martha M. "The Code of an Author's Editor." *Medical Communications* 5 (1977): 7-9.

As a freelance editor, Tacker developed a code to inform authors about her understanding of her duties and rights as an editor. Such a code can be effective at the beginning of an editing project because the code gives authors an opportunity to explain what they expect and desire from the author-editor relationship and to preview what the author's editor can do for the author. In particular, Tacker expects appropriate credit for editing a manuscript, in part, because proper credit "will serve to increase an editor's pride in his or her work and stimulate the production of high quality results" (9).

219 Targ, William. "What Is an Editor?" In *Editors on Editing: An Inside View of What Editors Really Do,* rev. ed., edited by Gerald Gross, 3-31. New York: Harper & Row, 1985.

Targ's comments, which are excerpted from his autobiography, *Indecent Pleasures,* offer bits and pieces of advice that center on a central theme: being an editor requires dedication to editing. It is a seven-day-a-week job. Editors must read manuscripts at home and after hours, build a collection of reputable books, pay attention to the economics of producing books, and treat authors and other professionals with respect.

220 Taylor, Helen K. "What Is an Editor?" In *Editors on Editing,* edited by Gerald Gross, 3-6. New York: Grosset & Dunlap, 1962.

Among other things, "an editor is a man with a finger to the wind" (4) who is looking for publishable ideas and authors to publish those ideas. In temperament, "an editor is a man with a gregarious mind and a tender regard for human nature. . . . [and] a friend to all literary talent" (4). An editor must help shape an author's book, check an author's references, and sniff out libel. An editor is both a businessman and a gambler who recommends that an author's first, second, even third book be accepted for publication by the firm, even though the editor knows all three books will lose money for the firm. The editor is betting on books the author will produce later. And even though "there are more hazards, disappointments and weary hours to this job than one likes to count" (5), admiring a book fresh from the press makes an editor's job worth it all.

221 Thatcher, Sanford G. "Competitive Practices in Acquiring Manuscripts." *Scholarly Publishing* 11 (1980): 112-32.

Thatcher presents and analyzes the results of a twelve-question survey on competition for manuscripts among university presses. Fifty-one presses responded to the survey. Although most questions ask about how a press competes for manuscripts, some questions pertain directly to editors. For instance, in response to one question, respondents in large, middle, and small presses noted that editors pay a significant role in approving advance contracts. Also editors acquire manuscripts by travelling to another press's campus. Although travelling to another editor's campus is a touchy issue for some editors, Thatcher notes that an editor must have the liberty to contact the best authors in a particular field regardless of their campus affiliation. Otherwise, no press—small or large—would be able "to build a truly first-rate list of national scope and significance" (128). Comments from those who completed the survey suggest that manuscript competition is a mixed blessing. A respondent from a large press noted, "'it is a system-wide waste of editorial overhead and, when we lose, a waste of house editorial resources'" (130). However, a respondent from a small press said, "'aggressive publishing is, on the whole, a good thing, and competition is part of that'" (131).

222 Thurber, James. "Harold Ross." In *Editors on Editing,* edited by Gerald Gross, 246-52. New York: Grosset & Dunlap, 1962.

In a selection from his *The Years with Ross,* Thurber says that Ross was "the most remarkable man I have ever known and the greatest editor" (248). See 223 for annotation of *The Years with Ross.*

223 Thurber, James. *The Years with Ross.* Boston: Little, Brown and Company, 1959.

Harold W. Ross, the founding editor of *The New Yorker,* was a man of many faces. Thurber notes, "there were so many different Rosses, conflicting and contradictory, that the task of drawing him in words sometimes appears impossible, for the composite of all the Rosses should produce a single unmistakable entity: the most remarkable man I have ever know and the greatest editor" (13). In chronicling the development of Ross's magazine from 1924 until 1951 when Ross died, Thurber, a member of *The New Yorker* staff for many years, gives examples of the many-sided Ross. For instance, "Ross stood in awe and reverence of no writer" (78), but his attitude toward writers was not due to his great learning. Rather, "when he worked on a manuscript or proof, he was surrounded by dictionaries, which he constantly consulted, along with one of his favorite books, Fowler's *Modern English Usage*. He learned more grammar and syntax from Fowler than he had ever picked up in his somewhat sketchy school days. He read the *Oxford English Dictionary* the way other men read fiction, and he sometimes delved into a volume of the *Britannica* at random" (82). In fact, as Thurber notes, "the central paradox of Harold Ross's nature . . . [was] his magic gift of surrounding himself with some of the best talent in America, despite his own literary and artistic limitations" (92). Because Ross rarely read novels, he queried writers about obvious literary allusions that he didn't recognize and even seriously asked one *New Yorker* staff member if Moby Dick was the name of the captain or the whale. Because of his mercurial nature, Ross, according to Ogdan Nash, "'was an almost impossible man to work for—rude, ungracious and perpetually dissatisfied with what he read; and I admire him more than anyone I have met in professional life. Only perfection was good enough for him, and on the rare occasions he encountered it, he viewed it with astonished suspicion'" (123). "Ross had an obsessive reverence for Order and Organization" (139), yet he was flexible, "at once the most obdurate and reasonable of editors" (184). Many of Harold Ross's attitudes about editing are explained in Wolcott Gibbs's 31-point list outlining the theory and practice of editing *New Yorker* articles (129-35 and annotated under 80). For another biography of Ross see 85.

224 Toland, Robert. "Attitudes and Method: Complements of an Editing Process." In *The 577 Papers: Writing Processes, Editing Processes, Written Products,* vol. 2, edited by Roger E. Masse and Martha Delamater, 139-52. Las Cruces: New Mexico State University, Technical Communications Programs, 1983.
Toland recounts his personal growth as an editor by changing his attitude about editing and then by editing using a three-step process. To change his attitude, Toland had to correct a misunderstanding about what an editor does, not just proofread, but help authors transfer information to readers. To help authors Toland had to commit sufficient time to making editing choices that would solve manuscript problems. Once he corrected his misconceptions about how to edit a manuscript, Toland developed a three-stage method for editing manuscripts: "understanding content, discovering organization, and analyzing problems and making suggestions" (144). This method requires three readings of a manuscript (1) to understand its content and correct minor errors, (2) to outline the paper and find organizational problems and suggest ways to reorganize the work, and (3) to reread parts of a paper

that need more editorial effort. The three-stage approach is a systematic way to edit any paper.

225 Tripp, Edward. "Editors and the Editorial Committee." *Scholarly Publishing* 8 (1977): 99-109.

In responding to Giamatti's article (79), Tripp notes that the editorial committee of a university press does not become involved in the manuscript selection process early enough to safeguard that process. It is true, Tripp says, that the faculty editorial committee possesses the key that can lock quality in and mediocrity out, but the committee turns that key after other doors have been locked or unlocked by people who are not on the committee. "The problem is that the committee, unlike the editors, has not been hanging around the barn. When it finally locks the door, how can it be sure the horse is still inside?" (101). Editorial committees can become involved earlier in the review process by collaborating with editors to build a list of books. Committee members can help identify areas of scholarship that are becoming recognized as important, emerging fields and point out scholars who are doing important research. In terms of publishing philosophy, committee members should not reject manuscripts that challenge traditional academic ideas, explore nontraditional areas of scholarship, or present research findings in an unorthodox way. The committee should also become interested in books about teaching, which "no less than research, is the work of the universities, and therefore of their presses" (108).

226 *United States Government Printing Office Style Manual*. 28th ed. Washington: U.S. Government Printing Office, 1984.

"The *Manual* is primarily a GPO [Government Printing Office] printer's stylebook. Easy rules of grammar cannot be prescribed, for it is assumed that editors are versed in correct expression. As a printer's book, it necessarily uses terms that are obvious to those skilled in the graphic arts" (VII). Because the *Manual* prescribes style for government documents, it contains chapters on how to print the *Congressional Record;* Senate and House journals; and nominations, reports and hearings. Over 100 pages of the *Manual* constitute "a guide to the typography of the more important languages handled in the Office" (335), including Finnish, Greek, Russian, and Turkish.

227 University of Chicago Press. *The Chicago Manual of Style*. 13th ed. Chicago: University of Chicago Press, 1982.

"Two pervasive features characterize the present edition: it reflects the impact of the new technology on the entire editing and publishing process, and it spells out, in greater detail and with many more examples, the procedures with which it deals. It is, in short, a much more 'how-to' book for authors and editors than was its predecessor. In chapter 2, for example, a new section has been added on how to mark a manuscript and how to mark the type specifications on a script. Chapter 12, completely rewritten, begins with advice on how to make a table from raw data. Chapters 15 through 17, reorganized and greatly expanded, offer many more alternative methods of citation—the emphasis being on the most practical—and provide a wealth of examples. In chapter 18, clear step-by-step procedures for the mechanics of index making are set forth. The terminology and methodology of technological advances (in word processing, computerized electronic typesetting, and the like) are reflected most prominently in chapter 20, 'Composition, Printing, and Binding' (new to this edition), and in the Glossary, which now emphasizes typesetting and printing terms, excluding many items, formerly included, that were applicable only to the publisher's function. Other notable features of the present edition are chapter 4 ('Rights and Permissions'), rewritten in light of the new copyright law, and chapter 9 ('Foreign Languages'), which includes a new table of diacritics, a pinyin (Chinese) conversion chart, and data on several more languages" (vii). The *Manual* is divided into three parts: Bookmaking, Style, and Production and Printing.

228 Van Buren, Robert, and Mary F. Buehler. *The Levels of Edit*. 2nd ed. JPL 80-1. Pasadena: Jet Propulsion Laboratory, California Institute of Technology, 1980.

Van Buren and Buehler present nine types of edit and five levels used by the Jet Propulsion Laboratory (JPL). The nine types are coordination, policy, integrity, screening, copy clarification, format, mechanical style, language, and substantive. The levels (1 through 5) are based upon how many types of edit are used. Level 1 includes all types; level 5 includes coordination and policy. The levels of edit do not include extraordinary editorial functions, such as "providing additional or missing material.... [or] working with unusually difficult or time-consuming material.... [for instance,] editing copy written in a foreign language" (7). In short, "each level of edit consists of a range of effort from minimum to maximum, depending on the condition of the manuscript.... [and] the level of edit defines the quality of the end product but not the effort required to achieve it" (9). The levels of edit make distinctions between format ("the visual aspect" of a manuscript) and mechanical style ("the content of the publication" [11]). The authors also discuss distinctions between language and substantive parallelism (22-3). In practice, the levels of edit has "proved useful as a management tool for estimating and monitoring cost" (vi). See also 275 and 276.

229 Vaughan, Samuel S. "Letter from the Editor." In *Editors on Editing: An Inside View of What Editors Really Do,* rev. ed., edited by Gerald Gross, 39-52. New York: Harper & Row, 1985.

The book editor's job is to help authors publish their books, to represent the author. The editor has three roles as a representative: to represent the author in the publishing house; to represent the publishing house to the author; and to represent the reader. Vaughan's letter offers details about what the editor does to represent authors.

230 Vocale, Mary L. "Overcoming the Manuscript: An Editing Process." In *The 577 Papers: Writing Processes, Editing Processes, Written Products,* vol. 1, edited by Roger Masse, 57-73. Las Cruces: New Mexico State University, Technical Communications Programs, 1982.

The editing process is divided into three levels: "(1) getting in shape, (2) finding the problems, (3) solving the problems" (59). Getting in shape refers to attitude. Editors who approach the editing task conscientiously will do a more professional job than editors who are in a depressed or vindictive mood. Finding the problem entails reading a manuscript twice, once to become familiar with the paper's content, once more to look for possible problems. If editors cannot summarize the paper in outline form after two readings, they need to isolate the reason(s) why they can't summarize it. Solving problems requires a third reading while editing on two levels: larger and lesser problems. Larger problems are organization and content. Lesser problems include language and style. However, style "should be left intact" (66). A 21-item annotated bibliography on editing is included.

231 Wade, James, and Richard Marek. "Editing Nonfiction: In the Service of One Book and Many Readers." In *Editors on Editing: An Inside View of What Editors Really Do,* rev. ed., edited by Gerald Gross, 202-12. New York: Harper & Row, 1985.

An editor "is *not* the author's friend . . . he is the *book's* friend. . . . a reader's advocate" (204). To be a good nonfiction editor, one should not assume the expert's role, but enlist experts to comment on manuscripts. In fact, the editor should "give very little specific editorial advice [to the author] during the book's formation" (208). However, the editor should keep in mind the goal of nonfiction—to clarify, organize, and efficiently transmit information—and suggest manuscript changes that will achieve that goal.

232 Wales, Ruth W. "A Taxonomy of Editing Tasks." In *Proceedings 29th International Technical Communication Conference. Technical*

Editing, General

Communication—Charting the Course of Technology, W-116—W-117. Washington: Society for Technical Communication, 1982.

Editing, changing a document to improve its quality, is divided into four categories, which list questions about a document being (1) correct, (2) consistent ("Consistency is achieved by tracking items throughout the document to be sure of uniformity and agreement" [W-117]), (3) clear, concise ("Writing quality is the focus here. The editor is now more concerned with good or bad than right or wrong" [W-117]), and (4) coherent, complete.

233 Weeks, Edward. No Title. In *Editors on Editing,* edited by Gerald Gross, 216-31. New York: Grosset & Dunlap, 1962.

In a selection from *In Friendly Candor,* Weeks's memoirs, the author recalls his career as a book and magazine editor for *Atlantic Monthly.* Early in his editorial career, Weeks learned that "a first reader is no good unless he is outspoken" (219) and "the temptation to overedit is insidious" (221). Underediting, not recognizing changes in the relationship between editor and author, is also a liability. "[T]he editor's relations with his author can never be the same year in year out. They must be resilient and subject to the swiftest change" (223). The job of actually editing manuscripts is reserved for weekends. "[A]n editor's work week really begins on Friday afternoon when with his secretary's help he stuffs his briefcase with all the things he ought to have attended to during the week. Beginning Friday night and continuing through Sunday he reads his prizes and makes his discoveries, blueprints the next issue, and dreams up his big ideas for the future" (226). During the week, an editor is busy answering correspondence, attending meetings, and being "tossed and gored by a contributor" (228). In spite of the liabilities of editorial work, Weeks remarks, "the truth is we couldn't be paid to do anything else. Editing is in our blood" (228).

234 Wheelock, John H., ed. *Editor-to-Author: The Letters of Maxwell E. Perkins.* Dunwoody: Norman S. Berg, 1977.

Selected letters written from 1914 to 1947 by Perkins, editor at Scribner's, are addressed to well-known writers, unknowns, and unnamed persons and reveal themes in Perkins's view of the editor. One theme is the author's ownership of his or her book; editors should honor that ownership. Perkins writes to F. Scott Fitzgerald, "don't ever *defer* to my judgment" (30). To an unnamed critic, Perkins asserts, "a book, of course, has to arise out of the author, and what an editor must fear most is that he will influence the author too much" (231). In fact, Perkins notes, "the editors I know shrink from tampering with a manuscript and do it only when it is required of them by the author"

(230). Thus Perkins portrays himself to one critic as a common man. "You ask who I am," Perkins says. "I am, or at least should be if I fulfilled myself, John Smith, U.S.A. He is the man who doesn't know much, nor think that he knows much" (238). The ineffective editor violates that rule of commonness. "The trouble with reviewers, and with editors, is so simple that nobody gets it. They ought to just take a book and give themselves to it, and read it like a regular citizen and see whether they like it or not. They ought not to apply their standards and frames of reference, and all that, to it, until afterwards" (248). Another theme addresses the editor's role as an advocate for the audience, again "the ordinary unliterary citizen, who is the really important critic in the end" (43). In fact, Perkins tells one author, "if you make your audience mad, it doesn't make any difference how cogent is your reasoning" (212). A third theme is freedom of speech. Perkins championed free speech in his letters and criticized censorship, upholding the duty of the publisher to publish authors of literary importance, even if the publisher disagrees with those authors' viewpoints. To one unnamed critic Perkins notes, "nowadays, publishers are under pressure from all sorts of groups. What if they should trim their books to suit every point of view and every element of religious and racial pride? What, then, would remain of that one relatively free realm left, the republic of letters" (303).

235 White, Jan V. "Editors Don't Know Design? Nonsense!" *Folio* 12, no. 4 (1983): 65-6, 168.

Editors and writers are qualified to make a design decision if they know why a particular document is being published. Editors can work with designers to determine what it is that the editors want to say, but both editors and designers should recognize that "the purpose of editorial design is not to make a handsome piece, but a piece that *says something*" (66). If the editor has trouble communicating with a designer because the editor is uncertain of what good design is, he or she should show the designer samples of the type of design desired.

236 Williams, Frank O. "Design Desiderata and Editorial Considerations." *Scholarly Publishing* 3 (1972): 169-73.

The book designer's ideas should be solicited at the beginning of the publication process because from the beginning of a project both the editor's and the designer's ideas are important. Generally, however, design decisions that entail important financial issues are made by press directors. When a manuscript finally arrives at the designer's desk, the designer can perform only a "perfunctory and so rigidly predetermined" (171) role in the book's design. Design, however, is inherent in editing. Thus, it will be a progressive move when "editors, when they first discuss a manuscript with some prospective author, will look upon *their* performance as a designing effort—a far cry indeed from the implicit meaning of editing" (171). The misuse of the designer in the preparation of scholarly books probably stems from press editors who perpetuate the view that printed words are the only valid and enduring form of scholarship.

237 Williams, Miller. "The Writer and the Editor." *Scholarly Publishing* 14 (1983): 149-54.

Conflicts between the author and the manuscript editor are "almost wholly one of style" (151). Thus manuscript editors can set the style for the editor-author relationship in corresponding with the author. Generally, the editor writes two letters to the author, one introducing the editor as the person responsible for editing the author's manuscript and one included with the edited manuscript when it is sent to the author. In writing those letters, the editor should recognize that "it is presumptuous and perilous to assume that an author wants to be addressed by first name" (151). A patronizing tone, too, also is poor style. The editor will increase the author's faith in the editor's professionalism if the editor does not persistently split hairs. "Writers will suffer in peace, and even gladly, if they can believe that only those changes are made that should be made, and if those necessary changes are made with sensitivity and in a context of common sense" (154).

238 Witman, William D. "Using Reading Protocols to Edit Documents: A Case Study." In *Proceedings 34th International Technical Communication Conference,* RET-159—RET-161. Washington: Society for Technical Communication, 1987.

After reviewing a financial-aid document using standard editing techniques, Witman prepared a typed revision for a reader to analyze. The reader read the manuscript aloud into a tape recorder and made comments about the document. From the reader's comments, Witman learned "that my reader was not willing to read along passively from section to section. When the reader ran into new information, he immediately tried to fit the new information into what he had just read" (RET-161). Witman used the reader's comments to edit the document a second time, improving it by adding cues that assured his reader that whatever new information was not explained would be explained later.

239 Young, Bruce. "Manuscript Editing: Talent, Craft, and a Sense of Order." *Scholarly Publishing* 6 (1975): 227-33.

Manuscript editing is basically preparing a manuscript to be typeset and printed. Thus the manuscript editor, who must be a good speller, may markup, proofread, and index a manuscript. However, in performing editorial tasks, the editor must remember that the style of the manuscript belongs to the author. Effective editorial work is done "in a spirit of unassuming helpfulness" (230). "[M]odesty (genuine or assumed) and willingness to compromise" (231) are therefore characteristics the manuscript editors should possess. The editor should enjoy "bringing order out of chaos" (231). Craft is essential because for the average scholarly book about 80 per cent of an editor's time is spent on tasks that require little or no creativity—using the house rules to style the manuscript. The best way to become an editor is to know someone in the bookmaking business.

240 Zook, Lola M. "Editing and Editors: Views and Values." *Technical Communication* 28, no. 4 (1981): 5-9.

"Editing is utterly, remorselessly personal. . . . This means that 'the process of editing' is something each editor shapes and implements in his or her own way" (5). Zook lists five editorial values and viewpoints she holds. An editor must (1) be committed to trying to achieve an ideal by doing the best editing possible given specific objectives and time constraints, (2) set the standards for his or her performance, recognizing that "perfection is not a realistic goal" (6), (3) have command of the medium (basic editorial techniques should be second hand and an editor should be interested in many different subjects, have unlimited curiosity and possess "an absolute delight in information" [7]), (4) have critical judgment born from an understanding and appreciation of logic, order, and language, and (5) be able to work well with other people by controlling one's own behavior and practicing communication skills that promote a cooperative relationship with authors. These virtues describe a vocation "that, at its highest level, might truly be called 'an art'" (9).

241 Zucker, Ernest. "Stelco's Communication—Managing Reader Satisfaction (Audience Analysis) and Editorial Policy." In *Proceedings 26th International Technical Communication Conference. Technical Communication—Shaping the World We Live In,* M-191—M-195. Washington: Society for Technical Communication, 1979.

Zucker discusses three topics: (1) telephone surveys of readers to determine audience satisfaction, (2) case histories to market Stelco products through company-produced magazines, and (3) editorial policy. The editor's job is divided into seven procedures: (1) participation in a planning meeting, (2) getting approval of ideas for stories, (3) preparing copy and photographs, (4) ensuring technical accuracy of data, (5) submitting text and photographs to artists, (6) suggesting layout ideas, and (7) proofreading.

242 Zuppan, Jo. "Technology and the Manuscript Editor." *Scholarly Publishing* 13 (1982): 281-84.

Computers are often the focus of technological development, but editors should not overlook a number of other useful devices. For instance, "new forms of writing instruments . . . a dozen models of soft-tip fine-line pens are available at reasonable prices" (281). Such pens also come "in a rainbow of color. . . . Purple prose merits purple editing? The possibilities are endless" (282). Operating a copying machine "could make an ideal initiation rite for aspiring editors" (282) because it numbs one's mind. Correction fluids, self-adhesive correction tape, and advances in cellophane tape are also discussed. Certain electronic devices are included. Pocket calculators, for example, are not only useful for validating numeric sums but are "indispensable for figuring out expense reports following professional meetings" (284).

Editing, Technical

243 Abshire, Gary M., and Dan Culberson. *The Art of Technical Writing and Editing*. IBM Technical Report GTR 05.225. Beoblingen: IBM Corporation, 1978.
"[T]he whole point of editing, is to get an objective opinion—an appraisal—about how good the writing is" (6). To get such an appraisal the technical writer should consult with a professional editor who knows the craft of editing, who has "the skill of choosing, arranging, substituting, and rearranging words" (12). The authors contend that "editing is editing is editing" (16). There is no such thing as a technical edit or a light or heavy edit. Editing "comes in two flavors: good and bad" (16).

244 Allen, Arly, and Melanie Miller. "The Printer Talks About Editors." *CBE Views* 9, no. 3 (1986): 82-83.
Printers categorize editors of scientific and scholarly publications as either copyeditors or substantive editors. Printers also divide other printers into two groups: WYSIWYG ("what you see is what you get") printers and partner printers. The WYSIWYG printer is interested primarily in rapid turnaround time because the faster a project is completed the more competitive a printer is. Partner printers, however, are interested in providing specialized processes and services, so time is not the critical issue. Copy editors who share the fast turnaround philosophy work best with WYSIWYG printers. Substantive editors are primarily interested in quality and prefer working with partner printers.

245 Altman, Lawrence K. "Cheating in Science and Publishing." *CBE Views* 4, no. 4 (1981): 19-25.

Contrary to scientists who believe that cheating and fraud are rare in published scientific data, Altman says that cheating and fraud are prevalent. One reason such unethical activities occur is because scientific journal editors have vested interests which may mitigate against their investigating charges of fraud. And although scientists have trusted the peer review system to detect fraudulent research, that system has not been effective. Perhaps potential cases of fraud could be investigated by checking raw data when papers are critiqued. When fraud is uncovered, "editors have an obligation to publish . . . follow-up information" (24) explaining that a published paper was fraudulent. Otherwise, the original data remain uncorrected and are preserved.

246 Altman, Philip L. "The Council of Biology Editors." *Scholarly Publishing* 20 (1989): 218-226.

Altman recounts the history of the Council of Biology Editors (CBE) beginning in mid-1955 when a preliminary conference was held to consider problems biology editors face. Now CBE has an annual meeting which "provides a forum for the sharing of ideas leading to solutions of problems intrinsic to the journals of CBE members" (219). From that annual meeting, committees and task forces are organized to cope with specific editorial problems. Publications, like *CBE Views, Scientific Writing for Graduate Students, Editorial Forms: A Guide to Journal Management,* and *Illustrating Science: Standards for Publication,* are produced to help editors and teachers have references for answering editorial questions. In addition, CBE has been a leader in the creation of "three foreign associations of biological editors and a national association of earth science editors" (225).

247 Amsden, Dorothy C. "Exercise Your Visual Thinking." In *Proceedings 29th International Technical Communication Conference. Technical Communication—Charting the Course of Technology,* W-12—W-15. Washington: Society for Technical Communication, 1982.

Editors can use visual thinking to picture—both mentally and on paper—what an author is describing. When editors make rough drawings of a particular process to aid their understanding of what an author is saying, they should realize that other readers may also have difficulty understanding the text. Amsden suggests that editors include their rough sketches with the author's text when they pass on the text to the graphic artist. If a photograph is the best way to picture a description, the editor should determine the focus of the photograph. Editors can recommend graphics when an author compares data and when the steps of a procedures are included in the text. Editors need not possess excellent drawing ability because technical illustrators can produce professional drawings based on the editor's rough sketches. Authors may be reluctant to accept a drawing to explain data because they might consider it insufficient for sophisticated readers. The editor, however, is an advocate for the reader, and if the editor is confused by an author's text, readers might also be confused.

248 Amsden, Dorothy C. "Get in the Habit of Editing Illustrations." In *Proceedings 27th International Technical Communication Conference,* vol. II, paper WE 7A, W-147—W-154. Washington: Society for Technical Communication, 1980.

Not a formula, but a working approach can help editors improve illustrations for technical documents. An editor can begin using the working approach by determining an illustration's purpose in a manuscript. Then the editor can make judgments about the level of detail in an illustration. The editor also should identify missing information and spell out abbreviations, among other things. Amsden provides guidelines for editing graphs, diagrams, and drawings, emphasizing simplicity as a primary editing concern. "Unclutter the drawing. Remove unnecessary detail. Condense. Combine" (W-151). The use of heavy lines to indicate important parts of a technical graphic is also important. Editors also should consider reducing certain illustrations so that the sizes of illustrations in comparison to one another and in comparison to the type size do not create an imbalance.

249 Angell, Marcia. "Editors and Fraud." *CBE Views* 6, no. 2 (1983): 3-8.

Editors of scientific publications can do little to prevent fraud in research, but "editors do have the responsibility to be alert to any warning signals that appear in a manuscript and to follow up on them. When data fall into place too well or when there is little or no variance, then an editor should be skeptical" (5). Editors should be alert for seven types of fraud—fragmentation, loose authorship, duplication of publication, selection of data, trimming, plagiarism, and fabrication—and once fraud is detected, editors should question the validity of other works published by the errant researcher(s), warning readers that earlier studies may be invalid. If authors whose research is being scrutinized do not assure the editor that earlier studies are valid or do not retract their published results, the editor should retract the studies in question and tell readers of that action.

250 Annett, Clarence H. "Improving Communication: Eleven Guidelines for the New Technical Editor." *Journal of Technical Writing and Communication* 15, no. 2 (1985): 175-79.

New editors can become disenchanted if they have poor relations with their authors. By using the following eleven guidelines, editors can be friends with writers: (1) Only make changes to manuscripts that improve them. (2) "Look for innovation. . . . appreciate freshness and variety" (177). (3) Be punctual in processing manuscripts, including answering authors' queries and acquiring reviewers' comments. (4) "[L]earn something from each manuscript" (177) and teach the author about communicating. (5) "Temper your verbal and written comments, and keep the worst of them to yourself" (177). (6) Be fair by giving writers the opportunity to disagree with you. (7) "Don't be arrogant" [178], but sympathize with the author. (8) "Explain delays and changes to the author" (178). (9) Accept disagreements as part of your job and don't let them become major conflicts. (10) Ensure that deadlines or author satisfaction are not reason for sacrificing editorial quality. (11) Realize that most unedited manuscripts aren't of high quality and find the author's message and help convey it to readers.

251 Applewhite, Lottie B. "The Author's Editor." *Medical Communications* 1 (1973): 16-20.

Author's editors—"the medical editor with whom an author works at his own institution" (16)—have five roles to play. One, they are mechanics who help authors refine a manuscript by working with the mechanics of language, format, and assembly. Two, they are teachers who question authors to help them evaluate a paper's logic and to alert authors to data which may be further refined before being published. Three, they are interpreters who explain to the author what type of audience reads a particular journal, what editorial practices are preferred by a particular editor or journal, and why a manuscript may be delayed during the publication process. Four, they are advocates. Editors must champion an author's paper, if the editor believes the paper is good enough to deserve championing. Five, they are activists. Editors strive to ensure that authors follow scientific writing standards. Editors can improve the quality of scientific writing by organizing medical writing workshops.

252 Applewhite, Lottie. "Examination of the Medical/Scientific Manuscript." *Journal of Technical Writing and Communication* 9, no. 1 (1979): 17-25.

Editors, reviewers, and authors can evaluate a medical/scientific manuscript by consulting four aspects of the manuscript: "1. its medical/scientific contribution in reference to the intended audience (Gross Examination); 2. the contents and coverage of the topic (In-Depth Examination); 3. the manner of expression and the grammatical precision (Minute Examination); and 4. the completeness of the manuscript-package (Components of the Manuscript)" (18). Applewhite divides each aspect into subcategories and lists questions under each subcategory. For instance, Minute Examination is divided into four categories (paragraphs, sentences, word choice, and punctuation), and of the seven questions under word choice, one asks, "Are the appropriate units of abbreviations used?" (23).

253 Aronson, Milton H., and Robert C. Nelson. "Technical Reading, Writing, and Editing—No. 5." *Instruments and Control Systems* 36 (1963): 81-83.

In a series of six articles, published January through June in *Instruments and Control Systems*, the authors discuss causes of the breakdown in technical communication and determine that editors are a major cause of the breakdown. The fifth and sixth articles in the series are devoted to editing. The fifth article states that the editor has two functions, the mechanical function of producing publications and the educational function of working with authors so that they can communicate to readers. The mechanical function is secondary to the educational function, which can be performed by answering four questions: "1. What is the author trying to say? 2. Has he said it clearly? 3. Is it worth saying? 4. Do the level, background, perspective, and overlapping frame of reference permit the reader to understand it?" (83). Article six (254) is a continuation of article five.

254 Aronson, Milton H., and Robert C. Nelson. "Technical Reading, Writing, and Editing—No. 6." *Instruments and Control Systems* 36 (1963): 73, 75.

(No. 6 is a continuation of article No. 5 [253]). "The main point of a technical article should be made early in a manuscript" (73), and if it is not made early, the editor should locate the main point and put it at the beginning of the manuscript. To determine the main point, the editor can ask four questions: "1. What is the main point? 2. Is the main point identified in the manuscript? 3. Is it clouded by a lot of minor points? 4. Can the main point be separated from all other ideas and presented alone?" (75).

255 Atkins, Eldred E. "Comprehensive Publications Program: A Simplified Writing/Editing Approach That's 'Got it *All* Together.'" In *Proceedings 18th International Technical Communications Conference. The State of the Art,* paper #3-4, pp. 1-8. Washington: Society of Technical Writers and Publishers, 1971.

Atkins explains a nine-step procedure used to publish three IBM technical documents. The procedure was implemented because of a constant backlog of unfinished reports. After one year of using the procedure, editors reduced editing time by at least one third. Authors now have clear guidelines that require them to communicate with the Communications Department at the outset of a project, direct them to take responsibility for manuscript preparation, and enable them to prepare manuscripts that are more organized than they were before the guidelines were implemented.

256 Baker, Carole F. "The Publisher's Editors." *Medical Communications* 8, no. 3 (1980): 71-75.

The production process for a medical book requires numerous editorial functions performed by a series of editors: editor in chief or acquisitions editors, serials editors, developmental or project editors, sponsoring editors, managing editors, copyeditors, and production editors. After explaining the role of each type of editor in the publication process, Baker notes that one person may perform all of the editorial functions.

257 Balaban, Miriam, ed. *Scientific Information Transfer: The Editor's Role*. Dordrecht: D. Reidel Publishing Company, 1978.

Scientific Information Transfer is the Proceedings of the First International Conference of Scientific Editors held in Jerusalem in 1977. The Proceedings is "dedicated to the diverse aspects of editing towards advancing scientific information transfer—technical and sociological norms and practices, quality, refereeing and judgment, impact of new mechanical and organizational techniques, copyright, standards and style, economics, society and commercial publishing, primary-secondary-tertiary literature and their interfaces, and the philosophy and sociology of science. Scientists, editors, publishers and others concerned with information transfer have laid bare some of their attitudes, policies, practices, prejudices and problems" (x). For articles selected for annotation see "Editing a Photographically Reproduced Journal" (541), "Primary Publications and Modern Information Systems: Copyright Problems from the Viewpoint of Editors of Scientific Journals" (365), "How Editors Catalyze the Publication Explosion" (449), "Editors' Impact on Science Policies and Politics" (544), "The Editor as Mover or Retarder of Scientific Ideas" (359), "The Role of the Review Journals in Scientific Publication" (502), "Reports on Progress in Physics" (548) "Editorial Judgment in Scientific Periodicals" (517), "The Creative Role and Function of Editors" (497), "Can Editing be Quantitated?" (170), "Style! Why Bother?" (120), "An Editor's View of Standards and Standardization" (418), "Four Kinds of Style" (38), "Is a Good Editor a Good Publisher?" (348), "Editing a Photographically Reproduced Mathematics Journal" (542), "The Need for a Council of Social Science Editors" (386) "A Rational System for Editing and Publishing the Literature of Tropical Agricultural Resource Assessment and Development

Planning" (259), "Scientific Editing and Publishing for the Third World: A Review from the Tropical Products Institute" (261), "On the Information Transfer from Primary to Secondary Sources and from Secondary to Primary Sources—An Editing Experiment in an Interdisciplinary Field (Automatic Image Analysis)" (360), "How Services from the Institute for Scientific Information® (ISI®) Aid Journal Editors and Publishers" (509), "The Difficulties of Preparing the International Serials Catalogue. How Editors Could Help" (529), and "IFSEA: Towards an International Federation of Scientific Editors' Associations" (392).

258 Barnow, Renee K. "Setting and Clearing a Table: How an Editor Can Get Out of the Kitchen." In *Proceedings 29th International Technical Communication Conference. Technical Communication—Charting the Course of Technology,* W-18—W-21. Washington: Society for Technical Communication, 1982.

Editors may need to create, "set," or rewrite, "clear," tables, like chefs set or clear kitchen tables. Barnow gives examples of how to set a table from a text and how to clear a cluttered table. To clear a table an editor may "(1) make another table, (2) present some information in the text, (3) delete some material, or (4) leave it as it is and swallow hard" (W-20).

259 Baulkwill, W. J. "A Rational System for Editing and Publishing the Literature of Tropical Agricultural Resource Assessment and Development Planning." In *Scientific Information Transfer: The Editor's Role,* edited by Miriam Balaban, 523-42. Dordrecht: D. Reidel Publishing Company, 1977.

Changes in the reporting procedures of a governmental agency in England helped produce documents that are more useable to readers. The Land Resources Division (LRD), a scientific component of the Ministry of Overseas Development, evaluates land resources throughout the world and their potential for development. Before 1970, LRD was understaffed and reports tended not to separate supportive data, interpretation of data, and recommendations based on the data. Part of the problem could be traced to lax "editorial control of the documentary output at the early (field) stages" (529) of a project. With an infusion of more editorial personnel after 1970, LRD reports improved, but the relationship among different reports was still not clear. An analysis of the readership of various reports showed a need to distinguish between reports that recommended action and those providing scientific data. Scientific writers were given advice about how to prepare reports for specific groups of readers, and editors became more involved with the reporting process, resulting in "the editor's early involvement with the authors, even before writing begins, his continued collaborative action at the centre of scientific activity, and finally his compilation of several documents to produce a work of reference" (542).

260 Bennett, John B. *Editing for Engineers*. New York: Wiley-Interscience, 1970.

"[I]f professional editorial help is not available, editing is the manager's responsibility" (v). To help technical managers fulfill this obligation, Bennett explains how they can serve as effective editors. For instance, "to function effectively the editor must be able to recognize good writing and know its distinguishing marks" (3). Thus, "writing must be factually correct, complete, and understandable. . . . grammar, spelling, and punctuation . . . are secondary characteristics of good writing" (4). Once editors know what good writing is, they need to function as teachers, helping writers improve manuscripts, including giving advice on writing procedures. While conferring with authors, the editor "must make it abundantly clear that he and the author share a common goal; they are in no sense adversaries" (9), but "at every stage of the review the editor stresses the writer's primary responsibility for the manuscript" (10). During the review process, the editor should stress the importance of writing for a particular audience and the need for specific format requirements like headings. The entire editing process is carried out in three stages: "the first, to determine purpose, organization, and development; the second, to perform the major editing (but leaving substantial changes to be made by the writer); the third, to review the editing for completeness and consistency" (35). During that process the editor should give advice about graphics. The editor need not perform all editorial functions; a competent secretary can proofread and copyedit a manuscript. Graphic artists—visualizers—can also help the editor prepare a manuscript. Once a manuscript is prepared, the editor needs to distribute it because "a document has not truly been published until it is in the hands of the reader or readers for whom it is intended" (64). Editors also should develop a system to catalogue documents early in an organization's existence. Bennett includes appendices on readability, reference books, indexing and abstracting techniques, grammar, punctuation, compound words, capitalization, numerals, a sample style guide, and duplicating processes.

261 Blatchford, Shirley M. "Scientific Editing and Publishing for the Third World: A Review from the Tropical Products Institute." In *Scientific Information Transfer: The Editor's Role,* edited by Miriam Balaban, 543-51. Dordrecht: D. Reidel Publishing Company, 1977.

Blatchford lists the types of publications produced by the Tropical Products Institute (TPI) in England and briefly explains the purpose of each publication, its audience, and the procedures for publishing each publication. Because most TPI publications have been produced for a scientific audience, the publication of TPI's *Rural Technology Guides* for extension workers is a new venture. By working on the *Guides*, Blatchford learned that editors have to revise extensively scientific writing about research and development to make it suitable for nonscientific readers. The writing must be simple. Illustrations should be free of "cultural barriers" and should be realistic.

262 Bold, Harold C. "Manuscript Merit: Scientific Criteria and Objectivity in Manuscripts." In *Conference of Biological Editors: Report on the Special Meeting of European and North American Editors,* edited by Raymund L. Zwemer and Robert E. Gordon, 7-9. 1964.
"The primary factor in publishing manuscripts of high scientific merit is the Journal's reputation for doing so" (7). Maintaining quality depends on the way manuscripts are evaluation and the way authors are treated. For instance, editors can foster good editor-author relationships by rewriting peer reviews that are "sarcastic, vindictive and destructive" (7) so that authors are not offended. At the same time, the editor should ensure that peer reviews state a manuscript's flaws. Since quality also depends upon how manuscripts are evaluated, Bold cites fifteen criteria for evaluating manuscripts.

263 Boomhower, E. H. "Producing Good Technical Communications Requires Two Types of Editing." *Journal of Technical Writing and Communication* 5, no. 4 (1975): 277-81. (Also published in *Directions in Technical Writing and Communication,* edited by Jay R. Gould, 71-75. Farmingdale: Baywood Publishing Company, 1977.)
A technical document requires a literary editor and a technical editor, who may be one in the same person. "[T]he *literary editor* is principally concerned with the mechanics of writing and producing a document, while the *technical editor* is principally concerned with technical content and the techniques of developing good technical exposition" (278). Their duties overlap, but a technical editor must represent the reader to the writer and help writers hone their writing skills. Boomhower lists thirteen questions that the technical editor can ask to represent the reader to the writer.

264 Boro, Emily S., and Edwina B. Davis. "The Approach to Copy Editing at the *New England Journal of Medicine.*" *CBE Views* 9, no. 3 (1986): 86-87.

The *Journal* has no style sheet. However, four full-time manuscript editors follow certain rules, such as using English rather than Latin plurals, eliminating jargon, discussing galleys with authors, and checking "all drug dosages in the galley proofs against the author's original" (87). The references in a paper are also checked.

265 Borysewicz, Mary L., and A. J. Ladman. "Scientific Illustration for Editors in Medicine and Science." *CBE Views* 3, no. 3 (1980): 16-21.

Participants in a session of the 1980 Council of Biology Editors annual conference noted that simplicity is the best approach to integrating graphics in a journal. To prepare graphics, Hundley stressed that the production editor is the link between author and printer, while Porcher focused on the author's editor as an interpreter of graphics. Schaubert discussed the need for production standards, including consistent journal style and exhorted editors to follow eight guidelines, including developing guidelines for authors and artists. Porcher indicated that editors must be equally interested in illustrations and text, and Demerest reminded editors that art is prepared for an audience and should be easily understood by an audience and have a great impact on the audience. An eleven-item appendix, Publications on Illustration Techniques and Standards, is included.

266 Broadbent, Margaret. "Checklist for Copy Editors." *CBE Views* 8, no. 1 (1985): 36-38.

Broadbent's checklist is comprised of questions the editor should ask about accuracy (in spelling, grammar, alphabetizing, and cross-references), ambiguities, consistency, inserts, typography, queries to authors, figures, and assembling of the copy-edited manuscript.

267 Broadbent, Margaret. "Workshop in Copy Editing." *CBE Views* 3, no. 1 (1980): 17-19.

Broadbent offered eight 90-minute sessions on copyediting to teach basic copyediting to 25 students because so few New York publishing houses hire redactors who do not have experience. According to the results of the final examination, "about 80% of the class had grasped the fundamentals of copy editing: how to mark manuscript clearly for the printer; the difference between marking manuscript and proof; the need to follow house style; a feel for author's queries" (18). However, many students continued to rewrite copy, so Broadbent had to emphasize repeatedly that a copyeditor corrects clearly defined errors and eliminates inconsistencies. A copyeditor does not, however, alter an author's style. Broadbent provides a copy of the workshop syllabus.

268 Broer, Jan W. "Feedforward and Metaphoric Transfer—Natural Forces of Technical Authors and Editors." In *Proceedings 31st*

International Technical Communication Conference, RET-12—RET-14. Washington: Society for Technical Communication, 1984.

Feedforward and metaphoric transfer are global aspects of writing and editing. Feedforward is a process the writer and editor use to establish relationships among elements of a document and thereby communicate with an audience. Metaphoric transfer is a means of arranging a technical communication using a nesting series. To implement those global concepts, the writer/editor uses formators: graphics, titles, bylines, topic sentences, key words, outlines, and abstracts, for example. Writers and editors need to create formators when they are not present in a manuscript. The ultimate purpose of using formators is to create a technical document that will meet the readers' needs. See also Broer's "Feedforward, An Old Strategy for Modern Editors" (20).

269 Brogan, John A. "A Pitfall for Professionals." In *Technical Editing: Principles and Practices,* edited by Lola M. Zook, 87-91. Anthology Series, no. 4. Washington: Society for Technical Communication, 1975. ED 173 807.

When editors are exposed to poor technical writing they begin to think and write using poor literary style. When editors know that their editing decisions will be reversed by "literary incompetents," the editors fail to rewrite poor technical prose. Although editors may become more productive over time—produce more copy—their work will suffer unless they counteract their exposure to low-quality writing by reading excellent prose. Brogan advises editors to select a piece of good literature and "reread the same sentences and paragraphs, then read them again. Bathe your mind in the flow of their sound" (89), because repeated exposure to good writing is an antidote to constant exposure to low-quality prose. Editors should also analyze the writing of well-known stylists by asking how an author achieves a certain effect and then studying the author's prose to understand the author's techniques. Editors should study authors they enjoy, making the study a matter of personal satisfaction.

270 Bronson, Judith G. "Freelancing: Is It for You? How Do You Start?" *CBE Views* 10, no. 4 (1987): 51-53.

Editorial freelancing is a lonely life. The freelancer must make many decisions about money and labor on a variety of projects, and "about 30% of the necessary tasks [a freelancer must possess] have nothing to do" (51) with actually editing a document, Bronson says. Those who don't succeed as freelancers can't manage their time, can't talk about money comfortably, aren't competent, or can't deliver what they promise to deliver to their clients. Successful freelancers know their market and their product. They sell their skills and they sell quality, not price. See also 271, 272, 273.

271 Bronson, Judith G. "Prevention of Donkeyism: The Role of the Medical Author's Editor." In *Proceedings 28th International Technical Communication Conference,* W-10—W-13. Washington: Society for Technical Communication, 1981. ED 227 479.

The role of the medical author's editor is to keep "authors from making donkeys of themselves in print" (W-10). Editors can spare authors the indignities of donkeyism by pointing out common fallacies in medical manuscripts: *ad hominem* arguments, fortuitous fallacies (Did the author present data that represents the literature on the subject?), prodigious fallacies (reinventing the wheel), and begging the question or the "list-and-ignore error." (When authors forget to marshall opposing arguments, they also forget that "readers read papers not minds" [W-12].) Author's editors should also caution authors about being honest. For instance, arrogant claims ("no one would ever operate on the human heart" [W-12]) can lead to a loss of credibility. Issues about authorship are also important. Bronson makes two points about such issues. One, only those who made an intellectual contribution and who endorse the conclusions should be listed, and two, to list the editor as an author is unethical regardless of how much writing the editor did to produce the article, because "authorship is a statement of authority" (W-13).

272 Bronson, Judith G. "Ringmastering Your Own Three-ring Circus: Life as a Successful Biomedical Freelancer." *Technical Communication* 33, no. 4 (1986): 224-32.

"Most freelancers fail," writes Bronson, a freelancer. To succeed as a freelancer—indeed, to determine if freelancing is what a person is capable of doing—Bronson describes what the life of a freelance writer/editor is like. It's lonely, full of decisions, and requires business acumen. Bronson explains how freelancers can do market research by listing their skills and then explaining why clients would need those skills. She advocates direct mail as the best way to advertise those skills. Her diary for a typical week—a 62-hour week, "about the shortest I can expect" (231), she notes—exemplifies the wide variety of tasks a freelancer performs. See also 270.

273 Bronson, Judith G., and Sharon Boots. "Doing It All Yourself: Business, Work, and Self-Management for Freelance Editors." *CBE Views* 12, no. 4 (1989): 62-63.

In reporting on a presentation by Bronson, Boots says that Bronson addressed the question of why own your own business, and explained how to start and run your own business. If a person is looking for self-fulfillment, he or she should not be a freelancer because a freelancer must have self confidence to face rejection without crumbling. If, however, a person wants to provide a service that will make a profit, that is a good reason for being a freelancer. To start a freelance business, a person will need to investigate state and local laws to determine where to locate an office. The laws in some locations prohibit a person from working at home because of regulations regarding, for instance, the type of equipment a home can have. Bronson also discusses the relationship between a sole proprietorship, a partnership, and a corporation. Whatever business structure a freelancer chooses, he or she must not confuse revenue and profit and risk financial failure. But "if you're making money and doing it in a way you want to," Bronson says, "then consider your business a success" (63).

274 Bryson, Sheryl R. "Author's Editors." *Scholarly Publishing* 16 (1985): 159-73.

To determine "more about who author's editors are, where and how they work, and how they feel about what they do and about some of the issues that have been discussed through the years in the articles about them" (160), Bryson sent 419 questionnaires to editors. From the 140 usable questionnaires that were returned, she analyzed respondents' answers and found that most author's editors edit at various levels of editing many kinds of manuscripts and that they help authors in many other ways. She also provides statistics on salaries and job satisfaction. About the recognition an author's editor should receive for editing a manuscript, Bryson reports that most respondents did not think author's editors should be cited as co-authors, even if they thoroughly revised a manuscript, but they should be acknowledged in the final manuscript for their work. She recommends that author's editors (1) demonstrate to management that author's editors save an organization money, (2) recruit and train more author's editors, and (3) teach authors more about writing.

275 Buehler, Mary F. "Controlled Flexibility in Technical Editing: The-Levels-of-Edit Concept at JPL." *Technical Communication* 24, no. 1 (1977): 1-4.

Buehler discusses nine types of edit—coordination, policy, integrity, screening, copy clarification, format, mechanical style, language, and substantive. Five levels of editing are based on how many of the types of edit are used. For instance, level one uses all nine types; level five uses two types: coordination and policy. The types and levels of edit allow "controlled flexibility: the ability to meet a range of needs and demands, but within clearly defined limits" (1). However, extraordinary editing may be necessary, e.g., "editing copy written in a foreign language. . . . [or] editing transcribed tapes" (3). In such cases, job costs will need to be adjusted to account for extraordinary editing expenses. The levels of edit are also useful in training new editors, who can work on specific editorial tasks, and trainers can gradually increase the complexity of the entire editorial job. See also 228.

276 Buehler, Mary F. "Defining Terms in Technical Editing: The Levels of Edit as a Model." *Technical Communication* 26, no. 4 (1981): 10-15.
Editing is defined in various ways, even by those who are knowledgeable about editing. Confusion about what constitutes editing can be eliminated by defining editing as the levels of edit: coordination, integrity, screening, copy clarification, format, mechanical style, language, and substantive. Buehler defines each level. See also 228, 275.

277 Buehler, Mary F. "Patterns for Making Editorial Changes." In *Technical Editing: Principles and Practices,* edited by Lola M. Zook, 1-6. Anthology Series, no. 4. Washington: Society for Technical Communication, 1975. ED 173 807. (First published in *Proceedings 14th International Technical Communications Conference. Technical Communications: Man's Record of Reality,* edited by Harold L. Mensch, paper #86, 1-14. Washington: Society of Technical Writers and Publishers, 1967.)
To ensure that technical writing is clear, an editor can review a manuscript using six interrelated patterns: (1) relationships, (2) outline, (3) types of technical report information (introductory information, background information, information on the investigation itself, and judgments based on the results obtained), (4) elements of discourse (description, narration, exposition, and argumentation), (5) tables and graphs, and (6) quantitative statement. Patterns of language change, grammatical structure, and usage should be based on a conservative view of language represented by Fowler's *Modern English Usage* and Follet-Barzun's *Modern American Usage*.

278 Buehler, Mary F. "Rules that Shape the Technical Message: Fidelity, Completeness, Conciseness." In *Proceedings 31st International Technical Communication Conference,* WE-9—WE-11. Washington: Society for Technical Communication, 1984.
Rules can be cast in an if-then form. "*If* you are in church, *then* you should not applaud after the soprano sings" (WE-9). However, context helps determine the validity of a rule; at a concert, one might very well applaud after the soprano sings. "The essential elements of rules are context, behavior, and choice, along with the prescriptive force of the

rules themselves" (WE-9). Buehler formulates rules of fidelity, completeness, and conciseness using the if-then format and bases those rules on ethical considerations. When the three rules conflict with each other, audience is a key consideration for resolving conflict because to answer the question "what is unnecessary?" requires audience analysis. Conflict between conciseness and completeness can be resolved by giving ethical consideration a higher place on a hierarchy of significance than practical consideration: "the obligation of completeness is ethical, while the obligation of conciseness is practical. The ethical consideration should supersede the practical one" (WE-10).

279 Buehler, Mary F. "Similarities and Differences: A Key To Clarity." *1966 S[ociety of] T[echnical] W[riters and] P[ublishers] Convention Proceedings,* #27, 1-7. Washington: Society of Technical Writers and Publishers, 1966.
Clarity, which is vital to technical communication, entails writing and editing so that the reader receives only the meaning the writer intended without laboring over a text to understand what the writer is trying to say. Clarity can be achieved by using the principles of similarities (grouping similar things together) and differences (setting different things apart) in form and content. By using these principles, the writer and editor are building "normal expectation" in readers. Normal expectation in form includes the outline, "a list showing which subjects are similar, that is, of similar importance, and which are different, that is of greater or lesser importance" (4). Normal expectation in content includes definition and parallelism.

280 Buehler, Mary F. "Situational Editing: A Rhetorical Approach for the Technical Editor." *Technical Communication* 27, no. 3 (1980): 18-22.
The technical editor represents the author to the audience and the audience to the author. In this mediating role, the technical editor cannot rely only on grammatical or programmatic answers to questions about how to help prune a manuscript to communicate effectively with an audience because "a programmatic approach simply applies a set of rules to all situations" (19). A rhetorical approach is better. Although it applies grammatical conventions to a manuscript, a rhetorical approach also asks questions about effectiveness that can only be answered by making judgments about appropriateness. To determine the appropriateness of using certain language choices in particular contexts, the technical editor must possess "breadth of perspective. . . . investigative persistence. . . . flexibility. . . . rhetorical knowledge and taste. . . . empathy. . . . [and] self confidence" (22).

281 Buehler, Mary F. "Table Design—When the Writer/Editor Communicates Graphically." In *Proceedings 27th International Technical Communication Conference. Technical Communication—The Bridge of Understanding,* vol. 1, G-69—G-73. Washington: Society for Technical Communication, 1980. (Also published in *A Guide for Writing Better Technical Papers,* edited by Craig Harkins and Daniel L. Plung, 184-88. New York: IEEE Press, 1982.)

Drawing upon the *Bureau of the Census Manual of Tabular Presentation* Buehler examines tabular format, noting that a table must make sense and "must be legible under all conditions of use" (G-70) because tables are often abstracted from a context. The rational design of a table emphasizes similarities and differences using the stub, boxhead, and spanner. For instance, because spanners help readers to distinguish between data and its labels, field spanners should be placed in the field. Tables should also be legible, especially for microprinting (microfiche, for example). Buehler discusses legibility by referencing Tinker's *Legibility of Print*, which analyzes readability studies. Tables are a unique graphic because they require an editor to employ graphic techniques that normally cannot be applied to words and sentences, but "as in any other kind of technical communication, the writer/editor must think, above all, about the reader" (G-73).

282 Burkhart, Sue. "Status and Position of Editors." *Journal of Research Communication Studies* 3 (1981/1982): 457-58.

As rapporteur, Burkhart synthesizes three discussants' remarks about editing. The discussants note that editing is gaining recognition as an important task in the preparation of scientific papers, but editors still have identity problems because many scientist-editors "put editing in second place" (457). However, editing is a primary function in the publication of scientific papers because editors know how to use current technology to present scientific data so that authors effectively reach readers. Thus, all scientist-editors "must wear their editing hats as conspicuously as they wear their scientific hats" (458). Institutions can encourage editorial professionalism by providing resources to train and pay editors. However, authors should be trained how to use language because those who judge language—referees and editors—often begin their careers as authors.

283 Burr, William. *Why Technical Editors Act That Way.* Report 64-825-1195. Oswego: IBM Corporation, 1964.

Technical writers should have three insights into technical editors. One, a technical editor believes that writers and editors are professionally responsible for making technical writing clear and interesting for any intended audience. In fact, the audience is supremely important to the editor. Two, a technical editor believes the writer is the technical expert, and expects the writer to verify editorial changes so that technical accuracy will not be compromised. Advice about how to evaluate good writing, including an explanation of the categories of accuracy, clarity, grammatical correctness, and stylistic appropriateness, leads to insight three: a technical editor believes that the editor should do everything possible to help writers "prepare a manuscript that is clear, accurate, grammatically correct, and stylistically appropriate" (19). "In short," Burr advices authors, "act like an editor" (19).

284 Bush, Don. "Content Editing, an Opportunity for Growth." *Technical Communication* 28, no. 4 (1981): 15-18.

Technical editors often need to rewrite a technical author's manuscript, instead of merely ensuring that the manuscript is grammatically correct. Such content editors need to be perceptive and persistent and write well. Seven principles can guide the trainers of content editors: "Check accuracy. . . . Be skeptical. . . Stamp out 'creative' writing. . . . Preserve the idiom. . . . Remember the word is not the thing. . . . Remember that language changes. . . . Bury the stylebook" (16-17). Good editors, therefore, "learn the language, better and better" (17) so that they can facilitate information transfer, and establish a new set of editing priorities: technical accuracy, clarity, English correctness, and consistency.

285 Bush, Don. "Strategies for a Technical Editor." *The Technical Writing Teacher* 7 (1979): 19-23.

Technical editors can use a variety of strategies to help technical authors communicate with their audiences. For instance, charm, flattery ("If I can't compliment the author on his writing, I praise him for his exhaustive research" [20]), helpfulness, and common sense can be effectively used to help authors. These strategies are needed because technical writing, generally "very bad writing," requires a great deal of editing. But technical writers don't like to be edited, so courtesy is of paramount importance in editing. Bush says, "I try to give what I expect to receive: a great deal of empathy" (23).

286 Cantwell, Michael. "An Acquisitions Career in Scientific Publishing." *CBE Views* 11, no. 2 (1988): 21-22.

"[T]he primary pathways [to a career in acquisitions] are through sales, desk editorial, or science" (22). Cantwell, an acquisitions editor for Elsevier Science Publishing Company, came through the desk editorial department. An acquisitions editor will probably have "secondary" and "primary" acquisitions. Secondary acquisitions require an editor to manage existing titles. In managing a journal, the editor monitors finances and acts as the principal contact between the journal's editor and publisher. Primary acquisitions, on the other hand, requires securing new titles, and, again, financial skills are necessary, in addition to production and sales acumen. The editor must also possess interpersonal skills to interact successfully with authors and editors. The editor must determine which projects are appropriate for the publisher and take responsibility for the economic success of acquired titles.

287 Carbrey, Edward J. "Don't Bother with Editing—This Report Doesn't Need It." In *Proceedings 23rd International Technical Communication Conference,* 102-04. Washington: Society for Technical Communication, 1976.

A technical editor at Draper Laboratory not only edits documents in the generally accepted use of the word, but also makes sure that manuscripts move through the production process. If the editor does not perform all the tasks needed to produce a high-quality document, the author must perform editorial tasks. But authors, even those who are highly qualified scientists, may not know or care about how to produce a professional document. Therefore, editors must work with authors to produce a document. In fact, not the editor but the author is responsible for the printed document; however, unless the editor is satisfied with the quality of a printed document, that document is not finished.

288 Cederborg, Gibson A. "The Role and Rationale of Technical Editors." *Journal of Technical Writing and Communication* 5, no. 4 (1975): 283-86.

Qualified technical editors must function in several roles. They are "pilot readers," representing the writer's audience. They can change technical substance, very carefully, to improve readability. They are stylists, who express opinions about style given the type of publication under consideration. They "discern the thrust of the draft, and detect any deviation or drift from course" (286). They are copyeditors who believe "trifles make perfection."

289 Chapline, J. D. "The Editorial Function in Scientific Organization." *IRE Transactions Engineering Writing and Speech* EWS-3, no. 2 (1960), 48-53.

The problem of two cultures, raised by C. P. Snow, can be solved by discontinuing the practice of having technical writers write for scientists and instead having editors work with scientists to improve technical communication. Technical writers are specialists who are trained to write about a particular area of science, but editors are educated to use a "method for acquiring knowledge and understanding" (50) that can be applied to any scientific endeavor. While technical writers are subservient to scientists, editors are scientists' equals, sharing the communication task. "The full responsibility for technical accuracy falls upon the scientist, while the full responsibility for linguistic details falls upon the editor" (51). The editor edits by representing the scientist's audience and asking questions that focus scientific writing.

290 Chapman, Victor W., and Jean L. Owens. "Finding Solid Ground: Using and Articulating the Grammar of Technical Editing." In *Proceedings 32nd International Technical Communication Conference,* WE-67—WE-68. Washington: Society for Technical Communication, 1985.

By using three levels of editing—proofreading, style editing, and control editing—editors can develop standards for editing a document. Those standards should be codified in a style guide that includes instructions on every part of a document. The authors present eleven tips for creating a style guide. The tips focus on group meetings where participants debate issues of style to develop a manual.

291 Clark, B. F. "Initiating a Technical Editing Program for R and D Operations." *Journal of Chemical Documentation* 6, no. 4 (1966): 245-46.

Clark reports on a technical editing position that was established at one R and D laboratory. In addition to the position, a style sheet and a workflow diagram were prepared. Authors used dictation equipment to prepare drafts of papers that were edited by the editor. The technical editor did not ghostwrite reports but helped authors produce "more readable and valuable reports" (246). The editor maintained card files and rating sheets to chart a report's progress. In addition the editor taught authors about writing through a series of symposia and also helped authors prepare graphics for oral presentations of papers.

292 Clark, Nancy, and Barbara B. Reitt. "Dear Editor . . . ." *CBE Views* 8, no. 4 (1985): 19-21.

In reporting on Clark's presentation, Reitt notes that Clark focused on the editor's responsibility to communicate with the illustrator, noting that "the one indispensable specification that the editor must provide the illustrator is the point of the illustration" (21). The editor can provide that information by translating tabular matter into words. If such a translation is easy to do the table is probably well organized. Editors also should have authors explain the focus of a graphic and should teach authors to think of graphics as a means of communicating information. The test of a graphic's value is not its aesthetic appeal, but its success in persuading or informing the intended audience.

293 Clements, Wallace, and Robert G. Waite. "A Guide for Beginning Technical Editors." In *Proceedings 26th International Technical Communication Conference. Technical Communication—Shaping the World We Live In,* W-32—W-36. Washington: Society for Technical Communication, 1979.

A guide for beginning technical editors can establish uniformity in training new editors. Editors at Lawrence Livermore Laboratory developed such a guide, which was organized in five sections interspersed with philosophical remarks on technical editing. Section Four, "a systematic approach to editing technical manuscripts" (W-33) is the key section. The *Guide* is annotated in entry 294.

294 Clements, Wallace, and Robert G. Waite. *Guide for Beginning Technical Editors.* Washington: Society for Technical Communication, 1983.

In their *Guide* Clements and Waite examine the many facets of a technical editor's job, including a systematic approach to editing technical manuscripts. Throughout the *Guide* the authors insist that an editor's success is closely related to how well he or she interacts with people. As a skilled communicator, the technical editor works with scientists and engineers to reach a common goal: effective communication of technical data. Besides sound human-relations skills, a technical editor needs to know what he or she does and doesn't know "so that you *know* when you're not certain about a word or a point of usage and hence should look it up" (6). In using this knowledge, technical editors should realize that their "role is advisory but clearly subordinate" (9) to the author. "To be most helpful," the authors tell editors, "your editing should be restrained and inconspicuous" (9). In a seven-step approach to editing, the authors provide a model for preparing a manuscript for publication that focuses on working with the author and other publishing professionals. Step 2, editing the draft, is examined in detail, including how to edit graphics. Even so, four sections of the *Guide* are devoted to editing specific parts of the manuscript—references, mathematical material, tables, and illustrations. Editorial judgment is needed to edit the manuscript, so the authors state, "you are an *editor*, one who is expected to exercise due judgment in interpreting the rules you work by" (26). Clements and Waite summarize the major points of the *Guide* on pages 45-46.

295 Cochran, Wendell, Peter Fenner, and Mary Hill. *Geowriting: A Guide to Writing, Editing and Printing in Earth Science.* Falls Church: American Geological Institute, 1979.

The authors of *Geowriting* give advice to the writer of scientific papers on the entire document production process. Concerning editing and editors, Cochran, Fenner, and Hill tell authors "to see things as the editor sees them" (8), which means, in part, to take the reader's point of view. To help an author understand what the editorial function entails, the authors of *Geowriting* note that editors codify typographic style, size illustrations, ensure that an "author's captions are as clear and complete as possible" (25), select appropriate paper for printing a map, choose reviewers and evaluate manuscripts, and read proofs. The authors apply chapters on style and printing technology to the work of writers and editors. Writers are given specific advice on how to write an abstract, a review, and a press release. The authors include an annotated guide to references on writing, editing, and printing. The indexed checklist at the back of the book helps readers locate a particular topic quickly.

296 Cocks, Gary T. "Editing Articles about Recombinant DNA." *CBE Views* 1, no. 6 (1978): 4, 9, 13.

Cocks gives examples of incorrect usage of clone; hybrid, genetic, and enzyme nomenclature; molecular weight; and annealing. He concludes that editors will need to work with authors "whose energies in uncovering facts and generating hypotheses are not always matched by their thoughtfulness in describing their activities" (13).

297 Coggshall, Gordon. "Using the Core Sentence to Edit Poorly Written Technical Manuscripts." *Technical Communication* 27, no. 1 (1980): 19, 22-23.

Editors may need to identify a core sentence, a simple-subject/simple-predicate pair, "to pry logic from illogical prose, to extract meaning from poorly written technical manuscripts" (123). The five steps in identifying the core sentence are (1) identify sentence order (S-V-O, for example), (2) identify sentence type (simple, compound, complex, or compound-complex), (3) identify voice, (4) evaluate sense and grammatical correctness, and (5) identify what modifies what. Identifying core sentences is akin to sentence diagramming. Coggshall provides three examples of how to identify the core sentence.

298 Coin, Maxine D. "Epidemiology in Industry: Writing and Editing Opportunities." *Medical Communications* 8, no. 2 (1980): 44-45.

"[T]he epidemiologist in industry examines the medical and work histories, exposures, and mortality among a group of workers to determine if a disease or other effect has occurred or developed in an exposed group at a rate greater than in a comparable group" (44). Those who write epidemiological reports are thankful for help in preparing a report, and because the number of such reports is growing, writers and editors have many opportunities to help prepare epidemiological reports.

299 Collins, David N., and B. A. Jones. "Editing Slides and Other Graphic Aids." In *Technical Editing,* edited by B. H. Weil, 187-201. Westport: Greenwood Press, 1975.

"[T]he editor is the prime mover of the team which prepares graphic aids. He represents the artist to the author, and the author to the artist, to the advantage of both" (189). Editors not only plan and prepare slides but they also edit slides for style and content because "even one extra line of type makes every word harder to read, and extra detail in a slide drawing may make it completely incomprehensible" (197). The editor may have to rearrange an author's material so that it is presented clearly, concisely, and accurately.

300 Cord, Marian S. "Crossing the Blue Pencil Line." In *Proceedings 27th International Technical Communication Conference,* W-13—W-14. Washington: Society for Technical Communication, 1980.

A technical editor has the skills needed to cross the blue pencil line and become a technical writer. In many ways, technical writing and editing require reciprocal skills.

301 Cortelyou, Ethaline, and B. A. Jones. "Editing Illustrations for Technical Reports and Papers." In *Technical Editing,* edited by B. H. Weil, 203-15. Westport: Greenwood Press, 1975.

Illustrations and tabular materials often are less carefully edit than the text of an article or report, so editors should educate authors about the proper preparation of graphic materials. Both journal editors and report editors can instruct authors by giving them detailed instructions on how to prepare graphics. Editors can also prepare an illustration guide or report-preparation manual with examples of graphics, including examples of what an illustration will look like at 20 or 50% reduction and examples of how cropping can give a picture clarity.

302 Cortelyou, Ethaline. "Editing Tabular Data." In *Technical Editing,* edited by B. H. Weil, 217-29. Westport: Greenwood Press, 1975.

Cortelyou provides 23 style rules for a style guide addressed to authors on the preparation of tabular data. Such a guide is useful because it allows the author to prepare copy that will need less editing than is normally needed to edit tabular data. A guide also "will be a decided aid to good author-editor-typist relations" (218). In addition, Cortelyou provides a ten-point checklist for authors to help them make tabular data more understandable. A third list, twelve suggestions for arranging tabular data, offers suggestions, not definitive answers, because principles that affect how tabular data is interpreted can only be suggestive. In fact, technical authors may have difficulty even accepting editorial suggestions because technical writers have a strong sense of ownership toward their writing and tend to question an editor's authority when he or she suggests changes in a manuscript. "Any editing beyond style editing should therefore be offered as suggestions, no matter how technically competent the editor may be" (228).

303 Cox, Alberta L. "Editorial Services—Expressway Not Roadblock." In *Proceedings 34th International Technical Communication Conference,* MPD-40—MPD-42. Washington: Society for Technical Communication, 1987.

For editors to be expediters, they should follow five rules. Rule #1: The editor is responsible for a job from start to finish, so he or she must keep track of jobs during the entire production process. Rule #2: Editors should follow procedures and inform others involved in the production process about pertinent procedures. Rule #3: The editor should keep a written record of each job's location during the production process. Rule #4: The editor should educate clients. Rule #5: The editor should be attuned to clients' needs. Cox found ways to implement rules four and five in her workplace, thus improving the relationship of her publications group with authors and other departments.

304 Cox, Alberta L. "Some Language Choices of Technical Writers and Editors: Analysis of Questionnaire Responses." *Technical Communication* 33, no. 3 (1986): 140-43.

Results from a 16-item questionnaire on style, administered to 160 "editors and writers, with perhaps some managers and a few illustrators" (140) suggest that technical communicators disagree about what is correct style. For instance, when asked to evaluate "the data is incomplete," 29% of the respondents agreed that the sentence is correct, 44% said maybe it was correct, and 27% said it was incorrect. In determining correctness in style, "audience is all-important" (142), because documents should be functional for their intended audience. "The burden is on the editor to be sure of the audience" (142) when evaluating correctness in style.

305 Cox, Barbara G. "The Author's Editor." *Mayo Clinic Proceedings* 49 (1974): 314-17.

Most scientists are not trained to write, so they need assistance from an author's editor. The author-editor relationship works best when it is a person-to-person relationship because the editor needs to consult with the author to ask questions about a manuscript's focus and to gather data "to fill in gaps that the author unwittingly leaves" (316). During the editorial process, the editor's purpose is to help the author construct a logical and clear argument for the targeted audience. At the same time, the editor serves readers and the publisher. Once editors complete the editing process, they should meet with authors to explain manuscript changes and to encourage the author to produce a revised manuscript. Such an editorial meeting has long-term benefits because the author and editor can learn about each other's work habits and develop a relationship that allows for differences in style. An additional benefit is that "the written product represents the synthesis of two minds" (317).

306 Cox, Barbara G. "A Protocol for Author's Editors." *CBE Views* 12, no. 2 (1989): 23-24.

"[A] personal approach to authors lays the groundwork for the most fruitful kind of collaboration" (23). For Cox that personal approach entails meeting with the author to discuss a manuscript before editing it, editing the manuscript, and meeting with the author again to discuss the revised manuscript. By meeting with an author and gathering details about the purpose of the manuscript, Cox believes that the author has a chance to recognize that Cox is a professional with a background in medical communication and a good team member who is committed to the author's paper. By editing the manuscript using an editorial critique, "a document that comprises all my questions and comments about the paper and the rationale for changes" (23), Cox justifies her editorial judgments. If she cannot meet an author who lives in a distant city, she calls the author. For the final conference, she "may send the manuscript back with an audiotape in lieu of a conference" (24). Cox says that the editor who uses a personalized editorial process, becoming the author's personal tutor, is teaching authors to become better writers.

307 Dan, Bruce B., and Winfield Swanson. "The Biomedical Editor and 'Breakthroughs,' Real and Contrived: Dealing with Authors and the Press." *CBE Views* 10, no. 6 (1987): 103-04.

Scientific research should be translated into language that the layperson will understand, and the best way to reach the layperson is through television. To prepare scientific information for television, the editor should recognize that "television doesn't deliver facts, but impressions; not information, but perceptions" (103). When scientists are interviewed for television, they should explain scientific facts without exaggerating or lying so that the layperson can understand them. The authors advise scientists, "say something important in a catchy way if you want it on TV" (104).

308 Dancik, Bruce P., and Leslie A. Cameron. "Who Is the Author?" *CBE Views* 12, no. 4 (1989): 66-67.

Scientific articles have become shorter over the years, but the number of authors per article is increasing, from 1.84 authors per article in 1955 to 3 authors per article in 1985. The increase in the number of authors may not be legitimate and editors can use a four-point criteria to determine who is a legitimate author of an article. In addition, editors have ethical and legal responsibilities concerning the authorship of articles they review and publish. Legally "editors who carefully follow established procedures and do so in good faith are not at substantial risk" (66). Ethically, editors should consider exposing those who claim to be legitimate authors but are not "known to the field, although this obviously has legal implications" (67). Editors can also write editorials about ethics and publish in each journal issue a statement about what constitutes ethical authorship.

309 Day, Robert A. *How to Write and Publish a Scientific Paper.* 2nd ed. Philadelphia: ISI Press, 1983.

In the Preface Day states, "the purpose of this book is to help scientists and students of the sciences in all disciplines to prepare manuscripts that will have a high probability of being accepted for publication and of being completely understood when they are published" (x). Written from the perspective of a managing editor and publisher, Day's book is designed to give specific and practical instructions to authors. In particular, chapter 16, "The Review Process (How to Deal with Editors)," explains how authors' papers are reviewed. The review process begins and ends with the editor who initiates the process by making a preliminary decisions about whether a manuscript should be reviewed and ends the process by writing a letter of acceptance or rejection to the author. If the editor chooses to review a manuscript, it has met two preconditions; it has a proper subject and it is in the proper form (complete and formatted according to editorial style) for the particular journal. Then the editor initiates the paperwork needed to trace the paper through the review process and enlists appropriate reviewers. After reading reviewers' reports, the editor sends either a reject or a modify letter to the author. Day explains three types of rejection letters. Authors can elect to write the editor and explain that reviewers misread the paper, but when two reviewers cite the same problem, generally there is a problem. "Occasionally, a referee may be biased, but hardly two of them simultaneously. If referees misunderstand, readers will" (86). However, authors "should never be afraid to talk to editors. With rare exceptions, editors are awfully nice people. Never consider them adversaries. They are on your side" (85). Indeed, both editors' and reviewers' "primary function is to help you express yourself effectively and provide you with an assessment of the science involved" (90) Day tells authors, adding, "it is to your advantage to cooperate with them in all ways possible" (90).

310 De Quattro, James. "Getting It Right with the Author." In *Proceedings 26th International Technical Communication Conference. Technical Communication—Shaping the World We Live In,* W-46—W-48. Washington: Society for Technical Communication, 1979.

An editor's job is not finished until the author accepts an editor's changes to the author's manuscript. To help authors accept editorial changes, editors should meet with authors and ask questions that cause the author to consider the actual audience, not the editor as audience. Editors should be prepared to explain why they marked a manuscript the way they did, but they should recognize that "disagreement is the beginning of editing" (W-47), and disagreement does not have to include animosity if the editor is candid and humane in discussing manuscript changes with the author. Author-editor relationships can also be improved by using brackets instead of deletion marks because brackets do not efface text and they can be erased if the author chooses to include the bracketed material in the final draft. Marginal notes should be brief. De Quattro recommends using "a question mark or a neutral comment such as 'Please clarify'" (W-48). Author-editor conferences should not exceed a hour. "Consider how the author must feel," De Quattro remarks, "for whom the conference may be a series of unwelcome surprises" (W-48).

311 DeBakey, Lois. "Rewriting and the By-Line: Is the Author the Writer." *Surgery* 75 (1974): 38-48.

Editors of scientific journals should not rewrite an author's paper, making it acceptable for publication. Editors can make nonsubstantive changes, but rewriting is a form of deception and "has some of the same educational, ethical, function, aesthetic, and economic implications as ghostwriting" (40). Educationally, editors have little success in teaching author about writing by rewriting their manuscripts. The author misses the opportunity to apply composition principles to a scientific article. In fact, if editors do not establish high literary standards, authors will continue to produce scientific articles lacking in literary quality. Ethically, editors who rewrite promote a false impression of the author's abilities, which are the basis for academic rewards. Functionally, an editor "may unwittingly impose his personal concepts, convictions, or biases on an article that he rewrites, or he may introduce inaccuracies" (42). Aesthetically, editors impose their character on a work, thereby depriving authors of their own style. Economically, when editors expend resources to rewrite, they increase publishing costs. In an informal survey DeBakey conducted, editors agreed that when an editor rewrites an author's submitted article, subsequent articles by the same author show no improvement in the author's writing skills. The solution to editorial ghostwriting is to teach scientific authors to do their own writing, which is their duty.

312 DeBakey, Lois, and F. P. Woodford. "Extensive Revision of Scientific Articles—Whose Job?" *Scholarly Publishing* 4 (1973): 147-51.

Editors can heavily revise a manuscript with its author's approval and publish it (the radical view) or they can admonish the author (without rewriting a single word) to rewrite the manuscript (the conservative view). Both views are extreme and a middle ground between the two is the best way to educate authors about manuscript revision. The intermediate course of editorial action requires the editor to ask the author to revise a manuscript by sending the author a detailed list of suggested revisions, including "paragraphs that are verbose or out of place, sentences that bear two interpretations" (149-50). An example of an edited paragraph or two may also help the author revise the paper. When the author returns the revised manuscript, the editor "should edit it with sole reference to the reader's comfort, show the results to the author, and publish without delay" (150). Ethics is also at issue. An editor who extensively revises a manuscript "may be conniving at fraud if he insists too much on his own standards and method of expression without adding his name to the by-line" (150).

313 Dean, W. M. "Techniques of Creative Technical Writing and Editing." In *Proceedings 23rd International Technical Communication Conference,* 70-76. Washington: Society for Technical Communication, 1976.

Editors can use problem-solving techniques to answer questions about editing. Dean explicates and applies five problem-solving steps to editing—"1. Getting facts, 2. Defining the problem, 3. Finding possible solutions, 4. Evaluating the possible solutions, 5. Implementing a solution" (70). For instance, step two is central to technical communication because technical communication deals with open-ended problems that have a variety of solutions. To find solutions to problems, the editor should make judgments after allowing an idea to incubate, considering the graphic representation of an idea, tapping the unconscious, seeking ideas, and asking questions. "Remember that the best way to get a good idea is to get lots of ideas" (75).

314 Deming, Lynn H., Eva Dukes, Barbara Y. Myers, and Sudha Prasad. "Fine-Tuning Technical Editing." In *Proceedings 35th International Technical Communication Conference,* WE-40. Washington: Society for Technical Communication, 1988.

The authors highlight essential elements of tables, equations, grammar, and punctuation—aspects of technical editing that tend to be neglected. Proper construction of tables entails preparing uncluttered data with captions and adding footnotes when needed. For equations, the editor must decide which typesetting styles and notational systems are best. Grammar and punctuation also include knowledge of spelling, vocabulary, and syntax.

315 Dukes, Eva P. "Gullibility Is for the Birds." *Technical Communication* 21, no. 3 (1974): 6-11.

"Even trustworthy persons may mislead us unwittingly" (6), so editors and authors should "check and recheck data" (7) to ensure that it's correct. Besides normal lapses in memory and related distortions of data, the desire to be loved is the fundamental reason for error, "the underlying motivation for conscious and unconscious efforts to please" (6). To aid technical editors and writers in checking facts, Dukes provides an annotated list of references in engineering, physics, chemistry, architecture (one reference), and miscellaneous references (science and technology, style manuals, and general information).

316 Dukes, Eva P. "Some Authors I Have Known." *Technical Communication* 28, no. 4 (1981): 27-31.

Dukes sorts authors into six categories—the hostile/distrustful type, the know-it-all type, the cooperative author, the vicious author, the perfectionist, and the ideal author—and gives examples of each type of author. The best author for an editor to work with is the ideal author who "must prize quality while maintaining an objectivity that precludes squabbling and displays of petulance" (30). In the best author/editor relationship both parties work toward a common goal without trying to assign blame to the other party. "[O]nly the common objective—the work itself—counts" (30).

317 Eastwood, S. "The Author's Editor in the Setting of a University or Research Center." *Journal of Research Communication Studies* 3 (1981): 211-16.

Editors of scientific authors are cost effective because such editors can educate authors about writing and publishing and such editors help "produce well written manuscripts and process them efficiently" (215). Many scientific authors need writing instruction and because the author's editor communicates with the author throughout the preparation of the manuscript, the author's editor is in an excellent position to ensure that the intended audience will not misunderstand the author's meaning. Author's editors are also valuable in shepherding a manuscript through the publication process. Authors and journal editors should investigate the use of author's editors to evaluate and prepare manuscripts.

318 Eastwood, Susan. "Dissemination of Scientific Information from the Author to the Public: The Other Gatekeeper." *Medical Communications* 10, no. 2 (1982): 54-62.

As the rules of scientific communication change, so must the ways change in which scientists communicate scientific data. Historically scientists have published research findings without regard for personal economic gain. That practice has changed and scientists now labor under conflicting rules that, on the one hand, require publication for promotion and, on the other hand, require nondisclosure if proprietary rights for a discovery are sought. To achieve objectivity in scientific communication, three gatekeepers may become influential: scientific information services and citation indexes, unaligned reviewers, and author's editors. Eastwood sees author's editors as particularly useful gatekeepers because the author's editor is a natural liaison between the scientist and the rest of the publication community, including the audience. Author's editors can give practical and ethical advice to authors and thereby enable them to make informed decisions about publication dilemmas.

319 Eastwood, Susan. "Editors' Problems and Resources." *CBE Views* 2, no. 4 (1979): 10-18.

Eastwood reports on presentations about citation analysis, copyediting, readability, and publication responsibilities that were given at the annual conference of the Council of Biology Editors. Citation analysis—determining the number of times an article is cited in the scientific literature—"can afford a retrospective check on peer review" (11) by analyzing an article's impact factor in relation to how the peer reviewers evaluated the article. In addition, when articles treating related topics demonstrate a cluster pattern, significant areas of research may be developing. In the presentation on copyediting, the speaker noted that beginning about 1963 copyediting standards declined because the educational system neglected the rules of grammar and punctuation. Copyediting is an important function in the publication process because the copyeditor helps ensure that a manuscript is accurate and styled. The results of readability studies, another focal point among presenters, have shown that readers are influenced by microvariables (size and legibility of type and length of the line, for example) and by macrovariables (for instance, page layout). Even though "the most readable page has a ragged margin achieved with some judicious use of hyphens" (14), editors continue to use justified margins because editors favor style or aesthetics over readability. Editors should use legibility analysis to decide what is stylistically most readable. Editors have other publication responsibilities according to another presenter who listed an eight-fold mission for science journals. To help accomplish that mission, editors can use reader surveys. In fact, a study of authors who submitted manuscripts to one journal found that most of the authors agreed that the editing of their manuscripts was useful. The presenter also affirmed that editors are needed to fulfill the publishing mission because "the ultimate goal of a publication is to achieve quality with minimal editing" (17), including literary quality. "Without editors, quality control would be lost" (18).

320 Eastwood, Susan. "A Fine Portrait." *CBE Views* 3, no. 4 (1980): 26-27.
In commending Tacker's article "Author's Editors: Catalysts of Scientific Publishing" (440), Eastwood notes that scientists often need editorial assistance to produce a literate scientific article. To help authors, editors should recognize that the working relationship between an author and an editor is ideal for teaching an author how to "harness his or her innate sense of logic to the end of translating well-designed research into a well-designed manuscript" (27). Eastwood qualifies Tacker's understanding of the editor's responsibility to the author by saying that the editor may need to help the author determine the manuscript's purpose when that purpose has been lost during the writing process. In their manuscripts, authors should acknowledge editorial assistance.

321 Eastwood, Susan. "Is the Editor an Author: A Gentle Conspiracy." *Medical Communications* 5 (1977): 10-12.
Authors can become inured to having their manuscripts rewritten by editors. "Soon, the author tells the editor s/he hasn't time to wade through messy drafts, wants to see fresh copy only, and defers to the editor's adept rendering of the manuscript with relief" (11). For the editor, the urge to rewrite a manuscript can be compelling. Such gentle conspiracies can be avoided when the editor begins teaching the physician-author how to write a research manuscript. Editorial instruction includes disabusing authors of their belief that elegance is the hallmark of good writing. A scientific manuscript should be straightforward, the more so, the better. The editor can outline questions that lead the author systematically and painlessly through the preparation of a manuscript.

322 Eastwood-Berry, Susan, and Gillian F. Brown. "Substantive Manuscript Editing: Approaching the Minotaur." *CBE Views* 10, no. 5 (1987): 83-84.

An editor's job is to make certain that the author is clearly understood and cannot be misunderstood. To fulfill that job an editor can use one of three approaches. As a samurai, the editor "confidently slices through the manuscript, rewriting, querying the author on the copy as necessary, and requesting a conference only when, for example, the data appear to support a conclusion somehow different from the author's or when otherwise thoroughly perplexed" (83). As a didactic escort, the editor "explains each change in detail" (83) to the author. As a California holistic, the editor "leads the author strategically through the logic of 'thought components' of the manuscript as the author has expressed them" (83). Eastwood-Berry endorses the California holistic approach. She also explores the relationship between substantive and copyediting. Although the differences between the two may be a matter of scale, one way to distinguish between them is to say that copyediting problems can be solved by appealing to an unequivocally right or wrong answer. Substantive editing problems require greater judgment because substantive editing is the recasting of material, so the substantive editor is a closer collaborator with the author than the copyeditor is.

323 Feinberg, R., Bernice Ennis, and Salmon R. Halpern. "Getting Doctors and Editors Together: A Panel Discussion from AMWA Editors Section." *Medical Communications* 1, no. 3 (1973): 6-11.

An editor may have difficulty working with physician-authors because they listen selectively, respond automatically, and practice ritual behavior. That is, doctors hear what they want to hear and conform to accepted procedures. They are also clanish, defending each other against outsiders' criticisms. In addition, doctors lead a hectic life that is antithetical to producing "an organized, well thought-out paper" (9). Editors by contrast enjoy a "leisurely pace" and are "at a comfortable distance from direct attack by readers" (9). Editors need to pursue patient and constructive involvement with physician-authors because the private practitioner can prepare useful articles for the medical profession. However, the current editorial policy of many journals may hasten the extinction of practitioners' articles because of the harsh criticism that is often leveled against their manuscripts. And even though articles by practitioners may be flawed, private practitioners need clinical studies.

324 Fogelberg, Paul. "The Future of Copy Editing As I See It." In *Scholarly Communication Around the World. Proceedings of a Joint*

Global Conference, 68-69. Washington: Society for Scholarly Publishing, 1983.

Speaking as "a small-scale editor working in a country with a small population [Finland]" (68), Fogelberg describes the traditional model of copyediting and develops two scenarios that reflect modern copyediting practices. In the traditional model, editors were interested solely in a manuscript's scientific content, so the printing foreman made obvious corrections. The modern approach eliminates the printing foreman and focuses either on minimizing the editor's work (Scenario 1) or minimizing the author's work (Scenario 2). In Scenario 1, authors and referees shoulder a significant burden of the editing task. In Scenario 2, editors and referees shoulder the burden. In the future either scenario could work, but a combination of both also is possible.

325 Forscher, Bernard K. "Preferred Background for Manuscript Editors: English or Science?" *CBE Views* 8, no. 3 (1985): 5-7.

An editor of science manuscripts must understand science, the idiom of the particular science for which a paper is written, and the reason a paper is written. If an editor understands scientific principles, he or she will not push "an observation further out onto the limb than the facts warrant. 'X may be related etiologically to the development of Y' cannot be restated as 'X causes Y'" (6). The editor also will recognize the difference between slang or jargon and the idiomatic language of science. Idiomatic language is necessary and has an influence on an author's credibility; jargon or slang is not credible. The editor should recognize that scientists write papers to earn a living, so the editor must be aware of and responsive to the publishing constraints under which authors labor—"the need for speed, accuracy, clarity, and the trappings of validity" (7).

326 Forscher, Bernard K. "Principles of Manuscript Editing." *American Medical Writers Association Bulletin* 18, no. 2 (1968): 1-5.

Editing an author's manuscript can be divided into three aspects—technical, internal logic and consistency, and readability. The technical aspect includes correcting mistakes in spelling, grammar, punctuation, and usage. Forscher discusses particular problems with medical writing. "Editing for technical aspects usually requires slow examination of each sentence," Forscher admits, but "editing for internal logic and consistency requires an uninterrupted reading of the complete paper" (4). Readability, the third aspect of editing, "relates to how easily the reader can collect from [an article] the information or message the author intended to present" (4). Technical writing may be complex and readable, but not ambiguous and readable.

327 Forscher, Bernard K., and Susan P. Harmon. "The Mayo Clinic Approach to Editing." *CBE Views* 12, no. 4 (1989): 60-61.

Mayo Clinic authors can choose to have their manuscript edited by the Section on Publications, which offers five levels of editing from proofreading to the entire range of services offered by the Section, for instance, "verifying and typing references in appropriate style, retyping the manuscript, obtaining any necessary permissions to print or reprint figures" (60), but editors do not verify statistics. The Section on Publications also proofreads papers (including galley proofs) and submits manuscripts to journals. Editors regard editorial changes as suggestions that authors can disregard.

328 French, Burr J. "Internal Editing of Technical Papers and Articles." In *Technical Editing,* edited by B. H. Weil, 31-40. Westport: Greenwood Press, 1975.

The technical article is not mandatory reading, as a technical report is, so authors and editors of technical articles must appeal to readers' interests. To appeal to readers, the technical article should be reviewed by a committee and an editor after the author's supervisor reviews and approves the technical data and the author's interpretation of the data. The editor reviews the document by asking questions about the intended audience and purpose. For instance, the audience's needs, interests, and backgrounds should be considered. Reader interest can be appealed to by organizing the paper carefully, using a good lead and discussing the most important point of the article first. Journal specifications should also be met and most journals prefer short instead of long articles. The editor can help authors by discussing article writing in "an informal session with the author before his first word is put on paper" (39). In fact, editors should inculcate two precepts into authors: "(1) Think before you write. (2) Do not write so that you can be understood; write so that you cannot be misunderstood" (39).

329 Fritz, John F. "Who Gets Credit as Author?" *Medical Communications* 13, no. 1 (1985): 1-4.

Fritz provides a flow chart an editor can use to help senior authors determine who should be listed as co-authors. In anesthesiology, for instance, one senior author decides who gets co-author status by checking potential co-authors' hands for blood or ink. Even then, the senior author needs to find out "whether the people with blood or ink on their hands contributed in a *creative* way that was *essential* to the success of the work" (3). To the extent that they did make that kind of contribution, they should either be co-authors or cited in the acknowledgments. Fritz recommends that in-house editors send copies of all communication about a paper under review to every co-author of the paper to protect the journal, the authors, and the editor.

330 Frost, David. "Author's Editors in the Workplace: Their Similarities and Differences." In *Scholarly Communication Around the World. Proceedings of a Joint Global Conference*, 76-78. Washington: Society for Scholarly Publishing, 1983.

Frost summarizes one session of the Proceedings of a Joint Global Conference in which four author's editors presented their view on editing. The author's editors agreed that authors should consider all changes an author's editor makes as suggestions. However, one group of editors believes that an author's editor should correct problems in a paper's format, including use of abbreviations or citations, or else a journal might return a paper for revision. Concerning book editing, even though no professional editing is done by staff members of the publishing house, publishers do not realize how available author's editors are for freelance book editing assignments. Breaking into freelance editing, however, is difficult without prior experience as an editor, but experience as an editor generally does not include an apprenticeship under an experienced editor. When an author's editor does get the opportunity to work with authors, he or she should train writers by meeting with them to explain why a manuscript change is reasonable. Authors can apply the principle associated with a particular change to future manuscripts.

331 Frost, David, and Karen F. Phillips. "Establishing a Clientele for a Freelance Writer and Editor." *CBE Views* 10, no. 6 (1987): 105-06.

Expertise is essential for successful freelancing, and the credentials that best demonstrate expertise are full-time employment as a writer and editor and a portfolio of projects. To apply that expertise, a freelancer needs to prospect for clients by reviewing classified ads in business, health, or education sections of the newspaper and sending letters to prospective clients. (The lag time between sending letters and landing assignments can be 18 months.) Fees are also discussed, but a freelancer's income "is likely to be irregular, even with a regular clientele . . . [so] if your lifestyle requires a regular income, freelancing may not be for you" (106).

332 Fuccillo, Domenic A., Jr. "A Survey of Services Offered Authors by Biological Editors." *BioScience* 14, no. 2 (1964): 23-24.

In reporting on a survey of 100 Conference of Biological Editors, Fuccillo notes that editors not only perform editorial work, but prepare graphics and copy for reproduction. The survey revealed that most editorial staffs serve over 20 authors each year. Editors generally either meet with authors in personal conferences or communicate by mail with authors before editing a manuscript. In the survey editors were asked to list faults in manuscripts they edited and of the seven major faults the top three are "wordiness, inattention to details of form, and ambiguity" (24).

333 Garfield, Eugene. "How IFSEA and Other Editors' Associations Are Helping to Professionalize Scientific Editing." *Current Contents* 41 (1983): 5-12.

Because editors of scientific journals face significant problems in producing journals, editors' associations, such as the International Federation of Scientific Editors' Associations, can provide resources to solve problems. Editors face problems of gatekeeping, deciding what should be published; "establishing the style and format for their journal" (6); marketing the journal; and convincing "administrators to budget time for editing" (6). To help editors cope with these problems, Garfield discusses various editors' associations, providing their addresses and explaining their purposes.

334 Garstka, Katharine, and Morgan D. Romans. "The Writer/Editor Relationship: A Docudrama." In *Proceedings 34th International Technical Communication Conference*, WE-77—WE-80. Washington: Society for Technical Communication, 1987.

In their playlet, Garstka and Romans create two characters, a writer and an editor, who argue about how to edit a computer documentation manual the writer has written. Throughout their dialogue, the writer and editor discuss the difficulties that attend editing and writing the manual, including the seeming inconsistency of editorial judgment. The writer says to the editor, "you know how different editors change different things." The editor responds, "just like writers write differently" (WE-79). The editor explains that different editors have different backgrounds, but they try to reach an agreement with an author about how to resolve discrepancies in editorial style. In one way, the editor tells the author, diversity among editors is an advantage for the author because "another editor might find a problem I overlooked—and don't you WANT to clear up all the problems and have the perfect document?" (WE-79). The playlet has two endings because the writer and editor couldn't agree on which ending was best.

335 Garvey, William D., and Elynor Sass. "Social Dimensions of Science: The Struggle Between Authors and Editors." *CBE Views* 3, no. 3 (1980): 9-11.

Scientific authors often develop a manuscript by first presenting it in local colloquia and then national meetings before submitting it to a refereed journal. Compared to a journal's requirements, colloquia are informal, so one struggle between authors and editors is the transition from the informal domain to the formal domain. Authors tend to see journals as ultraconservative (formal), especially since editors and referees often are selected because of their success in publishing within a conservative system. Yet, the system tends to weed out crank research which could impede scientific progress, and even though a genius initially may not receive the recognition he or she deserves, time will correct that injustice.

336 Genin, Michael S. "Turning Adversaries into Allies—Avoiding Tension in an Author-Editor Relationship." In *Proceedings 26th International Technical Communication Conference. Technical Communication—Shaping the World We Live In,* W-59—W-60. Washington: Society for Technical Communication, 1979.

Using "the arm-around-the-shoulder approach" (W-59) Genin applies certain techniques to assure authors that the author-editor relationship is a partnership. One technique Genin uses is to call the author as soon as possible after receiving an author's manuscript and tell him or her that the manuscript is interesting, but some parts of the text might need a little tinkering to make the entire manuscript excellent. After editing a manuscript, Genin meets with the author and, before handing the author the marked manuscript, explains that any changes he has made are suggestions. The author has the authority to determine which changes are necessary and which ones are not necessary or are incorrect. Genin tells authors to make sure none of his changes distorted the author's meaning. If the author reviews the edited draft alone, the meeting with the editor to resolve differing views of the editor's editing will be "shorter and smoother" (W-60) than an editorial meeting without the author first reviewing the manuscript. During the editorial meeting, if author and editor cannot reach agreement about a suggested change, Genin marks the change and suggests to the author that both editor and author think about a solution to the change at their leisure.

337 Gilbert, John R., Christy N. Wright, Janis I. Amberson, and Amy L. Thompson. "Profile of the Author's Editor: Findings from a National Survey." *CBE Views* 7, no. 1 (1984): 4-10.

In a survey of "175 people thought to be scientific author's editors" (4), the authors gathered data about author's editors, including demographics, salaries, type of work, and co-authorship between author and editor. Given the population they surveyed, the authors conclude "that the 'typical' author's editor is a woman with an MA degree and 14 years of editorial experience who works in a university/medical school setting or a government agency. She has been in her current position for 9 years and earns approximately $26,000 a year. She does primarily creative or substantive editing of biomedical research papers, advises authors on publication strategies, and conducts writing workshops. She has strong opinions about acknowledgment and co-authorship and often feels underrecognized. Yet she does not want to be recognized for work that has been re-edited by the author" (9).

338 Gildenberg, Philip L., Robert J. White, and Jonathan Cohen. "Responsibilities of Clinical Editors to Patients." *CBE Views* 8, no. 3 (1985): 30-31.

Editors of publications directed to clinicians should ensure that potential articles are reviewed critically by competent reviewers, that authors frankly acknowledge inconclusive data, that articles be placed in a context by being published with other articles "on the same topic, in the same or subsequent issues" (31), that the legal implication of publishing misleading data be considered because "the records of journals have been and may increasingly be brought into court battles over malpractice" (31), and that patients be protected from any possible misuses of faulty data. Not only journal editors but author's editors need to consider the potential harm to patients due to manuscripts that are poorly prepared.

339 Glen, H. W. "User Attitudes to Scientific Editing—Just Change the 'Was's' and 'Were's'." *Journal of Research Communication Studies* 3, nos. 1-2 (1981): 221-27.

Editors can help authors who are required, but unwilling, to have their work edited by pointing out four main types of mistakes: (1) grammatical, mechanical, spelling, and syntax errors; (2) stylistic errors resulting from failure to follow an organization's style guide; (3) logic errors; and (4) diction errors resulting from the author's use of jargon or inflated language. In pointing out such errors, editors must be sensitive to authors' feelings. Sarcasm or criticism can destroy a working relationship that may have taken years to develop.

340 Golley, Frank B. "Ethics in Publishing." *CBE Views* 4, no. 4 (1981): 26-30.

The potential for unethical behavior among scientific authors has increased since scientists have lost their status as members of a tightly knit subculture and have become influential in helping formulate political decisions. "When a subculture can maintain the proper size, personal communication can be maintained, the ethical system can be transmitted informally, and the reliability and honesty of communication will be high" (29). Science, however, has been fragmented by being incorporated into the larger culture, resulting in the problem of validating scientific results. Publication is a major way to validate scientific results, especially when manuscripts are peer reviewed. However, the rapid expansion of the number of publishing outlets creates a further validation problem that is often solved by using quantity of publication as the measure of an author's success as a researcher. The scientific publishing complex then becomes a source of political activity because promotion, power, and money are the by-products of a successful publications record. Editors can also be influenced by these outcomes because commercial publishers select people for editorial positions that are regarded as prestigious positions. Efforts to rectify ethical breeches of publication standards will be successful when society is not fragmented and social groups are able to police their members' behavior.

341 Gould, Jay, ed. *Directions in Technical Writing*. Farmingdale: Baywood Publishing Company, 1977.

See "Producing Good Technical Communications Requires Two Types of Editing" (263), "An Editor's Viewpoint on Preparing News Releases" (626), and "Readability Techniques for Authors and Editors" (373).

342 Griggs, Tim. "Editing in Nigeria—An Informal Study." *Journal of Technical Writing and Communication* 13, no. 3 (1983): 247-58.

Griggs's experience as an editor in Nigeria suggests that "international organizations are fooling themselves" (258) if they hire people with advanced degrees for communication positions in the Third World believing that those people, because of their degrees, will perform well. A candidate for a communication position in the Third World does need editorial and layout experience and should be capable of adjusting to an environment where getting a job done correctly and on time is the exception rather than the rule. Equipment, for example, often malfunctions. ("During my two years," Griggs recalls, "I had two telephone calls: both were wrong numbers: this record was not exceptional" [251].) The technical support to repair equipment or to provide needed supplies was unavailable or available only through the black market. The postal service was unreliable. Griggs found that it was more expedient to send an urgent letter to a party in Nigeria via London so that the letter could be sent back to Nigeria because "this bizarre system actually saved time" (252). In trying to launch an internal journal, Griggs learned that "the more complex the job, the less of it should be let out of sight" (255). He didn't follow that principle at the outset of his new journal enterprise and in working with an outside printer found that most of the articles for the first issue of the journal had to be typeset at least three times before anybody could even begin to proofread them. Griggs's experience convinced him that practical, not theoretical, training in the editorial enterprise is most useful for working in a country like Nigeria.

343 Gross, Alan G. "Style and Arrangement in Scientific Prose: The Rules Behind the Rules." *Journal of Technical Writing and Communication* 14, no. 3 (1984): 241-53.

A study of the editorial practice of one biology journal shows that the editors and referees paid close attention to style and arrangement. However, when making changes in authors' manuscripts or when suggesting changes, editors and referees did not follow the conventional wisdom on style and used satisficing, a problem-solving technique that does not promote a best solution, to make changes in arrangement. Stylistic changes were "made either for the sake of clarity, simplicity, concision, or specificity" (252); "'fluency and elegance in style'" were secondary considerations (251). Thus, "stylistic changes are tactical choices made within the context of strategic presuppositions about the impersonal and descriptive nature of scientific prose" (252). Problems of arrangement were resolved by using satisficing. The editorial process included authors' opinions because authors accepted and rejected editorial advice.

344 Grossblatt, Norman, and Gillian F. Brown. "Professional Standards for Author's Editors." *CBE Views* 7, no. 4 (1984): 21-22.

In reporting on a workshop led by Grossblatt, Brown notes that participants discussed ways to maintain the integrity of professional standards. Although participants recognized that competence is critical for an author's editor to be professional, they were divided in their understanding of how to ensure competence. Some favored certificate programs and others supported the test of author satisfaction as a basis for determining competence.

345 Grossblatt, Norman, and Gillian F. Brown. "The Review Article: What Authors and Author's Editors Should Know." *CBE Views* 10, no. 4 (1987): 65.

The purpose of a review article is to evaluate the literature "on a narrowly defined subject." The author's editor can help an author prepare a review article by checking the accuracy of references, recommending headings to organize a paper, suggesting the use of a table when data need to be summarized, and selecting appropriate words for a context.

346 Hageman, Mary S., Louise M. Vest, and Patrick M. Kelley. "Editorial Dialogue: An Alternative Writer-Editor Relationship." In *Proceedings 28th International Technical Communication Conference,* W-38—

W-40. Washington: Society for Technical Communication, 1981. ED 227 479.

Hageman, Vest, and Kelley propose Editorial Dialogue which is based on Buber's, Briggs's (15), and Johannesen's thinking about the dialogic *I-thou* relationship. In particular, the authors cite Johannesen's six major components of dialogue and develop general guidelines for those six components. The authors maintain that dialogue works during "tough-minded" editing session, if the editor has developed an I-thou relationship with the writer. In fact, disagreement, if handled in a dialogic relationship, allows the editor to "make decisions contrary to the writer's desires without damaging their relationship" (W-39).

347 Harkins, Craig, and Daniel L. D. Plung, eds. *A Guide for Writing Better Technical Papers*. New York: IEEE Press, 1982.

See "Contextual Editing: The First Step in Editing Sentences" (142) and "Table Design—When the Writer/Editor Communicates Graphically" (281).

348 Harris, Michael. "Is a Good Editor a Good Publisher?" In *Scientific Information Transfer: The Editor's Role,* edited by Miriam Balaban, 359-61. Dordrecht: D. Reidel Publishing Company, 1978.

The good editor of scientific publications can be a good publisher, and in fact, in scientific publishing often the editor ultimately becomes the publisher. When editors do become publishers they need to have training and talent for executive responsibilities, particularly managerial responsibility. Editors, however, have distinct functions that a publisher does not have. The editor is the one who works closely with the author. The editor also chooses the manuscripts that will be published and those choices determine "the quality, the reputation, and in the final analysis, the success of the publishing company" (361).

349 Hartley, Herbert L. "Should an Editor Edit or Rewrite Submitted Articles?" *Medical Communications* 3, no. 2 (1974): 8-10.

Hartley compares the editorial policies at two journals, one where authors rewrite articles to conform to the journal's understanding of good writing and the other where the editor rewrites articles even if the author is "the world's leading authority on the subject" (9) of the article. Hartley recommends to editors an eclectic approach concerning the rewriting of articles. If the editor finds an article easy to read, the intended audience probably will find the article easy to read. However, if the editor has difficulty reading an article, he or she should rewrite the article, even if that entails cutting a paper into pieces and reassembling the pieces into a logical sequence.

350 Hasch, Jean, and Val Chepeleff. "Wearing the Production Editor's Hat." In *Proceedings 29th International Technical Communication Conference. Technical Communication—Charting the Course of Technology,* G-23—G-26. Washington: Society for Technical Communication, 1982.

The production editor makes sure that the printer gets a manuscript that is ready to be printed. Unfortunately, a production editor's duties often are unassigned, so those duties fall to someone by default. To avoid such a haphazard approach to producing a document, someone, preferably the graphics director, should be assigned the production editor's duties, which include being involved with a document from the earliest stage of a document's development. The production editor's involvement throughout the stages of a document's development will help preclude "last minute rushes [which] always cost extra—in vendor charges, overtime requirements, or gray hair and on-the-job stress" (G-25). When a document is sent to the printer, the production editor not only gives explicit instructions for printing and binding the document, but reviews the document to make sure it is complete and accurate. "Completeness is essential; the printer will ONLY do what the instructions specify!" (G-26). The production editor should examine a proof copy of the document to check the quality of the printing and the order of the pages.

351 Haughness, Norman. "The Technical Editor as Tactician." *Technical Communication* 15, no. 3 (1968): 18-19.

The technical editor should employ tact and diplomacy to help authors prepare manuscripts for publication. Using tact and diplomacy means keeping "to a minimum the introduction of your personality into discussion of the editing. . . . [maintaining] a healthy respect for the competence, *in his field,* of your technical collaborator" (18), and selecting which of your views must be accepted: "Be sure the point at issue is significant enough to outweigh the damage to the spirit of cooperation that must follow a jaw-to-jaw confrontation and put-down of your collaborator" (18).

352 Hawley, G. G. "Publisher Editing of Technical Books." In *Technical Editing,* edited by B. H., Weil, 155-66. Westport: Greenwood Press, 1975.

The editorial function for producing technical books can be divided into three levels. At the top level, the editor works with management to determine what type of books to publish, to procure books, and to decide which of the procured books to publish. The editor must appreciate "author's problems, whether they seem trivial or abstruse"

(158). At the second level, the editor encourages authors to fulfill their publishing contract and evaluates authors' manuscripts. The editor is a salesperson and a critic, able to tell the difference between a good and bad book. At the third level, the editor prepares the manuscript for the printer by copyediting the work and communicating printing specification to the printer. In all these levels, the editor "'must apprehend ethical meaning—the discriminating capacity between right and wrong'" (165).

353 Henderson, Arnold C. "Editing for the First Half Second: The Perceptual Process and the Technical Editor." In *Proceedings 28th International Technical Communication Conference,* W-49—W-52. Washington: Society for Technical Communication, 1981. ED 227 479.

Misperceiving, not seeing what really is present in a visual, is a major problem. Readers, generally in the first half second of viewing a visual, will misperceive the visual. A quick-sketching technique can alert editors to potential perception problems an audience might have. To use that technique, Henderson recommends that editors show a "chart, map, photograph, or slide to a few colleagues, giving them perhaps 5 seconds to look. Then have them sketch it—from memory" (W-49). Types of mistakes readers will make include lumping things together that are in proximity to each other, completing incomplete things, "grouping similar shapes together . . . [and] simplifying and distorting complex shapes to approach shapes" (W-52) readers prefer. Testing visuals is important because readers often are frustrated by a page layout that makes clues to the data difficult to find.

354 Hewitt, William F. "Editors and Their Needs." *Medical Communications* 2, no. 1 (1973): 14-17.

Analysis of survey results from 100 editors shows that at least 25% of the editors surveyed agree on 16 editorial needs. The top two needs are for standardization guides and editorial workshops. Surveyed editors also suggested topics that could be developed to aid editors. The 20 topics cited include judging the reliability of authors' sources, writing editorials, and understanding facets of the editor-publisher relationships.

355 Hobel, Marlene A., and Kathy L. Urbach. "Establishing a System for Technical Editing." In *Proceedings 35th International Technical Communication Conference,* WE-37—WE-39. Washington: Society for Technical Communication, 1988. (Also published in *Southeast Regional Conference of the Association for Business Communication Proceedings,* edited by Binford H. Peeples and Glynna E. Morse, 7-

12. Houston: Association for Business Communication, 1988. ED 308 565.)

The authors developed and implemented a system of technical editing in their firm by conducting two workshops, one for editors, one for branch office staff. At the first workshop, editors established three basic tenets: editing can be divided into levels; each level should be clearly defined; "each level must be assigned a credible time range" (WE-37). Using Buehler's system of editing levels as their model (see 276), the editors determined how much time a level would take. Editors estimated that proofreading would take one hour for 10-12 pages. During the second workshop, branch office staff were asked to edit one "page of poorly written technical prose" (WE-38) and then told to stop after 30 seconds. That's the amount of time an editor has per page when asked to edit a 100-page report in about an hour. Follow-up to the workshops included developing record-keeping procedures, providing authors with credible editing of their manuscripts, and continuing to market the editing system.

356 Holmes, Patricia C. "The Importance of the Editing Function: A Persuasive Presentation." In *Proceedings 32nd International Technical Communication Conference. A Mission to Communicate,* MPD-8—MPD-10. Washington: Society for Technical Communication, 1985.

Holmes describes a slide presentation that she prepared to educate engineers and engineering managers about the editorial function in the preparation of proposals. Her presentation includes describing the editor's general goals ("the five C's of correctness, conformity, conciseness, clarity, and content" [MPD-8]), giving examples of edited text, and explaining the differences between proofreading and editing. Holmes notes that because of the slide presentation, management recognized how valuable editing is and how much time it takes. Managers even added items to the information editors requested from authors and recommended that editors reject manuscripts that did not provide that information.

357 Howe, M. Rita. "Editor and Author: A Professional Relationship." *CBE Views* 9, no. 3 (1986): 69-74.

Authors are not editors and editors are not authors, but when authors and editors complement each other during the preparation of a manuscript, they develop mutual respect. Respect is the result of editors and authors negotiating resolutions for manuscript difficulties. Whether an author works toward resolution of manuscript difficulties depends on where the author fits on a cooperation scale. Howe provides examples of authors that fit on various points of the scale. Authors who are cooperative do not abdicate their control of a manuscript but do consider the validity of changes an editor suggests. Ultimately, "if editors and authors were to understand each other better, it would seem to follow that the anonymous third party known as the reader would be better served" (69).

358 Huth, Edward J. "Cooperation Among Editors—the Council of Biology Editors." *IEEE Transactions on Professional Communication* PC-18, no. 3 (1975): 113-15.

Huth says, "by 'cooperation' I am going to mean 'agreement on publication style.' And by publication style I shall mean all those conventions that govern our use and presentation, in published papers, of scientific terms, units of abbreviation, bibliographic references, structure of tables—in brief, all the details that go together to convey a scientific *message*" (113). Huth says that such uniformity will help authors prepare manuscripts, save journals money that is now used in the "redactorial handling of papers" (113), and make articles easily understandable to a journal's targeted audience. Huth cites the *CBE Style Manual* as a major source that will help editors achieve uniformity in scientific publications. Comments by other editors on Huth's presentation conclude the article.

359 Isenberg, Artur. "The Editor as Mover or Retarder of Scientific Ideas." In *Scientific Information Transfer: The Editor's Role,* edited by Miriam Balaban, 161-65. Dordrecht: D. Reidel Publishing Co., 1978.

Evidence suggests that Dr. Velikovsky's scientific writings have been suppressed because editors and reviewers of scientific scholarship use excessively conservative standards to judge new scientific theories. This conservatism is a problem because it can retard scientific advancement. For instance, Gregor Mendel's work, because "editorial fiat denied him access to the leading botanical journal of his day[,] . . . languished in an obscure periodical until it was re-discovered more than a generation later, a generation during which much progress might have been made" (161). Likewise, Velikovsky's work has been suppressed by scientific journals, even though a number of his predictions have been substantiated by other scientists. In choosing between two evils, "excluding true new scientific insights and including pseudo-science" (162), the editor should choose the latter and "make the relevant scientific channels of communication available . . . [to new theories] so that they can be tested, examined, discussed—dispassionately, objectively, thoroughly, rigorously: no more, no less" (164).

360 Jesse, Andreas. "On the Information Transfer from Primary to Secondary Sources and from Secondary to Primary Sources—An Editing Experiment in an Interdisciplinary Field (Automatic Image Analysis)." In *Scientific Information Transfer: The Editor's Role,* edited by Miriam Balaban, 581-86. Dordrecht: D. Reidel Publishing Company, 1977.
Secondary literature (indexing and abstracting journals, bibliographies, computer databases) can be coordinated to help authors and editors keep informed about new primary sources in the sciences. Coordination includes editors and authors in interdisciplinary fields communicating among themselves and constructing a bibliography that can be continuously updated.

361 Johnson, Margaret N. "The Technical Editor: An Obsessive-Compulsive Personality?" In *Proceedings 32nd International Technical Communication Conference. A Mission to Communicate,* WE-39—WE-40. Washington: Society for Technical Communication, 1985.
Obsessive-compulsive editors have a behavioral disorder that makes them misfits. Such editors alienate other professionals by insisting on standards that even the editors cannot maintain. The antidote to the obsessive-compulsive disorder requires afflicted editors to maintain a sense of humor and see perfection as an ideal, "not an achievable goal" (WE-40). Part of recognizing the inevitability of producing imperfect documents is a joint recognition of individual fallibility. Once editors recognize the legitimacy of that inability to be perfect, they can begin to work with people throughout an organization. Editors who recognize their fallibility do not abolish standards, but do the best job they can and then "relinquish control" (WE-40) to prevent unnecessary delays in the publication process.

362 Kantrowitz, Michael, B. "Split Shifts: You Can't Please All the Readers All the Time." *Conference Record of the IEEE Professional Communication Society,* 158-60, October 1985.
After administering a cloze test and a questionnaire to readers of edited and unedited technical documents and analyzing readers' responses, Kantrowitz found that editing helped technical and nontechnical readers' understand the texts. However, the two audiences also demonstrated a split shift. Technical readers rated the edited texts low and nontechnical readers rated texts high. And even though the technical audience understood the edited text better than they understood the unedited text, they had less approval of the edited text than they did the unedited text. Kantrowitz concludes that even though "editing has

a direct value in enhancing the comprehensibility of a text for varied audiences" (158), readers' attitudes of edited text are complex. Thus, "sometimes editing helps; sometimes it actually hurts" (158). [Note: Page numbers of this article are out of order. The article begins on page 160 and proceeds to 161, 158, and 159.]

363 Kantrowitz, Michael B. "What Price Technical Editing? Phase 1: Reaching a Lay Audience." *IEEE Transactions on Professional Communication* PC-28, no. 1 (1985): 13-19.

A study comparing lay readers' responses to unedited and edited manuscripts showed that edited manuscripts aided readers' comprehension, decreased reading time, and increased message acceptance. Unedited manuscripts negatively affected all three areas. Forty lay readers were randomly assigned to read either an edited or nonedited treatment of one of five passages excerpted from a technical report. Each reader was given two different passages: one with deletions, one intact. When considering whether to edit a document, managers ought to recognize "that if the lay reader's comprehension, reading time, or message acceptance is important, then editing should be a high priority" (18).

364 Kass, Jerry. "Editing Mathematical Copy." *Journal of Technical Writing and Communication* 2, no. 4 (1972): 307-30.

"[T]he editor of mathematical copy must give as much consideration to the typographer as to the reader" (308). The editor must pay particular attention to any potential typographical errors that could arise because of ambiguity in the way mathematical symbols are set. For instance, when an author chooses to use handwritten notations, Greek letters like iota or omicron can be confused with the English i and o. Errors of ambiguity increase in proportion to the complexity of an equation. Thus, Kass notes, '*set everything 'tight' unless there is a definite reason not to do so*" (315). To explain how particular notations should be set, Kass includes examples of signs of aggregation, subscripts and superscripts, square root signs, vector notations, and arrays. "As long as mathematical rules are not violated, the editor can present copy pretty much as he wishes" (320). However, rules for setting mathematical copy should result in clear communication of concepts. The editor will have to temper the setting of mathematical notations with practical issues: budget, schedule, and the typesetter's technical limits.

365 Katzenberger, Paul. "Primary Publications and Modern Information Systems: Copyright Problems from the Viewpoint of Editors of Scientific Journals." In *Scientific Information Transfer: The Editor's*

Role, edited by Miriam Balaban, 43-48. Dordrecht: D. Reidel Publishing Company, 1978.

Editors of scientific journals should "take a position on the copyright question" (46) raised by the distribution of reprographic copies among libraries. International copyright laws do not speak adequately to the reprographic problem, so individual countries have made laws governing the distribution of articles copied from scientific journals. But editors should participate in the development of codes or laws that influence the quality of journal publication, including issues surrounding the freedom of the press and censorship.

366 Kaye, Myra. "Selective Dissemination of Information at the Research Frontier—The Editor's Role." *Journal of Research Communication Studies* 3, nos. 1-2 (1981): 133-43.

"We have created information transfer services highly suitable for *technology*" (135), Kaye says, but those services may not promote science. For instance, technology provides information in large quantities, but scientists at the frontier of scientific research do not need masses of facts. Frontier scientists need stimulation to think about scientific ideas, and they need ethical guidance in their interaction with other scientists when they talk about new scientific developments. Editors can protect that interchange somewhat by requiring scientific authors to acknowledge peer reviewers. "The association of the reviewer with a particular paper should also obviate the theft, conscious or unconscious, of ideas" (141). Editors can also protect the audience by requiring authors to publish a statement in their papers saying that they followed appropriate safety guidelines. Editors should not publish papers that do not make that assertion.

367 Keller, Mark. "De Mentis Editorus." *Medical Communications* 7 (1979): 145-51.

Authors can get their scientific papers published by thinking like an editor. In a humorous tone, Keller says that editors like manuscripts double spaced, so an infallible piece of advice is, "get a secretary who double-spaces everything" (151). Editors also use referees, but the ultimate decision to publish rests with the editor. Keller cites one editor who chooses referees with opposite viewpoints so that one will wholeheartedly recommend that a paper be published while the other referee will unmercifully damn the paper. "It is obvious who then gets to cast the tie-breaking vote" (150). When an editor accepts a manuscript, authors should also accept changes that conform to the journal's style because a fundamental rule of editing is that editors who do not enforce style rules will one day regret their lax practice. See also 517.

368 Kelley, Patrick M. "Charting a New Course for Technical Writing and Editing: Technical Writing and Editing as Dialogue." In *Proceedings 29th International Technical Communication Conference. Technical Communication—Charting the Course of Technology,* W-62—W-65. Washington: Society for Technical Communication, 1982.

To write or edit by dialogue is the truest form of communication "because dialogue is characterized by the intense empathy of one person for another" (W-62). The theoretical bases of dialogue as found in Martin Buber and Carl R. Rogers can be articulated as six principles of dialogic conduct: "1. Genuineness, 2. Accurate Empathic Understanding, 3. Unconditional Positive Regard, 4. Presentness, 5. Spirit of Mutual Equality, and 6. Supportive Psychological Climate" (W-64). One major way to apply dialogue in technical writing is through tone.

369 Kelley, Patrick M. "High Tech/High Touch: A Trend in Technical Writing and Editing." In *Proceedings 31st International Technical Communication Conference,* WE-106—WE-108. Washington: Society for Technical Communication, 1984.

Referencing John Naisbett's *Megatrends*, Kelley cites the trend toward high tech/high touch, which means that technology is accepted only when it is accompanied by an emphasis on human qualities associated with touching. Naisbett discovered the high tech/high touch trend by conducting content analysis of newspapers, so Kelley used content analysis of selected papers from three International Technical Communication Conference Proceedings to identify the high tech/high touch trend in technical communication. His analysis confirms the trend toward high tech/high touch in technical communication. In particular he found that dialogue, as defined by Martin Buber and Carl Rogers, is becoming the basis for writer/reader and writer/editor relationships in technical communication.

370 Kelley, Patrick M., and R. L. Sims. "Theory-Based Technical Editing in Practice: It Doesn't Get Any Better Than This." In *Proceedings 32nd International Technical Communication Conference. A Mission To Communicate,* WE-25—WE-26. Washington: Society for Technical Communication, 1985.

One of the authors used the other author's theory about editorial dialogue to replace linear editing with dialogic editing. In linear editing writers and editors work independently in a linear sequence, creating an antagonistic relationship. When six guidelines on editorial dialogue were practiced, I-thou relationships replaced us-them relationships and the quality of reports improved.

371 Kendall, Bonnie L. "Editing in Dentistry: An Emerging Specialty." *American Medical Writers Association Journal* 3, no. 3 (1988): 5-6.
Every year the dental profession produces thousands of articles, 200 to 300 books, and materials on dental management and research. Because of the amount of dental literature published each year, every major city in the U. S. has a need for people to write and edit dental literature.

372 Landreman, Dolores M. "Selling in Technical Communications—The Mark of the Professional Editor." In *Proceedings 22nd International Technical Communication Conference,* 380-84. Washington: Society for Technical Communication, 1975.
"[T]he basic purpose of a technical communication is to sell a discovery, an idea, a device, a material, a procedure, a concept, or some other newly available or newly appreciated item" (380). Yet technical writers seldom understand how they can sell their ideas effectively. Technical writers may even feel insulted if a technical editor suggests that their drafts do not show sufficient evidence that the selling function has been used adequately. In discussing ways technical documents can be made into sales documents, Landreman notes that in the technical article the Introduction, Discussion, and Conclusion should be sales or future oriented. The Introduction should show how a product can benefit a customer. The Discussion supports the Introduction by convincing the customer that a real benefit is being offered. The Conclusion should add more evidence to convince the customer to purchase the product—and its benefits. Landreman cites three effective types of conclusions (speculative, conversion, and inspirational). The Recommendations also can be sales oriented. When the Recommendations ask readers to make yes or no responses to each recommendation, readers come to a clear decision about whether to buy a product.

373 Laner, Frances J. "Readability Techniques for Authors and Editors." In *Directions in Technical Writing and Communication,* edited by Jay R. Gould, 136-47. Farmingdale: Baywood Publishing Company, 1977.
"In general, neither authors nor editors study in depth what the needs of the reader are or how best to serve him" (146). Readability studies can help authors and editors prepare more readable documents by explaining how readers read. For instance, when a document's text is the primary consideration, how margins and captions are used can either add or detract from the text. In terms of type, serif is superior to sans serif. Editors who understand how to create a readable document

can give authors advice throughout the development of a manuscript so that authors prepare a better, more readable, document.

374 Last, John M., and John Gilbert. "Is 'Creative Editing' Ethically Acceptable." *CBE Views* 9, no. 4 (1987): 117-18.

Participants in a workshop seemed to agree that an editor can revise extensively an author's manuscript if the author is involved actively in the editing process; if the author cites the editor's efforts in the paper, even making the editor a co-author; and if the senior author takes complete responsibility for the published work. Most participants agreed that for an editor to create a manuscript out of an author's notes and unanalyzed data is "a serious breach of ethics" (118).

375 Layton, Edward. "Editor-Author Relationships: Both Can Win." *IEEE Transactions on Professional Communication* PC-16, no. 3 (1973): 57-59, 172.

Scientists read technical articles for intellectual stimulation, so technical writers should prepare interesting and easy-to-read articles. Editors can help a writer achieve that goal by using a booklet of author's aids. Such a booklet could include information about audience ("the reader is not a mirror image of the writer" [59]), theme (authors should produce one theme per article), and outlining. The author's aids booklet allows the editor to focus his or her editing on details, not major changes in an author's work.

376 Lehr, Dolores. "Three Roles of a Technical Editor." In *Proceedings 31st International Technical Communication Conference,* WE-65—WE-69. Washington: Society for Technical Communication, 1984.

In addition to serving as a proofreader, copyeditor, and substantive editor, an editor is also a resource person, instructor, and standards bearer. As a resource person, the editor provides "information on correct style to writers, typists, managers, and other personnel" (WE-65) and can enhance this role by developing a library of technical books, periodicals, and specialized dictionaries and by circulating those materials to writers. As an instructor, the editor tutors writers in one-on-one conferences, in seminars, or workshops. As a standards bearer, the editor has the task "of establishing and maintaining publication standards—both written and graphic" (WE-66), to include written standards that the editor continually updates.

377 Leibrandt, Thomas L., Jonathan Cohen, and Maureen O'Sullivan. "Opportunities for Author's Editors in Medical/Surgical Teaching Programs." *CBE Views* 12, no. 6 (1989): 111.

Normally, research physicians in training programs in general surgery are required to publish the results of their scientific research. Author's editors can assist the research physician by helping him or her prepare (1) a manuscript that is publishable, (2) a talk for the hospital or a medical conference, (3) grant proposals, (4) slides that present a case study or research results, and by teaching scientific writing, preferably on a one-on-one basis.

378 Levreault, E. P. "Who's On Third?" *Journal of Technical Writing and Communication* 2, no. 2 (1972): 133-37.

Using the analogy of a baseball game, Levreault traces the author's (hitter's) progress with a manuscript around the bases. The technical editor plays third base. However, Levreault recommends that editors not be restricted to third base, but be allowed to play early in the game. The editor can help the pitcher (program manager) by doing what a third-base player is supposed to do—quality control as the manuscript goes from base to base. When the editor is involved early in the game, the team saves time, team members work together well, and the quality of the team's product is improved.

379 Lindberg, Helen A. "Keeping a Sense of Humor." In *Proceedings 26th International Technical Communication Conference. Technical Communication—Shaping the World We Live In,* W-87—W-91. Washington: Society for Technical Communication, 1979.

After trying unsuccessfully to work as an editor with a demoralized group of engineers, Lindberg analyzed her situation and decided to change her work habits, change her part of her relationship with authors, and change the recording system that traced documents in progress. In changing her work habits, Lindberg took a more relaxed view of herself, decided to compromise even when she knew she was right, planned her work so that it could be completed in a reasonable amount of time, found a comfortable place to work, kept studying grammar, and labored to edit consistently. In changing her relationship with authors, she decided to review an author's manuscript with the author when the author was not distracted, not to rewrite an author's work, to phrase all comments to the author in positive terms, to motivate authors to take a technical writing course, to instruct authors using humor, and to encourage authors to have controversial or multiauthored papers reviewed by a team. In changing the way documents were traced, she helped develop an office log to record a document's location and a cover sheet that would stay with a document from the draft to the final copy. At each stage of a document's journey, the person responsible for a document would initial and date the sheet. Lindberg's efforts helped restore to the engineers a group spirit, and she recognized once again that "the technical editing tool most essential to a successful career, most difficult to obtain, and most easily lost [is]—a sense of humor" (W-91).

380 Losano, Wayne A. "Political Editing, Minimizing the Technical Editing Delay." In *Proceedings 23rd International Technical Communication Conference,* 109-12. Washington: Society for Technical Communication, 1976.

Technical editors should not allow technical managers to interfere with the production of manuscripts. Managerial intrusion into the report-production process can be minimized by following a four-step approach where managers influence a manuscript in the early stages of its development, steps one and two, "before the researcher or author can too strongly imprint his own personality upon his work and before outside influence will be too seriously resented" (110). The third step, manuscript review, is limited to the technical writer or editor. During the fourth step, pre-publication review, management is less likely to intrude in the manuscript preparation cycle. Editors can help managers relinquish control of editorial functions by explaining tactfully that managers have too much status and earn too much money "to be bothered with such pedestrian considerations as grammatical accuracy and stylistic niceties" (111).

381 Lufkin, James M. "Observations of a Godfather." *1979 S[ociety for] S[cholarly] P[ublishing] Proceedings,* 70-71, Washington: Society for Scholarly Publishing, 1980.

In his acceptance speech for being named Godfather of the Society for Scholarly Publishing, Lufkin says scientists need to write intelligently to readers. To do so, scientists need to understand what readers do and do not know and what they want to know. Editors can help scientists communicate by asking them to generalize scientific data when communicating with a lay audience. "[M]ost scientists recoil in horror from the very idea" (71) of generalizing scientific data because they have been trained to be exact. But a democracy depends upon public policy based on information, scientists and editors need to recognize the importance of the social implications of what they say and do.

382 Lytel, Allan. "What Kind of Editor Are You?" In *Proceedings of the Seventh Annual National Convention, Society of Technical Writers and Editors,* 81-90. Washington: Society of Technical Writers and Editors, 1960.

An editor needs to understand a writer's problems and ask questions about a manuscript's audience and about the manuscript itself. Although editing can be divided into three levels, a professional editor sees a document as a whole. Lytel includes an editor's job description.

383 McCafferty, James W. "Constructive Editing." In *Handbook of Technical Writing Practices,* edited by Stello Jordan, vol. 2, 908-24. New York: Wiley-Interscience, 1971.

If an editor can be compared to a camera that gives a static view of an action, a constructive editor is a dynamic camera that photographs a subject from different angles to produce a focused image. To do a constructive edit, the editor must know a report's audience, purpose, subject matter, and author. Knowing the author means working with him or her to prepare a manuscript for publication, which culminates in a meeting where the editor attempts to help an author eliminate any error from the manuscript by explaining comments on the edited copy. To help authors achieve consistency, the editor should be conversant with company style and have a grammar book, dictionary, and style guide at hand as references. Because technical editors may also be writers and coordinators of the publication process, the role of a technical editor is expanding and the trend is "to develop writers who can edit and editors who can write" (919), to provide "total publications service, with the writer-editor at the hub of the communications circle, making everything else turn" (920). McCafferty includes an appendix of common editing problems (capitalization, punctuation, abbreviations, bibliography and reference format, and equations).

384 McCall, Mary A. "The Value of a Scientific Editor." In *Proceedings 22nd International Technical Communication Conference,* 390-92. Washington: Society for Technical Communication, 1975.

A scientist needs an editor to help prepare scientific documents. Most scientists do not have the high-level skills in language and writing necessary to communicate scientific knowledge effectively, even though they should produce high-quality scientific reports for four reasons. One, publication of scientific data can advance science and the career of the publishing scientist. Two, language fluency "enhances a scientist's creativity and writing ability" (391). Three, scientific data should be expressed so that readers think as authors will them to think. Four, precision in language usage will increase publication possibilities. Scientists who lack the ability to write high-quality reports should seek editorial help.

385 McCarron, William E. "Confessions of a Working Technical Editor." *The Technical Writing Teacher* 6 (1978): 5-8.

Technical writing, technical editing, and proofreading are distinct activities. Technical writers are not technical editors and proofreading is not editing. In particular, the technical editor must consider the report's audience when reading the report, ask questions about how well the report is prepared according to technical reporting standards, and talk with writers. In many ways, "the process of technical editing is remarkably like grading a student paper" (6). Technical editors may also need to create one document out of various technical reports and proofread a document, but "proofreading is proofreading; it is not technical editing" (7). In short, technical editing, "next to technical writing itself, is the most demanding task placed on the report writer in science and industry" (7).

386 McCartney, James L. "The Need for a Council of Social Science Editors." In *Scientific Information Transfer: The Editor's Role,* edited by Miriam Balaban, 473-84. Dordrecht: D. Reidel Publishing Company, 1977.

Social science journals could benefit from a council of social science editors because a council could address policy issues that editors need to face if they want to improve the dissemination of social science information and preserve the editorial role in which they function. A council would not make policies, because most social scientists are "fearful of centralized decision making in their professional societies" (477). The policy questions a council raised could be resolved by other groups. The council should seek to be international and interdisciplinary. "A council should be embracive and not try to draw its boundaries too narrowly" (478).

387 McCormick, Barbara S. *How To Function as a Schizoid Editor.* Washington: Society for Technical Communication, 1977.

Most technical editors produce "literary, rewrite, grammatical, style, copy, production, and layout edits" (1). The diverse skills required to be a technical editor can cause the editor to be schizoid, wondering exactly what his or her function is. Editors can overcome this schizophrenia by recognizing what each editorial function requires and by accepting the challenge of performing multiple functions. Those functions can be divided into two broad classifications: technical and literary. McCormick provides a table outlining the relation between those two functions. Because the technical editor is of primary concern to McCormick, she gives details of the responsibilities for the technical classification, including audience ("the editor is the rhetorical, syntactical interface between technology and the ultimate reader/user" [9]), rewrites ("the rewrite responsibility requires that the editor 'intuit' from the draft's contents, just what it is the writer is trying to say, and to whom the material is directed" [11]), and style ("discounting correct grammar, syntax, and punctuation, etc., the decisions as to aspects of style are the editor's choice" [13-14]). Technical editors can also function as copyeditors and production/layout editors. However, the goal in all editorial activity is "not letting a document out of our hands until it has had the best treatment we can give it throughout all phases of the editorial process" (17).

388 McGhee, Patricia L. "Technical Tact." In *Proceedings 26th International Technical Communication Conference. Technical Communication—Shaping The World We Live In,* W-107—W-109. Washington: Society for Technical Communication, 1979.

Five basic techniques can help technical writers and editors communicate with technical personnel. One technique, interpreting and applying knowledge of personalities, is divided into five types: ridiculous meticulous, the plodder, eager to learn, anything goes, and the cloud climber. Another technique, liaison, focuses on the role of the technical communicator as "scapegoat, educator, salesman, and trouble-shooter" (W-109). To gain knowledge of technical subjects, writers and editors can use a technique of asking appropriate questions at the right time by eliminating inappropriate questions. Professionalism, another technique, "encompasses tact, flexibility, sincere interest, high performance standards, [and] dependability" (W-109).

389 McGough, David L. "Production Editor: Key To New Effectiveness." In *Proceedings 17th International Technical Communications Conference. A New Decade in Communications Effectiveness,* edited by Byron F. Hylen and Robert R. McDaniel, paper W8-4, 1-5. Washington: Society of Technical Writers and Publishers, 1970. (Also published in *Technical Editing: Principles and Practices,* edited by Lola M. Zook, 71-76. Anthology Series, no. 4. Washington: Society for Technical Communication, 1975. ED 173 807.)

The production editor coordinates the activities and products necessary to produce a document on time. McGough calls the editor's coordinating activities convergence and breaks those activities into three parallel and simultaneous aspects: inputs, production effort, and end results. "The editor's primary task is to focus all of them, all of the time, with equal emphasis, toward the final book" (2). To ensure that the production processes converge, the editor first should establish sequence and identity by labeling all manuscript components, second should conduct a troubleshooting review, and third should budget editorial time to solve problems, review drafts of an author's work, and advise printing of manuscripts with long lead times. Even though technological developments may change the way documents are produced, the successful use of such developments depends on production editors.

390 Marcus, Judith H. "The Proof of the Editor Is in the Editing." In *Proceedings 35th International Technical Communication Conference,* MPD-91-92. Washington: Society for Technical Communication, 1988.

To test potential editors to make a hiring decision, Marcus used a five-page report containing most of the editorial problems an editor in Marcus's department would have to deal with. Prospective editors were given instructions on how company documents are edited and a copy of the company's style manual. Candidates were to edit the report at home and mail it back within one week. Results of the editing test revealed that candidates with impressive resumes edited poorly, "ignoring gross inconsistencies among parts of the document, and making only cursory efforts to follow the logic of the text" (MPD-91). Some candidates with little or no scientific background edited well. Over seven years, those who have been hired based on high test results have become successful editors.

391 Martinsson, Anders. "Foreign Editing of Foreign English." *Earth and Life Science Editing* 9 (1979): 6-7.

Although nonnative speakers of English have primary responsibility for submitting papers that are written in fluent English, editors of English language publications also must assume responsibility for the fluency of a nonnative writer's English. Editors can share this responsibility by having a paper reviewed and then sending it to a linguist or they can send the paper first to a linguist. They can seek help from retired professors to prepare manuscripts. Editors at the World Health Organization help nonnative writers of English by using translators to prepare an English copy of a difficult text that the author has written in his or her native tongue.

392 Martinsson, Anders. "IFSEA: Towards an International Federation of Scientific Editors' Associations." In *Scientific Information Transfer: The Editor's Role,* edited by Miriam Balaban, 635-38. Dordrecht: D. Reidel Publishing Company, 1977.

A global federation of scientific editors from many disciplines would enable editors to attain more professional status. Such a federation could identify professional editorial tasks, like reducing journal costs. Editors can help reduce journal costs, because the hidden costs of rewriting and retyping texts are part of the editor's responsibilities. The editor can assist scientists applying for a copyright. The editor can become an active educator, teaching authors in groups about reporting scientific results. Editors also can publish papers about scientific editing. An International Federation of Scientific Editors could help integrate scientific methodology and writing, elevate scientific editing to the level of other academic activities, initiate and enforce publication standards, encourage the development of courses that teach authors and editors publishing methods, and provide a forum for answering questions about editorial practices.

393 Martinsson, Anders. "Scientific Editing in the Spectra of Disciplines, Languages and Communication Techniques." *Journal of Research Communication Studies* 3, no. 4 (1981/1982): 355-66.

Martinsson believes that editors can enhance their professionalism by considering editing as an international activity, not one limited to English-language publications; by teaching authors about the manuscript production process, especially in light of the increased use of camera-ready copy; by resisting the "oppressive promotion of the terms *Chairperson* and *Ms.*, the latter of which those of us who do not have English as their mother tongue cannot pronounce—it becomes an 'ums' or a 'mess'" (364); and by continuing to improve the quality of conferences on editing.

394 Marx, Joanna M. "Editing in a Multilingual Environment." *Journal of Research Communication Studies* 3, no. 4 (1982): 405-09.

As rapporteur, Marx synthesizes participants' comments about science editing in multilingual contexts. Since the lingua franca for science is English, a paper published in another language should include a long summary, figure legends, and table captions in English. An abstract in English will increase the paper's chances that abstracting and indexing services will list the paper and thereby increase its dissemination. When editing scientific papers, editors should remember that they are responsible for the quality of a published article, but quality is secondary to the paper's scientific value. And although editors must correct errors, improvements should not violate an author's style. In an international context, editors should ensure that the translation of a text does not distort an author's meaning. "The editor has to combine a good linguistic competence and a reasonable scientific insight" (408). Although the editor's native language should be English, the editor's knowledge of the author's native tongue is helpful.

395 Masse, Roger E. "Solutions to a Technical Editor's Problems: A Selected Bibliography on Technical Editing." In *Proceedings 32nd International Technical Communication Conference. A Mission to Communicate,* WE-29—WE-32. Washington: Society for Technical Communication, 1985.

In a 66-item annotated bibliography, Masse groups articles under three categories: Discovering the Roles of a Technical Editor, Discovering

Effective Editing Processes and Techniques, and Discovering Effective Techniques for Working with Authors.

396 Mazzatenta, Ernest. "GM Research Improves Chemistry between Science Writers, Editors." In *Proceedings 22nd International Technical Communication Conference,* 153-57. Washington: Society for Technical Communication, 1975. (Also published in *Teaching Technical Writing and Editing—In-House Programs That Work,* edited by James G. Shaw, 55-60. Anthology Series, no. 5. Washington: Society for Technical Communication, 1976. ED 172 264.)

At editor workshops for General Motors (GM) managers who edit reports, attenders learn how to apply information that they learn about editing. A major objective of each workshop is to help GM writers and editors determine what "is either correct, preferred, or allowed in technical writing" (154). That objective is partially realized when managers learn, for instance, that a combination of active and passive voice in technical writing is preferable. That objective also is forwarded when workshop attenders critique each other's editing and learn that their editing is based on incorrect information about language or that they overedit documents. Managers also learn how to apportion editorial efforts within their departments by realizing that "the higher the report goes, the lower the editorial input should be" (156). Mazzatenta cites favorable reviews of the workshops by workshop alumni, including the remark of a young editor-supervisor who said, "'you know, that course is working for me. My people tell me I'm a much better editor now'" (157).

397 Meckel, Susan R., and Kathleen H. Sauer. "Five Concepts for Effective Interaction between an Artist and Editor/Writer." In *Proceedings 29th International Technical Communication Conference. Technical Communication—Charting the Course of Technology,* G-38—G-40. Washington: Society for Technical Communication, 1982.

To function as a team, editors and artists should understand each other's roles. Editors can read literature about the graphic arts (six sources are cited) and artists can read literature about language (four sources are cited) to become familiar with the other's area of expertise. In addition, editors and artists should determine the focus of a document at the outset of a project, allocate nonoverlapping responsibilities to one person, and communicate daily so that problems are resolved quickly.

398 Meyers, Manny. "Diatribe of a Technical Editor." *Chemical Engineering* 75 (1968): 184, 186.

Because editors are servants, they want to help promulgate technical information by making manuscript changes that will increase readability. Yet some engineers and technicians (Meyers identifies three types) resist editors' help. Those with the Oedipus syndrome do not want to improve a manuscript because they believe it is fine as it is. Zealots have no editorial knowledge but cite and interpret regulations for readers. The new-wave engineer uses jargon and dares readers to guess what he or she is saying.

399 Mitchell, Constance. "The Editor's Multiple Roles in Transmitting Information to the Public." *Medical Communications* 10, no. 2 (1982): 40-44.

Mitchell discusses "the editor as *middleman*; the editor as *dress-rehearsal audience*; the editor as *expert reader*; the editor as *tabula rasa*; and the editor as *conciliator, negotiator, or mediator*" (41). As dress-rehearsal audience, the editor's initial response to a document can give authors insight into how an audience will react to their writing. As *tabula rasa* the editor reflects the audience's lack of knowledge about a topic. As conciliator, negotiator, and mediator, the editor can break a deadlock among various people who are working on a manuscript by becoming "an advocate of one of the viewpoints represented" (43).

400 Monagle, E. B. "Error Pattern Analysis Applied to Technical Writing: An Editor's Guide for Writers." In *Proceedings 28th International Technical Communication Conference,* W-81—W-84. Washington: Society for Technical Communication, 1981. ED 227 479.

By developing a numbered list of errors authors make, an editor can edit manuscripts by referring authors to numbered errors. In developing her error pattern analysis, Monagle constructed 18 classes of errors, but found that 80 percent of all errors "were in the placement of commas, the lack of hyphens with compound nouns and adjectives, and the failure of spelling out numbers of ten and below" (W-82). She distilled all errors into four numbered categories: "(1) Awkward Syntax, (2) Choice of Word, (3) Lack of Colon for Lists and Definitions, and so forth" (W-84) and (4) commas, a category which had subsections because of the many uses of commas. To use Monagle's method, the editor circles errors on an author's paper, numbers the errors, and provides a Master Sheet of the Most Common Errors when returning the author's paper.

401 Morgan, Peter. *An Insider's Guide for Medical Authors and Editors.* Philadelphia: ISI Press, 1986.

Addressed to medical authors and editors, "the *Insider's Guide* is intended to be a companion, not a textbook. It is replete rather than complete, thematic rather than systematic, argumentative rather than dogmatic" (viii). Thus throughout the book, Morgan introduces fictional characters—Drs. Nojarg, Relso, and Lucid—in a hospital setting who discuss the relationship between authors and editors and the use of medical language. Because Morgan addresses medical authors, he discusses the writing process and cautions authors against the use of jargon and pretentious language in print. Of style he says, "the style of a scientific report makes no attempt to impress; it forswears any claim to excellence; it imitates rather than innovates; and it bears no trademarks of the author. Its straightforwardness assures us that the author believes the research can stand on its own without the support of rhetoric, and its simplicity reduces the chance that we will misunderstand what the author is trying to say" (25). Authors are also advised to use IMRAD (introduction, methods, results, analysis, and discussion) in preparing a medical paper. To editors, Morgan gives advice about how to treat numbers, figures, and tables in a manuscript. For numbers, "the rule of economy and clarity in writing applies just as well to numbers: say as much as possible, as clearly as possible, with as few numbers as possible" (38). "Medical editors," Morgan notes, "like almost all hard-boiled journalists, find criticism more credible and more interesting than praise, and are more likely to publish it" (56), so authors should writer letters to the editor that "make one point. Make it clearly and quickly. Cut out repetition, unnecessary detail, and empty phrases" (56), just one out of eight pieces of advice Morgan offers about writing letters to the editor. Morgan also discusses editorials, case reports, and review articles. In addressing the need for consistency, Morgan explains citation systems (Harvard, author-year, numeric-alphabetic, order-of-citation), saying "medical editors have opted for the order-of-citation system (also called the Vancouver system), which assigns numbers to citations in the order in which they appear in the text and lists references the same way" (70). Morgan also discusses peer review, saying that from his experience "the more critical a review, the more likely the editor is to believe it. Editors usually have no difficulty in appreciating, unaided, the positive features of a scientific paper; what they want to know from the reviewer is whether there is anything seriously wrong with it" (75). Also "peer review is not a democratic process. One 'nay' vote may carry more weight than four 'yeas,' especially if the 'nay' comes from a methodologist or biostatistician" (75). Of ethics Morgan says there are four types of authors who commit breeches of ethics—the innocent blunderer, the pyramid builder, manipulators, and desperadoes. Collaborative researchers should assign one author—the corresponding author—to shepherd the manuscript through the review, rewrite, and publication process. In discussing advertising in journals,

Morgan calls the charge that "scientific editors will favor studies that support an advertiser's product or that challenge a competitor's" (96) senseless. He also explains the importance of having a journal indexed when an editor starts a new journal.

402 Morris, Ann, and Kate Kelly. "A Personal Approach to Working with Authors." *CBE Views* 12, no. 6 (1989): 114.

"Editors should not need to tame authors" but should establish a collaborative relationship with them. Such a relationship begins when the editor meets with the author at the outset of a project. As the project progresses, editors should communicate with authors in simple language by clearly stating any problems. However, editors need to provide an author with details about what they do to edit a manuscript. Editors should also prepare a list of instructions about usage, graphics, and handbooks authors can consult, and be advocates and teachers of authors.

403 Mundy, Della. "Professional Recognition for Authors' Editors—An Update." *Medical Communications* 11, no. 4 (1983): 92-98.

In reviewing the literature on authors' editors, Mundy cites three issues in that literature: 1. working conditions, 2. recognition, and 3. education. Concerning number one, she says that when companies advertise editing jobs as clerical positions, authors' editors are kept in "lower-paid lower-prestige positions" (93). Mundy's discussion about recognition of authors' editors focuses on the credit editors should receive for helping to prepare an article for publication, including whether an editor should be named as a co-author. She notes that ghostwriting may misrepresent the listed authors' authority as the interpreter of data. Mundy also recommends that more courses in medical writing/editing be offered at colleges and universities and that teaching positions for such courses be created in academic institutions.

404 Myers, Barbara Y. "A Classification of Author-Editor Relationships: Toward Team-Centered Relationships." In *Proceedings 31st International Technical Communication Conference,* WE-116—W-119. Washington: Society for Technical Communication, 1984.

Myers groups the literature on author-editor relationships into editor-centered, author-centered, and team-centered. She endorses the team-centered approach because "the skills and caring that result from practicing editorial dialogue ('high touch,' if you will) are extremely important" (WE-118).

405 Newman, Julliana. "Medical Education: The Editor's Role." *CBE Views* 12, no. 5 (1989): 79-80.

Pharmaceutical companies market their products to physicians through company-sponsored symposia on medical issues. When reporting on such meetings, an editor should maintain a balance between presenting medical problems and the possible pharmaceutical remedies. To maintain that balance, editors can follow four procedures. One, list presenters, titles, and salient points of a presentation. Two, verify the information from a presentation with the presenter. Three, when writing about the presentation, "avoid generalizations and speculations about the data presented" (79). Four, determine whether changes in the copy you write are ethically acceptable. Ask why a change is needed. Editors should follow these four steps because when educational publications are judged by the FDA to be advertisements, the FDA applies stringent regulations to the publication to intensely scrutinize the publication.

406 Nisley, Rebecca, Penelope Allen, and Ellen M. Chu. "Editing Tables." *CBE Views* 7, no. 4 (1984): 28-29.

Of the elements of a table, the title "should be a succinct but independent statement of the topic" (29). Heads should be flush left, not centered, unless centering is absolutely necessary. The table itself should be complete; the data pertinent, meaningful, accurate, and consistent; the format clear: "trends should be apparent and space should not be wasted" (29).

407 O'Connor, Maeve. *Editing Scientific Books and Journals: An ELSE-Ciba Foundation Guide for Editors*. Kent: Pitman Medical, 1978.

Published in the United States as *The Scientists as Editor: Guidelines for Editors of Books and Journals*. See 408.

408 O'Connor, Maeve. *The Scientist as Editor: Guidelines for Editors of Books and Journals*. New York: John Wiley and Sons, 1979.

The Preface states, "the purpose of this books is to describe and discuss the many facets of editing scientific books and journals and to explore the responsibilities of editors towards authors, readers and science itself" (vi). At the outset, O'Connor acknowledges that scientific editors, to master the facets of editing, must use knowledge and possess intuition. While editors must "be familiar with the standards and usages of their disciplines . . . the ability to choose the best work to publish remains an indefinable and elusive talent owing as much to intuition as to a deep knowledge of the subject" (2). To assist editors in satisfying their need for knowledge, O'Connor discusses the process of acquiring, editing, and producing books and journals. For instance, chapter 4 is devoted to refereeing with the advice that the editor should be flexible. "[I]f it is obvious that a particular manuscript needs no refereeing, the editor should simple accept it for publication, or reject it, as the case may be" (32). Throughout the book, O'Connor addresses ethical issues as she does when discussing plagiarism (37-38). She discusses manuscript editing, the topics for chapters 5 and 6, in part, by detailing the elements of a scientific paper. (How to cite references is given specific attention in Appendix 7, one of ten appendices that include topics like a publisher's contract with an author, information on copyright, guidelines for book reviewers, and a list of editors' associations.) She also includes chapters on the printing process, from design to reprints; reading and marking proofs ("Correcting minor errors such as the omission of a comma or full stop in references may seem fussy, but it is good for both the printer and for future authors if the editor/proofreader always demands a high standard of consistency even at this level" [102]); editing conference proceedings ("The conference editor should discuss policy with the journal editor and resolve major differences before telling contributors what kind of papers to prepare" [112]); starting a new journal, with comments about page charges and advertising; editing a journal ("[T]he editor should at all times exercise firm but flexible control over what goes into it [a journal] and how the material is processed and presented to readers" [128]); and editing in the future, with particular emphasis on electronic publishing; however, "no software program yet devised can cope satisfactorily with the countless different circumstances an editor should discuss individually with authors" (148). In sum, O'Connor notes, "editors will still be needed for electronic journals for the same reasons as they are needed for paper ones—to control the quality, quantity and form of what goes into the system" (153). Therefore, "editing is clearly no job for an amateur" (149).

409 Orenberg, Cynthia L., and Kelley Osborn. "Professional Data Survey of Editors or the Great Alchemy Trick." *Medical Communications* 8 (1980): 133-39.

Orenberg and Osborn present and analyze the results of a questionnaire they mailed to members of the American Medical Writers Association. One hundred ninety two respondents answered questions about salary ranges, pay satisfaction, education, employers, and geographic locations. Based on their findings the authors recommend ways medical editors can improve their professional status. "We can, in effect, engage in a little alchemy, and use the results of our survey to turn the seeds of our discontent into real gold for us all" (139).

410 Otto, Gilbert. "Some Frustrations and Responsibilities of the Editor." *CBE Views* 9, no. 3 (1986): 67-68.

Editors should educate authors, not replace them by rewriting their manuscript or by acting as "a literary technician" (68). In fact, "the detached editorial review is most beneficial" (68) to authors. Writers usually can find the problems in their manuscript that the editor found, but to do so, writers need to let the manuscript alone for a month before going back to it and preparing a final draft. That month delay is comparable to the value an author gets from a peer review of a paper.

411 Peterson, Dart G., Jr. "Developing the Editor-Author Relationship." In *Proceedings 23rd International Technical Communication Conference,* 85-88. Washington: Society for Technical Communication, 1976.

"[S]uccessful editors and authors develop the ability to work together, and it is the editor's task to lead in this development with each new author" (88). To lead in the development of the author-editor relationship, the editor can ask a series of questions about the job situation, about how the editor works with authors, and about the author-editor relationship. Just as an old adage tells writers to inform, not impress when they write, so the editor can ask if he or she edits to inform or to impress. An editor can listen to what an author says about a topic and translate oral language into written language. To "dejargonize" a writer's language, the editor can learn the meaning of the author's jargon.

412 Philler, Henry, and Harlan Matheson. "Artists and Editors Incorporated." In *Proceedings 14th International Technical Communications Conference. Technical Communications: Man's Record of Reality,* edited by Harold L. Mensch, paper #24, 1-14. Washington: Society of Technical Writers and Publishers, 1967.

Before the reorganization at Aerospace San Bernadino, editors and artists worked in separate buildings and were listed under separate organizational charts. After reorganization, editors and artist work in the same building to produce reports and briefings. The editor coordinates the preparation of a manuscript and has even assumed more responsibility for the administrative duties artists performed so that artists have time to integrate graphics with text. The editor has also relieved the artist of much reworking of art and of proofreading text that is integrated with graphics. The next phase in integrating the communication process will include the author. Editors will work with authors, teaching them how to compress and unclutter documents to save the audience time.

413 Power, Ruth M. "Who Needs a Technical Editor?" *IEEE Transactions on Professional Communication* PC-24, no. 3 (1981): 139-40.

Managers who are having trouble producing technical documents—their own or their staff's—should consider hiring an editor. The ideal candidate would have technical training, but people with technical training usually find that editing does not have the opportunities, salaries, and prestige that technical jobs offer, so humanities majors fill many technical editing positions. Power provides a checklist that supplies 21 aspects of a technical editor's job description so that employers can determine if they need a technical editor.

414 Rainey, Kenneth T. "Technical Editing at the Oak Ridge National Laboratory." *Journal of Technical Writing and Communication* 18, no. 2 (1988): 175-81.

Rainey describes the work of the Oak Ridge National Laboratory, focusing on the Technical Publications Department (TPD). The editing process of the TPD "requires intense and careful verification" (177) of technical reports' documentation. Consistency is also vital and the author's editor ensures that manuscripts meet publication requirements by coordinating the efforts of production personnel. "The assigned editor is responsible for the job from start to finish, rather than for parts of the total editing job" (178). Rainey describes the five levels of edit Oak Ridge editors use and notes that TPD wants editors to have both humanities and scientific credentials, but verbal skills are more important than technical background.

415 Reitt, Barbara, David Frost, and Kevin Brennan. "How Does a Free-Lance Editor/Writer Build a Clientele?" *CBE Views* 9, no. 4 (1986): 115-16.

Freelance editors/writers can build a clientele by possessing demonstrated expertise in a particular discipline and seeking potential clients. A freelancer can document his or her expertise by a resume and portfolio, and find clients by combing classified newspaper ads, even those advertising full-time positions for editors/writers. Referrals also help build a business, and the freelancer should consider all authors of a multiauthor project as potential clients. Once freelancers land a project, they can negotiate fees, but kills fees, advances (30 to 50% of the costs), and renegotiation options protect freelancers.

416 Renkonen, K. O. "Manuscript Merit." *Conference on Biological Editors. Report on the Special Meeting of European and North American Editors,* edited by Raymund L. Zwemer and Robert E. Gordon, 10, 1964.

A small, local science journal can attract good manuscripts that over time will contribute to general scientific knowledge. Such journals should not focus entirely on readers, but should consider being a proving ground for young scientists just starting their careers.

417 Reynolds, Helen. "Problems of a Government Regulatory Agency in Scholarly Publishing." In Scholarly Communication Around the World. Proceedings of a Joint Global Conference, 122-24. Washington: Society for Scholarly Publishing, 1983.

As the Food and Drug Administration's Bureau of Foods grew in size and importance, Reynolds was asked to be in charge of its effort "to develop and operate an internal manuscript review system, and to edit and publish a serial and some books" (123). She chronicles the evolution of the FDA review system, stressing that editors have a major part in ensuring that any material published by FDA personnel, particularly scientists, does not violate FDA policy.

418 Rigg, J. C. "An Editor's View of Standards and Standardization." In *Scientific Information Transfer: The Editor's Role,* edited by Miriam Balaban, 311-19. Dordrecht: D. Reidel Publishing Co., 1978.

More work needs to be done to develop adequate international standards for the preparation of scientific publications. Three types of standards are necessary: minimum specifications (what should be required on the title page, for instance), unification (paper size), and perfection, which cannot be achieved but should be aimed at. A major impediment to creating standards is conservatism in publishing. Rigg cites eight areas where standards should be improved, including bibliographic identification and proof correction.

419 Schmid, Anne M. "The Freelance Medical Editor." *Medical Communications* 8, no. 3 (1980): 84-87.

Freelance is an archaic term that should be replaced by "consultant acting as a medical editor" (84). The consulting editor can find work by preparing a curriculum vitae that includes the consultant's skills, rates, and availability. To ply the vitae, the consultant can contact medical publishing houses, prepare a plan to produce a conference publication for medical directors, contact medical journals about a position as managing editor, and discuss the publication needs of corporate training centers with their directors. Once a client agrees that a publication is needed, the consultant should prepare a schedule and budget in preparation for negotiating a contract.

420 Schmid, Anne M. "That Mysterious University Editor." *Medical Communications* 4, no. 2 (1975): 7-9.

What do university medical editors do? They locate articles for physicians and even keep an index of published articles in a particular specialty; write abstracts, grants, obituaries, and public relations pieces; and edit monographs and chapters for textbooks. In editing manuscripts, Schmid meets with the authors after they have completed a first draft and asks them to explain the article to her and identify the journal they want it to be published in. She then edits for clarity and conciseness and always checks the accuracy of citations. She rewrites (not ghostwrites) manuscripts when they need to be rewritten.

421 Schwager, Edith. "The Redactor's Responsibility." *Medical Communications* 5 (1976-77): 24-27.

The redactor has two important functions: help authors say what they want to say and improve a manuscript by making it succinct "without overriding the author's style" (24). To do that work, redactors must organize and retain all valuable information; must understand what the text says, which can be a problem for redactors who are not scientists but who edit scientific text; must verify the accuracy of data; and must know and use good grammar. "[A] person who does not excel in grammar, style and spelling hasn't a prayer of succeeding in the profession of editorship" (27).

422 Schwager, Edith. "Writer vs. Editor: Why Not Allies?" *Medical Communications* 4 (1976): 2-5.

"Writer and editor don't have to be Damon and Pythias, but the don't have to carry on a vendetta either" (2). Editors can encourage good author-editor relationships by helping authors clarify their meaning, not impose meaning on authors' writings. To help an author, editors must establish their authority by citing the source of authority for changes they make in a manuscript. While documenting changes is an editorial talent, the editor also must be flexible. "The editor doesn't have to win 'em all" (5).

423 Scott, Denise. "The Editor in a University or Research Center." *Medical Communications* 8 (1980): 88-90.

The editor in a university or research center should have the wonder of a child surrounded by books, the ability of a philosophy student to think clearly and logically, and the experience of an author who has been edited. The editor should also recognize that authors innately resist being edited. Such resistance is valid because editing attacks, challenges, and questions the writer's competence. Ideally, however, the editor is a collaborator with the author. To be a successful collaborator, the editor must understand what a text says. "Editing something one does not understand is a contradiction in terms" (89). Although editors at the University of California, San Francisco, work with a variety of authors and even do "a lot of rewriting" (89), "in a nutshell, the responsibility of an editor is to see that papers get published" (90).

424 Serenkin, Harriet. "Results of the 1982 E[ditorial] F[reelance] A[ssociation] Work Profile and Rates Survey." *EFA Newsletter* 7, no. 5 (1983): 5-8.

The EFA survey categorizes freelancers according to skills and experience, yearly salaries, and rates for various editorial skills.

425 Shaefer, Patricia. "Editor to Artist—Object, Communication." In *Proceedings 20th International Technical Communications Conference,* 157-61. Washington: Society for Technical Communication, 1973.

The editor can help "the artist help the author look good" (161) by communicating with the artist using the language of art, by using clear instructions, by eliminating unnecessary callouts and captions, by asking the artist to create missing scales, and by giving the artist freedom to produce effective art. "Tell him the problem, tell him the size, tell him what is available for his use" (161).

426 Shampo, Marc A., and LeAnn M. Stee. "Medical Editing: Classification of Cases." *American Medical Writers Association Journal* 2, no. 3 (6-9): 1987.

Medical manuscripts are compared to 10 types of patients, for example those needing emergency treatment, major or minor surgery, or a second opinion. The analogy of papers to patients shows how complex editing is and helps medical writers understand that editorial judgment distinguishes editors from each other, just as the use of surgical techniques distinguishes physicians from each other. The analogy also points out the need for editors, like physicians, to develop a good bedside manner.

427 Shnitzler, Robert K. "What the Writer Expects the Editor To Do." In *Proceedings of the Seventh Annual National Convention, Society of Technical Writers and Editors,* 73-79. Washington: Society of Technical Writers and Publishers, 1960.

Speaking as an author, Shnitzler tells what an author expects from an editor. In general, the author expects the editor to help him or her produce a carefully-crafted manuscript that readers can understand. The editor-author relationship is based on mutual confidence, so the editor can assume that technical data in a manuscript is correct and complete. However, the editor should have enough technical knowledge to spot problems in the use of symbols, notations, and abbreviations and should correct such errors. When making suggestions for changes, the editor should be able to support a suggestion by appealing to an authoritative reference. But before an editor makes a radical change in a manuscript, he or she should consult with the author. And in no way should the editor edit out the author's style, unless it interferes with the manuscript's meaning. The greatest sin an editor can commit is losing an author's manuscript.

428 Shore, Joseph N. "How Specific?" In *Proceedings Seventeenth International Technical Communications Conference. A New Decade in Communications Effectiveness,* edited by Byron F. Hyden and Robert R. McDaniel, paper #W2-1, 1-3. Washington: Society of Technical Writers and Publishers, 1970.

Of the triad composed of semantics, clear writing, and specificity, specificity is of most concern to the production-line writer/editor. "If the use of semantics is to attain a type of truth, and the use of language, including 'clear writing,' is to limit communication within historical confines, the purpose of specificity is to attain totally useful communication" (3). The technical writer/editor can help generate "inescapably useful documents" by employing all appropriate techniques of writing and graphic arts. He or she also should use all the necessary control methods to guide a draft through the production process.

429 Sideris, George. "Creativity in Technical Editing." In *Proceedings 18th International Technical Communications Conference. The State of the Art,* paper #6-10, pp. 1-7. Washington: Society for Technical Writers and Publishers, 1971.

Because technological innovations can be used in unforeseen ways, an editor should be creative by editing technical reports or articles so that they appeal to a wide readership. The editor should "insure that the ideas are free to circulate on their own, meet other ideas, and give birth to new ideas" (1). Such creativity in editing is different from craftsmanship, which helps a reader understand a technical document but does not widen the readership. The creative editor should help authors broaden their view of readers' needs.

430 Simons, John L. "The Technical Aspect of the Technical Editor's Job." In *Proceedings 24th International Technical Communication Conference,* 268-69. Washington: Society for Technical Communication, 1977.

Editors can improve the quality of technical documents by training authors to write well. Such training would entail preparing a report writing manual; conducting a training program of lectures, workshops, and seminars; and participating in one-on-one critiques of a document with its author. Company editors should develop a training program because time constraints do not allow them to refine each manuscript as much as they would like to refine it, and "no editor . . . can have the same insight as the observer/investigator/designer who is developing the project" (269). Editors are best able to develop a training program (rather than consultants) because editors are familiar with the company's authors, knowing their strengths and weaknesses. In-house training can help the editor make excellent documents superb instead of making poor documents tolerable.

431 Simons, John L. "The Technical Editor as a Decision-Maker." In *Proceedings 27th International Technical Communication Conference. Technical Communication—The Bridge of Understanding,* vol. 2, W-27—W-29. Washington: Society for Technical Communication, 1980.

In performing their job, technical editors make many decision that can have far-reaching effects. Technical editors "must adopt a positive, aggressive attitude about making those decisions" (W-30). Although technical editors are not perceived as decision makers, they make decisions about documents—decisions that have major economic repercussions on the editor's employer. The editor's decision-making powers are expanded when deadlines require completed documents that may not go through an extensive approval process. An assertive attitude about decision making is enforced when an editor earns authors' and managers' acceptance.

432 Simpson, Amy. "Editors and Usability Testing: A Perfect Match." In *Proceedings 32nd International Technical Communication Conference. A Mission to Communicate,* MPD-65—MPD-67. Washington: Society for Technical Communication, 1985.

A usability test is designed to determine if a product's intended user can use it for its intended purpose. Editors are ideal participants in a usability test because they are the first persons to use a writer's document. Simpson provides a checklist for editing documents, based on her experience with usability tests. From that checklist, editors learn that headings should be succinct, the index should be thorough, and material should be repeated if readers really need it. The goal of usability testing is to provide to the author needed information in a usable form, so an editor can learn about an audience's needs through being involved in user testing. Using usability testing, the editor also can solve problems before a document is produced, leaving fewer flaws in the published product.

433 Sims, R. L. "Buck." "Dialogue: The Key to Professionalism in Technical Communication." In *Proceedings 30th International Technical Communication Conference,* W&E-35—W&E-37. Washington: Society for Technical Communication, 1983.

During a one-year internship, Sims successfully used dialogic editing, proving to himself that a dialogic relationship between writer and editor is practical in the real world. In a dialogic relationship, editorial changes are not final until the author approves of the changes. In all but three cases Sims was involved in writers liked editorial dialogue and cited Sims's inadvertent editing errors which occurred because he was unfamiliar with technical issues. Dialogue resulted in excellent manuscripts, according to reviewers, and "the reviewers did not recommend major changes in any papers that resulted from good dialogic editing sessions" (W&E-37).

434 Smith, Frank R. "Editing Technical Illustrations." *Journal of Technical Writing and Communication* 3, no. 3 (1973): 177-204.

Technical editors evaluate illustrations when they are rough art, finished art, and production art. When evaluating rough art—art produced by the author of a technical document—the editor adds and deletes, simplifies and elaborates. "His concern is primarily with message and only secondarily with tone, style, and appearance" (178). The editor suggests changes in illustrations after understanding what message the author intends to convey. If the editor cannot understand that message, he or she should talk with the author and ask "dumb" questions about the illustration's message and purpose. It may be that the editor's questions will cause the author to consider amending the graphic so that readers are satisfied with the information presented. After an illustrator prepares finished art, the editor proofreads it and makes changes according to editorial style. In editing production art, the editor, in counsel with the illustrator, discusses layout of illustrations. The editor also integrates text and art "so that they are mutually supporting" (203-04). The editor should develop a positive relationship with illustrators because "the clear, precise figure interpreted and embellished by the well chosen word can be the product only of the cooperative union between the illustrator and his friend the editor" (204).

435 Smith, Howard. "Author's Editors: Responsibilities and Professional Standards." *Journal of the American Podiatry Association* 72, no. 9 (1982): 473-75.

In reviewing the literature on author's editors, Smith points out that the author and the author's editor must have a mutual respect for each other to achieve a team goal of publishing a manuscript. The author's editor's responsibility as a member of that team includes editing at three levels (technical, copyediting, or redaction; substantive; and creative editing); advising the author about the publication process by making suggestions for graphics, layout and design and by processing galleys and page proofs; and teaching the author about writing. Smith includes Tacker's list of five professional standards. See Tacker's "The Code of an Author's Editor" (218).

436 Smith, Terry C. "Who Says Editing Can't Be Fun(ny)?" *Technical Communication* 34, no. 1 (1987): 34-36.

Editors of technical documents may discover unintended examples of humorous prose. For example, "'in the event that the equipment needs to be stored while awaiting installation, it is preferred that it be stored in a warehouse before it is unpacked'" (35). Smith cites other problems with punctuation, diction ("'After the first attempt failed, we decided to try a sillier [should be similar] scheme'" [36]), and transitions to provide examples of fun(ny) technical writing, advising editors to scrutinize graphics and text.

437 Solla Price, Derek J. de. "Ethics in Scientific Publication." *Science* 144 (1964): 655-57.

To regulate the flow of scientific information, scientific publication should "*be considered a privilege consequent upon the finding of something which people may need to read, rather than as a duty consequent upon the spending of time and money*" (656). Thus editors should refuse to publish articles where authors are cited because they helped conduct research but participated little in preparing a publishable article. Referees and editors should be particularly anxious to reject "insufficient or padded" bibliographies.

438 Stapleton, Paul. "Western Editors and Third World Writers." *Scholarly Publishing* 17 (1986): 278-87.

Western editors have an obligation to help Third World scientists publish their research findings. Third World scientists have a great deal of difficulty understanding and conforming to Western publication requirements, but their work should not be rejected out of hand because it does not conform to those requirements. Rather, editors should take special care to help Third World scientists. Editors can donate their time to edit a paper from a Third World scientist, ask referees to evaluate the paper's content without regard for poor presentation of the content and then prepare thorough reports that charitably explain how to amend the paper for publication. An editor can draft a revision of a promising paper and provide the author with materials on preparing scholarly papers. As an example of editorial help, Stapleton describes a series of workshops he created to improve the writing of Third World scientists. In helping Third World scientists, Western editors should not discriminate against developing countries by using cost or selection standards that Third World authors cannot reasonably be expected to meet.

439 Swee, Cathleen E. "Defensive Editing." *Medical Communications* 6, no. 2 (1978): 15-17.

Defensive editing occurs when editors prevent antagonism between themselves and authors by avoiding "misunderstanding, resentment, and negativity from the author" (15). To practice defensive editing, editors should watch their diction when conversing with authors. For instance, revisions are *suggested* revisions. Instead of commands ("Delete this") the editor queries the author: "Could this sentence be deleted?" Editors should also practice constructive revision by asking the author for clarification of how he or she is using a word or phrase. The editor can support suggested revisions by appealing to appropriate references.

440 Tacker, Martha. "Author's Editors: Catalysts of Scientific Publishing." *CBE Views* 3, no. 1 (1980): 3-11.

A scientific author's editor should be recognized as a bona fide participant in the preparation of scientific articles for publication. Although authors are ultimately responsible for their written work, editors can help authors to "communicate scientific data and ideas effectively" (4). Most scientists need an editor's help because they do not have the training or have not acquired the skill to be effective communicators of scientific information. The author's editor provides the needed training and skill by applying three levels of edit—technical, substantive, and creative—to an author's document. The more substantive or creative editing an editor performs, the greater the need to acknowledge the editor's help somewhere in the published paper. Although some may object to an author getting help from an author's editor, such objections fail to consider the valuable tasks an author's editor can perform, including serving "as the author's production manager" (7) to prepare a manuscript for publication. Author's editors also can serve as educators who do not edit manuscripts, but "indicate on the drafts where changes are necessary or desirable and to raise questions at appropriate points, a level of edit we might call educational editing" (9). The author's editor is not a ghostwriter, and his or her contributions should not be recognized with co-authorship. See also 320.

441 Thompson, Marilyn A. "Easy Does It: Author and Author's Editor." In *Proceedings 32nd International Technical Communication Conference. A Mission to Communicate,* WE-64. Washington: Society for Technical Communication, 1985.

The relationship between an author's editor, "the editor who works with authors as they write," and the author is based on an implied contract that promises partisan alliance. The author's editor is dedicated to seeing the author's work printed, but to do that, the author's editor is a devil's advocate who evaluates the paper from a journal's perspective to find flaws that the journal editor could cite as evidence for rejecting the paper. The author's editor also teaches the author about scientific composition by writing notes in the margin of an author's manuscript and by using humor judiciously.

442 Tyson, Thomas H., and Thomas E. Abbott. "Grassroots Technical Communication." In *Proceedings 18th International Technical Communications Conference. The State of the Art,* paper #4-3, pp. 1-3. Washington: Society of Technical Writers and Publishers, 1971.

To promote better technical writing at the Atomic Energy Commission's Savannah River Plant, the Plant's Technical Procedures Office produces *Technical Writing Tips,* a two-page bulletin, issued at irregular intervals. The bulletin generally has a lead problem-solving article followed by regular features on graphics ("How to Improve Your Figure" and "How to Set Your Table"). Miscellaneous features include a section where readers can match words and definitions. The bulletin "has succeeded in keeping before our community of engineer-writers the goal of effective communication, the interest of Management in the subject, and the aims of the Technical Procedures Office" (3).

443 Urbach, Kathy L. "From Writing to Editing: The Transition." In *Proceedings 34th International Technical Communication Conference,* WE-89—WE-91. Washington: Society for Technical Communication, 1987.

To become a technical editor, former technical writers will need to learn new aspects of time management and author-editor relationships. "Editor's deadlines," for instance, "are ... much more strict and limiting" (WE-89) than author's deadlines. The writer turned editor must also learn how to turn personality conflicts into productive relationships, which will include teaching authors the craft of writing. Because each author presents different challenges to the editor's job, the editor must be flexible, must choose an editorial approach to a project based upon the writer's ability, the document's purpose, and the audience's needs.

444 Wagner, Carl B. "The Technical Side of Technical Editing." In *Proceedings 29th International Technical Communication Conference. Technical Communication—Charting the Course of Technology,* W-112—W-115. Washington: Society for Technical Communication, 1982.

"[G]ood technical editors possess technical knowledge" (W-112); that knowledge distinguishes them from literary editors. The technical editor uses technical knowledge to back-up authors, much like a right fielder backs-up the third baseman. Wagner objects to those who believe that too much technical knowledge can hinder technical editors from representing audiences that have little technical background. He asserts, "only too little knowledge can prevent the editor from understanding the reader's point of view" (W-114). Thus editors are encouraged to "be interested in the subject. Probe, dig, and learn. You can't learn too much!" (W-114).

445 Wall, Tom. "Working with the Graphic Artist: Advice for Technical Communicators." In *Proceedings 33rd International Technical Communication Conference,* 137-40. Washington: Society for Technical Communication, 1986.

Editors who manage artists are responsible for meeting artists' needs. Editors can meet those needs by recognizing that artists need uninterrupted time to concentrate on creative planning. Artists also need to communicate directly with authors so that instructions about a project are not distorted by being passed through a number of intermediaries.

446 Ward, James H. "Editing in a Bilingual, Bicultural Context." *Journal of Technical Writing and Communication* 18, no. 3 (1988): 221-26.

As an editor in Puerto Rico, Ward says that an editor in a bilingual, bicultural context must be sensitive to linguistic problems and authors' expectation of an editor. In a bilingual context where Spanish is a major language, linguistic problems include the use of apostrophes to indicate possession and the inversion of certain common phrases (white and black for black and white). Linguistic problems of usage and semantics are intensified when two languages do not have a common way to express an idea. "Pundits enjoy pointing out that machines 'run' in English but only 'walk' (andar) in Spanish" (224). Linguistic issues are secondary to commonly held perceptions in Hispanic culture that a writer's words should not be edited. In fact, "criticism of what an individual produces—no matter how constructive the criticism—can be construed as belittling the person" (225). Even peers don't edit their peers' work. So the audience must fend for itself when interpreting a writer's work, especially since the Hispanic writer writes to impress. "Obviously the intervention of a third party, an editor, is considered unnecessary and even undesirable" (225). However, changes are underway to revise the traditional view of editing so that more technical information can flow from Spanish-speaking to English-speaking countries.

447 Weil, B. H. "Psychological, Educational, and Professional Aspects." In *Technical Editing,* edited by B. H. Weil, 1-16. Westport: Greenwood Press, 1975.

Technical editors should possess unique abilities because they are called upon to perform several functions in an organization. Psychologically, editors should develop positive relationships with authors by being interested in what authors write and by being willing to help authors throughout the development of a manuscript. The editor also must develop positive relationships with management, illustrators, and publishers while keeping the readers' needs and interests constantly in mind. As an educator, the editor can prepare an in-house style manual and organize and conduct training courses on writing. The teaching technical editor performs a real service to his or her organization. Professionally, the editor may be called upon to perform a variety of roles in an organization, as a representative of management, as a staff member, as a member of a service division, or as a member of a team. To serve in any of these capacities the editor should possess the requisite technical and editorial expertise to function successfully as a technical editor.

448 Weil, Benjamin, ed. *Technical Editing.* Westport: Greenwood Press, 1975.

According to the Preface, "in essence, the book is a review of the field of technical editing from the 'what,' 'why,' and 'how' standpoints, with a touch of 'when' and 'where.' 'What' is edited falls into the categories of papers, reports, slides, tables, figures, journals, business magazines, books, manuals, abstracts, and translations, to mention but a few. 'Why' they are edited is clear—to maximize their communication impact. 'How' they are edited to accomplish this varies with the medium, and ranges from 'structuring' technical articles to deleting extraneous data from slides. 'When' and 'Where' are concerned with timeliness and timing" (vii). See "Psychological, Educational, and Professional Aspects of Technical Editing" (447), "Editing Technical Reports" (635), "Internal Editing of Technical Papers and Articles" (328), "Editing Organization-Sponsored Magazines and Newsletters" (566), "Editing from the Patent Standpoint" (622), "Editing and Publishing Technical Abstracts for Internal Use" (459), "Editing of Technical-Society Journals: The Editor's Viewpoint" (496), "Editing the Technical Business Magazine" (553), "Editing Technical News Releases" (625), "Publisher Editing of Technical Books" (352), "Editing Technical-Equipment Manuals" (589), "Editing Slides and Other Graphic Aids" (299), "Editing Illustrations for Technical Reports and Papers" (301), "Editing Tabular Data" (302), "Editing

Translations" (637), and "Other Aspects" (460).

449 Werner, Yehudah L. "How Editors Catalyze the Publication Explosion." In *Scientific Information Transfer: The Editor's Role,* edited by Miriam Balaban, 113-21. Dordrecht: D. Reidel Publishing Company, 1978.

Editors can refrain from increasing the amount of data published by journals (1) by encouraging authors "to publish comprehensive papers each of which is a whole, meaningful entity with its own merit" (116), (2) by refusing to publish "a lip-service" book review, (3) by allowing authors to cite unpublished works in the references to their papers, and (4) by not assessing authors page charges. Editors, like authors, should "learn to derive personal satisfaction not so much from the number of pages they edit and publish but, rather, from the level of importance of each page" (119).

450 Whalen, Elizabeth. "The Author-Editor Relationship: Observations and Suggestions." *CBE Views* 11, no. 1 (1988): 5-7.

"The road to successful relationships between authors and editors is paved with simple paradoxes: 1) tactful honesty, 2) gentle firmness, and 3) flexible consistency" (7). Two truths will help the editor travel that road. One, authors want their work published, and two, their egos are involved in their manuscripts. Those two truths lead to guidelines about how editors can work successfully with authors. Editors can communicate with authors about problems; ask an author's permission to do something only when a choice is available; expect confrontation at times, but find out why an author is upset, correct the problem if possible, and tell the author what was done to resolve the problem; and expect only occasional praise from a few authors.

451 Wilhelm, John R. "Technical Writing and Editing in a Multinational Environment." In *Proceedings 34th International Technical Communication Conference,* WE-190—WE-192. Washington: Society for Technical Communication, 1987.

When Americans work as technical editors in an unfamiliar culture like Europe, they should study the country's culture and anticipate problems associated with a multinational environment. Problems include degree of formality (Europeans are quite formal), amount of data required to submit a successful proposal, level of testing ("Many companies in other countries . . . put their equipment in the field. If it works, there is no problem. If it doesn't, they fix it" [WE-190]), and degree of control (In Europe, the creator only unveils a product when it is finished). Cultural distinctions have implications for editing. For instance, in Germanic cultures deadlines are sacred, even though working overtime to meet a deadline is unacceptable. Thus a typist could deliver a manuscript on time with "only half of it typed" (WE-192). Translating and typing (in several languages) are also problematic. Even how paper is measured can cause problems. "U.S. paper is measured in inches. European paper adheres to the metric system. . . . Metric holespacing only fits metric binders" (WE-192). However, the writer/editor is responsible for overcoming those problems to produce effective technical communication.

452 Williams, Graham. "The Role of the Editor in Australia." *Journal of Technical Writing and Communication* 5, no. 3 (1975): 167-80.

To make effective judgments, the editor in Australia must be knowledgeable about both production and technical editing because both roles are generally combined. Thus, the editor must be knowledgeable about typography, layout and design, and paper. For example, in editing a technical manual, the editor's duties "fall into three main areas: information collection; text scheduling; editing, assembly, and verification" (173). Williams suggests that the editor be involved in all three areas from the beginning of a project. In bridging the gap between specialists and nonspecialists, the editor can follow a nine-point approach Williams outlines that emphasizes quality. "The editor's motto should be that of the young lady on the desert island who told her male companion, 'I'd know—that's who'd know'" (176). Williams also cites survey results to demonstrate that "editing, like writing, is at bottom a subjective activity" (179), a matter of judgment.

453 Wilson, Peggy L. "Medical Publishing: An Editor's Viewpoint." *Medical Communications* 6, no. 4 (1978): 9-15.

The growth of technical publications has highlighted the need for editorial training. In particular, increased publication of medical texts will foster a competition among authors where the best written manuscripts will be profitable and the others will be remaindered. Editors can help medical authors prepare well-written texts, but institutions that require physicians to publish should share the responsibility of helping authors. Wilson outlines seven ways such institutions can help, including fostering a relationship between editors and physicians so that editors are perceived as members of a professional team.

454 Woods, Mary P. "An Editor's View of Indexing." In *Proceedings 26th International Technical Communication Conference. Technical Communication—Shaping the World We Live In*, W-158—W-161. Washington: Society for Technical Communication, 1979.

The editor should prepare the index for a technical document less than book length. Woods explains basic principles of indexing using 3x5 cards and discusses the Key-Word-in-Context (KWIC) computer system. The KWIC index "prints out a list in which the pertinent words in a title are permuted" (W-160).

455 Zimmerman, Muriel. "Reducing by Design: A Checklist for Editors." In *Proceedings 30th International Technical Communication Conference,* W&E-18—W&E-20. Washington: Society for Technical Communication, 1983.

Editors can reduce the size of a document by adjusting its design. In particular, the trim size can be changed to allow more print on each page; the text area or type page can be enlarged (by adjusting margins); the number of columns per page can be increased ("A multi-column format will accommodate considerably more words per page, reducing the number of pages required" [W&E-18]); type size (particularly of headings) can be set smaller; leading can be reduced to delete excessive white space; and illustrations can be scaled down. In many cases, redesigning a document does not affect readability adversely. However, "redesign is not a substitute for editing, but it is a useful adjunct technique, particularly valuable in any situation in which lower production cost is a goal" (W&E-19).

456 Zook, Lola M. "Lessons Learned—Not Always By Choice." In *Proceedings 27th International Technical Communication Conference,* vol. II, W-31—W-36. Washington: Society for Technical Communication, 1980.

Zook divides her lessons into four categories: lessons she wishes she didn't have to learn, lessons she wishes she would have learned sooner, lessons she never learned, and lessons she is still trying to learn. Under lessons she wishes she hadn't had to learn Zook notes, "you can't do everything" (W-32); editing is a matter of making choices that involve compromise. But choice allows the editor to take control of a situation and plan for success. Under lessons she wishes that she had learned sooner, Zook points out that she and everyone else underestimate how long a project will take. Under lessons she never did learn, Zook includes never learning that shortest is best. Just because a phrase is not essential does not mean that is isn't useful. A bare bones sentence may not read well. Under lessons she is still trying to learn, Zook cites using the ear to "judge whether prose is effective" (W-33). In addition, she is still learning about defining the problem, applying editorial skills with care so that authors are treated with respect, and understanding the role of the editor as a bridge between two people. "Editorial skills are simply an aid in bringing author and reader together" (W-35).

457 Zook, Lola M., ed. *Technical Editing: Principles and Practices.* Washington: Society for Technical Communication, 1975. ED 173 807.

Technical Editing is an anthology of articles published in the *Proceedings* and Society for Technical Communication journals from 1965-1974. Zook chose articles "that present a broad and flexible view of the editorial job, and that show respect—or self-respect—for the functions the editor serves" (iii). See "Patterns for Making Editorial Changes" (277), "The Editor as Generalist as Well as Specialist" (46), "A Logical Approach to Editing Proposals, Reports, and Manuals" (632), "Stalking the Troublesome Hyphen" (102), "Editing by Dialogue" (15), "The Art of Editing" (54), "Production Editor: Key to New Effectiveness" (389), "Editing the Small Study Proposal" (630), and "A Pitfall for Professionals" (269). Zook includes a bibliography "of papers and articles that deal with the work of the technical editor or have strong relevance to that work" (92).

458 Zook, Lola M. "Technical Editors Look at Technical Editing." *Technical Communication* 30, no. 3 (1983): 20-26.

The results of a 28-item questionnaire administered to more than 60 technical editors and managers provide data about what technical editors do and are expected to do. For instance, technical editing duties are difficult to define because the variety of editorial contexts defy the codification of editorial norms. However, common problems, like managers' and writers' lack of understanding of the editor's function in an organization, suggest that many editors need more status to operate effectively. Yet, most editors like their jobs, especially the diversity of projects and people they work with. "This diversity is the most demanding but also the most rewarding attribute of the editor's job" (23). In evaluating qualities editor need, managers cited interpersonal skills, and when hiring an editor, they look for good communication skills as the most important measure of an applicant's editorial abilities. Changes in editorial life include the use of computers in editing and the decrease in the quality of written products. Decline in the quality of written products indicates that editors are being confronted with the fact that different types of publications have various value to the organization, and more time and money will be spent on the more valuable publication. However, the editor's "proper objective is to do *the best work possible under the constraints that exist*" (25).

Editing, Types of Publications

Abstracts

459 Schoengold, Morris D., B. H. Weil, and Mary A. Mento. "Editing and Publishing Technical Abstracts for Internal Use." In *Technical Editing,* edited by B. H. Weil, 62-79. Westport: Greenwood Press, 1975.

Technical abstracts for internal use are found in in-house bulletins prepared for technical personnel in a research organization. Technical abstracts are important because they allow technical personnel to be informed about important articles in technical journals, articles that technical personnel might not otherwise be able to read. Editors can ensure that these abstracts are useful to readers by keeping informed of the organization's information needs, by training abstracters, and by maintaining a well-balanced staff of technical experts. "If the editor can determine how the research person reads, what he expects from an abstract, how he uses it, and the best method of presenting the information, he is well on his way toward being a good editor" (65). The authors recommend that abstracts begin with a topic sentence, and the authors note that "informative abstracts are usually the most popular and useful" (67) compared to indicative abstracts. Section headings and a subject index help readers find information easily as does a highlight page, a one-page summary of the most critical references. The authors also discuss methods of printing a bulletin and ways to prepare file cards of the abstracts.

Advertisements

460 Weil, B. H. "Other Aspects." In *Technical Editing*, edited by B. H. Weil, 257-65. Westport: Greenwood Press, 1975.

Technical editing includes editing technical advertisements and publicity materials, proceedings and compendia, technical-process manuals and handbooks, and technical specifications. To edit technical advertisements and publicity materials, the editor must not overedit, "destroying creative freshness of approach" (258). To edit proceedings and compendia, the editor ideally is the expert in charge of the program so that he or she can solicit appropriate papers and edit them. To edit technical-process manuals and handbooks, the editor must compile information from a variety of sources and edit documents that often have been prepared by engineers. To edit technical specifications, the editor applies editorial skills to the work of other professionals.

Anthologies

461 Jordan, Stello. "Acting as an Editor." In *Proceedings 19th International Technical Communications Conference,* 109-10. Washington: Society for Technical Communication, 1972.

As a co-editor for an anthology by 35 authors, Jordan recounts problems with authors that contributed to a six-year elapsed time from beginning to completion of the anthology. He advises other editors of similar projects to (1) demand strict time limitations for authors' manuscripts, six months for the final manuscript with partial submittals during that time, (2) work with the publisher to establish a production schedule that will accommodate both editor and publisher, (3) construct a work flow chart and update it throughout the project, and (4) maintain records to track all chapters in the project.

Booklets

462 Ainsworth, Richard A. "Job Opportunity: Freelance Booklet Editing." *Writers Digest* 48, no. 7 (1968): 49-52, 92-93.

To prepare a booklet, the freelance editor will need to consult a printer, an artist, and a photographer and talk with those professionals in their own technical terms. To determine who might need a booklet prepared, the freelancer can consult the yellow pages. Ainsworth advises novice freelancers to begin a freelance career by accepting a small project as a public service for an organization. When charging for freelance editing, the freelancer should know cost factors—such as printing costs—and should base fees on time by determining what his or her working day is worth and multiplying the daily rate by the number of estimated days he or she will spend to produce the booklet. Then,

Ainsworth advises freelancers, ask for "one third of the total fee on assignment, one third on approval of the publication, and the remainder on delivery of the finished copies" (52). After a booklet is prepared, "the final test of your ability as a freelance editor," Ainsworth notes, "is to leaf quickly through the pages you have prepared and read or look at only what catches your eye immediately" (92). If the quality of the booklet is supported by such an analysis, "you have just become an editor" (92).

Books

463 Abinder, Paul. "Editing the Illustrated Book." In *Editors on Editing: An Inside View of What Editors Really Do,* rev. ed., edited by Gerald Gross, 233-38. New York: Harper & Row, 1985.
Editing "books about essentially visual subjects, where the illustrations are absolutely essential to the context of the book" (233), requires skills in addition to those needed to edit any other book. Sizing, cropping and captioning; acquiring reproduction rights ("there is no uniform, clear-cut law covering reproduction rights to the visual arts in this country" [236]); and making decisions about a reproduction of illustrations in black and white (regular offset, duotone offset, or gravure?) are among the duties that are needed to edit illustrated books. In addition, the editor must work closely with the designer and production specialists.

464 Balfour, Bernice. "Another Speciality: Freelance Textbook Copyediting." *Writer's Digest* 49, no. 1 (1969): 53.
Balfour notes that "the most important qualification [for a freelance editor] . . . aside from a solid foundation in the English language, is some previous experience in copyediting, preferably in a book publishing house." Although the copyeditor's duties include leaving major decisions to the author, Balfour queries the author or publisher if she has questions about the manuscript. When she edits a complicated text for a publisher located long distances from her, she edits one or two chapters and sends them to the publisher for comment.

465 Beneduce, Ann. "Planting Inflammatory Ideas in the Garden of Delight: Reflections on Editing Children's Books." In *Editors on Editing: An Inside View of What Editors Really Do,* rev. ed., edited by Gerald Gross, 258-64. New York: Harper & Row, 1985.
The editor of children's books has a special responsibility to the intended readers. "Editors have a duty . . . to consider its [a book's] effect on the child's mind, personality, and character and on his or her developing interests. . . . It's the editor's job to guard them from misinformation" (260). Thus, the editor should have training in child and developmental psychology. One goal of editing children's books is to offer children insights and inspiration, not adult fear and

disillusionment. Books for children should set them on fire with an idea. "Books for children should be 'inflammatory' in this sense" (264).

466 Brass, Alister. "The Editor of a Medical Book." *Medical Communications* 8, no. 3 (1980): 80-83.

The editor of a technical book has divided loyalties between the publisher and the author. To satisfy the publisher, the editor should look for new authors, "the young, bright, enthusiastic people who have a need to publish. They are the ones who will work with you, be eager to produce their manuscripts on time, and tend to be cooperative" (81). But the editor also should establish ground rules early, so that authors do not explode with rage when the editor begins marking the author's manuscript by considering the intended audience. Establishing the ground rules includes determining which illustrations are necessary and informing the author about house style. In serving both publisher and author, the editor needs to be willing to let the author win if the author demands than an issue be settled to his or her satisfaction.

467 Colby, Jean P. "Editing Children's Books." In *Editors on Editing*, edited by Gerald Gross, 98-104. New York: Grosset & Dunlap, 1962.

When editors consider whether to accept a manuscript, they ask practical questions about a manuscript's potential sales, the author's willingness to revise a manuscript, and what future writing an author might do. "Of course," Colby tells authors, "the whole business of your manuscript's being accepted or rejected boils down to—what are your particular editor's set standards?" (101). Colby lists eight standards that she believes are essential, if a children's book is to be successful. She also tells authors, "to write well for children *you must like them, understand them, and respect them*" (104).

468 Dellon, Hope. "Editing the Mystery Novel." In *Editors on Editing: An Inside View of What Editors Really Do,* rev. ed., edited by Gerald Gross, 214-20. New York: Harper & Row, 1985.

The mystery novel market is not particularly lucrative, so editors of mystery novels must have an "honest enthusiasm" for a project. That enthusiasm generally springs from a recognition that a mystery novel has "essential attributes . . . readability, pace, reasonable fairness to the reader (the crucial piece of evidence should not be withheld, except perhaps in a thriller, where the emphasis is on the chase rather than the puzzle), and the convincing creation of an orderly universe in which questions are answered and wrongs put right" (215-16).

469 Epstein, Edmund L. "Editing Quality Paperbacks." In *Editors on Editing,* edited by Gerald Gross, 71-76. New York: Grosset & Dunlap, 1962.

Quality paperbacks enjoy good sales even though the paperback editor may not be able to identify the buyers. "Who goes in and planks down a dollar and a quarter for a collection of documents about the American 19th Century?" (73). Epstein surmises that many Americans read such books *after* graduating from school. "Perhaps after all Johnny learns to read *after* he leaves school, and what he reads for fun is what he should have been reading for credit. If this is so, education is suffering from neglect of deeply ingrained amateurishness which imbues all enthusiasts for learning. They will not be taught; but they will learn" (75). Epstein address a second question: What type of books sell as quality paperbacks? Poetry doesn't because a successful quality paperback "sells more than 6000 copies a year" (73), given Epstein's criterion. Books on music (except opera synopses) and literary criticism also do not sell well. But books on art and American history do sell well. What about novels? "[T]he whole field of quality paperback novels and works on literature is a quagmire whose sunken paths are not even known to the oldest natives. Who can tell what will succeed?" (74). Documents, however, like diaries and collections on historical topics are "very important in quality paperback" (75). About editing quality paperbacks, Epstein says, "perhaps intuitive editing is the best editing; it means that you trust to your own personality rather than to abstract parameters of taste" (76). Epstein is certain that many people are reading the books he publishes, even if he can't clearly identify his audience. He believes that his "are responsible, intelligent, sensitive people, and are rapidly becoming more so. How many editors can make that statement?" (76).

470 Harter, Helen. "Textbook Editing." In *Editors on Editing,* edited by Gerald Gross, 84-92. New York: Grosset & Dunlap, 1962.

A textbook editor is responsible for asking a myriad of questions about the development of a text, but generally is not given authority to answer those questions. "There is no area in which he is free to use his judgment, but his work is an unending series of decisions which cannot be referred to anyone else" (92). The editor asks questions about audience, members of textbook selection committees, teachers, children, sales people; about content ("Is the author talking over the children's heads?" [86]); about organization and structure (the use of headings, for example); about production of the text ("'Will it be all right to change the order of the activities? The columns do not break right this way'" [90]); and about facts: "Sometimes a fact is challenged. If it is wrong, it must be corrected. If it is right, the textbook editor must produce sources of information to provide it" (91). Yet the editor must be a person "who must never lose his temper; about whom everyone can gripe and be sarcastic, but who must never answer back except in the gentlest and most polite terms; who must offer his ideas humbly, with the preface that they are just his opinion and probably wrong" (91).

471 Hartwell, David G. "Editing the Science Fiction Novel." In *Editors on Editing: An Inside View of What Editors Really Do,* rev. ed., edited by Gerald Gross, 222-31. New York: Harper & Row, 1985.

The science fiction (SF) novel is a category of general fiction, "a response to a specific audience demand" (222). The successful science fiction editor recognizes the unique readership of SF, an isolated cultural all its own. "The SF world is conscious of its separateness from the rest of literature and of publishing and has its own culture, which reveres the 'pros' who write and edit" (225). Thus, "if there is a single commandment for the SF editor, it must be: you cannot ignore the established SF culture and its standards" (225). Even SF art is clearly defined; "the appeal is escapist" (228). And terms like space warp, hyperspace, and hyperdrive are cliches that writers use to voice the real concern: "the characters and the environment and their thoughts and feelings and interactions" (230).

472 Kefauver, Weldon A., ed. *Scholars and Their Publishers.* New York: Modern Language Association, 1977.

"What is recorded here are the three formal papers read at the opening session of a forum on the subject 'The Scholar and His publisher' that formed a part of the program of the Ninety-First Annual Convention of the Modern Language Association of America, held in New York City on 26-29 December 1976, together with reconstructed transcripts and digests of the substance of three workshops that followed the opening session" (3). See annotation for "The Decision to Publish: Scholarly Standards" (129). The other articles in the volume are entitled "The Decision to Publish: Economic Factors," "The Scholar as Publishing Author," "Workshop: The Publisher's Reader," "Workshop: The Publishing Contract," and "Workshop: The New Reprographic Technologies as a Solution to the Problems of Scholars and Publishers."

473 Lee, Marshall. *Bookmaking: The Illustrated Guide to Design and Production.* 2nd ed. New York: R. R. Bowker Company, 1979.

Part II of *Bookmaking,* which discusses editing books, is divided into three sections: the profession, basic knowledge (agent and author relationships, contracts, copyediting and style, and proofreading), and procedures, including design and production procedures. At the outset, Lee notes that although the editor is the link between the author and the publisher, protecting both parties' interests, "the editor is primarily the publisher's representative and in contract negotiations must try to make the best terms possible in the company's favor" (376). Thus an editor must be a diplomat. In addition, those editors who edit copy should be good writers. "[E]very working editor does a considerable amount of writing in the course of making manuscripts work, and the success of the editor depends to a large extent on how good this writing is" (381). Lee outlines the editorial hierarchy and lists seven routes for becoming part of that hierarchy, noting that "increasingly, editors hire people with agency experience, because agents today perform many editorial functions" (387). Agents, like editors, may be called upon to negotiate between editor and author, especially when "an editor [is] faced with an especially difficult author" (394). About the typical book contract Lee says, "the best insurance against trouble is to make contracts only with people you feel are honest and reliable—and make the contracts simple and clear. Generally, a contract that only a lawyer can understand is a bad one" (400). In discussing copyediting and style, Lee notes that "finishing a manuscript involves 5 functions: (a) correcting errors of typing, (b) correcting errors of fact, (c) correcting errors of grammar, (d) improving awkward sentences and paragraphs, and (e) styling and marking" (402). About correcting errors of grammar, he says, "'cleaning up' the grammar could mean stripping the book of its character or altering its tone. The rule should be hands-off unless a clear understanding is reached with the author or editor" (403). About style, Lee notes that "it has no independent value. . . . What style should prevent is the blurring, through repeated error, of a language's ability to express thought clearly, precisely, and subtly" (405). He also discusses stylebooks, dictionaries, British and American style. In introducing proofreading marks, Lee explains three ways to proofread a manuscript. The final section on bookmaking procedures begins with an explanation of two sources of books: the project born in the house and the project or manuscript born outside the house and brought in from outside. Of those projects brought into the house from outside, the ones submitted by packagers are a great advantage to a publishing house because packagers provide books that are ready to be sold upon delivery; the house staff have time to devote to other projects because the book is delivered ready for the market; and a house may not have had the technical expertise to produce the book. Any manuscript brought into the house should be followed in the house by a paper trail because lost manuscripts, art or photographs "can result in high-cost lawsuits" (420). The editor must work with marketers, even before a book is accepted for publication, to determine the sales potential of a manuscript. The editor can ask three questions to assess a book's marketability: "Will it sell? . . . Is it good enough? . . . Is it consistent with our publishing program?" (423). Although working with marketers can pose difficulties for editors, "conflict can be minimized if the editor takes a stand only on the element of editorial integrity and leaves it to the art director and marketing manager to battle over the question of effectiveness" (425). However, editorial integrity includes examining promotional and publicity copy so that misrepresentations of a book are eliminated. The editor also edits the book because "all manuscripts need *some* editorial work" (430). Authors, however, may not appreciate an editor's suggestions so editors should explain to authors "how permanent and embarrassing weaknesses are in a published book; how the author would later regret not having taken the opportunity to make changes when there was still time" (433). About design and production, Lee says that editors contribute to designers' understanding of what the book says and check to see if the book is being prepared accurately. Checking for accuracy is an eight-stage process extending from galley proofs to press proofs. "Once all the proofs have been checked and the book has gone to press, the editor can only pray that all will go well, and that the reviewers will not notice (and mention) the errors that will almost certainly remain" (447).

474 McCormack, Thomas. *The Fiction Editor*. New York: St. Martin's Press, 1988.

"The good editor's sensibility is such that he's gripped, bored, delighted, confused, incredulous, or satisfied . . . as the appropriate reader would be. This quality, sensibility, is absolutely essential" (5). In applying sensibility, the editor diagnoses an author's work (McCormack focuses on novels) to identify what the author can do to satisfy the work's axiom, the verbal expression of the author's desire for a certain effect on the reader. Thus the editor needs craft, not merely intuition. While intuition alerts editors to a problem, it doesn't necessarily tell them what the problem is. (Many editors don't learn craft in any systematic way because "young editors are taught very little, and nothing systematic. When they are assistants, the explicit tutelage from their bosses is usually confined to the other major aspects of the occupation— acquisition, 'publishing', handling authors" [23].) Consequently, editors diagnose only 80% of the problems in a work. "[M]y argument," McCormack says, "is not that editors never diagnose anything; it's that eighty percent isn't enough" (25). To aid editors in their diagnostic task, McCormack defines and discusses gad, prelibation, somacluster, axiom, and sensibility (gustant and salivant), among other diagnostic tools. Such tools are necessary because "fiction editing is hard, its subject is complicated and its etiologies are often deep below the surface" (80). Even though the craft of editing may be useful for writers, "the techniques I have been urging," McCormack notes, "in the approach to, and execution of, the job, is for *editors*. It's not meant to tell writers how to do it" (111). McCormack addresses editors because "a *good* editor could benefit, at some time or other, any writer who ever lived" (113).

475 O'Connor, Maeve. *How to Copyedit Scientific Books and Journals.* Philadelphia: ISI Press, 1986.

In the Preface O'Connor says, "this book aims to explain the [copyeditor's] job to new or would-be copyeditors, including the freelance workers and author's editors, in science or medicine" (ix). To begin that explanation, O'Connor notes that copyeditors of scientific books and journals are needed because the average author has little training in writing and a great dislike of writing so that "the written language is almost an alien one" (7) to such an author. Copyeditors, therefore, will need to learn how "to let authors say things their own way, provided they say them correctly—hence the First Edict of Copyediting: LEAVE WELL ENOUGH ALONE" (7). (All twelve edicts are listed on page 134.) O'Connor also discusses training for copyeditors and then explains how to process manuscripts, beginning with logging-in submitted journal articles. She notes, "accepted manuscripts may be copyedited either before or after the authors revise the refereed version, depending on journal practice" (15), but authors should "re-check copyedited manuscripts before the typesetting stage" (17). Copyeditors will use two kinds of markings: mark-up and copy-marking. O'Connor explains copy-marking in chapter 2 and mark-up in chapter 7. About queries to authors, she says, "keep your queries very short. Mini-essays on the finer points of grammar or the ten other possible ways of writing a sentence are unlikely to be appreciated" (26). Chapter 3, on substantive editing, is a discussion of the parts of the manuscript—titles, abstracts, headings, tables, figures, references—and issues related to content. For instance, O'Connor says, "copyeditors are not expected to correct scientific statements—but you can at least look critically at more general comments and check their correctness when possible" (33). Chapter 4, on language editing, explains style in terms of spelling, punctuation, grammar, syntax, and usage. Chapters 5 and 6 are devoted to mechanical style and touch upon such topics as en and em dashes, indentation, Syteme International (SI) units, numerals and equations, references, and graphics. Overall, "if journal style is flexible, [copyeditors should] use the author's style if it is consistent; otherwise impose a consistent style of your own" (69). O'Connor also explains three systems of reference citation (Harvard, sequential-numeric, and alphabetic-numeric) and encourages editors to verify references. "[F]ew journals go to the troubled of verifying from the original sources that authors' references are correct. If this task falls to your lot, the time you spend in the library will have the editor's blessing" (79). Chapter 7 explains how to mark-up and code manuscripts and compuscripts. Chapter 8 discusses a journal's cover, masthead, contents list, running heads (including biblid and Copyright Clearance Center (CCC) codes), and indexes. Chapter 9, on proofreading, outlines the three proofreading systems, but O'Connor notes that team and tape recorder proofreading are not satisfactory for proofing scientific and technical documents. "Proofreading is therefore often a solo job demanding concentration and self-discipline to keep the eyes traveling from manuscript to proof and back, and to stop oneself from falling asleep" (106). Chapter 10 is about copyediting books—textbooks, monographs, conference proceedings, and symposia proceedings—and includes advice about working with authors ("[P]rovide them with clear guidelines or instructions at an early stage" [123]); preparing prelims (to include colophons), end matters, and indexes; and writing blurbs. "In a 200-word blurb you might use the first two sentences to explain the need for the book or the reason why a conference or symposium was held. You could state the theme or purpose of the book in the next sentence or two, summarize the contents in four or five sentences, and end by naming the likely readership if this isn't already clear" (132). O'Connor includes two appendices—one on organizational addresses, including organizations that offer training to copyeditors, and one on further readings.

476 Parker, Mel. "Born to Be a Paperback." In *Editors on Editing: An Inside View of What Editors Really Do,* rev. ed., edited by Gerald Gross, 177-85. New York: Harper & Row, 1985.

Paperbacks have three loosely defined markets: male, female, and "crossover" (both male and female). An editor must identify the market for a paperback and consider the means of distribution, either supermarkets or bookstores. If an editor can identify a book as primarily a supermarket book, that's good, "because the greatest number of paperbacks are still distributed through supermarkets" (179). Editors also can sell paperbacks by acquiring reprint rights through auctions. However, reprint editing doesn't allow for "creative interplay between editor and author" (183), which many editors find satisfying.

477 Sifton, Elisabeth. "The Editor's Job in Trade Publishing." In *The Business of Book Publishing,* edited by Elizabeth A. Geiser, Arnold Dolin, and Gladys S. Topkis, 43-61. Boulder: Westview Press, 1985.

Editors in trade publishing acquire books, decide which ones to accept for publication, edit them, and help get them published. Editors can acquire books from the slush pile, from published manuscript (works that can be translated, for instance), literary agents, and other publishing houses. Those are passive ways to acquire books. Editors also must seek books actively, even invent books by thinking up ideas authors can use to write books. Editors make publishing decisions by asking questions about the quality of the book and the market for such a book. In choosing books, and editor's "editorial equilibrium is continually reestablished and found anew on a balance between risk and prudence, between a desire to feed established tastes and interests in the reading public and to encourage the new, the uncertain, the innovative, the not yet proven" (50). In editing a book, an editor should work for the author by not asking for manuscript changes that are not in accord with the writer's natural style, and editors should not ask writers to write better than they are able to write. This means editors "should behave a little differently with each book: pliant and agreeable, pleasantly coercive, impatiently dictatorial, demanding and fussy, meekly inquisitive, or soberly encouraging" (54). By responding to books individually, the editor advises the author about how to improve a book while honoring the author's authority over the book. Sifton notes, "making comments on other people's work is always fraught with danger" (56). To publish the book, an editor needs to be efficient and keep track in writing of where a book is in the publication process. Editors can help differentiate a book from competing books by explaining the book's unique allure to people in and outside the publishing house. As in the other functions the editor fulfills, in marketing the book, the editor mediates among people who work together to produce the book.

478 Stainton, Elsie M. *Author and Editor at Work: Making a Better Book.* Toronto: University of Toronto Press, 1982.

In the Preface Stainton says, "herewith, from a swarm of notions about writing and publishing, I've sorted out a gaggle of problems, a pack of problem-solvings, a flock of helpful hints, a pod of *dos* and *don'ts,* and a pride of comforting thoughts. This brood of ideas follows the primordial order: the first part is addressed to authors, the second to editors. A third part adjures each to consider the other" (ix). In the first part, Stainton addresses authors about editors by recommending openness. "The worst mistake an author can make after finding that an editor has altered a meaning is to say flatly, 'Stet—erase your editing, since it changes the meaning.' He should think of the next reader, and the next" (25). In the second part, to editors, Stainton recommends compromise ("Frequently editors must be satisfied with the good . . . but the better editor will be disappointed" [27]); scrutiny ("Major reorganization or rewriting often is not necessary, but dogged attention to innumerable details is" [27]); and tact ("An adroit editor will intersperse compliments to the author among the queries and quibbles. A little praise, honestly put, will make that editor seem more human—and more credible" [27]). Stainton also gives specific advice about prefaces and introductions, grammar, transliterations ("when an editor is scheduled to work on a manuscript derived from lectures, attending one or more of the lectures is sure to be useful in the editing" [34]), sexist language, and repartee ("When an author scribbles in the margin: 'Nitpicking!' respond neatly: 'Who wants nits?'" [41]), among other topics. She concludes the second section by saying, "a good editor tries to get inside the author's skin and help present the author's ideas—no matter whether the editor agrees or disagrees" (42). About the author-editor relationship, the topic of section three, Stainton makes this distinction, "the good writer is more amenable to suggestions than the bad writer" (45). Even with "crazy and nasty authors . . . [the] editor is the agreeable diplomat who offers suggestions, considers compromises, and even withdraws from the controversy if necessary" (47). Information on how to prepare indexes is includes in section three. Two final chapters, annotated lists of dictionaries and books on style, complete the book with the admonition about style books that "one can follow all their rules and write badly" (71).

479 Thornton, John. "The Truth About Trade Paperbacks." In *Editors on Editing: An Inside View of What Editors Really Do,* rev. ed., edited by Gerald Gross, 164-75. New York: Harper & Row, 1985.
Thornton gives a "short if sweeping" history of trade paperbacks, pointing out that trade paperbacks began as a means of encouraging mass literacy, but that is not the aim of most trade paperback programs today. Rather, most programs want the trendiest books and hope to publish a few big sellers. After recounting the history of trade paperbacks, Thornton explains the various ways editors produce trade paperbacks: reprinting public-domain books like Dover Books does, reprinting hardcover editions or printing a paperback and a hardcover of the same book at the same time, buying paperback reprint rights for hardcover books (increasingly hard to do), and, most commonly, producing an original trade paperback.

480 Topkis, Gladys S. "Book Publishing: An Editor's-Eye View." In *Scholarly Writing and Publishing: Issues, Problems, and Solutions,* edited by Mary Frank Fox, 73-98. Boulder: Westview Press, 1985.
Topkis's discussion of scholarly and textbook publishing focuses on who publishes scholarly works and textbooks, who chooses the books

to be published, what the role of the contract is in the publishing process, and what part editors play in the book publishing process. Editors are involved throughout the publication process because they acquire manuscripts by visiting campuses and academic conferences, knowing what courses in a discipline use textbooks that the editor's house does not publish, and learning the textbook preferences of instructors at different kinds of school. An editor also evaluates book proposals to build a list, asks authors to submit manuscripts, authorizes professional reviews of manuscripts, chooses reviewers, "and interprets their reports for the decisionmakers, trying to convince them of the manuscript's merits and ultimate profitability—sometimes despite a negative view" (81). Editors, however, may collude with an author to seek desirable reviews. Editors may also have to reject manuscripts that they have fought for. In fact, editors may have to compete with other editors in the same house for limited resources. With such varied responsibilities, editors, often due to understaffing, have a heavy workload, "and, editors, with the best will in the world, are often simply unable to get through the stack of things to be done" (92).

481 Topkis, Gladys S. "The Editor's Job in Professional/Scholarly Publishing." In *The Business of Book Publishing: Papers by Practitioners,* edited by Elizabeth A. Geiser, Arnold Dolin, and Gladys S. Topkis, 62-79. Boulder: Westview Press, 1985.

Topkis compares editors of professional books with editors of trade books and textbooks. Professional books—books written by authors for their peers, not a general or classroom audience—are produced by university presses, monograph houses, and professional divisions of large houses. The editors of professional books "'find' books in two ways: by literally searching in the most likely places for manuscripts in progress or under contemplation and by dreaming up the idea for a book and convincing the right person to produce it" (67). Thus an acquisitions editor, who must have network-building skills, visits institutions that employ scholars, reviews professional journals, and pursues clues that might lead to a published book or series of books. Although editors propose books to the house, they rarely decide which books to accept. They try to enhance a prospect's change of publication by soliciting reviews (hopefully favorable) by outside authorities, by seeking books with institutional subsidizes for publication, and by exploring foreign sales. At the same time, editors ply the backlist because in many scholarly houses sales from the backlist contribute up to 70 percent of a house's annual income. Because the market for professional books is composed mainly of authors who write or consult scholarly books, an editor works with a relatively small group of people. The editor must be careful not to alienate authors who could hinder the editor's efforts by telling colleagues about supposed or actual mistreatment at the hands of an editor. Within the house, editors have "a great deal to say about the production and marketing of their books and considerable power in dealing with other departments" (76). Yet, the editor can be caught in loyalties between an author and the house and be damned by both. Compared to trade or text editors, the professional editor's job is not highly competitive, but the workload is onerous. One reward of the job is the gratification editors feel for working with books that they perceive to be valuable beyond the economic sense.

482 Wollheim, Donald A. "Editing the Mass-Market Paperback." In *Editors on Editing,* edited by Gerald Gross, 77-83. New York: Grosset & Dunlap, 1962.

Because paperback books evolved from pulp magazines, the paperback editor should appeal to the former pulp reader, but the editor also needs to be aware of developments among best sellers, the literati, and good literature. Once an editor acquires manuscripts, they must be edited and prepared for the printer. A title and art work must be considered. At the same time, the paperback editor works on any other paperback books at various stages in the product process for which he or she is responsible. For editors to learn what materials will satisfy the paperback audience, they must read "stock" novels—Western novels, detective novels, adventure novels—"because this kind of literature is not analyzed and taught in classes; it can only be learned by reading it" (81).

Computer-Based Education Lessons

483 Van Eps, Barbara J. "Editing Computer-Based Education Lessons." In *Proceedings 28th International Technical Communication Conference,* W-114—W-116. Washington: Society for Technical Communication, 1981. ED 227 479.

Van Eps describes a process for editing instructional computer lessons on the PLATO system. Each lesson is edited, user tested, and edited again. When editing lessons, the editor should consider the visual appeal of the on-screen lesson. In fact, "editors check carefully that the graphics are complete, clear, and attention-grabbing as well as educational" (W-115). However, the editor's primary job is to "ensure that the directions are extra clear, helping students feel comfortable" (W-115).

Customer and Service Information

484 Halliday, Roy. "Editing Customer and Service Information in Kingston." In *Kingston Information Development Procedures Manual,* i-16. Kingston: IBM Corporation, 1987.

Halliday outlines editing procedures for IBM documents produced at Kingston, New York. The Preface states, "this document is intended for Kingston information developers and their managers as well as for the editors. It lists the editing assignments and explains the procedures for editing outlines, drafts, and production-cycle jobs. It also describes what editors check at the various stages in the writing and publishing cycles" (ii). Much of the text is composed of lists, for example, on what to do to complete a quick edit, a limited technical edit, or a full technical edit. The document can be requested from IBM Corporation, DSD Technical Library-Learning Center, Dept. 65P/687, Neighborhood Road, Kingston, NY 12401-1041.

Direct Marketing Copy

485 Brady, Thomas B. "Editing Copy for Easier Reading, Better Results." *Direct Marketing* 43, no. 6 (1980): 30-38.

Brady presents nine editing techniques for direct marketing copy, including the admonitions to edit for short words, sentences, and paragraphs; "edit for useless copy and negatives" (34); "edit for a personal, conversational tone" (36); and "edit for 'calls to action'" (38).

Encyclopedias

486 Tomlinson, Graham. "The Social Construction of Truth: Editing an Encyclopedia." *Urban Life* 15, no. 2 (1986): 197-213.

Tomlinson worked as an associate social science editor for a major university press and from that experience determined that the requirements under which editors labor determines the truthfulness of a publication. The particular project Tomlinson worked on was an updated edition of a one-volume encyclopedia of the social sciences. Tomlinson's job as one of several associate editors was to write articles for the updated version of the encyclopedia. All associate editors had a quota to meet—500 lines of copy per week—and a rule to follow—*"never get information from another encyclopedia or reference book"* (202). The quota was unrealistic if editors properly researched topics, so editors adapted to the situation by violating the rule to meet the quota. Associate editors also learned how to meet the quotas by using certain practices. For instance, "free-lancing allowed the associate editor to shift responsibility; underediting and paraphrasing permitted associate editors to 'speak the same language' as senior editors and thereby avoid the vulnerability of using original sources. In the more extreme instances, when backed into a corner, associate editors turned to the practices of losing and thin-airing" (207). Tomlinson concludes that when an organization determines that it will report the truth, those members of the organization who are given the authority to determine what the truth is will "develop strategic adaptations to the real, practical constraints" (210) that are part and parcel of the conditions under which the organization works. Tomlinson speculates that those organizations with the "boldest truth claims" may be the same organizations that employ the most truthful adaptations.

Journals

487 Armstrong, J. S. "Creative Obfuscation." *Chemtech* 11 (1981): 262-64.

A study to determine the readability of professional management journals showed that difficult reading, according to the Gunning Fog Index, is associated with high prestige. Thus, "clear communication is not appreciated. Faculty are impressed by less readable articles. Lack of clarity is especially helpful when content is poor" (264).

488 Avi-yonah, M. "Editing the IEJ: A Personal Memo." *Israel Exploration Journal* 23 (1973): 267-72.

Avi-yonah provides a historical context for his editorship of the *Israel Exploration Journal* (*IEJ*), beginning with his copyediting and proofreading lessons under L. A. Mayer. In developing the *IEJ*, Avi-yonah notes that editorial staff changes were frequent and the makeup of the editorial board changed "at least as many times as France changes her governments and/or her methods of voting" (270). Editors used the fruit salad approach to selecting articles, with any scoop overriding whatever had been planned for print. "We prefer a readable scoop in hand to a lot of dry-as-dust writing, learned but dull" (271).

489 Axelby, George S. "Problems and Procedures in Editing a Professional Technical Journal." *IEEE Transactions on Professional Communication* PC-16, no. 3 (1973): 54-56.

The goals and policies of a professional journal include publishing helpful and accurate technical information, keeping contributors informed of the status of their manuscripts, and defining editorial procedures in writing. A journal's staff can be organized in one of three ways to achieve that goal. The first type of organization, the most flexible, gives associate editors the bulk of the authority to manage the publishing of papers. The editor therefore has the lightest workload compared to the other two types of organizations. But the quality of published papers may suffer if publication deadlines are disregarded because associate editors assume that other associate editors are supplying the publisher with articles. In a second type of organization, the associate editors and the editor function as a selection committee. That type of organization yields the best technical papers, but the editors must travel to a common meeting place and editors will have unequal work loads depending on the number of manuscripts submitted in a particular area of interest. A third type of organization is a blend of the first two. The editor receives and sorts all articles and then sends articles to associate editors based on their interest in an article's topic. Under the third approach, the workload is rotated and editorial favoritism toward an institution or author can be reduced. However, whichever type or organization is used, "no material should be scheduled for publication without the editor's knowledge and consent" (56).

490 Bain, Anne Lee, and John Rutledge. "Editing and Publishing Scholarly Book Reviews: A Dialogue." *The Journal of Academic Librarianship* 11 (1986): 355-59.

In a dialogue, a library bibliographer and an editor of a history journal discuss the problems of reviewing books. One purpose of book reviews is to create a record of books available for scholars. Editors of large journals would expect that the books the journals review should be part of the collection of any major research library. Editors choose books for review based on several factors, including the author's and publisher's reputations. The review process can take several years if reviewers are delinquent with the reports or a review can be delayed until problems of libel, for instance, are resolved. Generally such a problem is addressed by the editor who edits and returns the review for an author's consideration. The most difficult book to review is a Festschriften. Some Festschriften "really defy review" (359).

491 Barclay, William R. "Some Observations on Editing a Medical Journal." *Medical Communications* 6, no. 4 (1978): 24-26.

Speaking as the editor of *The Journal of the American Medical Association*, Barclay says that he has complete editorial freedom, but his principal editorial constraint is financial. "[A]dding even two pages per week for one year over what is authorized could cause a deficit of $100,000" (25). He also outlines an editor's responsibilities, which are to select manuscripts, rewrite manuscripts, and supervise the production of manuscripts. Barclay advises editors to read literature to develop the literary talent needed to write "in a concise, clear style that is a pleasure to read" (25).

492 Barry, Brian. "On Editing *Ethics*." *Ethics* 90, no. 1 (1979): 1-6.

As the new editor of *Ethics*, Barry encourages authors to submit original manuscripts, not ones "covering well-trodden ground" (5). Barry will rely on associate editors "to stimulate contributions, to suggest topics for review essays and symposia, to advise me about manuscripts, and to work with authors to ensure that everything is done to make all the articles we publish as immune to substantive criticism and as free from stylistic blemish as is humanly possible" (4). Barry concludes by explaining how a manuscript is processed at *Ethics*.

493 Beeson, Paul B. "Lessons Learned from Editing a Geriatrics Journal." *Journal of the American Geriatrics Society* 32 (1984): 849-50.

Beeson learned from editing the *Journal of the American Geriatrics Society* that geriatric medicine is tremendously diverse as witnessed by submissions to the journal on a wide range of topics. In fact, he says, "I think it would be difficult to cite any other medical journal that regularly receives contributions from such a wide spectrum of disciplines" (850).

494 Benedek, Elissa P. "Editorial Practices of Psychiatric and Related Journals: Implications for Women." *American Journal of Psychiatry* 133 (1976): 89-92.

After analyzing responses to a questionnaire about procedures for selecting editors, articles, and reviewers for the major journals in psychiatric-related fields, Benedek concludes that notwithstanding some noteworthy exceptions, little is being done to encourage women to publish professional papers or to be members of editorial boards. In fact, a majority of the journals in her study have a disproportionate number of women authors and board members given the number of women working in psychiatry. For instance, "only 3 of the responding journals had a female editor-in-chief. Most editorial boards had a preponderance of male members" (89), and procedures for selection of editors and articles did not include sufficient safeguards to protect women from discrimination. The same can be said for blind review (Only six journals reported using blind review) and review by women of articles pertaining to women (Only six journals reported using such a review philosophy and "these were not . . . the same 6 journals that reported blind review" [91]).

495 Bishop, Claude T. *How To Edit a Scientific Journal*. Philadelphia: ISI Press, 1984.

Bishop's book focuses on the review process for scientific journals, but he also asks questions about editors, associate editors, the editorial office, and ethics. Scientific editors, as Bishop defines them, "are directly involved in selecting the contents of their journals and only indirectly in the subsequent publisher's functions" (9). Thus scientific editors should be scientific researchers, actively involved in their own research. "It is important for an editor to know where new, exciting work is being done and by whom, and to retain an appreciation of quality in experimental work. Furthermore, authors want to be judged by people who are playing the game" (12). Ideal editorial candidates are "scientists who are productive and happy in a secure position, not involved in a competitive situation with respect to their career advancement" (17). Editors should serve a four- or five-year term unless they neglect their duties, in which case they should be replaced immediately, "before irreparable damage is done to the journal" (21). Bishop also discusses editorial boards, outlining six editorial systems, but states that "small editorial boards are easier to manage and tend to develop stronger interests in their journals" (30). In choosing an editorial system, the journal will need copies of operating manuals for each participating editor. Editors and editorial boards also will need to make policies about the role of the journal and inclusion of advertising, book reviews, special issues, and Festschrift in the journal. About the review process, Bishop notes, "the proponents of unrestricted access to publication have failed to distinguish between the formal and informal systems of communication in science" (43), and cites a number of reasons why anonymous (not blind) peer review is needed. To choose referees for peer review, editors should consider the members of "an editorial board of knowledgeable scientists whose areas of expertise reflect the major topics within the editorial scope of the journal" (54). Authors cited in submitted papers are also potential referees. Bishop provides examples of forms that editors can give to peer reviewers to evaluate manuscripts and advises editors "to maintain good relations with referees: keep to a stated, minimum interval between requests for reviews from the same referee; provide feedback when a referee's advice is not followed or when reports have been particularly helpful; acknowledge every report and say 'thank you'" (73). A chapter on ethics discusses publication fraud and the ethics of multiple authorship, duplicate submissions and confidentiality of referees and editors. Bishop believes that "possibly the most important ethical responsibility of editors is to preserve confidentiality in their review systems" (83). Editors must also keep track of manuscripts and Bishop recommends that editorial assistants, "vigorous self-starters who can keep things moving, including their editors" (88), should relieve the editor of the administrative demands of processing manuscripts. Bishop provides a variety of sample forms for processing manuscripts and says, "each journal should have an operations manual that spells out what needs to be done, and who does it, at each stage in the review process" (100). Indeed, a journal's database is a good source for determining the journal's performance. Editor's also need to know about printing so that "their journals appear on time" (108). The printing process includes copyediting, and "a useful and time-saving guide is to limit revisions by copy editors to correction of errors; rephrasing should only be contemplated when there are obvious ambiguities or unclear expressions" (110). After a journal is printed, editors should ensure that the leading information service in their journal's field indexes the contents of their journal because, for one reason, "coverage by information services represents the best possible publicity" (129).

496 Bliss, Allen D. "Editing of Technical-Society Journals: The Editor's Viewpoint." In *Technical Editing,* edited by B. H. Weil, 91-102. Westport: Greenwood Press, 1975.

Bliss explains the editorial process by tracing a manuscript from its receipt by an editor to its publication. The process begins with editorial philosophy. The editor's concept of what type of journal he or she is editing determines which articles are appropriate for the journal. At the same time, the editor's concept of the journal's purpose should not be inflexible, so that the limits he or she establishes are unreasonable and indefensible. If a manuscript fits within an editor's philosophy, referees judge the paper and write a report of their judgment. The editor uses referees' reports to make a decision about publishing a manuscript. Bliss cites "three broad causes for declining papers (rejecting is an ugly word)" (96). Once a paper is accepted, the technical-journal editor makes decisions about style and printing procedures. Although authors proof their galleys, a member of the editorial office also should proof the author's proof "to approve alterations, check queried details, prevent expensive rewriting, and avoid style-breaking changes" (101). Given the editor's wide-ranging responsibilities, Bliss sees the editor "as a minister, physician, lawyer, and teacher to those scientists whose literary souls have been placed in his charge" (102).

497 Borysewicz, Mary L. "The Creative Role and Function of Editors." In *Scientific Information Transfer: The Editor's Role,* edited by Miriam Balaban, 261-64. Dordrecht: D. Reidel Publishing Co., 1978.

The editor is creative in that he or she is the force that presents new, true, and important ideas to one part of the scientific community. As a presenter of ideas the editor is a catalyst who assumes the roles of "colleague, counsellor, [and] advisor [in which] tact and diplomacy are imperatives" (261). Tact and diplomacy are particularly needed when the editor tries to transform an oral presentation into a journal article. Borysewicz also says that editors "are more than surrogate readers. We are rather the mediators between authors and the particular audience that concerns us" (263). However, a journal's audience also should and can be involved in the editorial process, especially through corresponding with the editor. When a journal encourages correspondence between readers and editor and when readers have a favorable opinion of the journal, the editor "has some tangible basis for his editorial decisions" (263).

498 Braceland, Francis J. "Editing Circa 1976." *American Journal of Psychiatry* 133, no. 1 (1976): 76-79.

"[W]e find returning manuscripts one of our most unpleasant tasks," Braceland notes, even though "we try to give voice to many points of view and many research paths that appear promising" (76). While editorial boards can give helpful advice about the value of a manuscript, "it is of course the Editor who must assume final responsibility for the fate of all manuscripts" (77).

499 Braceland, Francis J. "On Editing the Journal: *Ave Atque Vale.*" *American Journal of Psychiatry* 135, no. 10 (1978): 1148-55.

After recounting a brief history of the *American Journal of Psychiatry* (*AJP*), Braceland reviews some of what he learned during a 13-year tenure as editor of *AJP*. After assuming the editorship of *AJP*, Braceland initiated a referee system for peer review, even though one study has shown that peer review is a notch or two above chance as a method for evaluating whether a paper should be published. About advertising in the journal he reports that the staffs of those advertisers who place ads in *AJP* know what ads *AJP* will accept. Braceland believes that the physicians who read *AJP* are professionals who will not dispense a substance simply because they saw it advertised. About editing, Braceland states, "the editor must . . . possess dogged independence" (1151). Because medical findings can be used by the media to injure the medical profession, part of the editor's job is to remind writers how the media operate. Thus the editor should be wary of miraculous discoveries. "The half-life of some of these well-publicized discoveries is very short, and the editor must be concerned about misleading his readership" (1152). In dogged independence, the editor must select manuscript based on merit, not on an author's reputation. "[W]e are publishing his work, not his biography" (1153). The editor seeks—and edits for—succinct expression of ideas. About the future of journals, Braceland is optimistic.

500 Broadbent, Margaret. "Standardization in Production of Journals: A Black and White Case?" *IEEE Transactions on Professional Communication* PC-18, no. 3 (1975): 123-26.

In addition to being detail oriented, organized, disciplined, and diplomatic, a good copyeditor possesses judgment. A good copyeditor knows when to break the rules. The copyeditor's task falls into three categories: format marking, internal copyediting, and procedural checking. As the manager of five journals with different format requirements, Broadbent explains how copyeditors strike a balance between uniformity and diversity when copyediting those journals. "[A]n expert copyeditor knows instinctively when black and white rules should be broken" (124). However, as journals become more reliant on camera-ready copy from authors, publishers should enforce form and style standards so that editors do not begin making a habit of correcting authors' copy, which could be costly. In a discussion following Broadbent's remarks, participants commented on citation systems that only require first initials of authors. Of the participants "40 percent do check references for accuracy and 60 percent do not" (125).

501 Brooks, Cleanth. "The Life and Death of an Academic Journal." In *The Art of Literary Publishing: Editors on Their Craft*, edited by Bill Henderson, 88-99. Yonkers: The Pushcart Press, 1980.

Brooks recounts his editorship of *The Southern Review* (with Robert Penn Warren), noting that Eudora Welty and Katherine Anne Porter were early contributors. Not all the contributors were established author because, as Brooks notes, an editor must take chances by publishing unknown authors. If an editor only publishes established authors, the editor "will simply market other people's notions of literature—not encourage experiments or develop new talents" (93). Brooks also discusses the economics of publishing a university literary magazine, saying that if the university faces financial difficulties the funding for a university magazine is usually cut. Even if funding is not cut, the editor, underpaid and overworked, "is bound to a sweatshop trade" (97).

502 Chigier, Norman. "The Role of the Review Journals in Scientific Publication." In *Scientific Information Transfer: The Editor's Role*, edited by Miriam Balaban, 179-82. Dordrecht: D. Reidel Publishing Company, 1977.

The review journal provides general scientific information to potential scientists, such as undergraduate science majors. Review journals are essential because scientific articles are so specialized that they are difficult to understand for those who are not experts in the particular scientific field. Because review journals are directed to a general audience, their articles should be written clearly by experienced writers. The responsibility for judging how well an author writes "lies clearly and definitely in the hands of the editor" (181). If the editor has access to a referee who can make an educated judgment on a subject, the editor "prays and hopes that the referee will help him make that judgment" (180), but ultimately the editor is responsible for judging an article's quality.

503 Corliss, John O. "Labor of Love: Reflections of a 'Small Journal' Editor." *CBE Views* 5, no. 4 (1982): 5-8.

Besides the lack of time and money that present hardships to the small journal editor, "an editor's biggest headache comes in a form, allegedly human, known as *authors*" (6). Authors are uncooperative, irresponsible, and, at times, stupid. Corliss unveils the commandments of, for, and by the author that codify authors' follies. For example, commandment three states, "Thou shall not create a title for your paper that reveals its subject matter in any comprehensible way" (7). The more obscure the title, the more it will impress the editor, reviewers, and readers. But the commandment goes on to note that according to authors the opinions of editors, reviewers, and readers are not important. Despite authors' inflated view of themselves, their work must be edited. The editor edits—labors over—authors' manuscripts because he or she does not think it is fair to reject them just because they possess stylistic and editorial infelicities. At the same time, the editor does not have the resources to counsel the author about how to rewrite a manuscript. Editing labors, Corliss notes, are labors of love.

504 Crandall, Rick. "We Need Research on What Constitutes Good Journal Papers—and Good Editing—Not Guesswork on How to Improve Manuscripts." *American Psychologist* 42, no. 4 (1987): 407-08.

Crandall states that research on the editorial review process among journals has shown that the process has no validity or reliability . Of those findings Crandall says, "the lack of reliability and validity in the editorial review system is a professional disgrace" (408). Therefore Crandall calls for a commitment to do the research necessary to test and improve the review system.

505 Daroff, Robert B., and Bruce P. Squires. "The Role of Journal Editors in Promoting Good Scientific Writing." *CBE Views* 12, no. 5 (1989): 83.

Reviewers and editors often evaluate a manuscript for publication in less than optimal conditions, and the quality of writing may be the determining factor in whether a manuscript is accepted for publication. Thus editors should demand that authors produce "carefully written high-quality manuscripts." If authors do not accept that standard, everyone else who reads the manuscript—reviewers, editors, and members of the intended audience—will do more work than they should do to understand the writer's meaning.

506 DeBakey, Lois. *The Scientific Journal: Editorial Policies and Practices: Guidelines for Editors, Reviewers, and Authors*. St. Louis: The C.V. Mosby Company, 1976.

The Scientific Journal is divided into two general sections: "editorial policies, which usually require major decisions; and editorial practices, which involve minor decisions, often about format or mechanical style" (viii). Those two sections are preceded by two chapters that discuss (1) the purpose of scientific journals ("a journal should publish what is *new, true,* and *important*" [1] and what is comprehensible) and (2) the editor's responsibility, which can be divided into editorial and administrative functions. The first major section of the book, on editorial policies, is subdivided into chapters on reviewing and special types of manuscripts. DeBakey establishes twelve guidelines for reviewers, including "*a reviewer should not discuss a paper with its author*" (19), even though inexperienced reviewers may consider a discussion directly with the author of points of difficulty or disagreement a "natural and reasonable" thing to do. "Specific prohibition of the practice is therefore necessary, because the other reviewer [a second reviewer] and the editor may have differing opinions, and the author may be led into undue optimism by having 'cleared things up' with the reviewer who made contact with him directly" (19). DeBakey also discusses the problems associated with reviewing a manuscript that the reviewer evaluated for another journal and rejected, the types of files the editor can establish to track manuscripts, and the editor's responsibility when reviewing a manuscript with an experimental design that is ethically questionable. DeBakey believes that when editors evaluate a manuscript, they should "apply ethical as well as other criteria. To meet his responsibility, the editor will require not only a mechanism for determining whether ethical standards have been maintained, but also a policy for disposition of manuscripts that do not meet these standards" (29). She also addresses issues related to the multiple publication of a paper or presentation, advertising policies, the distinction between by-lines and acknowledgements, and ways to determine publication date ("In general, the date of receipt of the original version protects both the author and the editor" [48] from disputes about how to establish a manuscript's date). Under the section titled Special Types of Manuscripts, DeBakey discusses editorials; abstracts ("Editors who publish large numbers of abstracts [that are published as submitted] . . . risk being embarrassed by the possibility of an author's undetected insertion, in an abstract, of a political statement or a caustic comment about a rival researcher" [56]), transactions, proceedings, minutes, and news items; solicited and remunerated manuscripts; letters to the editor commenting on published articles; publication of symposia or conference papers in a journal; and book reviews. Because the purpose of the book review is to tell readers if a book is relevant and significant, "good as well as poor books should be reviewed" (64). In fact, the reviewer should determine how long a review to write, "and, indeed, he may write a long critique of a poor book on an important subject in order to point out all the flaws or deficiencies" (65). The second major part of the book, on editorial practices, is divided into two parts: references and format. These two sections are prefaced by chapters on what to say under the Information for Authors section of a journal, (Throughout the book, DeBakey counsels editors to anticipate potential conflicts by stating editorial policy clearly in the journal, particularly in the Information for Authors section), copyright ("Fair use" is ill defined in the copyright law), and errata ("The temptation to make as little as possible of a published mistake should be resisted" [82]). The section on references addresses the citation of titles, unpublished or inaccessible information, verification of bibliographic references ("[T]he editor who is serious about serving his readers should assume the responsibility of having references verified at the journal's expense" [89]), and copyediting, which is "best limited to essential changes that can be fully and indisputably justified" (93). In the section on format, DeBakey discusses the role of the journal's cover as a reference tool for librarians and readers, the use of running heads or foot lines to provide a complete citation for each page in an article, the masthead, special features in the final unbound issue of a volume (title page and indexes, for instance), subject and author indexes (The editor can assist indexers in determining key words and standard terms that should be used to index articles), and finding practices. Because librarians may strip advertisements from journals before having the journals bound, the editor neither should print scientific and nonscientific material back to back nor interleave advertisements with scientific material.

507 Fearing, Bertie E. "The Education of an Academic Journal Editor." In *Proceedings 29th International Technical Communication Conference. Technical Communication—Charting the Course of Technology,* E-41—E-43. Washington: Society for Technical Communication, 1982.

When she accepted the position as co-editor of *Teaching English in a Two-Year College,* Fearing thought she was accepting a plush job. She didn't realize "that in reality my life as an editor would be consumed with endless mundane chores . . . [including] lugging 800 pounds of journals three times a year to the post office" (E-41). One of the most significant problems she encountered was the need to educate authors. She addressed that problem by pointing authors to the journal's guidelines. When a manuscript with "feculence of style is accepted" (E-42), she or another editor either work with the author to revise the manuscript or rewrite it. As an editor, Fearing looks for manuscripts with excellence in content and presentation, although such manuscripts are rare.

508 Feiner, Arthur H. "Notes on the Dynamics of the Problems of Editing Psychoanalytic Journals." *Contemporary Psychoanalysis* 23 (1987): 676-88.

Establishing selection standards for psychoanalytic journal articles is complicated by the paradox of trying to satisfy both romanticism and classicism (the Apollonian and Dionysian traditions). On the one hand, editors trained in the psychoanalytic tradition want to be accepting. On the other hand, they must make editorial decisions based on standards. Editors face the dilemma of being either elitists or libertarians. Feiner insists that editors must set standards and advances four criteria for editorial judgment of a manuscript: enlightenment, originality, respectful scholarship or erudition, and literateness. He warns editors against committing the virtuous or affective fallacy ("A paper despite its failings (i.e. its lack of originality, enlightenment, or erudition) may appeal still to our positive feelings" [684]) and the intentional fallacy ("a confusion between the causes for a work's existence, what it is supposed to do, and what has actually been achieved" [686]). When "setting standards in a responsible way" (688), editors must use their ability to judge a manuscript, but they also must respect authors, readers, and the psychoanalytic profession. See also 513.

509 Garfield, Eugene. "How Services from the Institute for Scientific Information[R] (ISI[R]) Aid Journal Editors and Publishers." In *Scientific Information Transfer: The Editor's Role,* edited by Miriam Balaban, 587-95. Dordrecht: D. Reidel Publishing Company, 1977.

Editors can assure the scientific worth and retrievability of articles published in their journals by subscribing to information retrieval services and implementing seven suggestions to improve a journal's format. Data from information retrieval services, like those provided by the Institute for Scientific Information, allow editors to determine what has been published on a particular topic. Such knowledge can help peer reviewers evaluate manuscripts. Editors should have their journals cited in an abstracting service so that abstracts of their journals' contents will be made available to the scientific community. Editors can ensure that citations to journal articles are retrievable by following seven suggestions, including prominently displaying the volume and issue number on the Journal's contents page. Although publishers may consider retrieval services as inimical to journal publishing, especially when such services offer subscribers copies of journal articles, Garfield says those services promote subscriptions to good journals.

510 Garfield, Eugene. "Idiosyncrasies and Errors, or the Terrible Things Journals Do to Us." *Current Contents* 2 (1983): 5-11.

Journal editors can help citation indexers, librarians, readers, and researchers save time by printing journals that are easy to cite. For instance, the size of a contents page can make it either easy or difficult to reproduce in *Current Contents*, an index of scientific literature. Incomplete or ambiguous addresses of authors can make more work for citation indexers and increase index expenses, which are passed on to consumers. Garfield says that an author's address should be placed on the first page of an article. False publication dates (journals published in 1982 having a 1981 publication date, for example), "the dispersion of references throughout the text of an article" (9), the misspelling of authors' names, and the confusion of volume and issue number of journals that cite their volume and issue and those of their parent journal are costly problems that prevent indexes from delivering information quickly and accurately. Garfield suggests that editors recognize that they hurt their readers when inaccuracies, ambiguities, and misspellings are allowed in a journal. Readers waste time trying to fine articles that are inaccurately cited and authors are not given the recognition due them. Failure of a journal to publish issues on schedule also injures authors because their papers are not available to indexers and that means, in practice, that authors' data are being withheld.

511 Glen, John W. "Ethical Problems of a Physical Science Editor." In *Scholarly Communication Around the World. Proceedings of a Joint Global Conference,* 60-61. Washington: Society for Scholarly Publishing, 1983.

By recognizing potential ethical problems among authors, editors, and referees of learned journals, editors can forestall the occurrence of ethical breeches, which are breeches of confidence. Editing a scholarly journal depends on trust among the people who evaluate and publish articles, and when that trust is betrayed, ethical problems arise. Those involved in evaluating and publishing articles can safeguard trust by fulfilling their official duties. For instance, the referee's duty is to give fair, professional opinions of a manuscript's merits and not to use data from a manuscript to promote his or her interests. Editors can refuse to use referees who produce biased reader's reports. Editors also should refrain from sending papers to referees who clearly disagree with a paper's views. Editors themselves can promote ethical conduct by not changing an author's meaning unless the author agrees to a change. When working with nonnative speakers, the editor should ask an author to supply a reference copy of the paper in the author's native language should any ambiguity need to be resolved. If difficulties in meaning persist, the editor should consult with the author to resolve those difficulties before sending the manuscript to the printer.

512 Glidewell, John C. "Reflections on Thirteen Years of Editing *AJCP.*" *American Journal of Community Psychology* 16 (1988): 759-70.

Glidewell constructed an ideal model of the editor and compared his editorial performance with that model. The ideal journal editor evaluates and selects manuscripts based on their rigor in analyzing an issue and their ability to advance or change a discipline's direction. Glidewell applied this model to reviewers' conflicting evaluations and recommendations to shape his journal and decided that conflicting reviews prompt the editor to refine his or her editorial vision. "An editor can find in conflicting reviews the standards that not only admit radical ideas, methods, and findings but also are firmly respected by those creative scientist-practitioners who strive to enable the advance of the discipline" (768). However, requests for promotion and tenure reviews of authors published in his journal caused Glidewell to wonder, "could it be that, once a journal became prestigious in its field, one's career depended more on whether one had published in that journal than on what one had published there" (769).

513 Grotstein, James S. "The Dynamics of Editing." *Contemporary Psychoanalysis* 24, no. 2 (1988): 350-54.

In responding positively to Feiner's article on editing (509), Grotstein notes that editors take a dialectical position between maintaining standards and encouraging contributions "which the Establishment organization needs in order to maintain its position against the encroachment of complacency, decadence, and solipsistic starvation" (352-53).

514 Hargrove, Eugene C. "On Editing *Environmental Ethics.*" *Environmental Ethics* 7 (1985): 291-92, 320.

Hargrove does not believe that the referee system "really provides any benefits" (291), but he uses referees, realizing that they only give advice; the editor accepts or rejects manuscripts. Hargrove does not like an author to ask him to read a manuscript before the author sends enough copies of the article for reviewers because Hargrove believes that he is being asked to predetermine what the review process should determine. After accepting a manuscript, Hargrove edits "lightly but enough that nearly all papers in the journal have a distinct unity of style" (292). But editing is time consuming. "I am performing a full-time job as a managing editor," he notes, "on a half-time basis" (320), so sometimes issues are late.

515 Hoge, James O., and James L. W. West, III. "Academic Book Reviewing: Some Problems and Solutions." *Scholarly Publishing* 11 (1979): 35-41.

Academic book reviews are not accorded much credit as a bona fide publication because often they are poorly prepared. As editors of a journal dedicated to academic book reviews, Hoge and West recommend that editors treat academic book reviews with the same care which scholarly articles are given. Editors should find qualified reviewers (the best available), referee the reviews, ask authors to revise reviews, not limit the amount of space a review can take, allow reviewers to document their review with footnotes (if necessary), and "give considerable attention to the tone of a reviewer's comments" (39) because "reviewers need spice, sting, wit, and even humour if they are to be successful" (39). "The editor must develop his own 'ear' for tone" (39), and, after forewarning reviewers that reviews are not accepted automatically, reject reviews that are unpublishable.

516 Huibregtse, Edward J. "Editorial Processes of the *IBM Journal of Research and Development.*" In *Proceedings 18th International Technical Communications Conference. The State of the Art,* paper #8-9, pp. 1-4. Washington: Society for Technical Communication, 1971.

Because the *IBM Journal of Research and Development* primarily carries articles by IBM employees, the journal's editors recruit manuscripts from authors who either will report the results of their work in "the form of a journal-style manuscript" (2) or who may be encouraged to prepare a manuscript for the journal. Submitted manuscripts are refereed by three reviewers—two internal and one external. An Advisory Board composed of senior managers also reviews papers for "business policy considerations" (3). When editors reject a manuscript, they explain to authors why the manuscript is not acceptable and offer suggestions for improving it. When a manuscript is accepted, one editor prepares it for the printer and another editor reads the final draft. That procedure,

Huibregtse notes, "has sharpened our editing and has led to a considerable reduction in the alterations made in proof" (4).

517 Keller, Mark. "Editorial Judgment in Scientific Periodicals." In *Scientific Information Transfer: The Editor's Role,* edited by Miriam Balaban, 195-201. Dordrecht: D. Reidel Publishing Company, 1978.

Keller discusses the journal editor's judgment in reference to referees, negative results, style, and ethics. About referees, Keller says that the editor must develop a list of good referees, but it is the editor who makes the decision whether to publish a manuscript. When the editor believes referees' advice is incorrect the editor "must have the courage sometimes to go against their advice" (197). An editor, therefore, may publish negative results, even if referees counsel against such publication, because "a negative result may be an important positive truth" (197). However, an editor should only print data in a manuscript that the author authorizes, unless the journal's style requires certain changes (spelling labour as labor, for example) or unless an author's statement misrepresents fact. Even when editors believe an experiment was unethical, "their duty is to publish the report of what has been done, once it has been done" (200), if they deem the study publishable. Science editors should not judge a scientist's morality "any more than they should be the censors of unsavory ideas" (201). However, the editor can append a statement to the author's article "condemning the experiment" (201). See also 367.

518 Krevitt, Beth I. *A Baseline Study of Current Journal Practices in the Life Sciences.* NSF-C769. Report No. NSF-SIS-75-001-1. Rockville: Westat, Inc. and Aspen Systems Corporation, 1974.

Krevitt's study focuses on the economics of publishing scientific journals. Part 2.6, based on data from a random sample of 42 journals from 30 societies, discusses editorial costs. Krevitt proposes the use of an editorial processing center to reduce costs because such a computerized facility shared in common by editors and publishers would, for instance, "greatly reduce the need for extensive reproofreading [of manuscripts, proofs, and galleys] by everyone" (2-15) because the amount of repetitious typing could be decreased. Computerized lists of reviewers could also reduce costs by reducing the amount of time an editor spends determining who is available to review a manuscript. Krevitt says, "it is our belief that an integrated file of reviewers and manuscript information capable of being accessed on-line and from many vantage points would be of even greater usefulness as a tool for the selection of reviewers" (2-27). For instance, "the task of maintaining and searching a file to determine the status of the manuscript could be merged with the task of selecting reviewers and dispatching the manuscript. All such information would have to be recorded only once" (2-29). Computers might also help decrease text editing costs, which Krevitt says are high. "In the 10-15 percent of the cases where text editing does occur, it takes about ten minutes per manuscript page. If an on-line text editing system were available to the editor or redactor and the manuscripts were in the available data base, then the task of text editing might be a more feasible one. Instead of just suggesting changes, the editor might, in the same amount of time, create a document containing the suggested revisions and send it back to the author with the original. It is also possible that some 'minor' revisions could be performed in a similar manner" (2-32—2-33). Krevitt estimates that "a reviewer spends a total of six hours recommending the acceptance of a manuscript and 6.25 hours recommending a rejection" (2-34). Authors can add to editing costs by not following a journal's style rules. "The degree to which the author does not adhere to the specified rules directly affects the cost of redaction. A redactor will spend, on the average, seven minutes per manuscript page redacting a 'typical' manuscript" (2-35).

519 Mann, Charles. *Editing for Industry*. London: William Heinemann, 1974.

Mann's book is an overview of the multifarious aspects of the job of a house journal editor. A house journal can be a newspaper, so Mann consider the industrial editor as a journalist who "must not only have acquired the skills of fact-finding and persuasive writing and be able to judge the relative value of stories and features. He must also have a first-class technical knowledge of presentations, layout, the use of photography, and modern printing techniques" (3-4). Mann discusses each of these skills throughout the book while providing comments about the editor's role in the organization. For instance, "the editor's loyalty is bound to his employers. If he has any doubts in the matter, he should not accept the job" (13). About a journal's content, Mann notes, "anyone can string words together into sentences and paragraphs— the editor's job is to ensure that they are in readable form" (20). Editors must also be good managers who meet printing deadlines, train employees, and continually make judgements. "Judgment must continually be exercised on the treatment to be given to stories, the research necessary, the positions they are to occupy in the paper, the number of pages they need and the size of illustrations, whether pictures of personnel should be included, or colors should be used" (160). To educate editors about technical aspects of publishing—

photography, design, typography, printing—Mann devotes chapters 7 through 14 to these topics. Chapter 15 addresses libel and copyright.

520 Minick, Phyllis. "The Author's Editor/The Journal Copy Editor." In *Proceedings 26th International Technical Communication Conference. Technical Communication—Shaping the World We Live In*, W-118—W-121. Washington: Society for Technical Communication, 1979.

At the Scripps Clinic and Research Foundation the editorial office corrects the grammar, punctuation, and spelling of manuscripts and correlates text, graphics, and references. Author's editors in that office not only train authors in scientific writing, but read page proofs for authors and prepare a variety of written products—"grants, speeches, book chapters or introductions, laymen's translations of technical subject matter, rewrites of transcripts from recorded talks, etc." (W-120).

521 Moossy, John, and Yvonne R. Moossy. "New Editors, Old Problems." *CBE Views* 8, no. 4 (1985): 14-15.

Journal editors—whether new or seasoned—face the same kind of problems, including finding and working with good referees ("The editors should maintain a file on referees with comments on the adequacy of their reviews and their performances" [14]) and selecting articles that meet ethical guidelines. In working with authors, editors should not neglect to write a prompt letter of receipt of the manuscript because that letter sets the tone for the editor-author relationship.

522 Moossy, John, and Linda Sears. "Workshop for New Journal Editors." *CBE Views* 10, no. 6 (1987): 101-02.

To operate effectively as a journal editor, a person should have an editorial policy, a manual of operating procedures, record-keeping forms, and a word processor. One of an editor's responsibilities is "to keep impeccable renewal records to maintain copyright, which could be bought by others if allowed to lapse" (101). Many editorial difficulties—problems with authors, questions about the order of authors' names on a manuscript, and complications with editorial board members who want preferential publication treatment—can be solved by reference to a well-defined editorial policy.

523 Morgan, Peter. "Biomedical Journal Editing as a Career." *CBE Views* 11, no. 1 (1988): 3-5.

In summarizing the job of an editor of a scientific journal, Morgan says that the editor "determines the content of the journal . . . . makes changes in accepted papers . . . . sets the journal's format and style . . . . [and] play[s] an administrative role" (3). To qualify for an editor's job, a person must have the ability to amend poor writing and to work with authors, copyeditors, and printers. Drawbacks to an editor's job include meeting deadlines, "hiring and training competent copy editors" (4), and facing off with authors. Editing has its rewards, particularly public recognition of an editor's influence. Although most editors of scientific journals are recruited from the ranks of successful scientists, editing is still seen as an adjunct activity, not a recognized profession. Morgan predicts that scientific editing will gain status in time.

524 Murray, Robert G. E. "What *Is* an Editor For?" *CBE Views* 6, no. 1 (1983): 14-19.

In answer to the question he poses in the title of his article, Murray says that the science journal editor promotes science by selecting articles, working with authors to help them express themselves clearly, and by abhorring "affectation and falsehood" (18-19). Fulfilling those duties is often complicated by dilatory referees and editors themselves. For instance, editors should be following up on referees who do not meet their report deadlines and should be "refereeing the referees' report" (16) to translate useful information to authors. Editors also need to take responsibility for the evaluation of a manuscript because editors, not referees, guard a journal's integrity. The editor is also "a friend in court and a strong supporter of the rights of authors" (17).

525 Nisbet, J. D. "Editing the Journal." *British Journal of Educational Psychology* 44 (1974): 221-23.

During his seven-year tenure as editor of the *British Journal of Educational Psychology,* Nisbet processed a total "of a little over 1,000 papers and about 1,500 books. Perhaps this does not seem too much of a burden, until one realises that it amounts to one new paper every third day for seven unrelenting years" (222). During his editorship, he did not reject a paper because it was poorly written, but he admits that finding someone who is willing to rewrite another author's paper is difficult. According to Nisbet, the most common failing among authors is writing too much by including too many details and not identifying a thesis that could help give their reports a clear organizational pattern.

526 Oates, Joyce C., and Raymond J. Smith. "On Editing *The Ontario Review."* In *The Art of Literary Publishing: Editors on Their Craft,* edited by Bill Henderson, 142-50. Yonkers: The Pushcart Press, 1980.

The editor "is a kind of God" (143), Oates says, who takes various artists' singular works and "creates a small unanticipated community that has never existed before and will never exist again" (145). The editor does not compile, but creates, and that act of creation results in a work of art.

For a little magazine like *The Ontario Review*, the editor is responsible for seeking and developing new voices.

527 Porter, J. R. "Challenges to Editors of Scientific Journals." *Science* 141 (1963): 1014-17.

Editors of scientific journals can enhance the communication of scientific data by rigorously evaluating manuscripts and working with other professionals to promote the storage, retrieval, and dissemination of scientific literature. In evaluating manuscripts, journal editors should realize that science will be served if the lasting value of a manuscript is evaluated before it is published, not afterwards. To establish a manuscript's value, editors need to ensure that manuscripts are thoroughly reviewed. Editors also can serve professional scientific societies by initiating discussions on how scientific information can be disseminated most effectively. Editors should initiate such discussions if they want to have a voice in the future of scientific communication. Editors should take a stand on language usage, too, and protest sloppy writing. In addition, editors should work with librarians, indexers, documentalists, journalists, and broadcasters to promote scientific literature. As historians, "editors of scientific journals and memoirs should follow the rule 'that every official obituary or memoir include a statement regarding the location and condition of the private papers of the scientist concerned'" (1016).

528 Porter, J. R. "Challenges to Editors of Scientific Journals II." *Journal of the Washington Academy of Sciences* 63, no. 4 (1973): 129-34.

In addressing editors of scientific (primarily biology) journals, Porter calls upon those editors to help solve problems related to a narrow interpretation of confidentiality and to the use of imprecise language. Although editors must be vigilant in resisting censorship and plagiarism, the most pressing problem editors face is the dissemination of scientific information to nonscientists who make policy decisions about funding for scientific enterprises. Porter tells editors to explain scientific ideas in terms that nonscientists can understand when the audience is the public. "If science is to receive continued support from politicians, and the public in general, more articles must be transmitted through the media that explain the significance of science in our complex society" (132). Because complex issues require scientists to establish new priorities for the way science can be used best to solve those issues, Porter sees editors as the ones who can help interpret science so that the new priorities are accepted by the public. In other words, "science must become more sensitive and responsive to demands by those providing the support and having to live with the resulting technologies" (133-34).

529 Poyen, Jeanne. "The Difficulties of Preparing the International Serials Catalogue. How Editors Could Help." In *Scientific Information Transfer: The Editor's Role,* edited by Miriam Balaban, 597-601. Dordrecht: D. Reidel Publishing Company, 1978.

Because "it depends mainly upon primary journals to make the information they publish easily retrievable" (601), Poyen recommends that journal editors follow six rules to help indexers catalogue data for easy retrieval. Among the rules Poyen lists are two rules about titles. Only one title should be highlighted on the cover, front page, masthead, and spine of the journal and that title should be spelled out fully.

530 Rodman, Hyman, and Jay Mancini. "Problems and Satisfactions of Journal Editors." *Scholarly Publishing* 8 (1977): 239-45.

Rodman and Mancini sent a questionnaire to 33 editors of sociology journals to determine what satisfied and dissatisfied those editors about their jobs. "On the whole, the data show a considerable mount of satisfaction and relatively little dissatisfaction" (240-41). However, both structured and open-ended questions on the questionnaire confirmed that "the quality of submitted articles, delays by referees, and time pressures on editors were frequently noted as problems" (244). The authors conducted their study because, although editors of scholarly and scientific publications are generally seen as vital to the publication process, not much evidence has been gathered about their part in that process.

531 Rose, Richard. "Editing an International Interdisciplinary Journal." *PS* 19, no. 1 (1986): 88-90.

To edit an international and interdisciplinary journal, the editor should not try to satisfy geographical quotas for accepting articles, but should encourage authors to show how research restricted to one locale could be applied to other countries. To achieve that goal, Rose recommends interdisciplinary refereeing, "the real test of a journal's interdisciplinary character" (89). (Rose's journal's editorial board is composed of scholars living in nine countries, so articles are refereed by scholars in two or three different countries.) An editor also should strive "to maintain professional standards without falling victim to disciplinary vetoes" (90).

532 Selle, Elaine B. "Publishing Association Journals." In *Proceedings 25th International Technical Communication Conference,* paper M-4B, 257-62. Washington: Society for Technical Communication, 1978.

Selle outlines the job of an editorial manager of a society's journal, explaining how to fund a journal and how to process manuscripts. To fund a journal, the editorial manager can seek subscribers (members and nonmembers); assess page charges and submission charges, which are considered advertising fees; sell back issues, reproduction rights ("Societies," Selle notes, "should first be sure that they own all copyright privileges, including rights for republication" [258]), and reprints; and solicit advertising. To solicit advertising, the editor needs to use a publications audit (to determine the journal's audience) and a publisher's representative. The editor will need to educate the publisher's representative about the journal, and support the representative by producing issues on time and "by providing free copies to advertisers, agencies, and prospects" (259). The editor also can produce revenue by selling the journal's mailing list to other organizations for promotional mailings. To process manuscripts, the editor will use a review system (editorial board, peer review, or a combination of both), will have the manuscripts edited (both content editing and copyediting), and will work with production personnel. In working with production personnel, the editor first will choose a production facility. Selle recommends that editors select one facility that can meet all the journal's publication needs. Second, the editor should know how to ask for a bid, so Selle provides a list of printing functions the editor can ask about in seeking bids. Third, the editor needs to become conversant with printing processes and terms. The editor will want to become familiar with the many types of paper, because "in many instances it represents 40% to 50% of the total printing bill" (261). Above all, the editor should enlist the printer who understands the publisher's goals and feels that he or she can satisfy those goals in as much as reaching those goals depends upon the printer.

533 Senders, John W. "I Have Seen the Future, and It Doesn't Work: The Electronic Journal Experiment." *Scholarly Publishing in an Era of Change, Proceedings of the Second Annual Meeting,* edited by Ethel G. Langlois, 8-9. Washington: Society for Scholarly Publishing, 1981.
An effort to establish an electronic journal failed, but Senders predicts that the ideal system, one where authors, editors, and publishers can compose, review, and distribute manuscripts electronically, will eventually emerge because electronic publishing is less costly than the print system. The publishing experiment Senders participated in failed because the system could not do what users wanted it to do. For instance, it did not speed up the exchange of scientific information and it did not allow interactive groups to function as a journal staff would. System users discovered that when it became too difficult to accomplish tasks through the system, the tasks were not accomplished.

534 Shephard, David A. E. "What Do Editors Do?: The View of a Medical Journal Editor." *Medical Communications* 7, no. 4 (1979): 204-09.

A medical journal editor has eight roles to play, including lock-keeper (maintaining a concern for quantity and quality), advocate for author and reader, and educator. As an educator, the editor publishes writing that serves as a model for physician-authors' writing. Shephard also believes medical journal editors should study medical journalism to manage a journal effectively and should work toward standardization of citations among medical journals.

535 Simon, R. I. "Journal Editing as a Subversive Activity: *Curriculum Inquiry* and the Curriculum Field." *Curriculum Inquiry* 10, no. 2 (1980): 107-13.

Simon objects to disciplinary boundaries that predetermine colleagues' relationships before the colleagues read each other's work. As editor of *Curriculum Inquiry*, Simon's mission is "to subvert the institutionalization of curriculum" (108). Simon evaluates the impact of *Curriculum Inquiry*, not by readership surveys or authors' citation of articles published in *Curriculum Inquiry*. "Rather, I look for the appearance of *CI* articles on course reading lists, in in-service handouts, and as reprints in new textbooks" (111). Simon also realizes that a journal editor wields power: an author may receive tenure because an editor published an author's article. To wield power in a principled way, Simon considers the editor's role by asking questions. Do exploratory data deserve publication? How much time should an editor take to process an author's manuscript? How can an editor recognize and eliminate editorial bias? How much should the editor encourage an author to revise a manuscript? "We have sometimes encouraged second and third rewrites only to finally reject the manuscript. Is such a policy unfair?" (112).

536 Smith, Frank R. "The Editorial Process." Paper presented at the Annual Workshop on the Teaching of Technical Writing, Carbondale, October 1979. ED 177 584.

As the editor of *Technical Communication* (*TC*), Smith explains the editorial process at *TC*. That process is governed by the editor's vision of the journal—its purpose, audience, literary quality, and physical characteristics. Editors have a clear vision of what the journal is, so when they advise authors to rework a manuscript, editors are trying to fit the manuscript into this vision of the journal. Smith advises authors to query an editor about a potential article because the letter of inquiry saves time for both author and editor. At *TC* unsolicited manuscripts are refereed and if the referee recommends that an article be rejected, the referee needs to state reasons for the rejection in two forms: in language that will not offend the author and in candid language that the editor will read to understand exactly why an article was rejected. Patience is a key ingredient in the production process because three months to one year can elapse from the submission of a manuscript until its publication.

537 Smith, Frank R. "The Education of a Society Journal Editor." In *Proceedings 29th International Technical Communication Conference. Technical Communication—Charting the Course of Technology,* E-110—E-111. Washington: Society for Technical Communication, 1982.

When Smith accepted the editorship of *Technical Communication* he had to learn technical, interpersonal, and psychological skills. He had to learn layout and design because he knew little about typefaces or type sizes, page layout, photo sizing, and paper qualities. He also had to learn how to work with a distant printer. Smith did not understand printer's terminology, so he had to deal with "innumerable misinterpretations, mistakes, and delays" (E-111). Because *Technical Communication* is operated by volunteers, Smith "had to learn how to locate, recruit, and motivate people to work for nothing" (E-111) and he had to learn how to work with a board of directors. He also had to learn about rejecting manuscripts so that authors would revise and resubmit their papers the way he wanted them revised. And he had to learn "how to accept and exercise absolute authority over the content and organization of a publication and how to accept the responsibility that goes with the authority" (E-111) because he learned that "in this editor's job, there is no other authority" (E-111).

538 Smith, Frank R. "Publishing the Small Society Journal." In *Proceedings 25th International Technical Communication Conference,* 266-71. Washington: Society for Technical Communication, 1978.

An editor's image of his or her journal—its purpose, audience, literary quality, and physical characteristics—determines his or her actions in editing the journal. However, the way an editor sees those facets of the journal is based, in part, on economic and substantive constraints. In particular, *Technical Communication* is published under "pretty narrow" budgetary restraints because it accepts no advertising and relies upon general revenues of the society. It also is published under substantive—content—constraints because of its broad, yet specialized audience. But content also suffers from lack of research. Smith notes that technical communicators are not doing research of their profession to gain a better understand of it. Thus technical communicators "tend to keep saying the same things over and over" (268). Because technical communicators are prone to rehashing old ideas, suitable articles for *Technical Communication* are hard to find, so the editor hunts for articles in proceedings and the journals of other professional communication organizations. When a reviewer rejects a manuscript, he or she explains the rejection "(1) in tactful language that can be passed on to the author, and (2) in blunter statements for the benefit of the editor, who must make the final decision and who needs to know the plain facts" (269). Unfortunately many manuscripts are so poorly written that they would fail the requirements of a freshman composition paper. For Smith, a manuscript with poor mechanics can distract his attention and weaken his objectivity.

539 Soltani, Poori. "Problems of Editing a Library Journal in a Developing Country." *I[nternational] F[ederation of] L[ibrary] A[ssociations] Journal* 2, no. 3 (1976): 147-53.

Developing countries face publishing problems that could prohibit the production of high-quality library journals, but in Iran, the editor of one library journal has overcome these problems by appealing to a work ethic rooted in human concern. That ethic must overcome manpower, reader, and financial and technical problems. For instance, the low number of professional librarians in Iran limits the number and quality of contributions to a journal, so the editor guides volunteer writers to appropriate subjects and explains the rules of writing. The audience for a library journal is also problematic because many types of library professionals read the same few library journals. A good editor satisfies those groups "without publishing a muddled and inconsistent magazine" (150). Economically resources for publishing a journal are scarce and printing procedures hinder the production of a professional journal. For instance, printing workers' lettering is not right until the editor corrects it—"often more than six times" (151). Yet, the editor can appeal to "personal and emotional human ties" (152) to make a journal work. Because human relations are so important, Soltani advises editors in developing countries to choose publication committee members "who are well read, creative, fair, modest, who have enough motivation not to do everything for the sake of money, and who have respect for mankind" (152). Indeed, the editor in chief should respect others' creative talents.

540 Spalding, B. P. "An Editor's Perspective." In *Workshop Proceedings. Shaping our Destiny: Techniques for Moving Up in Higher Education,* edited by Ernestine M. Copas, Helen H. Mills, Patricia L. Dwinell, M.

Louise McBee, and Betty J. Whitten, 22-24. Athens: University of Georgia, 1981. ED 234 714.

Recounting her experience as a journal editor, Spalding encourages women in the conference to write for history journals, even writing impressionistic studies like literary criticism. However, she cautions her audience not to accept the editorship of a journal because editorial work will not count toward promotion and tenure. If a person does accept the editorship of an academic journal that person should demand adequate space, personnel, and budget to produce the journal. "Get involved with editing," Spalding says, "only if you've got nerves of steel, adequate time, and the kind of professional help you need" (24).

541 Taft, Earl J. "Editing a Photographically Reproduced Journal." In *Scientific Information Transfer: The Editor's Role,* edited by Miriam Balaban, 25-27. Dordrecht: D. Reidel Publishing Company, 1978.

Mathematicians view their "subject as a permanent one" (26), so they find a photographically reproduced journal acceptable because "they do want their things to come out very very early and they do want them to appear in a nice and what they regard a permanent form" (27). In comparing his journal to ones in the same discipline that are typeset, Taft notes that both types publish the same kind of articles.

542 Taft, Earl J. "Editing a Photographically Reproduced Mathematics Journal." In *Scientific Information Transfer: The Editor's Role,* edited by Miriam Balaban, 415-18. Dordrecht: D. Reidel Publishing Company, 1978.

Although direct reproduction of mathematics journals is rare, such journals could become popular, especially as the technology for reproducing direct copy improves. Advantages of not typesetting articles, but photographically reproducing them, include saving time. Also "the author is assured that what he submits is what will appear" (418), typographical errors included. Photographically reproduced articles are also efficient for international journals because "all languages and alphabets are equal to the camera" (418). However, the preparation of copy is critical, so Taft asks authors to retype papers if they aren't camera ready. But stylistic requirements—instructions about references, footnotes, and title, for example—need not be rigidly enforced.

543 Thomas, Garth J. "Editing a Basic Science Journal." *IEEE Transactions on Professional Communication* PC-18, no. 3 (1975): 186-89.

Thomas says that because "basic science is concerned with very abstract propositions about experience" (186), it is not concerned with information explosion. Its readership is quite small and the format for publishing basic science is the long article based on a complex argument. That format is not reducible to "information in bits that you could put into all kinds of combinations" (188), such as abstracts and microfilm. Economic problems that arise because of format requirements should be solved by reducing journal publication costs, not by changing the format of data from basis science. Garth also believes that the referee system is evil, but is better than no system at all. However, respondents who commented on Thomas's remarks generally supported the referee system.

544 Viza, Dimitri. "Editors' Impact on Science Policies and Politics." In *Scientific Information Transfer: The Editor's Role,* edited by Miriam Balaban, 157-60. Dordrecht: D. Reidel Publishing Co., 1978.

Unfortunately, the scientist can only be successful by conforming to conservative standards of scientific inquiry: "never take the risk to create, it is an expensive hobby, it fails often, it disturbs always" (168). Editors of scientific journals can take the lead in changing this situation by formulating and enforcing scientific research policies and refusing to publish papers that do not subscribe to those policies. Viza advocates the creation of an international body of such scientific editors.

545 White, Stephen W. "Editing Ethics and Strategy." In *Workshop Proceedings. Shaping Our Destiny: Techniques for Moving Up in Higher Education,* edited by Ernestine M. Copas, Helen H. Mills, Patricia L. Dwinell, M. Louise McBee, and Betty J. Whitten, 25-29. Athens: University of Georgia, 1981. ED 234 714.

Written from the perspective of an editor who is advising authors how to get their work published in academic journals, White's article stresses that the author should know about and become involved in the publishing process. Authors can learn about the editorial process by reading books about publishing, learning "how to look at . . . [a] journal board editorially and politically" (26), and visiting newspaper editors. Authors can also influence editorial policy by reviewing an article, writing editors and suggesting that they edit out sexist language in their journal, solicit articles from particular authors, and add to their editorial boards members who will represent underrepresented groups of people like women and minorities. Authors' comments can be effective in changing editorial policy because "editors cannot operate in an informational vacuum, so the more inputs they have from a variety of channels, the better editorial products they will likely produce" (27).

546 Wolper, R. S. "Why I Edit—And Keep Editing—A Journal." *Scholarly Publishing* 13 (1982): 149-55.

Wolper edits *The Scriblerian*, because, he says, "I love the journal" (155). Along with two other editors, Wolper writes, edits, and pastes up reviews of eighteenth-century scholarship that appear in *The Scriblerian*. After being one of its editors for 13 years, Wolper has learned to write better. He has also learned to concentrate on a work of scholarship to prepare a review of it. Wolper believes that his work, as he says, "allows me to give something back to the eighteenth century" (153). To give that something back, all three editors consider no job too menial. "[T]o conquer, we have stooped (and lifted)" (150). He also asserts that no amount of money could repay him for the work he does, even the paste-up which "is dull and repetitious and demanding (in a trivial way) and exacting and uninteresting. Yet because I love the journal, I am not discontented with paste-up. At the end I even whistle (a little)" (155).

547 Woods, David. "Editing and Writing Problems of Medical Publications." *Medical Communications* 1, no. 1 (1972): 9-14.

The foremost problem a medical journal editor has is obtaining a usable manuscript because many physicians don't have time to or don't feel comfortable producing a manuscript. However, "so long as submitted material has facts, logic, and form, most editors are prepared to overlook its literary shortcomings" (10). Once a manuscript is acquired, the editor has two obligations to the author: not to distort the manuscript through editing it and to send the author a galley proof. The editor also has responsibility to the journal's audience and by using questionnaires and surveys, the editor can find out what the audience wants and how the audience evaluates the journal, "even if there are lies, damned lies, and magazine readership surveys" (11). Reprint requests also alert editors to topics that interest the journal's audience. The editor also can consider the audience by vividly presenting data to keep readers' "attention from being diverted to more sinful pleasures than reading medical journals" (13).

548 Ziman, John M. "Reports on Progress in Physics." In *Scientific Information Transfer: The Editor's Role,* edited by Miriam Balaban, 183-87. Dordrecht: D. Reidel Publishing Company, 1977.

The editor for a science review journal acquires manuscripts over a long period of time with the help of editorial advisors. First, though, the editor considers the journal's audience to instruct authors how to write for that audience. In determining what the journal will cover, the editor should look ahead and consider what readers will think is important next year. The editor also should review certain topics every few years. In looking for appropriate authors to write on appropriate subjects, Ziman suggests that editors use inexperienced authors who might be mentored by a senior author. Authors should be paid for their work because then the editor can reject work that is not satisfactory. One unsatisfactory idiosyncrasy is authorial bias, which happens when the works of an author's rivals "somehow or other are not given quite sufficient balance" (186). The editor should also send delinquent authors reminders even though "it is several years between commissioning and getting" (187) authors' papers.

Magazines

549 Abend, Jules. "The Care and Feeding of Stringers." In *Handbook of Magazine Publishing,* edited by Marjorie McManus, F18-F21. New Canaan: Folio Magazine Publishing Corporation, 1977.

Magazine stringers—freelancers—require tender loving care. "Make no mistake, ladling out generous portions of symbolic chicken soup with the loving care of a mother is the key to keeping nonsalaried stringers ready and eager to take on your occasional news or feature assignment" (F18). Because stringers are important to a magazine, the editor should be responsible for mothering stringers, which entails paying and supervising them. To locate stringers, the editor can consult the *Editor & Publisher Yearbook* or wire services. When an editor sees a wire service story that he or she likes, the editor should get the writer's name and address and contact him or her about being a stringer. Not only must the editor follow-up on stringers by sending them his or her magazine and notes praising the writer's work, the editor must supervise stringers. Good supervision requires giving clear and concise instructions to the stringer about assignment requirements, including length of story and the stringer's deadline.

550 Anderson, Elliott. "Cheek by Jowl: On Reading, Angels, and the Threat from Within." In *The Art of Literary Publishing: Editors on Their Craft,* edited by Bill Henderson, 203-11. Yonkers: The Pushcart Press, 1980.

Soliciting economic support from an angel or angels—a person or persons who donate money to a magazine—is one facet of a small literary magazine editor's job. As the editor of *TriQuarterly,* Anderson recounts two of his experiences with angels and notes that the relationship between a magazine and a nonprofit organization is superior to the relationship between a magazine and a for-profit organization because for-profit organizations measure literary quality by economic standards. The most difficult relationship, however, is between the magazine and an individual angel. Quality is a major issue when public funding is in view. For instance, support from the National Endowment for the Arts is often disbursed equally with little regard for literary quality. Without standards, public money given to support literature fractures "what is already a fractured audience, certifying in the process standards of mediocrity in the literary interests of no one" (211).

551 Barnett, Dick. "Sixteen Hints for the New Products Editor." In *Handbook of Magazine Publishing,* edited by Marjorie McManus, F30-F31. New Canaan: Folio Magazine Publishing Corporation, 1977.
Barnett provides 16 insights for the editor who publishes information about new products. For instance, he says that samples are particularly useful when an editor is asked to publish advertisements for "interesting but questionable items" (F30). The editor may want to request a sample of such an item. A sample is also useful when the editor wants to print a photograph of the item and needs to prepare the photograph. The main reasons an editor should acquire a sample is so that he or she does not promote a product that readers will find to be worthless.

552 Black, Theodore W. "Staff Memo on Editing . . . for the Specialized Magazine." *The Quill* 57, no. 5 (1969): 12-14.
As an editor for *Machinery* magazine, Black often rewrites authors' articles because "few of our authors are . . . able to convey ideas clearly and succinctly for *our* specialized audience" (12). To rewrite articles, Black weeds out illustrations that are not pertinent to the article, organizes the article's content, prepares headings and decks, edits for consistent tone, relays instructions to the printer about how to prepare photographs, writes captions for illustrations, writes the author's bibliography, asks the author to review the manuscript, and assembles the article for production. Of this process Black notes that editing is a matter of judging and selecting, of determining what should and should not be included in a publication. Good editors also recognize that making decisions is an imperfect process that results in imperfect articles. However, editors keep editing, trying to use better judgment as they become more experienced editors.

553 Bland, William F. "Editing the Technical Business Magazine." In *Technical Editing,* edited by B. H. Weil, 115-32. Westport: Greenwood Press, 1975.
The editor of a technical business magazine should try to increase readership of an article by presenting an article using headlines, illustrations, and organization. For instance, well-written technical articles have a good outline, but good editing makes the outline transparent to the reader. Illustrations also can help present an article, but a good illustration tells readers something. Typography can also be used to highlight key points in an article. For instance, to use a variable-

speed reading technique, "the editor has to write a story within a story, making the skeleton story read smoothly without being jumpy, and at the same time making it fit into the complete story" (125). Editors have three sources for articles—staff, contributors, and meeting papers. Meeting papers can be a good source of information, but require "adroit and laborious editing" (129) to make them into good articles. Once a staff-written article is completed, the technical business magazine editor checks the writer's sources because the editor wants to publish accurate information. Authors are not encouraged to read galley or page proofs because authors can change their minds easily about how to say something once they see their prose in type.

554 Chadbourne, Bill N. *What Every Editor Should Know About Layout and Typography*. Arlington: National Composition Association, 1979. Speaking to magazine editors, Chadbourne says, "your ideas to attract readers are wasted if the copy itself isn't readable" (4). Readability includes good layout and typography, which are editorial responsibilities. To fulfill those responsibilities, editors need to know how to measure type (points, picas, and inches), how to use a sizing wheel ("There is no excuse for an editor handing his printer a batch of photos and the instructions, 'make 'em fit!'" [26]), how to use white space, and how to crop and box photographs. Editors can use a variety of layout patterns (single theme, total design, and modular, for instance) and ad profiles (pyramid right, half-pyramid left, and ganged, for example) to produce a distinctive magazine. Chadbourne also discusses cutlines (captions), copyfitting, and typesetting, showing ways to create a dummy using either the paste-up method or diagram method. He advises editors, "don't forget to allow time for 'review' of the material by your own bosses. Be sure to let them see the job at a stage in which changes can still be made. By waiting until the 'blue line' stage your costs may skyrocket" (37).

555 De Voto, Bernard. "The Constant Function." In *Editors on Editing*, edited by Gerald Gross, 209-15. New York: Grosset & Dunlap, 1962. To celebrate *Harper's* centenary anniversary, De Voto explains that *Harper's* is a magazine of critical inquiry that offers expert judgment to the most intelligent reader. *Harper's* makes a profit without subsidies because "all subsidies rig the market; they are in restraint of trade" (210-11). If *Harper's* were subsidized, it could not provide in-depth reporting of events in retrospect to amend and correct the record. The editor's role in preparing such journalism rests on a "sovereign principle: the widest possible freedom of discussion" (214). And even though advocates of particular positions may have a legitimate claim, a magazine of critical

inquiry cannot take a position on whether a claim is legitimate. Not taking a position "is the upper ether of editorial skill and integrity, and the life of the magazine hangs in the balance" (214).

556 "Editors on Editors." In *Handbook of Magazine Publishing*, edited by Marjorie McManus, F3-F15. New Canaan: Folio Magazine Publishing Corporation, 1977.

Six respondents and a moderator discuss how editors can "evaluate, motivate, and compensate their staff" (F3). Respondents noted that motivation begins with the editor, who should not need to see his or her name attached to a product. The editor is pleased just to have contributed to the product. Writers, on the other hand, want their names identified with a product. Perhaps the most critical aspect of an editorial chief's job "'is to recognize the best work when it's done'" (F6). About hiring editorial personnel, one respondent noted that the editor has to be able to find the right employee and to pay that person whatever is necessary to accept the job. Paying people well gets their "'full, undivided attention'" (F7). But money is only one source of motivation. Freedom also motivates. Staff members should be given the freedom to grow professionally. They can initiate assignments and express themselves through their work. Editors should give staff members appropriate credit for their successes. In discussing labor unions, one participant noted that unions interpose themselves between the editor and the printed page, which is harmful to the editor who needs independence. Most of the respondents were skeptical about the value of readership surveys, because, as one participant noted, editors are the experts about editing, not readers. To find a good editor, a person should find someone who has successful experience, someone who is charismatic and attracts other quality employees, someone who has a vision of what the magazine should accomplish. But "'the end product of a magazine is really not the self-expression of the editors, but the willingness to submerge themselves—to some extent—to put out the product'" (F12). One participant compared editors to a person in sales, though editors may have more sensitivity than a salesperson.

557 Elfenbein, Julien. *Editor's Manual: Editorial, Production and Publishing Procedures*. New York: The American Journal of Nursing Company, 1970.

Elfenbein's *Manual* is intended to be a comprehensive guide for nurses who produce association magazines. The nurse-editor's job is divided into three parts: editorial, production, and publishing. The first part, editorial, is a discussion of the role of the editor ("It is the editor who breathes life into the magazine" [2-3]) and types of editing, noting that "the editor should not impose her style of writing on a contributed article or tamper with [an] author's idiomatic usage" (3-1). Also included are sections on how to treat the editorial page ("The anonymous editor is a bad policy" [4-3]); how to write nonfiction articles, obituaries, headlines and captions; how to treat letters to the editor ("Send galley proofs of a controversial article or editorial to a selected list of twenty or thirty readers inviting comment. These galleys should be sent in advance of publication" [13-1]); and how to handle contributors. The production section, the second part of the *Manual*, discusses, among other things, magazine design, typography, visuals, and paper stock. Chapter 21 is devoted to copy preparation and proofreading, with instructions about printer's and author's errors. Part three, publishing, includes data on circulation, advertising, copyright, and libel.

558 Ferguson, Rowena. *Editing the Small Magazine*. 2nd ed. New York: Columbia University Press, 1976.

The small magazine is produced by an organization and is not a commercial magazine. The editor of a small magazine must understand his or her readers; "the magazine must talk *to* people, not *at* them" (12). For a small magazine to talk to readers, editors must plan each issue and "by far, the biggest part of editorial planning is dreaming up ideas for content" (29). Content should follow from purpose, the message of the magazine. "The message will reflect the group's purpose and will likely attempt to sell the readers on the significance and importance of the organization; in other words, it will try to keep the membership interested, active, and growing" (35). An editorial board is one source of advice about the magazine's content; "the board can advise *what* to do but has little judgment as to *how*. The latter is the responsibility of the editorial office" (210). Even planning is advisory because the editor's "is the final word on the magazine" (45). In executing plans, the editor will procure manuscripts. As a rule "the more substantial the magazine, the less writing can be expected of the editor" (49). The editor of a large magazine can cultivate staff reporters by teaching them what stories the magazine is interested in, how to locate sources for those stories, and how to report the story. Editors can also contract with freelance writers, but editors should tell a freelancer exactly what he or she is being asked to write. Complete instructions help ensure that the freelancer will prepare a useful assignment. When working with writers, "the editor's job is to stimulate and release the author's energy and imagination, not to put him in a strait jacket" (69). Ferguson explains how to evaluate a writer's abilities, how to handle unsolicited manuscripts, and how to calculate payment for a manuscript. The editor also may work with a photographer to acquire pictures for the magazine, so Ferguson explains how to evaluate pictures. To process a manuscript, the editor will need to understand copyreading, typestyling, and copyfitting. "To copyread means to make the manuscript grammatical, that is, to bring it in line with good English usage; to make it stylistically consistent; and, by making minor modifications, to enhance its readability" (110). To type-style means establishing typographic design. Ferguson suggests that editors be inventive so that each issue's design varies somewhat from the basic design of the publication. To copy-fit means making the text and graphics fit aesthetically the amount of space allotted for each issue. Copyfitting includes layout and the cropping of pictures. Once an issue is in proof, proofreading is necessary. Ferguson discusses types of printing—offset, letterpress, photocomposition—noting that offset printing can look like letterpress, so "the possibilities of offset should not be underestimated" (161). The final copy of a small magazine should appeal to readers' emotions without causing them to recognize any changes in the magazine, unless an editor wants "to change abruptly an unpopular or ineffective policy" (182). An editor can appeal to readers' emotions by using the "we" frame of reference. "One of the editor's major responsibilities is to cultivate a we-are-all-in-this-together psychology, without which the cutting edge of the periodical is blunted" (204).

559 Glenn, George A. "The Art of Being on Time." In *Handbook of Magazine Publishing,* edited by Marjorie McManus, F44-F47. New Canaan: Folio Magazine Publishing Corporation, 1977.

"There is no question in my mind," Glenn says, "that on-time and quality editorial do go hand in hand" (F46). The key to meeting deadlines is cultivating the habit of thinking about being on time. Conditioning begins when an editor thinks mathematically. Glenn notes that an editor is able to produce just over four pages of copy each day. In turn, editors should know the productivity rate of staff members so that editors can establish checkpoints to monitor an employee's timely performance, should schedule deadlines, and should plan the major features of a year's issues. To meet deadlines, an editor also needs to exert self-discipline and adhere to a daily personal schedule that might include daily staff checks to determine what problems might slow down the magazine's progress. Tools like a bulletin board can be effective in outlining and visualizing an issue. Glen describes how a magazine was revitalized by the techniques he recommends and concludes that editorial creativity is fostered when the editor has time "to come up with fresh ideas" (F47).

560 Hanson, J. J. "The Editor as a Publisher." In *Handbook of Magazine Publishing,* edited by Marjorie McManus, F24-F26. New Canaan: Folio Magazine Publishing Corporation, 1977.

Hanson does not want his employees worrying about how to cut costs; rather, he wants them to think about increasing revenues. Editors can increase revenues by realizing that they are in the business of gathering and disseminating information. As gatherers and disseminators of information, they should consider ways to market information. For instance, by developing special issues of a magazine to attract new advertisers editors can encourage advertisers to spend more on advertising. Creating a newsletter is another way to increase revenues. The editor could produce a newsletter for each type of manufacturing company. Special interest seminars and trade show services are also activities that can increase revenues. Or the editor can tape significant trade show events and sell the cassette to interested readers. Hanson advises editors to set up a panel that would test new products or services for advertisers.

561 Hargreaves, Thomas G. "The Manager as Editor." *Management World* 7, no. 6 (1978): 12-16.

Hargreaves discusses the steps an editor can take to initiate and operate a company magazine. To begin a company magazine the prospective editor must "obtain the blessing of the company's most senior executive" (13). Then the editor communicates with printers to learn about printing techniques and processes. The editor should also solicit advertisers to finance the magazine. By enlisting a committee made up of executives, the editor gathers potential contributors to the magazine. Preparing a magazine for publication is a time consuming effort so editors should "be prepared for the many hours of typing, editing, proofreading, and correcting which go into a publication" (16). Editors also can avoid certain pitfalls associated with misspelling names or omitting reference to people who should have been included in an issue of the magazine.

562 Jacobi, Peter. "The Art of Magazine Editing: An Introduction." *Folio* 12, no. 9 (1983): 83-84, 86, 88, 214.

"Magazine editing is a calling," Jacobi states, and "the task is easier to learn than to teach, more to be experienced than read about, more to be assimilated and refined by trial and error than to be absorbed from lectures" (83). The editorial task can be divided into micro- and macro-editing. Micro-editing is editing at the word, style, and structure levels. Macro-editing is editing by establishing goals and determining the tone of the magazine. The outcome of magazine editing should be an influential publication with permanence that is directed to an audience.

Both micro- and macro-editing focus on audience. The audience determines whether a magazine is worth reading, but the editor must convince readers that his or her magazine is worth readers' attention. To do that the editor must plan so that every issue is comprised of material that attracts readers' attention. In essence, "serving the audience is what all the work of editor and staff reduces to or expands to or amounts to" (214).

563 Katzel, Jeanine, and Leo Spector. "How To Measure Readership in Depth Without Going Bankrupt." In *Handbook of Magazine Publishing,* edited by Marjorie McManus, F41-F43. New Canaan: Folio Magazine Publishing Corporation, 1977.

Katzel and Spector explain how the Editorial Quality Audit (EQA) is used "to measure the readership of all feature articles and to monitor editorial performance" (F42) of *Plant Engineering.* The EQA, which is composed of nine questions, is answered by "nine panels of 25 readers each, for a total of 225 members" (F42) to evaluate articles after they have been published. When the results of the EQA are tabulated, they help measure editorial performance. Editors also have used the EQA to assess articles before they are published.

564 Kobak, James B. "The Editor as Marketer: A Heretical but Correct Approach." In *Handbook of Magazine Publishing,* edited by Marjorie McManus, F37-F38. New Canaan: Folio Magazine Publishing Corporation, 1977.

Kobak lists 42 Editorial Truths about magazines. For instance, editorial content sells magazines, so editors are marketers. As marketers, editors must sell readers on the desirability of reading the editor's magazine. The editor may need to trick people into reading an article. If a magazine does not have a defined rationale, the magazine will not survive. "If an editor cannot describe the editorial rationale of his or her magazine in ten words, the editor doesn't have one" (F37). If advertisers do not know the editorial rationale, they are selling an imaginary product that promises what it cannot deliver. Kobak also lists 35 Editorial Why Don't We's, including Why don't we take the pages that market the magazine away from the editor? Why don't we state the editorial rationale? Why don't we tell the editor to communicate that rationale to people who produce and buy the magazine? Why don't we get the editor to review the various departments of the magazine to determine if they fit the editorial rationale? Why don't we "teach editors the economics of publishing?" (F38).

565 Kruse, Benedict. "The Editor as a Dictator." In *Handbook of Magazine Publishing,* edited by Marjorie McManus, F21-F23. New Canaan: Folio Magazine Publishing Corporation, 1977.

The editor can increase productivity and personal satisfaction by using a dictation machine to create a first draft or to conduct an interview. However, dictation is not a cure-all. Dictated copy must be transcribed, so although dictated materials can be completed sooner than materials that are typed, dictation may be more time consuming than traditional methods of drafting a document, especially for short jobs. When used for an appropriate assignment, dictation may shorten the amount of time it takes to prepare a first draft. And since the preparation of the first draft generally takes the most editorial time, dictation allows the editor to spend the time saved on preparing the first draft in refining the manuscript. For example, "for an article of 1,700 words, first draft writing time by dictation is generally under two hours. Editing time is at least an hour . . . . By contract . . . [it takes] four to six hours of typewriter time for the same assignment" (F23). Kruse also discusses synergistic writing where a writer and a subject expert work collaboratively to produce a manuscript. "The writer . . . dictates while the other person listens and interacts" (F23).

566 Lane, John C. "Editing Organization-Sponsored Magazines and Newsletters." In *Technical Editing,* edited by B. H. Weil, 41-50. Westport: Greenwood Press, 1975.

To be effective, a publication must have a clearly defined purpose and that purpose is inextricably linked with readers' needs. So for an editor to make effective decisions about the publication, he or she must understand the publication's purpose. For instance, decisions about types and quantity of graphics and length of articles should be based on the publication's goals. Lane lists fifteen duties for which the editor is solely responsible (enlisting authors, making writing assignments, preparing editorials, for example), but even those duties require that the editor have "a thorough understanding of his publication's basic purpose and specific objectives" (50).

567 Lippke, James A. "Editing the Industrial Magazine—Career Opportunity and Gateway to Technical Marketing Field." In *Proceedings Fifteenth International Technical Communications Conference. New Developments in Technical Communications,* paper W-4, 1-4. Washington: Society for Technical Writers and Publishers, 1968.

Industrial editors can work in technical marketing because part of an editor's job is to promote products. To promote products, the editor must compare them, giving readers an accurate view of a product's worth to the marketplace. Full disclosure of a product's assets and liabilities is the best way to promote a product so that a reader's time is not wasted. Lippke says that the industrial magazine editor has a responsibility to help readers by publishing product comparisons and in-depth behind-the-scene reporting. Readers will not pay for editorial and advertising information, but advertisers will. Unfortunately, the combination of reader desire for in-depth reporting and advertiser desire for editorial that helps sell products puts the editor in a potential bind. "Hence the editor of today and tomorrow will have to have courage" (4).

568 Littledale, Harold. "The Reader Responds." In *Handbook of Magazine Publishing*, edited by Marjorie McManus, F27-F28. New Canaan: Folio Magazine Publishing Corporation, 1977.

As the editor of *Training Magazine*, Littledale reports on the success of binding Editors' Information Cards into each issue of the magazine to solicit readers' responses to articles in a particular issue. "Do our readers take the bait?" Littledale asks. "Absolutely. An average of 150 cards are mailed to us each month (our circulation is 40,000)" (F27). Data from the cards help advertisers understand the market for *Training Magazine* and help Littledale determine what topics future issues of the magazine might explore. Littledale also publishes the information amassed from the cards under a department in the magazine titled 'Feedback' and believes that that department has potential to build readership. The cards also are useful for conducting research on national training trends, for instance the staffing and cost of training programs.

569 Mann, Jim. "Evaluating Your Editorial Product." In *Handbook of Magazine Publishing*, edited by Marjorie McManus, F28-F30. New Canaan: Folio Magazine Publishing Corporation, 1977.

A consultant or a magazine's publisher should evaluate the publisher's magazine every two or three years using a scientific analysis to find out if the magazine has the characteristics it claims to have. Although the editor should participate in such an assay, he or she should not conduct it because good editors trust their instincts. The scientific approach might have a negative impact on the editor's ability to edit instinctually. To conduct the assay, a publisher or consultant should determine the magazine owner's definition of the magazine's publishing purpose and objectives. Then the consultant should find out if the editor and owner share the same definitions of purpose and objectives. He or she should also determine whether the editor is pacing the magazine's content. Is it far enough ahead of the readers so that they continue to buy the magazine or is it so far ahead of readers that they feel lost? The consultant also should determine if everyone in the organization is working to achieve the purpose and objectives.

570 Mann, Jim. "How To Take Your Magazine's Temperature." In *Handbook of Magazine Publishing,* edited by Marjorie McManus, F47-F50. New Canaan: Folio Magazine Publishing Corporation, 1977. Mann offers 10 tests for determining whether a publication is effective. For example, Test 2 asks if the magazine's editorial content has disturbed people. If the disturbance is based on editorial comments, then the stir most probably is a sign of editorial vigor. If the disturbance can be traced to people in other departments than editorial, then the stir may be a sign of trouble. Test 5 asks whether the current issue of the magazine is quite similar to the same issue two years ago. Of Test 5, Mann says that a widely heralded change sends a clear message to advertisers and readers that the editors believe they made a mistake in promoting a failure. Such changes are clear signs of mismanagement. Test 8 asks if advertising sales staff waste time seeking advertising unrelated to the magazine's editorial content. If the sales force is wasting time doing that, the editor should recognize that magazines can advertise effectively only if they match readers' advertising and editorial needs.

571 McCabe, Edward. "More Tips for the New Products Editor." In *Handbook of Magazine Publishing,* edited by Marjorie McManus, F31-F32. New Canaan: Folio Magazine Publishing Corporation, 1977. Ten tips for processing new product items include advice to take a camera and sheet of cardboard to trade shows to create new product photographs. The cardboard can be used as the background and the camera flash as the light source. McCabe also compares selecting a trade name to walking through a minefield. "Learning to step with assurance through this minefield can be painful. 'Fiberglas' with one 's' is a trademark. Fiberglass with two is not" (F32).

572 McManus, Majorie, ed. *Handbook of Magazine Publishing.* New Canaan: Folio Magazine Publishing Corporation, 1977.
The *Handbook of Magazine Editing* is divided into fourteen sections: starting the new magazine, management, finance, ancillary activities, publishing law, editorial, advertising sales, graphics, circulation, fulfillment, printing, production, paper, and promotion. For annotated articles under the editorial section see "Thirteen Steps to Editing a Successful Magazine" (578), "Editors on Editing" (556), "How to Run a Roundtable" (581), "The Care and Feeding of Stringers" (549), "The Editor as Dictator" (565), "The Editor as Publisher" (560), "The Reader

Responds" (568), "Evaluating Your Editorial Product" (569), "Sixteen Hints for the New Products Editor" (551), "More Tips for the New Products Editor" (571), "The Editor as Marketer: A Heretical but Correct Approach" (564), "What about the Editorial Page" (574), "How to Measure Readership in Depth without Going Bankrupt" (563), "The Art of Being on Time" (559), and "How to Take Your Magazine's Temperature" (570).

573 Mayes, Herbert R. *The Magazine Maze: A Prejudiced Perspective.* Garden City: Doubleday & Company, Inc., 1980.

In his autobiography, Mayes recounts his career as a magazine editor, particularly with *McCall's* and *Good Housekeeping*. Mayes's premise throughout the book is that "the editor is the most meaningful person on a magazine" (11), and that most meaningful person "must know how to be boss" (26). Throughout his book, Mayes provides insights about magazine editors. "There is no school for training editors. About editing all is empirical" (25). "Normally an editor may reserve to himself the right to cut a manuscript but never the right to add or change an author's point of view" (69). The editor "relies on subconscious impulses. Hunch. Intuition. Instinct. He needs wisdom more than learning" (75). "Editors are big on insight and subconscious impulses" (125). "When editors are relegated to second place their enthusiasm wanes and innovations are few" (173). "An editor's job is to edit. He is under no compulsion to be a peerless writer or conversationalist or entertainer" (220). "An editor acquires as much authority as he is willing to risk assuming" (238). "[T]he editor is, or should be, part showman; and if he isn't part showman, he is only part editor" (242). About editing magazines, Mayes notes that he never found a typical reader, that the "prime objective of a magazine is to survive." (88), that "vital to a magazine are the regular columns intended to capture readers' issue-to-issue attention" (119), that "circulation, and *only* circulation . . . is what gives an editor the key to how he's doing" (122) because "readership scores are no guarantee to big sales" (124), that clarity "is the most important ingredient in writing for a mass-circulation magazine" (131) and that "editing is part of anything that concerns a magazine's welfare" (240).

574 Peter, John. "What About the Editorial Page?" In *Handbook of Magazine Publishing,* edited by Marjorie McManus, F39-F41. New Canaan: Folio Magazine Publishing Corporation, 1977.

Historically, editorial pages in magazines allowed editors "to sermonize from the editorial pulpit" (F39); however, the editorial page is no longer a standard magazine feature. In some cases the editorial page has been replaced. For instance *Time* gave birth to the publisher's letter, a casual report that explains how the magazine covered a story. But business editors still prefer printing an editorial page because they believe that the editor is an expert in his or her field, and as an expert, the editor can make controversial comments with which readers and advertisers will agree. The editorial page also allows the business editor to assess concerns that apply to his or her particular industry. And the editorial page can personalize the magazine while enhancing the editor's reputation as an authority. However, "the trend in writing the editorial page is towards a more relaxed and informal style. Preaching is out" (F41).

575 Pratt, Marianna. "Editing an Association Magazine for a Diverse Readership." In *Proceedings 25th International Technical Communication Conference,* paper M-4B, 263-65. Washington: Society for Technical Communication, 1978.

As a managing editor, Pratt discusses procedures she uses to produce *Agricultural Engineering*. Since the audience for *Agricultural Engineering* is quite diverse, the feature article for each issue is selected given the number of readers who have similar technical interests. If a feature article is written by an outside writer with a ponderous style, it is rewritten. The editor advises authors about suitable topics for articles and an Editorial Board evaluates each article's technical content. Post cards in every issue of the magazine, reader surveys, and the number of advertising pages are ways to evaluate a magazine's success in reaching readers. Preparing the magazine to reach readers on time is the managing editor's job. Pratt notes that the managing editor's attitude toward meeting deadlines is critical because that attitude is the basis of the magazine's staff's attitudes about meeting deadlines.

576 Purdy, Ken. "The Fruit of the Bittersweet." In *Editors on Editing,* edited by Gerald Gross, 253-60. New York: Grosset & Dunlap, 1962.

Magazine writers and editors have distorted views of each other. The writer thinks that the editor's day is "an eight-hour vacation" (254) when in reality the editor's days are propelled by pressure from the publisher about circulation, which must be increasing. Editors also have an idealized view of the writer's life. Editors reason that because writers don't have bosses, they don't experience the daily pressures of the magazine business. Writers, however, live by their ideas. If a writer can't come up with ideas, if the writer has a bad week, the writer isn't paid. Time is the writer's bane. The editor, who is being paid a salary, can justify the expenditure of time on a seemingly useless activity by believing that the activity someday will lead to a profitable relationship.

"If a writer does the same thing he's cheating himself" (258). Purdy concludes by listing five observations on how to be an editor and one on how to be a writer.

577 Singer, Mark. "The Editors Reach Out." *The Nation* 219, no. 10 (1974): 306-09.

Is the role of an alumni magazine to educate or to express alumni opinion? In addressing that query, Singer cites various alumni magazines, particularly *Harvard Magazine*, and suggests that in the 1960's magazines reported verbatim campus events. By doing that, magazines "gained additional attention and prestige" (307). However, at present, editorial freedom isn't even acknowledged as a part of the editor's job at many institutes of higher education. Because editorial freedom is linked to economics and audience, the editor of an alumni magazine should determine what the relationship is between constituency and finances. The editor also will want to ask how free the university is because the editor's authority is derived from the university's concept of freedom. In some situations, "'magazine editors walk a razor's edge because they're dealing with a group of readers who like their alma mater but don't necessarily want to hear the truth about it'" (308).

578 Spectorsky, A. C. "Thirteen Steps to Editing a Successful Magazine." In *Handbook of Magazine Publishing*, edited by Marjorie McManus, F1-F2. New Canaan: Folio Magazine Publishing Corporation, 1977.

Among Spectorsky's thirteen observations are the beliefs that audience must be the publisher's central concern if the magazine is to be successful; that readership surveys help the editor to become a follower, not a leader; that variety must be based on a well-established editorial viewpoint; that committee's cannot create; that second guessing readers makes the publisher look down upon readers and makes readers wary of the publisher; that radical changes in design and content are a sure sign of a magazine's financial demise.

579 Stefanile, Felix. "A Revolution of Twerps." In *The Art of Literary Publishing: Editors on Their Craft*, edited by Bill Henderson, 186-202. Yonkers: The Pushcart Press, 1980.

Federal grants have allowed twerps to establish small presses that flood the marketplace with bad poetry. Most twerps don't last very long because they depend on government money and mass markets. Little magazine editors that develop magazines that survive have experience in the magazine business, build their magazines over time, and maintain a backlist. Stefanile says those editors have either a "shared aesthetic" or "eclectic" philosophy of publishing poetry. "The shared aesthetic editor has a strong soul, on the heavenlier side of bigotry. . . . The eclectic editor has a strong stomach, which he masks behind a faint, occasionally bilious smile" (192). About the government's approach to publishing poetry Stefanile says that excellence is not measured by popularity. For those who want to start a little magazine, Stefanile gives two pieces of advice: get a job and hang on. He also discusses the economics of selling issues of the magazine and the need to ask poets to help sell their own work.

580 Tucker, Carll. "Our Curious Business". *Saturday Review,* November 12, 1977, 64.

Because a magazine is an evolving community, editors should make editorial decisions based upon "an ongoing collaboration between readers, editors, and advertisers." However, editors in being sensitive to readers' ideas should not be intimidated by readers. That holds true for relationships with advertisers. When fear pollutes editorial judgment, a magazine's readers will distrust and dislike the magazine.

581 Weiss, Bernard. "How To Run a Roundtable." In *Handbook of Magazine Publishing,* edited by Marjorie McManus, F15-F17. New Canaan: Folio Magazine Publishing Corporation, 1977.

Weiss explains how a roundtable is arranged and conducted to produce articles for *Patient Care.* Roundtable members are selected six to twelve weeks prior to the roundtable so that they can help prepare its agenda in collaboration with a *Patient Care* editor. To bring participants together for the roundtable, *Patient Care* has them flown to a hotel or resort where they meet on a Friday night and Saturday. Roundtable meetings are tape-recorded and a photographer takes pictures during the meeting. A moderator ensures that the participants discuss topics on a practical level and answer the questions that were developed for the agenda. (Weiss provides a copy of the Guide for Moderators.) After the moderator reviews the transcript of the roundtable, the editor produces an article that is reviewed by a panel. Then the editor rewrites and polishes the article for publication.

Manuals

582 Atlas, Marshall A. "The User Edit: Making Manuals Easier to Use." *IEEE Transactions on Professional Communication* PC-24, no. 1 (1981): 28-29.

A user edit helps determine if a manual user can locate and use the manual's instructions "quickly, easily, and without error" (28). To conduct a user edit, a person should recruit someone—a user—who is unfamiliar with the machine for which the manual is written and ask the user to operate the machine by referring only to the manual. The errors the user makes will help determine what needs to be revised in the manual. The user also should talk about what he or she is doing, explaining what he or she is trying to do with the machine and how he or she is using the manual to operate the machine. Users can also suggest how to improve the manual. Editors should correct errors that the user edit uncovers, including any similar errors throughout the manual. Even before the user edit is conducted, the editor should perform a casual edit for the first draft of the manual. That edit will help eliminate obvious errors and will allow the editor to alert the writer early to obvious mistakes that might otherwise spread throughout the manual. Atlas cautions that the user edit is an "*editing* tool, not a scientific one. Although the final document will not be perfect, it will be much more usable than it was in the beginning" (29).

583 Batchelder, Susan K. "Friends or Foes? The Relationship between Writer and Editor." In *Proceedings 30th International Technical Communication Conference,* W&E-73—W&E-74. Washington: Society for Technical Communication, 1983.

Speaking as a technical manual writer, Batchelder recommends that writers use editors as consultants throughout a project. For instance, during the preparation of manuals, the editor can act as a consultant during the first two preparation stages—research and rough draft—by suggesting ways to structure the manual. In addition, the editor can help the writer analyze the manual's audience and give the writer information about the company's global publishing agenda. If editors help writers during the drafting stage, then when the editor officially reviews the manual, he or she has the opportunity to correct problems that he or she failed to correct on earlier drafts. Editorial effectiveness, however, depends on the three preconditions of the writer-editor relationship. "First, both must be professional. . . . Second, the editor must be a technical editor, not just a literary editor. . . . Third, the writer and editor must respect and trust each other enough to be direct in their dealings with each other" (W&E-73).

584 Berkow, Robert. "Editing *The Merck Manual*: A Historical Perspective." *CBE Views* 7, no. 2 (1984): 6-10.

In reviewing the editions of *The Merck Manual,* Berkow notes that the first edition of the *Manual,* produced in 1899, was unsophisticated and humorous in retrospect, given medical advances, but the first edition was "a noble effort for its time" (7). By the seventh edition (1940), an index was provided. The editor of the eighth edition, Dr. Charles E. Lyght, began using outside authorities to write the text. Before that, a small group of physicians consulted prominent textbooks and wrote material based on data in those texts. The problem with using authorities to write the text was that they wrote too much text, and each wrote in his particular style. Much editing was needed "to achieve brevity, clarity, and consistency without altering the factual content'" (8). Berkow edited the thirteenth edition (1977), which had grown to "10 times the number of pages of the 1st edition and almost 14 times the page area in square inches" (9). To produce the thirteenth edition, over 800 pages had to be excised by "cutting the leading between headings and lines, furiously reediting, and slightly enlarging page size" (9). Before the fourteenth edition (1982) was produced, review procedures were implemented and the *Manual* was put into a computer database in preparation for typesetting and indexing it in-house.

585 Buelow, Bernard J., and Donna D. Frost. "The Evolution of the Writer's and Editor's Role in Product Development." In *Proceedings 32nd International Technical Communication Conference,* WE-22—W-24. Washington: Society for Technical Communication, 1985.

When writers and editors passively participate in the development of computer documentation, they have little opportunity to improve the product because they are asked to write and edit materials after the product is completed. To convince management that they should participate actively in product development, writers and editors can conduct user and internal surveys. Data from those surveys can help show the wisdom of involving writers and editors early in the product development cycle. When writers do participate actively in product development, they must begin spending time with developers during the initial stages of a product's development. They also should take part in making decisions about the product. Editors will need to take a greater interest in technical issues while maintaining their concerns for producing documents with literary qualities. Editors will also find themselves taking more time to work on a product. For instance, they will develop style guides for each product to aid developers and writers as they create the product. One of the benefits of active participation is that developers begin to depend on writers and editors to represent the user so that a product will meet users' needs.

586 Davis, Edwina B. "Tips on Editing a Book or Manual." *Medical Communications* 13, no. 2 (1985): 33-36.

Twelve tips on editing include advice about checking the consistency of reference citations in a text with the list of references, using consistent style in the list of references, and citing abbreviations ("spelled out the first time they are used in the text, with the abbreviations in parentheses" [35]). Tip ten suggests that if editors realize that they are explaining a particular editorial change repeatedly to different authors, editors can set up a file of explanations. The file would consist of typed slips of paper—one for each change—explaining editorial changes. Then whenever an editor encountered an error and changed it, he or she could attach the appropriate typed slip to the place in the manuscript where he or she made the change.

587 Foehringer, Stephen B. "The Role of the Editor in Software Documentation." In *Proceedings 34th International Technical Communication Conference,* WE-203—WE-206. Washington: Society for Technical Communication, 1987.

The role of editors of software documentation is to ensure that writers follow correct formal style and to encourage writers to use creative style. Enforcing formal style should start at the beginning of a project to save editing time later when debatable points of formal style arise. For instance, editors should establish style for lists (ordered and unordered), capitalization (including "guidelines for various heading levels and figure captions" [WE-203]), commas, and tone ("especially in tutorials, the present [tense] is usually where the action is" [WE-205]). Clarity of presentation is also a matter of style and includes use of compounds, acronyms, and graphics. In fostering the use of creative style, the editor "encourage[s] writers to exercise some poetic license" (WE-206). By encouraging individuality of style, the editor can play a part in making "the difference between a lively, readable document and just another uninteresting manual that is a drudgery to read" (WE-206).

588 Harrington, J. Y. "Editing Computer Manuals." *Technical Communication* 27, no. 4 (1980): 14-17.

To edit a computer manual, the editor must represent the user and ensure that the manual is "accurate, retrievable, complete, and readily understood" (14). To shape the manual according to that criteria the editor reviews the manual at least three times. During the first review, the editor takes notes and determines whether the intended audience can understand and use the manual easily. During the second review, the editor edits words, sentences, and paragraphs for cohesiveness and evaluates the manual's layout. During the third review, the editor focuses on making the style consistent with particular emphasis on capitalization. Because the audience of computer manuals includes people who are not computer experts, editors must avoid producing manuals with jargon. Editors also must be able to motivate authors to accept editorial judgments. "Gentle with some, caustic with others—whatever it takes, the editor must gain the cooperation of the writers and motivate them to improve their manuals" (17).

589 Miles, Samuel A. "Editing Technical-Equipment Manuals." In *Technical Editing,* edited by B. H. Weil, 167-83. Westport: Greenwood Press, 1975.

The editor of a technical equipment manual should be actively involved in the earliest stages of a piece of equipment's development and should consider the scope and cost of producing a manual for that piece of equipment. Miles says that the technical equipment manual gives detailed instructions for operating and maintaining equipment and alerts operators to potential dangers in using the equipment. Because "the editor is the virtual captain of the intellectual ship" (173) the editor should assign copyediting duties to a competent assistant and should devote his or her efforts to preparing copy for reproduction. The editor follows or creates specifications to which the manual conforms. In addition, the editor's duties include providing writers with style sheets and developing "a consistent shortened nomenclature" (179). The editor must test the manual to determine whether the way the manual says the equipment operates is in fact the way the equipment operates. The editor also should be concerned about the costs for editorial work. Miles suggests that editorial costs "be exempt from competitive bidding and negotiated as a separate items after a rough draft has been approved" (182), because bids seldom account for the high editorial costs needed to produce a professional manual.

590 Vaughn, David E. "Employing the Sounding-Board Effect in Writing and Editing the Free-Style Manual." In *Proceedings 22nd International Technical Communication Conference,* 393-96. Washington: Society for Technical Communication, 1975.

Editors should initiate the sounding-board effect (SBE) to use "'emphatic projection' to participate in the feelings and ideas of our authors" (395). The SBE technique works well with a free-style manual, a custom-designed manual, because a free-style manual can be flexible and substantive. However, the SBE is effective only in a situation where the participants are coequal and respect each other. Under those conditions, the editor helps authors "grow" ideas by accepting and reinforcing a concept that will "grow and eventually bear fruit—the usable idea" (394).

Newsletters

591 Arth, Marvin, and Helen Ashmore. *The Newsletter Editor's Desk Book.* 3rd ed. Shawnee Mission: Parkway Press, 1984.

Because "all newsletters involve gathering stories, writing and editing, copying and distributing" (2), Arth and Ashmore explain how to prepare a newsletter from its inception to its distribution. The authors advise beginning newsletter editors to seek help from people within the editor's organization. "What about Maria, the lawyer, who just won the city award for best amateur at photography? Would she help shoot photos for publication? Or Sam, the treasurer—he's good at layout and pasteup—a natural (which many an editor is not)" (14). Training reporters, deciding between typeset or typewritten newsletters, and establishing lines of authority also are part of starting an organizational newsletter. Finding news is an ongoing task, once the newsletter starts. "Experienced editors of employee newsletters keep plenty of solid information coming at readers, and plenty of stories about the readers themselves" (36). In supplying information to readers, the editor "accentuates the positive and eliminates the negative" (38). "Yet the editor's basic function is to exercise subjective judgment—which, while it is educated opinion, is still opinion. The editor decides which stories to run and which to drop. Judgment. The editor decides which words, sentences and paragraphs stay in stories, and which go. Judgment. The editor knows that the journalistic ideal of complete objectivity is just that—an ideal" (41). To inform editorial judgment, the authors discuss how to gather news, with particular emphasis on interviewing, and how to write and edit stories. In promoting style books, the authors note that "having a stylebook means never having to say you're stymied by something stupidly small" (52). Because a newsletter's credibility is everything, editors should not necessarily avoid controversy. "Often, a controversy met head on, in print, with fair representation of all sides, can be honorably resolved. Ignoring criticism won't make it go away" (62). The authors devote chapter 5 to a discussion of writing headlines; chapter 6 to newsletter format, including instructions on type styles, copyfitting, and dummying; and chapter 7 to newsletter distribution, with particular attention to mailing the newsletter. The authors include appendices on style, headlines, formula stories, contracts, editing marks, and typesetting specs.

592 Beach, M. *Editing Your Newsletter*. Portland: Coast to Coast Books, 1980.

Editing Your Newsletter is written for the novice newsletter editor, so Beach explains how to produce a newsletter from the beginning point of setting goals to the ending point of mailing the newsletter. Beach recommends that beginning editors develop a goal statement because it helps them define their job and helps the organization know how to support the editor. Although the editor is responsible for preparing the newsletter, he or she will need to rely on others, generally volunteer labor to produce the newsletter. Training volunteers is therefore the editor's job, including training people how to gather news using interviewing skills. To evaluate writing the editor can use one guideline: "no sentence longer than fifteen words; no paragraph longer than five sentences; no article longer than five paragraphs" (16). Technically, the editor makes decisions about how the newsletter looks—how to determine whether it should be typeset (a 10-point list of how to find and work with a typesetter is included) or typed using word processing; how to create a masthead and nameplate; how to make headlines (using handlettering, words cut from other publications, transfer letters, or a typesetter or headline making machine); how to write and place heads; how to use graphics (think in thirds), including pictures (how to make a halftone, how to crop a picture, how to make a photomechanical transfer [PMT]); how to layout the newsletter to achieve balance, contrast, unity, and proportion (again, think in thirds); how to scale copy using the diagonal line, scaling wheel, or scaling ratio methods; how to build a light table; and how to print the newsletter (mimeograph, photocopy, or offset?), "the mimeo says, 'We do it ourselves,' the offset, 'We can afford to pay for printing.' Photocopied newsletters usually fall somewhere in between" (62); how to maintain a mailing list to distribute the newsletter.

593 Downing, Vincent F. "Newsletter Editor Save Yourself." *Medical Communications* 4, no. 1 (1975): 19-22.

"[A] newsletter is designed to retain members, not lose them" (19-20), so a newsletter editor's attitude "might include: credibility, caution, humility, and positivism" (19). For instance, humility can be encapsulated in the dictum, "he edits best who edits least" (19). To save him or herself from failure, the newsletter editor also will need to make decisions about newsletter production (including issues related to typography, illustrations, and layout), distribution, and finances. Concerning finances, Downing notes that the editor should know how much money is available to produce the newsletter and not exceed the budget to produce the newsletter. However, "cheap printing is no bargain" (21).

594 *How to Produce Newsletters: Newsletter Editor's Handbook*. Washington: Association for Educational Communications and Technology, 1979. ED 220 073.

Designed for editors who produce newsletters for voluntary organizations, *How to Produce Newsletters* recommends that an organization develop a mission statement that "will act as a kind of constitution, providing a permanent set of guidelines that can be consulted from time to time for clarification about the purpose and scope of the newsletter" (2). In fulfilling the mission statement, the editor will want to prepare a newsletter "that is lively, interesting, timely, and—above all—informative for all members" (7). To gather information, the editor can consult an organization's calendar of events and develop a plan for the newsletter's content. The editor can call upon people in the organization to write articles, but the editor should give specific instructions about the length and scope of an article. However, "people are more willing to cooperate if all they have to do is provide information, rather than write articles" (10). When editors edit a writer's prose, they should rewrite a selection "to fit the space and content requirements of the particular issue" (14), but in editing they should not change the facts, even though they may change the style. Editors also will be involved in the production and distribution of the newsletter. To produce newsletters, editors must decide which form of printing to use. If editors decide to typeset the newsletter, they should comparison shop for a printer. If an editor wants "a distinctive, goodlooking newsletter, have a graphic designer create a format" (22) for the newsletter. Instructions on how to state specifications for typeset format include the caution that "the same type made by different companies varies somewhat" (23), so the editor needs a format to make decisions efficiently. The production process—proofreading, dummying, pasting-up, and printing—also are discussed. To distribute the newsletter, the editor must make decisions about how to label the newsletter and what method of postage to use (indicia, meter, stamps). How to evaluate the newsletter using a readership survey is also discussed. Although editors should act on what they learn from a readership survey, they must not be too sensitive to the wishes of their readers. "Don't be afraid to take a stand," editors are told. "One of the purposes of a newsletter is to stimulate new ideas, and you can't do that by printing news that is mundane, lackluster, and insipid" (33).

595 Howe, Cynthia R. "Editing a Club Newsletter: Constraints and Freedoms." *The Serials Librarian* 1, no. 3 (1977): 273-79.

Having edited *The Green Rage*, a Sierra Club newsletter, on a volunteer basis, Howe discusses the pros and cons of her experience. On the con side, she says that the turnover rate of volunteers can be high. She realized that she could develop staff stability by fostering a sense of loyalty to the publication. That loyalty would include respect for her as the newsletter editor. She also recognized that the editor must tread a careful path when asking volunteers for help and must be prepared to "do his/her own part in keeping informed on issues, gathering information, and seeing that the operation is running smoothly" (274). In assessing the amount of work needed to produce the newsletter, Howe decided that editorial staff members would not have time to write articles. However, that decision meant that editors would spend more time editing articles by authors with a variety of writing skills. Because of funding problems, *The Green Rage* was issued bi-monthly instead of monthly, which caused the calendar of events and announcements about pending legislation on environmental issues to be outdated at times. However, on the pro side, Howe says, "the freedom and informality of editing a club newsletter more than made up for the frustrations" (276). And although she believes a full-time photographer and "space and enthusiasm for an active editorial and Letters to the Editor column" (277), would have improved the newsletter, Howe is satisfied with the improvements she and her staff made to make *The Green Rage* a more professional publication. Of lessons learned, she says that when the club members are motivated and have adequate resources to produce a newsletter, the newsletter editor's job can be rewarding.

596 Hutchinson, Michelle I. "Newsletter Know-How." In *Proceedings 35th International Technical Communication Conference,* CD-3—CD-4. Washington: Society for Technical Communication, 1988.

In explaining how the Toronto Chapter of the Society for Technical Communication received two awards for its newsletter, Hutchinson says the keys to success are newsletter design and content. For instance, good newsletter design has "high visual appeal" (CD-3) that can be achieved through the use of color, type, and layout. In addition, content must be balanced among news about the chapter, news about members, and information in useful articles. The content should also be proofread by "a top-notch proofreader" (CD-4). However, the editor should review articles for transitions between paragraphs, proper usage, and appropriate length. Hutchinson advises editors, "don't get caught writing all the articles yourself—that's not an editor's responsibility" (CD-4). The editor should recruit articles by announcing at monthly meetings the topics for upcoming issues and approaching members who might be encouraged to write an article for the newsletter.

597 Nanfria, Linda. *How to Publish an Organizational Newsletter.* Sacramento: Creative Book Company, 1976.

"The how to's in this brochure," Nanfria writes of her book, "are geared to a very low-cost newsletter, roughly $50 per issue, depending on the number of copies printed and excluding the cost of postage" (4). She points out ways to cut costs by using services of local organizations, for instance by using a local community college's print shop. Beginning newsletter editors are told from whom to solicit information for the newsletter and advised to "stay in close touch with the person who is mainly responsible" (8) for arranging the functions that need to be covered by the organization's newsletter. In fact, "it is up to you as editor," Nanfria notes, "to decide what you can or cannot include in your publication, based on the needs and interests of the [organization's] members" (12). To present the information editors choose to print, Nanfria recommends using news writing and feature writing styles and adding art that interests readers. She explains layout and pasteup procedures and suggests the use of special type to create "a more professional and more visually pleasing page" (21). A newsletters should be designed so that when it is mailed "Page One will be seen by everybody who handles it, and especially by the person who receives it" (23).

598 Nye, Marjorie M. "Producing a Student Chapter Newsletter People Want to Read." In *Proceedings 34th International Technical Communication Conference,* WE-156—WE-158. Washington: Society for Technical Communication, 1987.

Nye divides newsletter content into three categories: The Basics, The Frills, and The Fillers. The Basics include student chapter news and letters to the editor. The Frills are features, for example, articles on professional development or profiles of "faculty members, industry professional, STC officers, alumni, interesting students, interns, and corporations" (WE-157). The Fillers are items that attract readers, so the editor should select fillers, including graphics, that will encourage readers to read the entire newsletter. Nye advises editors to search constantly for individuals who can contribute graphics. The editor should also ask people to contribute articles to the newsletter. To solicit articles the editor "must be part diplomat, part salesperson, and part parent" (WE-157). Nye lists five general tips for soliciting articles and six tips for soliciting articles for student newsletters, including the advice to solicit articles early in the school year and to use alumni who can write articles or who can be interviewed by a reporter.

599 Potvin, Janet H. "Eight Steps to Better Newsletters." *IEEE Transactions on Professional Communication* PC-25, no. 4 (1982): 204-10.

"A high quality newsletter is produced by setting high standards for content, writing quality, style, and design; by maintaining them, and by consistently publishing on time" (210). Potvin explains an eight-step process for producing a quality newsletter beginning with an inventory of the existing newsletter. She also provides a list of possible contents for a newsletter. Decisions about cost and production alternatives come next. For instance, the editor will need to decide whether to typeset or typewrite the newsletter. Paper size, number of issues per year, and number of pages per issue are also cost considerations. After publication goals and an editorial philosophy are codified, the editor must outline the content for a year's issues and establish the deadline for each issue. Then the editor must fill each issue. Although estimates suggest that the editor "will have to generate approximately 50 percent of the copy for each issue" (207), the editor can recruit contributing editors to provide feature articles or fill regular columns as one method for providing copy for the newsletter. The editor also should ensure that the newsletter has a distinctive image, so that type, graphics, and white space entice readers to read the newsletter. In short, "a good design should not call undue attention to itself" (209), but should attract readers to the newsletter's content. Editing newsletter articles includes writing headlines and proofreading the issue once it is set in type. In proofreading, the editor should pay particular attention "to names and affiliations and to numbers: statistics, addresses, telephone numbers, and dates" (210). Although the process of editing is not difficult, "it requires planning, organization, coordination, and attention to detail" (210).

600 Wales, LaRae H. *A Practical Guide to Newsletter Editing and Design: Instructions for Printing by Mimeograph or Offset for the Inexperienced Editor.* Ames: Iowa State University Press, 1976.

Wales advises the newsletter editor to "be sure your duties and responsibilities are clearly understood by the officers and members of your group" (7). To fulfill those duties, the editor will need to understand the process of producing a newsletter. Thus Wales explains newsletter formats, including nameplates and mastheads; finances ("Seeking enough advertising to support each issue takes a lot of time and should not be done by the editor" [17]); typography; copyfitting; and headlines ("There are two major kinds of headlines (also called heads): label and sentence. . . . Reserve label headlines for your column headings. Use sentence headlines to introduce the contents of news stories" [22]). One chapter (5) is devoted to explaining the pros and cons of producing a newsletter by mimeograph and one chapter (6) to the offset method. Of the offset method, Wales tells editors, "your main production tasks for offset printing (other than typing or typesetting) are preparing the layout, keylining and pasting up" (35). A chapter on the use of photographs describes the Rule of Threes technique for taking pictures and includes instruction on captions ("Give your reader information; don't just describe what he or she can easily see" [40]), and instructions on screening, cropping, and scaling a photograph. About the overall design of a newsletter, Wales notes that "simplicity is the key" (44). Simplicity includes the use of white space ("Many editors forget that white space is just as important—and in some cases, more important—than a piece of artwork or a story" [44]), bold headlines, boxes, and illustrations (line or continuous-tone). "One good design technique is to repeat a piece of artwork—or a part of it—throughout the newsletter at appropriate points" (50). Wales emphasizes that good design and good content both take equal forethought when the editor plans a newsletter.

601 Weyand, Jerry. "Publishing an Internal Newsletter without a Full-Time Staff." In *Proceedings 34th International Technical Communication Conference, WE-108—WE-110. Washington: Society for Technical Communication, 1987.*

As an editor for an internal newsletter for computer end users, Weyand developed a newsletter that "has centered around seven essential elements: Content, Contribution, Consistency, Commitment, Criticism, Change, and Cost" (WE-108). Content has four major components: "purpose, scope, style, and accuracy" (WE-108). About accuracy, Weyand remarks that editors risk loosing readers' trust if a publication does not print accurate information. Weyand characterizes contributors as good writers (columnists and frequent contributors) and poor writers (occasional submitters and those who prepare developmental projects). Weyand advises editors to help the poorer writers by encouraging them to get editorial help from their organizations. Because every issue of a newsletter competes with previous issues, consistency means "quality of the appearance and content, and on-time distribution" (WE-109). One aspect of commitment is allowing contributors to express themselves and giving them credit so that they are committed to the newsletter. Handling criticism, however, is the editor's job, and the editor can encourage criticism by conducting reader surveys. Change is one result of criticism and Weyand notes, "if your newsletter does not grow—it may reach a point where it no longer serves its purpose" (WE-109). An editor also should determine newsletter costs by maintaining an itemized list of costs. That list will help the editor pinpoint expenses that can be reduced or eliminated.

Newspapers

602 *The Active Newsroom: IPI Manual on Techniques of News-Editing, Sub-Editing and Photo Editing.* Zurich: International Press Institute, 1961.

The *IPI Manual*, designed for Asian journalists, provides instruction on editing and designing a newspaper by focusing on the active editor, the editor who provides leadership for reporters. For instance, editors should train reporters to follow-up on stories so that "no reasonable question in a reader's mind should be left unanswered" (11). The editor can assist reporters in interviewing people by giving reporters "an idea of the importance of the person being interviewed" (20). When editing a reporter's copy, the sub-editor should "approach copy with a critical mind. Let him distrust figures. Let him insist on proper identification of people reported. Let him know the laws of libel" (26). Because "the public has no memory" (28), the sub-editor must provide a context for a news story. The sub-editor also should create effective headlines and rewrite copy so that the first sentence of a story explains the news in the story. Thus, sub-editors "learn not to be afraid of writing things as they would say them, in everyday direct language" (41). Typography, design, page makeup, and cropping pictures are also discussed.

603 Andrews, Sir Linton. *Problems of an Editor: A Study in Newspaper Trends*. London: Oxford University Press, 1962.

Problems of an Editor begins and ends with a question: "How should a newspaper editor edit?" (vii). (See also page 177.) Between the two questions are answers about how an editor ought to treat the staff, how an editor ought to relate to newspaper owners, and how an editor ought to view libel, among other topics. Andrews emphasizes the need for the editor to train reporters and to explain the role of newspapers in society. The author, a veteran of 37 years of newspaper editing, focuses on editing in his homeland, England.

604 Baskette, Floyd K., and Jack K. Sissors. *The Art of Editing*. 2nd ed. New York: Macmillan Co., 1977.

In 18 chapters and 3 appendices, the authors discuss the newspaper editor's job, including writing headlines, editing pictures, and deleting libelous statements from copy. They also address computer editing, but they affirm that "the copyeditor has talents that cannot be replaced by computers. . . . editing demands many intangibles—judgment, scholarliness, background, memory, aggressiveness, motivation, curiosity, imagination, discretion, cynicism, skepticism, and even some genius" (3). Good editing, however, begins with "the effort to help readers identify themselves with the news" (8) and progresses with "the endeavor to assure accuracy both in fact and in language" (12). In chapter 3 the authors describe types of editors and the technologies of receiving and transmitting the news. The authors preface their advice on how to edit copy (chapter 7) by noting, "copyeditors have no business changing a writer's style" (92). In chapter 17, editing the magazine section of the Sunday paper, the authors note, "newspaper techniques differ from magazine techniques" (373) and "unless an editor is also an artist he cannot hope to produce a superior [magazine] publication" (376). Appendix 2 is devoted to proofreading, particularly the guideline and book systems.

605 Bogart, Leo. "Editorial Ideals, Editorial Illusions." *Journal of Communication* 29, no. 2 (1979): 11-21.

Two surveys conducted in 1977, one of editors and one of the general public, show that "what [editors] think is good in a newspaper is in most cases not too wildly different from what they think readers like" (16). But readers may not like what editors think readers like. For instance, editors run entertainment features to draw readership; yet readers tended to rate informational pieces higher than entertainment selections. "A majority (59 percent) of the public would choose a paper devoted to news rather than one which just provided a news summary and consisted of entertaining features" (19). Bogart concludes that editors should be shaping public taste by using professional standards to choose a newspaper's content. If they do not follow those standards, editors subscribe to public taste as the basis for selecting a paper's content. See also 608.

606 Boyer, John H. "How Editors View Objectivity." *Journalism Quarterly* 58 (1981): 24-28.

Based on data from a 26-statement questionnaire on objectivity in news reporting completed by 50 editors, Boyer classifies three types of editors, Type I, II, and III. Type I editors believe that although objectivity is possible, it is not possible "in the conventional no-opinion mode" (25). Type II editors believe that objectivity is not possible. Type III editors believe that objectivity is only possible when facts are presented without any bias. Boyer cites two demographic variables—years the editor had served in his or her current job and size of newspaper the editor worked for—as salient features of the data. Boyer concludes, "considering the differences, especially between Types I and III, and Type II, it is remarkable that editors tend to express themselves much the same, i.e., in terms of balance, fairness and service to readers" (28).

607 Buser, Paul J. "Neither Stooges nor Wide-Eyed Radicals." *The Quill* 57 (1969): 24-26.

College student-newspaper editors have the responsibility to print materials that openly report what happens on campus, even if such reporting entails using obscenity. College student-newspaper editors desire to "confront traditional standards by reporting exactly what IS happening and presenting true reflections of society today" (26). The role of activist may entail other duties, such as speaking "at rallies, coffee houses, and community service clubs" (25) to interpret campus activities. The college student-newspaper editor's role is one with the professional journalist's role as defined by Hal Bruno of *Newsweek*: "'a politics of confrontation and journalism of involvement'" (24).

608 "Editors Tend to Agree on What Readers Want." *Editor and Publisher,* May 7, 1977, 9-10.

The results of a survey of 1,300 editors suggest, among other things, that newspaper "editors have a high degree of confidence in readers. What editors think is good in a newspaper is in most cases not too different from what they think readers like" (9). However, newspaper readership has declined because television has changed the way people look at the news. Because of television, readers consider journalism as a form of entertainment. Newspaper editors can adjust to the television's influence on journalism by preparing news that people want rather than preparing news that the editor thinks people should know. To attract readers, "'editors should learn to think visually'" and "think color" (10). See also 605.

609 Evans, George P. "Good Copyediting is Knowing Your ABC's." *The School Press Review* 51, no. 6 (1976): 1, 4, 10, 12, 15-16.

Accuracy, brevity, and clarity are the ABC's of copyediting. Unfortunately, copyeditors, the persons responsible for ensuring newspapers adhere to the ABC's, are "unsung heroes" and, thus, not the envy of student newspaper personnel. Yet, good copyeditors are indispensable if a newspaper is to be professional because copyeditors attend to details. "Nothing is too big or too small when it comes to editing copy!" (4). A copyeditor knows the fundamentals of language, follows a style book line by line, and guards against libel. Evans provides examples of student newspapers that needed copyediting.

610 Garst, Robert E., and Theodore M. Bernstein. *Headlines and Deadlines: A Manual for Copy Editors.* 3rd ed. New York: Columbia University Press, 1961.

The word *Manual* in the subtitle describes *Headlines and Deadlines* well. The book is a step-by-step approach to the job of newspaper copyediting, starting with an overview of newspaper organization (chapter 1). Next, the authors discuss the place of the copyeditor in that organization (chapter 2). ("The careful copy editor leaves nothing to chance. His object is not only to correct errors, but also to improve [copy]" [26].) Then, the authors review word usage, spelling, punctuation, and grammar. They emphasize writing leads and editing copy by giving incorrect examples that are corrected (chapter 3). They review copyediting marks (chapter 4) and provide an alphabetical list of abused words with examples of proper usage (chapter 5). The headline is the topic for the remainder of the book (chapters 6-11).

611 Holder, Dennis. "Challenging an Editor's Right to Reassign." *Washington Journalism Review,* April 1981, 10-11.

In suing the *Detroit Free Press,* a reporter claimed that her contract was violated when she was reassigned to a position that did not allow her to write for television, her speciality. The executive editor of the *Detroit Free Press* believes that editors cannot be restricted in their authority to determine what topics will be covered and who will cover a topic.

612 Jordan, Lewis. *News: How It Is Written and Edited.* New York: The New York Times, 1960.

Newspaper "editors have three basic tasks. They direct the work of reporters. They prepare news stories for publication. They decide how these stories shall be presented in the paper" (43). In performing those tasks, the editor's goal is to produce a good paper. To produce a good paper, editors also must copyedit reporters' prose, including checking for spelling errors, deleting libelous remarks, and creating headlines. In making corrections, editors must use a variety of sources—almanacs and atlases, for example—but the best source "is a good fund of general and special information in the copy editor's own head. One way to build up that fund is by close, daily reading of the newspaper he works for" (45). In writing heads the copyeditor focuses on the specific rather than the general. Also "normal English is better than headlinese" (46). About typography and illustrations, Jordan says, "artistically, make-up can have a good or a bad effect on the reader. . . . Consciously or not, he will be affected by the presence or the absence of balance and attractiveness" (50).

613 Joseph, Ted. "Reporters' and Editors' Preferences Toward Reporter Decision Making." *Journalism Quarterly* 59 (1982): 219-22, 248.

In reporting the results of two questionnaires sent to 900 national newspapers, Joseph notes that reporters preferred more reporter participation in management decision making than editors preferred. "Female editors, however, . . . might accept a more democratic environment" (222). Joseph also found that the smaller the newspaper the more reporter autonomy and that larger newspaper reporters want "substantially more participation than is allowed" (248).

614 Murray, J. Edward. "Editing Artists: The Men Around the Rim." *The Quill* 53 (1964): 12-15.

Because newspaper copyediting is an art, "no managing editor or news editor or copy desk chief can tell a copy editor exactly how to do a good job on each specific piece of copy" (12). However, the managing editor can motivate copyeditors by (1) establishing good morale in the news room, (2) selecting a good desk chief, (3) stressing the need for professionalism so that the copyeditor believes his or her job is vital to the newspaper, (4) providing opportunity for professional growth (for example, more formal education and specialization in one type of news), (5) encouraging the copyeditor to love the language by protecting it from deterioration, and (6) paying, praising, and recognizing good copyediting. One way to recognize good copyediting "is to condemn bad work and praise good work between editions" (15).

615 Murray, J. Edward. "The Editor's Right to Decide." *The Quill* 58 (1970): 16-18.

"[A]ny effort, by court action or otherwise, to dictate to the editor is both unconstitutional and ridiculously impractical" (18). If editors are not performing professionally, the answer to insuring fairness in newspaper reporting includes "vigorous criticism of the editor and his decisions. . . . both inside and outside the profession" (18).

616 Phifer, Gregg, and Thomas R. King. "Censoring ('Editing') the Comics." *Journalism Quarterly* 63 (1986): 174-77.

Walker Lundy, editor of the Tallahassee *Democrat*, did not publish comic strips that he considered offensive, if the strip fit one of five criteria, all of which promoted the belief that women are inferior to men. The comic most commonly excised was "Beetle Bailey." Of the readers who responded to Lundy's decision about eliminating certain strips, "67 opposed Lundy's action and 19 favored [it]" (175). Women tended to support Lundy's decision, but men tended to oppose it. Those who supported Lundy believed that he understood the problem and was doing a good job as an editor of dealing with the problem. Opponents had a variety of arguments, but frequently cited the problem of censorship. Since any comic strip could offend someone, where does the editor draw the line when deciding which comic strips to excise? The publisher of the *Democrat* said, "'probably the most sacred of all newspaper comment . . . is the comic page. Readers may be offended by the front page, outraged by the editorial page, or dismayed by the sports page—but their real fury emerges only when you tamper with the . . . comics" (177).

617 Randall, Starr D. "Effect of Electronic Editing on Error Rate of Newspaper." *Journalism Quarterly* 56 (1979): 161-65.

In a study of the Charlotte (North Carolina) *Observer*, Randall compared three types of copy: copy written before automation of the newspaper, copy written during an interim period, "marked by the use of computer-assisted typesetting," and copy written when the paper was fully automated. He concluded, "a newspaper—at least this particular newspaper—using a fully integrated electronic editing system does have fewer errors in spelling, punctuation, sentence construction, hyphenation and typography than a newspaper not using electronic editing" (163). Those results suggest that editors and publishers should not be unduly concerned about implementing complete electronic automation of the newspaper office. See also 618.

618 Randall, Starr D. "How Editing and Typesetting Technology Affects Typographical Error Rate." *Journalism Quarterly* 63 (1986): 763-70.

In an extension of a previous study (617), Randall compared error rates in three newspapers that converted from one technology to another technology. The study demonstrated that "the number of errors in spelling, punctuation, sentence construction, hyphenation and topography . . . is affected by the kind of typesetting and editing technology in use by a newspaper, specifically that the error rate will be highest with optical character recognition (OCR) technology, followed in descending order by perforator, hot-metal and video display terminal (VDT) technology" (763). Although editorial time was not a variable in the study, Randall notes that editing will take more time when the editor edits using a VDT, because, in addition to performing all the standard editorial functions, the editor will take on the additional job of proofreading copy.

619 Rowan, Carl T. "If I Were a Suburban Editor." *The Quill* 57 (1969): 12-15.

Because "the suburbs are to a great measure a product of white racism" (13), if Rowan were a suburban editor, he would begin "the process of disabusing suburban readers of the notion that somehow they can be an island unto themselves, forever untouched by the rats, the filth, the hunger, the hostility that exists in so much abundance within the inner cities of America" (12). He would publish facts about injustice, like the fact "that a black college graduate earns $13 more a year than does a white high school graduate" (13). And he would try to foster a sense of hope by showing that whenever integration is given a chance to work, it works "beautifully and in a heart-warming way" (15).

620 Solomon, William S. "From Craftspeople to Production Workers: Video Display Terminals and the Devaluation of Newspaper Copy Editing Work." *Communication* 8 (1985): 207-24.

The advent of the use of video display terminals in newspaper work has changed the traditional copyeditor's function from editing copy and writing headlines to coding copy and fulfilling a variety of newsroom jobs in preparation for a promotion away from the copy desk.

Management's view of the copy desk also has been influential in changing the nature of copyediting. "Management perceives copy *editing* work as being different from copy *desk* work" (215). Copyediting is just one of the many copy desk tasks. In addition, the use of the video display terminal (VDT) at the copy desk has made the copy desk a training ground for a variety of newspaper tasks. The VDT enables the user to learn design and layout techniques, for instance, and become proficient in a particular task. Solomon concludes that management has made the copy desk a place where people can be trained for specific jobs in the newspaper, but in doing that management has devalued copyediting.

Package Inserts

621 Benson, Harriet. "The Physician's Package Insert: An Editor's Perspective." *Medical Communications* 10, no. 2 (1982): 49-53.

Preparing a package insert, the final printed labeling for an FDA-approved drug, "can be a thankless, unrewarding assignment" (51) for an editor because the process of creating a package insert includes "numerous drafts, [and] meetings to resolve conflicting interests" which result in a final version with "barely a sentence to call you own" (51). However a package insert can be a valuable marketing and advertising tool, and it also is a legal document for product liability cases. To prepare an insert the editor should prepare a draft of the package insert during the initial stages of research development and work with scientists throughout the product's development to create an insert that can be "an excellent information resource for the physician" (53).

Patents

622 "Editing from the Patent Standpoint." In *Technical Editing*, edited by B. H. Weil, 51-61. Westport: Greenwood Press, 1975.

A published article that is based on a potential patent must be edited so that it does not have an adverse impact on the patent claim. The published article (or any other published literature associated with the patent claim) must not precede the patent application by more than one year or the application will be invalid according to U.S. patent law. So the editor needs to determine whether the date of publishing a proposed publication will conflict with the time frame for filing a patent. When editing articles related to the patent application, editors must not allow an article's claim to minimize the larger patent claims. Because patents must pass utility, novelty, and operability tests, the editor should request that the scientific author delete any comments comparing the results of the patentable item with previous results of other similar items. "Facts are facts, but the way in which they are presented has real meaning in editing from the patent standpoint. Such editing is no game, played between inventor and patent examiner, but is instead a serious effort aimed at approving the release of publications that protect the property rights involved" (61).

Presentations

623 Kamelgarn, Marilyn B. "How Does a Presentation Editor Help Clients Communicate?" In *Proceedings 31st International Technical Communication Conference,* VC-50—VC-52. Washington: Society for Technical Communication, 1984.

A presentation editor works with an author and an artist to prepare an oral presentation with graphics. After a working conference in which author, editor, and artist organize the presentation, the editor and artist storyboard the presentation. Storyboarding is useful because each visual can be moved easily and new visuals can be added easily. Once the author completes a final draft, he or she schedules a "dry run" of the presentation before an invited audience, including the editor. The editor critiques the presentation to correct visuals and to coach the author on platform skills.

Press Releases

624 Aulenbach, Betty. "Editors Tell What Bugs Them about Press Releases." *Advertising and Sales Promotion,* March 1969, 41-46.

In a survey of 238 business publication editors, 164 editors responded to questions about press releases, saying, for the most part, that too many poor quality press releases are sent to the wrong publications. In fact, most press releases that are sent to a publication are not used. "Of 152 respondents, 41 estimated they used 10% of releases received. An additional 24 said they found only 5% useful. Another 16 used less than 5%. The balance of 71 editors used over 10%. Of these, all but 20 used 30% or less" (41). Editors tended to see incomplete releases, poor reproduction quality, and the use of cheesecake as negate factors in news releases. Most editorial complaints, however, were divided into two categories: writing content and writing quality. One editor noted that releases should be short. The essential facts should be presented first. Poor photographic quality and outdated mailing lists were other complaints. One editor noted that "at least 10% of his mail is addressed to an editor who left 13 years ago" (45).

625 Bixler, Gordon H. "Editing Technical News Releases." In *Technical Editing,* edited by B. H. Weil, 133-51. Westport: Greenwood Press, 1975.

Because many news releases "use long sentences, noun writing, and words that mean nothing" (149), an editor should rewrite news releases "to serve his own readers better" (134). In fact, "by rewriting, an editor performs his greatest service" (134). When Bixler speaks of rewriting, he is referring to amplifying the news release so that it becomes a story for a magazine. Thus, "one part of technical editing . . . is rewriting to bring in supplemental information" (147). Bixler provides examples of rewritten news releases.

626 Shapiro, Sydney F. "An Editor's Viewpoint on Preparing News Releases." In *Directions in Technical Writing and Communication,* edited by Jay R. Gould, 88-95. Farmingdale: Baywood Publishing, 1977.

Speaking from the editor's viewpoint, Shapiro states that a a writer of news releases should know what interests a magazine's editor and readers, how to prepare a news release with useful information, and how to submit a news release that the editor can use easily. For instance, a news release must have a message because editors select releases that convey needed information to readers. Shapiro cautions writers, "don't try to put something over on editors" (91). When submitting a release, authors should "provide both a short title (2-3 words) and a suggested caption (8-10 words) which abstracts the release" (89), and regardless of the length of the news release, the writer should use concrete, specific language. Authors also should remember that "the easier a release is to edit, the more likely that it will be used—and the more likely that the proper facts will be included" (92). Authors may want to follow-up releases by telephoning an editor, a method which, if not overused, can help the news release be accepted. Photographs should be included with releases, but should not be used as substitutes for essential information that should be included in the news release. The quality of a photograph will determine whether or not it is used. Shapiro recommends not submitting photographs with "girlie shots." In fact, "a safe procedure, if you must use girls or men in your photos *for political reasons,* is to keep them to one side so that the editor can crop them out without ruining the product view" (93). Authors should mail releases "to editors by name and title" (95). Thus updated mailing lists, though costly, are worthwhile.

Proceedings

627 Harman, Eleanor. "Publishing the Proceedings." In *The University as Publisher,* edited by Eleanor Harman, 103-07. Toronto: University of Toronto Press, 1961.

Publication plans for the papers in a proceedings should begin when participants are asked to present papers at a congress. Participants should be given instructions about the type, length, and format of papers; the date papers are due for publication; limitations regarding graphics; and what languages are required for the papers and abstracts. Proceedings can be printed using offset or letterpress, but material prepared for offset printing "cannot, of course, receive much technical editing" (105). Letterpress printing requires "galley proofs, page proofs, and revised proofs" (105) so editors are needed to ensure that the quality of the proceedings is uniform. Reprints, regardless of the printing method, must be considered and sales of the proceedings should include consideration of foreign markets and the need for subsidization by the congress of the proceedings.

628 Johnson, Abby A. "From Transcript to Minutes: An Editorial Challenge." *Technical Communication* 31, no. 2 (1984): 20-23.

Preparing the minutes or proceedings from a transcript of oral presentations is "a task of translation" (20) because the editor's goal is to create a written record from spoken language, and spoken language is different from written language in significant ways. For instance, the editor will encounter "idiomatic expressions, typographical errors, and grammatical errors" (21) that may be difficult to translate into clear and logical prose. To cope with those expressions and errors, the editor can follow a three-step procedure: identify the task, delete inappropriate material, and emphasize key points. Johnson explains each step of the procedure, emphasizing the need for the editor to maintain a speaker's idiom. Proceedings/minutes "need not contain the obviously colloquial, such as 'we did a few sneaky things,' or 'this perked up our ears'" (23). Proceedings should include contractions and personal pronouns, which are typical of informal speech. However, the editor should not "function as a type of ghost playwright, fashioning characters through the refashioning of words... [because] the ideas belong to the speakers, no matter how inarticulate some might seem" (23).

629 Manten, A. A. *Symposia and Symposium Publications: A Guide for Organizers, Lecturers, and Editors of Scientific Meetings*. New York: American Elsevier Publishing Company, Inc., 1976.

"The editors of many symposium proceedings have never edited anything before and belong to the mass of scientists who have no concept of publishing beyond a desire to see manuscripts multiplied in print. This inevitably has its effects on the average quality of the final product, thus indirectly illustrating the value of thorough refereeing, the resoluteness of a scientific journal editor and the silent but indispensable efforts of journal copy editors" (19). Thus, Manten devotes chapter 9 to a discussion of the editor's role in collecting and preparing symposium papers for publication. At the outset of planning a symposium, editors should ensure that authors are informed of deadlines for manuscript submission so that submissions can be refereed and edited. Manten notes, "the editor would do well to publicly reserve the right to edit the content of manuscripts, with the aid of refereeing reports, himself, if the author does not submit his revisions in time [for publication]" (107). Ideally, manuscripts should be submitted three months before the symposium so that refereeing can be completed before the symposium. Then authors revise papers once based on referees' and symposium participants' comments. Manten also discusses CODEN, CIP, ISBN, and ISSN identification systems because these systems help "to establish networks of communication between publisher of scientific and technical information, international organisations, libraries, and secondary information services" (111). He recommends that the editor include a subject index in symposium proceedings and gives three examples of how subject indexes might be arranged.

Proposals

630 Rohne, Carl F. "Editing the Small Study Proposal." In *Proceedings 20th International Technical Communications Conference*, 97-99. Washington: Society for Technical Communication, 1973. (Also published in *Technical Editing: Principles and Practices,* edited by Lola M. Zook, 77-81. Anthology Series, no. 4. Washington: Society for Technical Communication, 1975. ED 173 807.)

The technical editor should manage the production of the small study proposal by using innovative methods of creating the proposal and by organizing a staff to produce the proposal. The editor sets the tone for the proposal by reading the proposal at various stages of its development and asking questions, especially about the proposal's technical section. However, Rohne advises editors to focus on consistency of the technical content and not to tamper with authors' style. The editor also directs the preparation of the final product's appearance by following the Request for Proposal. The editor is responsible for making sure appropriate resumes are prepared because resumes are a critical part of the proposal, especially proposals prepared by new companies. The professional activities section is an essential part of the resume because it provides details about a person's professional development, especially a person's technical skills and experiences that relate to the project under proposal. Rohne suggests using a checklist to prepare a proposal because a checklist "sequences necessary steps, assigns responsibilities, and provides daily visual status" (99).

631 Tracey, J. R. "Managing-Editing a STOP Proposal—The Technical Editor as Bookbuilder." In *Proceedings 21st International Technical Communications Conference,* 157-64. Washington: Society for Technical Communication, 1974.

"STOP stands for Sequential Thematic Organization of Proposals" (157). Under the STOP concept, the editor manages the development of a proposal so that the proposal group produces a unified book instead of a collection of essays. The editor begins the unification process by helping the proposal team develop an outline from the Request for Proposal. The editor then uses storyboards to prepare topics generated by the proposal outline. The storyboards, which contain a thesis sentence and ideas for supporting paragraphs and graphics, are reviewed by the proposal team during the proposal's preparation. Because the topics are reviewed by the proposal group, the editor's duties "in this new managing-editing role are to direct the discussion, critique the manner of presentation, annotate the Storyboards with the discussion results, stimulate brainstorming when needed and record its results, copy the Storyboards for management, and update the outline. Most important, he becomes a bookbuilder as well as an editor" (159). The editor also troubleshoots and edits the proposal. As a troubleshooter, the editor works with the author to revise a topic; the editor "does not work in a vacuum" (160). The editor also posts the critique of an author's topic along with the topic itself for the entire team to review. In essence, the editor practices cadre management, "leadership by the group" (161), which is necessary because a STOP proposal is a group effort; no one person has the skills necessary to produce an effective STOP proposal. The STOP technique also benefits publication of a proposal because the editor can gauge how much copy will be written each day and allot production workloads throughout the available time. However, the editor has to produce daily schedules for each phase of the proposal if he or she wants copy produced daily. The editor also must maintain a STOP proposal outline which enables him or her to control the location of each page of the proposal.

632 Vaughn, David E. "A Logical Approach to Editing Proposals, Reports, and Manuals." In *Proceedings 21st International Technical Communications Conference,* 18-25. Washington: Society for Technical Communication, 1974. (Also published in *Technical Editing: Principles and Practices,* edited by Lola M. Zook, 20-27.

Anthology Series, no. 4. Washington: Society for Technical Communication, 1975. ED 173 807.)

Editors can enjoy editorial work—even unscheduled, rush jobs—if they seek to balance speed against accuracy and quality. Although each editor will develop a personal system of editing, the editing process must be logical and must anticipate outcomes. To control those outcomes, the editor balances speed, accuracy, and quality. For example, editors can estimate how much time will be necessary to achieve a certain level of accuracy and quality by determining how long an editor will take to prepare a manuscript; "50 pages and 8 hours represents a reasonable day's work for one editor, assuming a difficult manuscript" (21). When applying editorial time constraints to proposals and manuals that are rush jobs, the editor should do what must be done first; then do whatever else can be done, if time permits. After editing a proposal, the editor should take time to review the introduction and summary, two critical parts of a proposal. Introductions to each section of the proposal also are critical "because they often carry the most powerful part of the message for the entire section" (23). Careful editing of a manual "helps achieve greater technical accuracy and shortens production schedules" (24). However, the key to manual writing and editing is the outline, which should be developed early in the project.

Reports

633 Cheney, Patrick, and David Schleicher. "Redesigning Technical Reports: A Rhetorical Editing Method." *Journal of Technical Writing and Communication* 14, no. 4 (1984): 317-37.

In rhetorical editing, the editor's purpose is to "make sure the report says the right things in the right way" (336). The rhetorical editing method is composed of five major steps: "identify the audience and purpose of the report; analyze the ideas in the draft report; synthesize the ideas into a well-focused revision; interview the author; and finish the report" (318-19). The bulk of the method is devoted to the analysis of an author's manuscripts leading to a ghostwritten revision. That analysis includes developing an array of ideas in the author's manuscript. Then the editor selects from the array those ideas that will satisfy the report's purpose and audience, imposing "order on the unstructured ideas of the array" (324). In discussing the ghostwritten revision with the author, the editor may realize that the ghostwritten report is essentially the same as the author's draft. If that's the case, the editor has authenticated the author's purpose and outline. If, however, the editor believes the author should revise the ghostwritten report, the editor can ask the author to use the ghostwritten report—"filling in blanks, answering your [the editor's] questions, and correcting inaccurate ghostwritten statements" (335)—to develop another draft. To illustrate their method, Cheney and Schleicher provide examples from an environmental impact report.

634 Ivens, J. Loreena. "Editing the Technology Assessment Report—Headache and Challenge." In *Proceedings 24th International Technical Communication Conference,* 244-48. Washington: Society for Technical Communication, 1977.

A technology assessment report is a "multidisciplinary and interdisciplinary study . . . [that considers how] technology might develop in the future and how it might affect or be affected by various relevant elements of society" (244). Because such a report is sizeable, decision makers need a condensed version that is "readable, visually interesting, and easily usable" (244). Ivens describes how she helped organize a condensed report on hail suppression by solving three editorial problems. In particular, she found out that italic subheadings beside the text allowed readers to determine easily the content of each section of the 400-page report. The subheads also were an indication of the quality of a section's organization. Subheads that could not be written easily indicated that a section needed to be rewritten.

635 Stephens, Irlene R., and P. M. Reyling. "Editing Technical Reports." In *Technical Editing,* edited by B. H. Weil, 19-30. Westport: Greenwood Press, 1975.

Although the duties of an editor of technical reports vary depending on the size of an organization, the purpose of editing remains constant: to ensure that reports are accurate and readable. To achieve this purpose, editors must develop good relationships with authors; the experienced editor will try to sell improvements to authors rather than tell authors to accept such improvements. Editors must maintain standards, preferably by using a style manual prepared by the editor's company. However, an editor must edit judiciously because "it is not the function of the editor to rephrase the report in his own literary style" (24). Rather, the editor primarily is seeking technical accuracy. When editorial supervisors are included in an organization's publishing hierarchy, they must have extensive knowledge of graphic arts and production procedures because they will coordinate efforts with graphic-arts and reproduction personnel.

Teaching Materials

636 Xin, Anting. "On the Principles of Editing and Preparing Teaching Materials." *Chinese Education* 16, nos. 2-3 (1983): 161-82.

Writers and editors of materials for elementary school children should learn how students think and should know how to write and edit materials that will promote the class struggle. Xin notes, "whatever the teachers and editors do not understand cannot be lucidly understood by other people" (172), so editors must "mix with the masses" (172) to understand how people live and then to translate that knowledge into lessons that will teach children "nature and social knowledge" (173). In analyzing numerous examples of educational materials for students, Xin says that one major purpose of the materials is to educate children about the virtues of communism. For example, in elementary textbooks, "the main ideological approach was to foster the concept of physical labor. . . . and a hatred for bloodsucking oppressors who reap without making any efforts" (163). In another text, an example of the wealth of four Chinese families "deepened hatred for those opposed to the revolution" (176). "Textbook editors," Xin notes, "must attend to simplifying and highlighting the crucial facts so that the lesson is orderly and uncomplicated" (178).

Translations

637 Smith, Julian F., and T. E. R. Singer. "Editing Translations." In *Technical Editing,* edited by B. H. Weil, 251-56. Westport: Greenwood Press, 1975.

"Fundamental requirements of a good translation include careful attention to shades of meaning; accurate rendering of technical terms into correct equivalents; appropriate use of trade terms or the jargon of the art concerned; and correct, appropriate use of abbreviations and symbols" (251). Editors commonly find that by comparison, translations from French require less editing than translations from German. However, in all instances, "when lucidity clashes with technical accuracy or the intended degree of precision, lucidity loses. No matter how strong the temptation to clarify, the original turbidity is to be retained" (254). If an editor believes that obscurity is not intended, he or she should correct the text or add a note explaining the problem. As a translating principle, Smith and Singer recommend translating using idea units instead of word units because excessive attention to individual words is a common problem that accounts for many poor translations.

Author Index

The numbers in this index refer to entry numbers, not page numbers, in the bibliography.

Abbott, Thomas E.: 442
Abend, Jules: 549
Abinder, Paul: 463
Abshire, Gary M.: 1, 243
Adams, Tom: 2
Ainsworth, Richard A.: 462
Allen, Arly: 244
Allen, Penelope: 406
Altman, Lawrence K.: 245
Altman, Philip L.: 246
Amberson, Janis I.: 337
Amsden, Dorothy C.: 247, 248
Anderson, Elliott: 550
Andrews, Sir Linton: 603
Angell, Marcia: 249
Annett, Clarence H.: 250
Applewhite, Lottie B.: 251, 252
Armstrong, J. S.: 487
Arnold, Edmund: 3
Aronson, Milton H.: 253, 254
Arth, Marvin: 591
Ashmore, Helen: 592
Atkins, Eldred E.: 255
Atlas, Marshall A.: 582
Aulenbach, Betty: 624

Avi-yonah, M.: 488
Axelby, George S.: 489

Bagby, Susan: 4
Bain, Anne Lee: 490
Baker, Carole F.: 256
Baker, John F.: 5
Balaban, Miriam: 257
Balfour, Bernice: 464
Barclay, William R.: 491
Barnett, Dick: 551
Barnow, Renee K.: 258
Barry, Brian: 492
Barzun, Jacques: 6
Baskette, Floyd K.: 604
Batchelder, Susan K.: 583
Baulkwill, W. J.: 259
Beach, M.: 592
Beeson, Paul B.: 493
Bell, J. G.: 7
Benedek, Elissa P.: 494
Beneduce, Ann: 465
Bennett, John B.: 260
Benson, Harriet: 621
Berg, A. S.: 8

Berkow, Robert: 584
Bernstein, Theodore M.: 610
Bessie, Simon M.: 9
Bestor, Dorothy: 10
Bishop, Claude T.: 495
Bixler, Gordon H.: 625
Black, Theodore W.: 552
Bland, William F.: 553
Blatchford, Shirley M.: 261
Bliss, Allen D.: 496
Blue, William F., Jr.: 147
Bogart, Leo: 605
Bold, Harold C.: 262
Bond, Sandra J.: 217
Boomhower, E. H.: 263
Boots, Sharon: 273
Boro, Emily S.: 264
Borysewicz, Mary L.: 265, 497
Bostian, Lloyd R.: 11
Boston, Bruce O..: 12
Boyer, John H.: 606
Braceland, Francis J.: 498, 499
Brady, Thomas B.: 485
Brass, Alister: 466
Brennan, Kevin: 415
Brett, Carlton E.: 13
Bridgewater, William: 14
Briggs, Nelson A.: 15
Brilliant, Alan: 16
Broadbent, Margaret: 17, 266, 267, 500
Broadhead, Glenn J.: 18, 19
Broer, Jan W.: 20, 268
Brogan, John A.: 269
Brogan, Marianne: 21
Bronson, Judith G.: 270, 271, 272, 273
Brookes, Martha H.: 22
Brooks, Cleanth: 501
Brooks, Paul: 23
Brouns, Virginia L.: 24
Brown, David H.: 25
Brown, Gillian F.: 322, 344, 345
Bryant, Mavis: 26

Bryson, Sheryl R.: 274
Buehler, Mary F.: 27, 28, 228, 275, 276, 277, 278, 279, 280, 281
Buelow, Bernard J.: 585
Burkhart, Sue: 282
Burr, William: 283
Burroughs, William: 81
Burton, Lydia: 29
Buser, Paul J.: 607
Bush, Don: 30, 31, 32, 284, 285
Butcher, Judith: 33

Cameron, Leslie A.: 308
Cantwell, Michael: 286
Carbrey, Edward J.: 287
Carruth, Hayden: 35
Carter, Edward P.: 36
Cederborg, Gibson A.: 288
Chadbourne, Bill N.: 554
Chapline, J. D.: 289
Chapman, Victor W.: 290
Charney, Patricia F.: 37
Cheney, Patrick: 633
Chepeleff, Val: 348
Chigier, Norman: 502
Chu, Ellen M.: 406
Clark, B. F.: 291
Clark, Nancy: 292
Clements, Wallace: 293, 294
Cochran, Wendell: 38, 295
Cocks, Gary T.: 296
Coggshall, Gordon: 297
Cohen, Jonathan: 338, 377
Coin, Maxine D.: 298
Colby, Jean P.: 467
Collins, David N.: 299
Commins, Dorothy: 39
Commins, Saxe: 40, 41
Corbett, William: 42
Cord, Marian S.: 43, 300
Core, George: 44
Corliss, John O.: 503
Cortelyou, Ethaline: 301, 302
Cox, Alberta L.: 45, 46, 303, 304

Cox, Barbara G.: 305, 306
Cox, Stephen: 26, 47
Cragg, Catherine: 29
Crandall, Rick: 504
Crichton, Jennifer: 48
Culberson, Dan: 1, 49, 243
Czarnecki, Barbara: 29

Dan, Bruce B.: 307
Dancik, Bruce P.: 308
Daroff, Robert B.: 505
Davin, Dan: 50
Davis, Edwina B.: 264, 586
Day, Robert A.: 309
De Quattro, James: 310
De Voto, Bernard: 555
Dean, W. M.: 313
DeBakey, Lois: 311, 312, 506
Delamater, Martha: 51, 141
Dellon, Hope: 468
Deming, Lynn H.: 314
DeVivo, Anita: 52
Di Battista, Michael A.: 53
Dolin, Arnold: 77, 174
Downing, Vincent F.: 593
Dukes, Eva P.: 54, 55, 56, 314, 315, 316

Eastwood, S.: 317
Eastwood, Susan: 318, 319, 320, 321
Eastwood-Berry, Susan: 322
Edmonds, Paul: 57
Edsall, John T.: 58
Elfenbein, Julien: 557
Ellis, Rachael: 59
Ennis, Bernice: 323
Epstein, Edmund L.: 469
Evans, George P.: 609
Evans, Nancy: 60

Fargis, Paul: 61
Farkas, David K.: 62, 63, 64
Farkas, Nettie: 64

Farrar, John: 65, 66, 67
Fearing, Bertie E.: 507
Feinberg, R.: 323
Feiner, Arthur H.: 508
Fenner, Peter: 295
Fensch, Thomas C.: 68
Ferber, Ellen: 74
Ferguson, Rowena: 558
Field, Leslie: 69
Fischer, John: 70
Fletcher, Marjorie: 71
Foehringer, Stephen B.: 587
Fogelberg, Paul: 324
Forscher, Bernard K.: 170, 325, 326, 327
Freed, Richard C.: 18, 19
French, Burr J.: 328
Fritz, John F.: 329
Frost, David: 330, 331, 415
Frost, Donna D.: 585
Fruge, August: 72, 73
Fuccillo, Domenic A., Jr.: 332
Fulton, Len: 74

Galassi, Jonathan: 75
Gardener, Christina: 76
Garfield, Eugene: 333, 509, 510
Garst, Robert E.: 610
Garstka, Katharine: 334
Garvey, William D.: 335
Geiser, Elizabeth A.: 77
Genin, Michael S.: 78, 336
Giamatti, A. Bartlett: 79
Gibbs, Wolcott: 80
Gilbert, John: 374
Gilbert, John R.: 337
Gildenberg, Philip L.: 338
Ginsberg, Allen: 81
Girodias, Maurice: 81
Glasstetter, Susan R.: 146
Glen, H. W.: 339
Glen, John W.: 511
Glenn, George A.: 559
Glidewell, John C.: 512

Goffstein, M. B.: 82
Golbitz, Pat: 83
Golley, Frank B.: 340
Goodman, William B.: 84
Gould, Jay: 341
Grant, Jane: 85
Grauerholz, James: 81
Griffin, George D.: 86
Griggs, Tim: 342
Gross, Alan G.: 343
Gross, Gerald: 87, 88
Grossblatt, Norman: 344, 345
Grotstein, James S.: 513
Grove, Laurel K.: 24

Hageman, Mary S.: 346
Halliday, Roy: 484
Hallinan, Edward J.: 89
Halpenny, Francess G.: 90, 91, 92, 93
Halpern, Salmon R.: 323
Hanson, J. J.: 560
Hargreaves, Thomas G.: 561
Hargrove, Eugene C.: 514
Harkins, Craig: 347
Harman, Eleanor: 94, 95, 96, 97, 98, 627
Harmon, Susan P.: 327
Harrington, J. Y.: 588
Harris, Michael: 348
Harter, Helen: 470
Hartley, Herbert L.: 99, 349
Hartwell, David G.: 471
Hasch, Jean: 350
Haughness, Norman: 351
Hawley, G. G.: 352
Hayes, John R.: 217
Hays, Robert: 100
Heatley, Kenneth R.: 101
Heffner, Maxine: 102
Henderson, Arnold C.: 353
Henderson, Bill: 103
Hewitt, William F.: 354
Hill, Iris T.: 104

Hill, Mary: 295
Hills, L. Rust: 105
Hmnnn, H. O.: 106
Hobel, Marlene A.: 355
Hoge, James O.: 515
Holder, Dennis: 611
Holder, Laurel N.: 107
Holmes, Olive: 108
Holmes, Patricia C.: 356
Horne, David: 109
Howard, William J.: 110
Howe, Cynthia R.: 595
Howe, M. Rita: 357
Howe, Susan: 42, 111
Huibregtse, Edward J.: 516
Hutchinson, Michelle I.: 600
Huth, Edward J.: 358

Isay, Jane: 112
Isenberg, Artur: 359
Ivens, J. Loreena: 634

Jacobi, Peter: 562
James, Rowena G.: 113
Janik, Carol J.: 217
Jarman, Brian: 114, 115
Jarrett, Beverly: 116
Jeanneret, Marsh: 117
Jesse, Andreas: 360
Johnson, Abby A.: 628
Johnson, Margaret N.: 361
Jones, B. A.: 300, 301
Jordan, Lewis: 612
Jordan, Stello: 461
Joseph, Ted: 613
Judd, Karen: 118

Kador, John: 119
Kamelgarn, Marilyn B.: 623
Kantrowitz, Michael B.: 362, 363
Kasher, Asa: 120
Kass, Jerry: 364
Katzel, Jeanine: 563
Katzenberger, Paul: 365

Kaye, Myra: 366
Kefauver, Weldon: 93, 472
Keller, Mark: 367, 517
Kelley, Patrick M.: 346, 368, 369, 370
Kelly, Kate: 402
Kendall, Bonnie L.: 371
Kewer, Eleanor D.: 93
King, Thomas R.: 616
Kobak, James B.: 564
Koski, Raymond J.: 121
Krevitt, Beth I.: 518
Kruse, Benedict: 565
Kubeck, James E.: 122, 215

Ladman, A. J.: 265
Landis, James: 123
Landreman, Dolores M.: 372
Lane, John C.: 566
Lane, Michael: 124
Laner, Frances J.: 373
Last, John M.: 374
Layton, Edward: 375
Leavitt, William D.: 125
Lee, Marshall: 473
Lehr, Dolores: 376
Leibrandt, Thomas L.: 377
Levreault, E. P.: 378
Lindberg, Helen A.: 126, 379
Lippke, James A.: 567
Lish, Gordon: 127
Littledale, Harold: 568
Litz, A. W.: 128
Lockwood, Willard A.: 129
Losano, Wayne A.: 380
Lufkin, James M.: 381
Lutz, Jean A.: 130
Lynes, Russell: 131
Lytel, Allan: 382

Maggiore, James G.: 135
Malcolm, Andrew: 136
Mancini, Jay: 530
Mann, Charles: 519

Mann, Gerald A.: 121, 137
Mann, Jim: 569, 570
Mann, Michele H.: 138
Manten, A. A.: 629
Marcus, Judith H.: 139, 390
Marek, Richard: 231
Markland, Murray F.: 140
Martinsson, Anders: 391, 392, 393
Marx, Joanna M.: 394
Masse, Roger E.: 141, 395
Mathes, J. C.: 142
Matheson, Harlan: 412
Maule, Harry E.: 143
Mayes, Herbert R.: 573
Mazzatenta, Ernest: 396
McCabe, Edward: 571
McCafferty, James W.: 383
McCall, Mary A.: 384
McCarron, William E.: 385
McCartney, James L.: 386
McCormack, Thomas: 474
McCormick, Barbara S.: 387
McCormick, Ken: 132
McEldowney, Dennis: 133
McGhee, Patricia L.: 388
McGough, David L.: 389
McManus, Majorie: 572
McNaughton, Harry H.: 134
Meckel, Susan R.: 397
Mento, Mary A.: 459
Meyers, Manny: 398
Miles, Samuel A.: 589
Miller, Melanie: 244
Minick, Phyllis: 520
Mitchell, Burroughs: 144, 145
Mitchell, Constance: 399
Monagle, E. B.: 400
Montgomery, Tracy T.: 146
Moore, Charles B.: 147
Moossy, John: 521, 522
Moossy, Yvonne R.: 521
Morgan, Peter: 401, 523
Morris, Ann: 402
Mount, Robert L.: 148

Mullins, Carolyn J.: 149
Mundy, Della: 403
Murray, J. Edward: 614, 615
Murray, Robert G. E.: 524
Myers, Barbara Y.: 314, 404

Nanfria, Linda: 597
Nelson, Robert C.: 253, 254
Nelson, Roy P.: 150
Nestor, Margaret B.: 151
Newman, Julliana: 405
Nin, Anais: 152
Nisbet, J. D.: 525
Nisley, Rebecca: 406
Nowell-Smith, Simon.: 154
Nye, Marjorie M.: 598

Oates, Joyce C.: 526
O'Connor, Maeve: 155, 407, 408, 475
O'Neill, Carol L.: 156
O'Neill, Stephen: 107
Orenberg, Cynthia L.: 409
Osborn, Kelley: 409
Osborne, Harold F.: 157, 158
Oskam, Bob: 159
O'Sullivan, Maureen: 377
Otto, Gilbert: 410
Owens, Jean L. Owens: 290

Paine, Sonia Kuryliw: 29
Parker, Mel: 476
Parsons, Paul F.: 160
Pascal, Naomi B.: 161, 162, 215
Paxson, William C.: 163
Pedwell, Susan: 29
Perkins, Maxwell: 164
Perkins, Maxwell E.: 165
Peter, John: 574
Petersen, Judy: 166
Peterson, Dart G., Jr.: 411
Phifer, Gregg: 616
Philler, Henry: 412
Phillips, Iris Hosse: 29

Phillips, Karen F.: 331
Phillips, William: 167
Plotnik, Arthur: 168
Plung, Daniel L. D.: 347
Plung, Daniel L.: 146
Podhoretz, Norman: 169
Porter, J. R.: 527, 528
Portugal, Franklin H.: 170
Potvin, Janet H.: 599
Power, Ruth M.: 412
Poyen, Jeanne: 529
Prasad, Sudha Prasad: 314
Prashker, Betty A.: 171
Pratt, Marianna: 575
Purdy, Ken: 576
Putnam, Constance E.: 172

Rainey, Kenneth T.: 414
Randall, Starr D.: 617, 618
Raphael, Phyllis: 173
Rawson, Hugh: 174
Ray, David: 175
Reed, Ishmael: 176
Reimold, Cheryl: 177
Reitt, Barbara: 415
Reitt, Barbara B.: 291
Renkonen, K. O.: 416
Reuter, Madalynne: 178
Reyling, P. M.: 635
Reynolds, Helen: 417
Richardson, Marie: 179
Rigg, J. C.: 418
Roberts, William C.: 181
Rodman, Hyman: 530
Rogers, Geoffrey: 182
Rogers, Trumbull: 183
Rohne, Carl F.: 630
Romans, Morgan D.: 334
Rose, Richard: 531
Ross, Peter B.: 184
Ross-Larson, Bruce: 185
Rowan, Carl T.: 619
Ruas, Charles: 111
Rubin, Harriet: 186

Rude, Carolyn D.: 187
Ruder, Avima: 156
Rutledge, John: 490

Sale, Faith: 188
Santino, Charles: 189
Sass, Elynor: 335
Sauer, Kathleen H.: 397
Schleicher, David: 633
Schlosberg, Jeremy: 190
Schmid, Anne M.: 419, 420
Schmitt, Wayland W.: 93
Schoeck, R. J.: 93
Schoengold, Morris D.: 459
Schuster, M. L.: 191
Schwager, Edith: 421, 422
Schwartz, Laurens R.: 192
Scott, Denise: 423
Sears, Linda: 522
Sedgwick, Ellery: 193
Selle, Elaine B.: 532
Senders, John W.: 533
Serenkin, Harriet: 424
Shaefer, Patricia: 425
Shampo, Marc A.: 426
Shapiro, Sydney F.: 626
Shephard, David A. E.: 534
Sheppard, R. Z.: 194
Shimberg, H. Lee: 195
Shnitzler, Robert K.: 427
Shore, Joseph N.: 428
Sideris, George: 429
Sifton, Elisabeth: 477
Simon, Henry W.: 196
Simon, R. I.: 535
Simons, John L.: 430, 431
Simons, Rayanna: 197
Simpson, Amy: 432
Sims, R. L. "Buck": 433
Sims, R. L.: 370
Singer, Mark: 577
Singer, T. E. R.: 637
Sissors, Jack K.: 604
Skidmore, Bill: 198

Smith, Frank R.: 434, 536, 537, 538
Smith, Howard: 199, 435
Smith, Julian F.: 637
Smith, Patricia N.: 200
Smith, Peggy: 201, 202
Smith, Raymond J.: 526
Smith, Sanford R.: 148
Smith, Terry C.: 436
Smylie, Patricia O.: 203
Soderston, Candace: 204
Solla Price, Derek J. de: 437
Solomon, Carl: 81
Solomon, William S.: 620
Solotaroff, Ted: 205
Soltani, Poori: 539
Spalding, B. P.: 540
Spector, Leo: 563
Spectorsky, A. C.: 578
Spencer, John D.: 206
Squires, Bruce P.: 505
Stainton, Elsie M.: 207, 208, 209, 210, 211, 478
Stapleton, Paul: 438
Stearns, Laurie: 212
Stee, LeAnn M.: 426
Stefanile, Felix: 579
Stein, Sol: 213
Stephens, Irlene R.: 635
Stevens, George: 214
Stith, Mary E.: 215
Strauss, Harold: 216
Swaney, Joyce H.: 217
Swanson, Winfield: 307
Swee, Cathleen E.: 439

Tacker, Martha M.: 218, 440
Taft, Earl J.: 541, 542
Targ, William: 219
Taylor, Helen K.: 220
Thatcher, Sanford G.: 221
Thomas, Garth J.: 543
Thompson, Amy L.: 337
Thompson, Marilyn A.: 441

Thornton, John: 479
Thurber, James: 222, 223
Toland, Robert: 224
Tomlinson, Graham: 486
Topkis, Gladys S.: 77, 480, 481
Tracey, J. R.: 631
Tripp, Edward: 225
Tucker, Carll: 580
Tyson, Thomas H.: 442

University of Chicago Press: 227
Urbach, Kathy L.: 355, 443

Valderrama, Victor: 148
Van Buren, Robert: 228
Van Eps, Barbara J.: 483
Vanderlinden, Katharine: 29
Vaughan, Samuel S.: 229
Vaughn, David E.: 590, 632
Vest, Louise M.: 346
Viza, Dimitri: 544
Vocale, Mary L.: 230

Wade, James: 231
Wagner, Carl B.: 444
Waite, Robert G.: 293, 294
Wales, LaRae H.: 600
Wales, Ruth W.: 232
Wall, Tom: 445
Ward, James H.: 446
Weeks, Edward: 233
Weil, B. H.: 446, 459, 460
Weil, Benjamin: 448

Weiss, Bernard: 581
Werner, Yehudah L.: 449
West, James L. W., III: 515
Weyand, Jerry: 601
Whalen, Elizabeth: 450
Wheelock, John H.: 234
White, Jan V.: 235
White, Robert J.: 337
White, Stephen W.: 545
Wiley, Iris M.: 215
Wilhelm, John R.: 451
Williams, Frank O.: 236
Williams, Graham: 452
Williams, Miller: 237
Wilson, Peggy L.: 453
Witman, William D.: 238
Wollheim, Donald A.: 482
Wolper, R. S.: 546
Woodford, F. P.: 312
Woods, David: 547
Woods, Mary P.: 454
Wright, Christy N.: 337

Xin, Anting: 636

Young, Bruce: 239

Ziman, John M.: 548
Zimmerman, Muriel: 455
Zook, Lola M.: 240, 456, 457, 458
Zucker, Ernest: 241
Zuppan, Jo: 242

Subject Index

The numbers in this index refer to entry numbers, not page numbers, in the bibliography.

Abbreviations, 29, 34, 383, 427, 586, 637
Abstracting and indexing services, 394
Abstracting techniques, 260
Abstracts, 20, 260, 295, 394, 448, 458, 459, 475, 495, 506, 509, 543, 625, 626
Acknowledgements, 329, 337, 506
  of artists, 150
  of author's editors, 403
  of editorial assistance, 274, 320, 440
  of freelance editors, 218
  of peer reviewers, 366
  printing of, 96
Acquisitions, 7, 23, 286, 480
Advertising, 405, 408, 460, 506, 532, 557
Agents. See Literary agents.
Agricultural Engineering, editing of, 575
Alice James Poetry Cooperative, 71

American Journal of Psychiatry, history of, 499
American Psychological Association, editorial practices at, 52
Angels, 550
Annotated Bibliography on Technical Writing, Editing, Graphics, and Publishing 1966-1980, An, Introduction
Anthologies, 461
Apollonian and Dionysian traditions, 508
Auden, W. H., 39
Arrangement
  editing of, guidelines for, 187
  satisficing decisions about, 343
Art
  captions with, 150
  commissioning of, 182
  cropping of, 150
  humorous, selection of, 150
  impact of, 265
  professional vs. technical graffiti, 148

Art (continued)
  report, 78
Articles
  determining authors of, 308
  recruitment of, 596, 598, 599, 553
Artist-editor relationships. See Editor-artist relationships.
Aswell, Edward, 69
Atomic Energy Commission, 442
Auctions, 476
Audience, 20, 213, 238, 278, 283, 285, 289, 292, 310, 317, 349, 357, 375, 382, 383, 387, 429, 443, 466, 469, 477, 497, 505, 538, 539, 548, 550, 553, 562, 569, 573, 574, 578, 580, 588, 591, 597, 598, 599, 604, 605, 608, 625, 633
  comprehension of, 363
  editor advocate of, 234
  editor's awareness of, 162
  editor's identification with, 70
  editor's knowledge of, 200
  emotions of, 558
  identification of, 126
  injury to, 510
  lay, 381
  male chauvinism, offense of, 209
  misperceptions of, 353
  needs of, 373
  nonscientific, 261
  nonscientists as, 528
  for paperback books, 482
  for science fiction books, 471
  soliciting response from, 568
  split shift, 362
  and style, 304
  survey of, 547
  in technical communication, 253, 328
  trust of, 601
  types of, 126

Audience (continued)
  and usability testing, 432, 204
  volatility of, 205
  writer's questions about, 263
Australia, editing in, 452
Author-editor correspondence, 105
Author-editor relationships, 20, 54, 82, 194, 229, 309, 316, 305, 310, 316, 321, 322, 336, 339, 346, 357, 402, 404, 433, 443
Author-furnished copy. See Camera-ready copy.
Author's aids, 375
Author's alterations, 52
  advice against, 94
  percent of, 73
  reducing cost of, 59
Author's editors, 274, 305, 318, 345, 338, 377, 414, 435, 440, 520
  as activists, 251
  as advocates, 251
  as article editors, 330
  as book editors, 330
  definition of, 251
  donkeyism of, 271
  education of, 403
  as gatekeepers, 318
  goals of, 199
  as interpreters of graphics, 265
  for journals, 317
  for medical manuscripts, 271
  recognition of, 403
  responsibility of, 320
  roles of, 251
  survey of, 337
  as teachers, 251
  working conditions of, 403
Author's errors, 557
Author's sources, judging the reliability of, 354

Authors
- advice to, about editors, 192
- authority of, 165, 302, 336, 477
- and children's books, 467
- as careful writers, 505
- common failure of, 525
- communication with, editor's, 119
- as contract negotiators, 159
- cooperation scale of, 357
- as creators of formators, 268
- credibility of, 271
- criticism of, 503
- delinquency of, 548
- and dislike of writing, 475
- donkeyism of, 271
- editor's liking for, 70
- as editors, 177, 283, 295, 443
- editors' praise of, 208
- education of. See Editors, as teachers.
- ethical breeches by, 401
- evaluation of, 558
- expectations of by editors, 427
- and experience of being edited, 173
- experienced and inexperienced compared, 214
- explanations to, 586
- and fraud, 249
- guidelines for, 255
- Hispanics as, 446
- and illustrations, 434
- impatience of, 186
- and inadequate preparation of manuscripts, 180
- and influence of journal policy, 545
- injury to, 510
- instructions for, 113, 402, 475, 548, 586, 594, 626
- knowledge of publishing process, 545
- life of, 576

Authors (continued)
- and manuscript changes, 73
- manuscript responsibility of, 260
- mathematicians as, 541, 542
- mentoring of, 548
- minorities as, 545
- mistakes of, 339
- motivation of, 556
- nature of, 450
- as needing editor's help, 440
- negotiation of by editors, 169
- new, 75
- of news releases, 625
- nonnative as, 216, 391
- passive, 138
- physicians as, 323
- as potential referees, 495
- praise of by editors, 209
- and preparation of camera-ready graphics, 26
- procurement of by magazine editor, 105
- promotion and tenure of, 512
- publishing duties of, 71
- queries by to editors, 536
- queries to, 266
- rejection of, 175
- remuneration of, 548
- resistance of to editing, 422
- respect of by editors, 219
- rewriting by, 410
- of scientific works for television, 307
- scientists as, 381, 384
- style of, 557, 587, 604, 630, 635
- support for, 205
- technical, 206, 285, 289
- as technical experts, 283
- Third World, 438
- and time limits, 461
- tips for, 206
- training programs for, 430
- types of, 316, 398, 478, 601

Authors (continued)
  women as, 494, 540, 545
Authorship
  criteria for, 437
  ethics of, 308
  and rewriting by editor, 311
Autobiographies of editors, 23, 144, 219, 233, 573

Back issues, 532
Backlist, 481, 579
Behrman, S. N., 39, 41
Bergu, Thomas, 144
Bias, avoidance of, 29
Biblid codes, 475
Bibliographic citation, 29, 33, 227, 383, 401, 418, 534
Bibliographies, padded, 437
Bids, 532, 589
Biographies of editors, 8, 39, 85, 222, 223
Blads, 182
Blind review, 494
Blueline, Introduction
Blurbs, 475
Book producers, 61
Book reviewer's guidelines, 408
Book reviews, 449, 490, 495, 506, 515
Booklets, 462
Books, 66, 448, 463-82
  acknowledge page of, 6
  acquisition of, 194, 477, 481
  advertising of, 83
  audience of, 469
  and author's editors, 330
  British rights for, 174
  catalog copy for, 83
  children's, 465, 467
  classical, 33
  commercial vs. literary, 196
  conference proceedings as, 475
  cover design of, 83
  decline in quality of, 183, 194

Books (continued)
  design of, 174, 236
  East Asian, 108
  economics of, 219
  editing of, 408
  illustrated, 463
  indexes of, 59
  jacket copy of, 174, 182
  jacket of, 196
  law, 33
  marketing of, 6, 83, 174
  mathematics, 33
  medical, 466
  monographs, 475
  music, 33
  on music, 469
  ownership of, 209, 234
  paperback, 468, 476, 482
  preparation of, for printing, 482
  production of, 6, 59, 174, 182, 256
  professional, 481
  scholarly, 480
  scholarly design of, 236
  science, 33
  sources of, 473
  subsidiary rights of, 174
  symposium proceedings as, 475
  technical, production of, 352
  textbooks, 464, 470, 475, 480, 481, 636
  trade, 481
  trade paperbacks, 479
Brennan, Maeve, 144
Buber, Martin, 15, 346, 368, 369
Bureau of the Census Manual of Tabular Presentation, 281
Busch, Niven, 196
Business managers, as allies to editors, 109
Business practices, enmeshed with editorial activities, 167
By-lines, 147, 268, 290, 506

Subject Index

CBE Style Manual, Introduction, 358
CIP, 629
Cadre management, 631
Cameo Test Cases, of Thomas Wolfe's novels, 69
Camera-ready copy, 21, 162, 393, 500, 542
Canadianization, 29
Capitalization, 29, 34, 260, 383, 587, 588
Captions, 182, 295, 552, 554, 587, 600
Carson, Rachael, 23
Censorship, 81, 111, 132, 154, 234, 429, 517, 528, 616, 635
Charlotte (North Carolina) *Observer,* 617
Cheating, in scientific publishing, 245. See Ethics.
Cheesecake, 624
Chicago Manual of Style, The, 227
Chrysalis Review, 127
Churchill, Winston, 23
Citation analysis, 319
Citation indexes, 318, 510
Clarity, 279, 284, 325, 356, 428, 487
Co-authorship, 329, 337, 374, 403, 440
CODEN, 629
Contracts, 159, 162, 221, 408, 473, 480, 591
Costs
　editorial, 518
　influence on quality, 194
　newsletter, 599, 601
Collaboration
　between author and editor, 306, 402, 422
　between editor and illustrator, 434
　ghostwriting, as a type of, 132
　among researchers, 401

Collaboration (continued)
　among writers, 132
Collaborative writing, 565
Communication cluster, 20
Communism, 636
Company Editor, The, 147
Compendia, 460
Complex organizations, role of editors in, 63
Compositors, 59, 76, 93
Compound words. See Hyphens.
Compuscripts, 475
Computer-Based Education Lessons, 483
Computers, 168, 182, 183, 458, 518, 533, 584, 588. See also Video display terminals.
Conference proceedings, 408
Consistency, 30, 62
Copy, scaling of, 592
Copyediting, 83, 473, 475, 495, 506, 558, 589, 610, 612, 614. See also Editing.
　ABC's of, 609
　APA standards of, 52
　approaches to, 324
　benefits of, 44, 45
　of books, 33, 475
　checklist of, 33
　compared to substantive editing, 322
　costs of, 17, 44, 180, 183, 500
　decline in standards of, 319
　edicts of, 475
　in Finland, 324
　and freelancers, 118, 464
　guidelines for, 11
　importance of, 319
　management's view of, 620
　marks for, 475, 610
　quality in, 52
　by secretary, 260
　sensitivity in, 11
　of textbooks, 464

Copyediting (continued)
  time per page in, 518
  types of, 118
  workshop on, 267
  writing, distinct from, 118
Copyediting, 118
Copyeditors, 604, 620, 629
  checklist for, 266
  description of, 209
  duties of, 155, 147, 182, 267, 500
  hiring of, 523
  job of, at Naval Weapons Center, 45
  judgment of, 500
  motivation of, 614
  need for, 212
  overediting by, 180
  perfection of, 33
  professionalism of, 118, 614
  qualifications of, 14
  qualities of, 604
  remuneration of, 212, 614
  use of style sheets by, 182
  training of, 17, 475, 523
  and WYSIWYG printers, 244
Copyfitting, 147, 554, 558, 591, 600
Copyholder, 134
Copying equipment, 148
Copyright, 96, 168, 365, 408, 506, 519, 522, 532, 557. See also Permissions.
Copyright Clearance Center codes, 475
Core sentence, 14
Correspondence. See Letters.
Council of Biology Editors, history of, 246
Council of social science editors, need for, 386
Crash editing, 114, 115
Cropping. See Photographs, cropping of.

Current Contents, 510
Curtis, Tony 178
Customer and Service Information, 484
Cutlines. See Captions.

Davis, Dorothy, 144
Deadlines, 198, 200, 456, 559, 575, 599, 601, 629
Design, 147, 235, 236, 435, 452, 455, 473, 519, 557, 596, 599, 600, 602,
Designer-editor relationships. See Editor-designer relationships.
Detroit *Free Press,* 611
Developing countries, publication problems in, 539
Dialogic editing, 56, 433. See also Editorial dialogue.
Dictation machines in editing, 565
Dictionaries, 32, 473, 478
Dinesen, Isak, 39
Direct Marketing Copy, 485
Documentation, computer, 585, 587
Double Axe, The, 41
Doubleday, 178
Dover Books, 479
Dreiser, Theodore, 39, 40
Dummying, 554, 591, 594

East of Eden (Steinbeck), 68
Economics
  of journals, 286
  of newsletters, 593
  of producing books, 219
  in production process, 162
  of rewriting, 311
  and scientific publishing, 318
Edge of the Sea, The (Carson) 23
Editing
  approaches to, 322, 452
  aspects of, 326, 507, 557
  in Australia, 452

Editing (continued)
  of author's style, 195
  best when least noticed, 91
  bibliography of, Introduction, 230, 395
  in bilingual, bicultural contexts, 446
  and book design, 236
  of books. See Books.
  British and American practices of, 29
  as a calling, 562
  case study of, 139
  categories of, 232
  checklist for, 185
  choices in, 456
  clarity in, 279
  compared to writing and proofreading, 300, 385
  complexity of, 130, 426
  comprehensive, 24
  compromise in, 478, 456
  and computers, 604
  contextual, 142
  control in, 290
  controlled flexibility in, 275
  coordination, 276
  copy clarification in, 276
  core sentences in, 297
  for correctness and consistency, 214
  costs of, 21, 180, 228, 275, 589
  crash, 115
  creative, 100, 199
  creativity in, 429
  debugging technique, rapid, 100
  decline of, 194
  defensive, 439
  definition of, 1, 105, 232, 239, 276
  deliberate, 157
  of dental manuscripts, 371
  as a developing profession, 95
  dialogic approach to, 15

Editing (continued)
  diplomacy in, 351, 497
  and disagreement, 310
  distortion in, 547
  of East Asian publications, 108
  editing marks in, 591
  electronic, 617, 618
  empirical nature of, 573
  error list for, 400
  estimating time for, 115
  in Europe, 451
  fiat vs. fact, 4
  of fiction, 474
  of foreign language, 108, 228
  freelance. See Freelance editing.
  goal of, 243, 387
  goodness vs. quality, 28
  history of, 124
  humor in, 119, 131, 163, 242, 361, 367, 436, 379, 441
  of illustrations, 434
  instincts in, 70
  integrity in, 276
  as an international activity, 393
  intuition in, 469
  job satisfaction of, 458
  judgment in, 91, 552
  language, 7, 276
  levels of. See Levels of editing.
  light vs. heavy, 200
  line editing, 83
  linear model of, 72
  and literary criticism, 157
  macro-, 562
  making language choices, 280
  manager's responsibility for, 260
  managing of, 291
  of manuscripts, 250, 228, 230, 177, 105
  manuscripts, editor's loyalty to, 90
  marketing of, 356
  at Mayo Clinic, 327

Editing (continued)
   mechanical, 7, 24, 276
   and the media, 499
   medical, 298, 306
   method of, 4, 294
   micro-, 562
   minimal, 137
   misconceptions of, 224
   in multilingual contexts, 394
   in multinational environments, 451
   myths of, 172
   need for, 169
   in Nigeria, 342
   nonfiction, 231
   of nonnative writers' works, 195
   objectivity in, 143, 606
   as an organic process, 188
   of organizational publications, 147
   pays its way, 209
   perfectionism in, 95
   of posthumous works, 69
   practice of, 88
   practices exposed, 192
   pressures of, 5
   principles of, 25
   problem-solving techniques in, 313
   process of, 5, 179, 224, 230, 240, 260
   processes and techniques, 395
   production, 72, 452. See also Production editor.
   professional status of, 282
   quality, maintenance of, 269, 319
   rate of, 174
   for readability, 195
   reading protocols in, 238
   research on, 362, 363
   reserved for weekends, 233
   of reviews, 588

Editing (continued)
   rhetorical approach to, 187, 280, 633
   rigors of, 169
   rules of, 278
   of scholarly works, 112, 149
   scientific, 257, 261
   screening, 276
   selective, 107
   self-, method of, 190
   for sense and effect, 214
   sensibility in, 474
   skill and art in, 54
   skills of, 456
   slash marks in, 184
   state of, 207
   status of, 458
   strategy of, 285
   study of, 136, 217
   style, 290
   substantive, 7, 199, 276, 322, 376, 475
   as subversive, 535
   survey of, 452
   system of, 354
   technical and literary, 387
   techniques of, 388, 485
   technological impact on, 227
   textual, 154
   theory of, 88
   in the Third World, 342
   time for, 115, 198, 255, 518, 632
   to inform, not impress, 411
   types of, 51, 199, 214, 243, 484
   use of brackets in, 310
   usefulness of, 319
   value of, 356
   values in, 240
   workshops at General Motors, 396
   and writing, compared, 181, 186
Editing, General, 1-242
Editing, Technical, 243-458

Subject Index

Editing, Types of Publications, 459-637
Editor in chief, 171
Editor-advertiser relationships, 580
Editor-artist relationships, 299, 397, 412, 425, 445, 447, 463, 623
Editor-audience relationships, 580
Editor-author relationships, 1, 11, 66, 91, 107, 153, 168, 175, 187, 199, 209, 210, 233, 234, 237, 250, 260, 287, 294, 334, 351, 352, 368, 369, 379, 388, 395, 399, 401, 411, 422, 426, 427, 439, 441, 447, 450, 453, 456, 477, 478, 481, 503, 523, 549, 557, 558, 573, 575, 576, 583, 588, 590, 623
Editor-client relationships, 303, 323
Editor-designer relationships, 182, 235
Editor-freelancer relationships. See Freelance editing.
Editor-illustrator relationships, 292, 434
Editor-management relationships, 107, 109, 380, 447, 473
Editor-printer relationships, 350, 352, 532. See also Printers.
Editor-publisher relationships, 354, 569, 603. See also Publishers.
Editor-referee relationships, 517, 524, 506. See also Referees.
Editor-scholar relationships, 50
Editor-staff relationships, 556, 603
Editor-to-Author: The Letters of Maxwell E. Perkins, 165
Editorial assistants, 189, 495
Editorial bias, 535
Editorial boards/committees, 79, 225, 494, 495, 498, 522, 531, 545, 558, 575

Editorial candidates, testing of, 12, 101, 390
Editorial conferences/meetings with authors, 305, 306, 328, 330, 332, 336, 420, 511
Editorial dialogue, 51, 346, 368, 370
Editorial Eye, The, Introduction, 12
Editorial fallibility, 361
Editorial Forms: A Guide to Journal Management, 246
Editorial freedom, 577
Editorial opinion, 103
Editorial page, 354, 379, 401, 506, 557, 574
Editorial personnel, hiring and paying of, 556
Editorial policies, 22, 107, 146, 506
Editorial Problems Conference, 110
Editorial process, 77, 178
Editorial quality, 63
Editorial staff, supervision of, 559
Editorial survey, 125
Editorial tasks, chrestomathy of, 47
Editorial work logs, 148
Editors
  abilities of, 447
  acquisitions by, 47, 66, 83, 116, 286, 477, 481
  as advocates, 174, 234, 402, 534
  as amanuensis, 75
  as archaeologists, 82
  associate, 489, 492
  attitudes of, 230, 593
  authority of, 107, 422, 537, 573, 597, 611
  as authors, 131, 392
  bedside manner of, 426
  bonding with authors, 56
  as book marketers, 83

Editors (continued)
  of books, 229
  as bosses, 573
  as businessmen and gamblers, 220
  as businesspeople, 6
  as California holistics, 322
  as catalysts, 497
  categorized by printers, 244
  censorship by, 6
  certainty of, 294
  characteristics of, 172, 240, 470
  as checkers of authors' sources, 553
  as collaborators, 39, 75
  college-newspaper, 607
  as common man, 234
  compared to electronic text-processing tools, 135
  compared to publishers, 191
  compared to scientists, 289
  compared to technical writers, 289
  compromise as, 7, 11, 198
  compulsions of, 168
  as conciliators, 399
  as confessors, 75
  constructive, 383
  as consultants, 583
  content, 284
  contributing, 599
  as copyeditors, 288, 352, 376
  correspondence of. See Letters.
  cost-effectiveness of, 63, 317
  as creators, 268, 526
  criticism of, 615
  as critics, 352
  as data gathers, 148
  day-in-the-life of, 188
  and deadlines, 559
  as decision makers, 135, 431
  dedication of, 219
  as designers, 235, 236
  desk references for, 168

Editors (continued)
  dialectical position of, 513
  and dictation machines, 565
  as didactic escorts, 322
  as diplomats, 75, 598
  as double agents, 75
  as dress-rehearsal audience, 399
  duties of, 39, 66, 87, 178, 332, 458, 523, 524, 537, 548, 552, 604
  and editing philosophy, 538
  editorial committee, relationship to, 79
  egotistical vs. considerate, 51
  as epigraphers, 151
  ethical responsibilities of, 437, 495. See also Ethics.
  evaluation of referees, 521. See also Referees.
  as expert readers, 399
  fallibility of, 157
  finding a good one, 556
  flexibility of, 422
  as fortune tellers, 153
  and fraud, 249. See also Ethics.
  as freelancers, 122. See also Freelance editing.
  function of, 143, 387, 421
  future of, 121
  as generalists, 46
  and ghostwriting, 311. See also Ethics.
  guidelines for, 265
  hierarchy of, 473
  hiring of, 101, 172, 413, 458, 473
  house journal, 519
  human-relation skills of, 294
  independence of, 499
  indoctrination of, 130
  influence of, 234, 523
  in-house, 182
  instincts of, 569

Editors (continued)
- international organization of, 544
- interpersonal skills of, 240
- as interpreters of science, 528
- intuition of, 408, 474
- as investigators of fraud, 245, 506. See also Ethics.
- as Japanese gardeners, 70
- job description of, 241, 382, 413
- job of, 322
- job satisfaction of, 274, 458, 530
- of journals, 338
- as judges, 174, 502
- judgment of, 208, 294, 426, 517, 580, 591
- knowledge of, 408, 444
- as lawyers, 496
- length of journal editor's terms, 495
- and librarians, relationship with, 90
- use of library by, 168
- life of, 576
- as listeners, 116
- literary, 75, 263
- loyalty of, 519
- of magazines, 175
- as managers, 182, 174, 519
- as marketers, 174, 560, 564
- as mechanics, 208
- as mediators, 75, 280, 399, 497
- meeting with author, the first, 145
- menial labors of, 546
- as ministers, 496
- model of, 512
- motivation of, 556
- as motivators, 138
- need for, 135, 413
- as negotiators, 169
- nurses as, 557
- obligations to authors, 547
- obsessive-compulsive, 361

Editors (continued)
- as parents, 598
- as participants in design process, 182
- perils of, 144
- as physicians, 208, 496
- as pilot readers, 288
- of poetry, 579
- as politicians, 75
- portrait of, 87
- power of, 535
- prejudice of, 193
- primary function of, 213
- professional standards of, 344
- as promoters of scientific literature, 527
- as proofreaders, 376
- as protolectors, 151
- as psychiatrists, 75
- as publishers, 174, 348
- as publisher's representatives, 473
- publishing of unknown authors by, 501
- qualifications of, 239, 414
- qualities of, 8, 573
- as quality controllers, 449
- and querying of authors, 11. See also Letters.
- questionnaires of, 274, 530, 606, 613
- and readability, 373
- as readers' advocates, 11, 130, 247
- reading for, 133, 269
- relation to designer, 182
- relaxation of, 148
- remuneration of, 199, 274, 282
- replacement of, 495
- of reports, 259
- research of, 170
- as resource persons, 376
- responsibilities of, 132, 139, 320, 438, 491, 506, 558, 612

Editors (continued)
  and revenues, 560
  and review process. See
    Review process.
  as reviewers, 89
  revising traits of, 130
  roles of, 75, 175, 229, 395, 534, 607
  as salespersons, 556, 352, 598
  as samurais, 322
  schizophrenia of, 387
  and scholarly publishing, 77
  of scholarly works, 112
  science, associations for, 246
  of science fiction, 471
  of science manuscripts, 325
  scientific, qualifications of, 495
  as seekers of authors, 466
  selection of, 340
  selection of books, role in, 192
  as shapers of culture, 124
  shortage of, scientifically trained, 180
  as showmen, 573
  as slow readers, 116
  as specialists, 46
  sponsoring, 72
  staff loyalty, 595
  standards of, 361
  as standards bearers, 376
  status of, 523
  student, 101
  and stylists, 269, 288
  substantive, and partner printers, 244
  suburban, 619
  success of, 123
  as supervisors, 635
  survey of, 354, 608, 624, 605
  as tabula rasa, 399

Editors (continued)
  as teachers, 11, 13, 26, 64, 69, 138, 173, 208, 250, 260, 274, 291, 301, 306, 311, 320, 321, 376, 392, 393, 402, 410, 430, 440, 441, 443, 447, 496, 534
  as team members, 121, 447
  technical, 158, 263, 283
  technical knowledge of, 427
  technical vs. literary, 444
  and television, 307
  temperament of, 220
  as third basemen, 378
  as third-grade schoolteachers, 153
  training of, 101, 172, 284, 282, 453, 573
  traits of, 130
  types of, 256, 481, 606
  university, 225, 72, 50, 420, 422
  and usability testing, 432
  and visuals, 247
  weekly activities of, 233
  Western Electric, duties of, 36
  wisdom of, 573
  as witches, 153
  women as, 613
    work load of, 332
    working life of, 168
    workshops for, 354
    would-be, advice to, 191
    as writers, 151, 473
Editors' associations, 333, 408
Editors' Information Cards, 568
Editorship, of journals, 540
Education of an Editor, The (Mitchell), 144
Educational materials, for authors, 442
Effectiveness of publications, tests of, 570
Electronic publishing, 45, 135, 408
Elsevier Science Publishing Company, 286

Encyclopedias, 486
England, editing in, 603
Environmental impact reports, 633
Equations, 314, 383, 475
Errata, 506
Errors, 315, 399, 400, 473, 618. See also Typographical errors.
Esquire, 127
Ethics, 318, 408. See also Legal Issues, Libel, and Plagiarism.
  of authorship, 271, 308
  and breeches of confidence, 511
  of co-authorship, 374
  and confidentiality, 495
  and duplicate submissions, 495
  and editor's duty, 58, 366, 511
  and editorial power, 535
  and fraud, 245, 249, 495
  and multiple authorship, 495
  and publication of unethical experiments, 517
  and publishing decisions, 16
  and questionable experimental design, 506
  and referee's duty, 511
  of revision, 95
  of rewriting, 311, 312, 374
  and rules for conflict resolution, 278
  and scientific publishing, 245, 340, 437
  and scientific research, 366
  and truth claims, 486
  and types of auctorial breeches, 401
Europe, editing in, 451

FDA and advertising, 405
FDA, Bureau of Foods, editing at, 417
Fair use. See Copyright.
Faulkner, William, 39

Federal subsidies, 579
Federation of scientific editors, proposal for, 392
Feedforward, 20, 268
Festschriften, 490, 495
Fiction, 213, 214
Field Guide (Peterson), 23
Figures, 134, 266, 401, 448
First reader, 233
Fitzgerald, F. Scott, 8, 128, 165, 234
Foreign languages, 207
  Chinese (pinyin) conversion chart, 227
  diacritics, table of, 227
Formators, 20, 268
Fountain House, 85
Fraud. See Ethics, and fraud.
Freedom of speech. See Censorship.
Freelance editing, 10, 37, 44, 101, 118, 122, 156, 162, 182, 183, 192, 203, 215, 218, 270, 272, 273, 330, 415, 419, 549
Freelancers
  care of, 549
  clientele of, 331, 462
  credentials of, 331
  experience of, 424
  fees of, 122, 331, 462
  hiring of, 122
  locating of, 549
  remuneration of, 215, 424, 549
  starting as, 156
  supervision of, 215, 549
  survey of, 424
  training of, 122, 156, 215
  types of, 156, 462, 558
French in English contexts, 29
Friendly Candor, In (Weeks), 233
Frontier scientists, 366
Future Shock (Toffler), 121

GPO style manual. See *United States Government Printing Office Style Manual.*
Gad, 474
Galley proofs, 59, 435, 473, 496, 547, 553, 557, 626
Gathering Storm, The (Churchill), 23
General Motors, 396
Genesis West, 127
Ghost playwright, 628
Ghostwriting, 291, 403, 440, 633
Good Housekeeping, 573
Government documents, 226
Grammar, 12, 31, 207, 226, 260, 266, 314, 326, 473, 475, 478, 610, 628. See also Errors.
Grant, Jane, 85
Graphics, 43, 78, 247, 268, 353, 435, 557, 587, 598, 599, 626, 631
  charts, 26
  cropping of, 301
  editing of, 294
  editor advises author on, 260
  graphs, 26
  guidelines for editing of, 248
  in journals, 265
  maps, 26
  photographs, 26
  reductions of, 301
  tables, 258
  test of, 292
Gravure, 182, 463
Green Rage, The, editing of, 595
Guidelining, explanation of, 147
Gunning Fog Index, 487

Halftones, 182
Handbooks, 460
Handlettering, 592
Happy Profession, The (Sedgwick), 193
Harper's, 555

Harvard Magazine, 577
Harvard University, 69
Harvard University Press, 93
Hawthorne, Nathaniel, Centenary Edition of, 93
Headings, 432, 475, 587
Headlines, 3, 147, 552, 591, 599, 600, 602, 604, 610, 612
Heads. See Headlines.
Hemingway, Ernest, 8, 128, 165
Herbst, Josephine, 144
Hesse, Herman, 111
High tech/high touch, 369
Hispanic culture, 446
Houghton Library (Harvard), 69
House journal. See Journals, house.
Hurston, Zora Neale, 144
Hyphens, 29, 34, 102, 319

IBM Journal of Research and Development, 516
ISBN, 629
ISSN, 629
I-thou relationship, 15, 346, 370. See also Buber, Martin.
Idiomatic expressions, 325, 628
Illustrating Science: Standards for Publication, 246
Illustrations, 33, 46, 248, 261, 265, 294, 295, 301, 434, 455, 463, 593, 600, 612
Illustrators, 150, 292
IMRAD, 401
Indecent Pleasures (Targ), 219
Indexes, 33, 156, 207, 227, 432, 454
Indexing, 12, 260, 510, 584, 629
Information retrieval services, 509
In-house style manual. See Style guides, in-house.
Institute for Scientific Information, 509

Interviewing, 565, 591, 592, 598, 602, 633
Iran, library journal in, 539
Israel Exploration Journal, history of, 488

Jargon, 325, 339, 401, 411, 588, 637
Jeffers, Robinson, 41
Johannesen, Richard, 346
Jones, Jim, 144
Journalism, 555
Journalists, Asian, 602
Journals, 401, 416, 448, 449, 487-548
  advertising in, 495, 499, 506, 532
  and author's editor, 441
  basic science, 543
  book reviews in, 495
  citations in, 534
  conservatism of, 335, 359, 544
  costs of, 358, 392, 491, 518, 543
  editing of, 408
  editor's philosophy of, 496
  editorial policy of, 323
  editorials on ethics in, 308
  editors' associations for, 333
  electronic, 533
  format of, 475, 506, 509, 510, 529
  funding of, 532
  history, 540
  house, 519
  indexing of, 360, 495, 506, 529
  and instructions to authors, 17, 506
  international and interdisciplinary, 531
  management of, 286
  manual of operating procedures for, 495, 522
  mathematics, 541, 542
  mission of, 319

Journals (continued)
  organization of, types of, 489
  photographically reproduced, 541, 542
  purpose of, 506
  readability of, 487
  record-keeping forms for, 522
  review process for. See Refereeing.
  scientific, 311
  social science, 386
  special issues of, 495
  staff of, 489
  starting of, 408
  style guides for, 367
  as suppressors of scientific data, 359

Kent State University Press, 53
Key-Word-in-Context (KWIC), 454
Kill fees. See Freelancers, fees of.

Labor unions, 556
Lady Chatterley's Lover (Lawrence), 81
Language, regional-specific, 166
Lardner, Ring W., 165
Lawrence Livermore Laboratory, 293
Layout, 46, 200, 241, 319, 435, 452, 554, 593, 596, 597
Leading, 134, 455
Lectures, 207, 430, 478
Legal decisions, Doubleday vs. Tony Curtis, 178
Legal issues, 29. See also Ethics, Libel, and Plagiarism.
  of editor's communication with authors, 174
  of lost manuscripts, art, or photographs, 473
  of publishing misleading data, 338
Legibility of Print (Tinker), 281

Letterpress, 182, 558
Letters, 34, 48, 54, 174, 196, 216, 237, 401
  editing of, 154
  of inquiry by authors, 536. See also Queries.
  of John Farrar, 67
  between John Steinbeck and Pascal Covinci, 68
  of Maxwell Perkins, 234
  of receipt to authors, 521
  of rejection, 65, 309
  of Saxe Commins, 41
  to the editor, 497, 506, 557
Levels of Edit, The, 28
Levels of editing, 12, 21, 45, 115, 228, 275, 276, 290, 327, 354, 382, 414, 435, 440
Lewis, Sinclair, 39
Lexicography, 12
Libel, 58, 132, 168, 209, 220, 519, 557, 602, 603, 604, 609, 612
Librarians and journals, 506
Line editing, 60, 168
Line length, formula for, 147
Line width, 134
List-building, editorial role in, 109
Literary agents, 66, 124, 197, 473
Literary criticism, 469
Literature, American, nonwhite, 176
Lockridge, Ross, 23
Logic, 43, 326, 339
Look Homeward, Angel (Wolfe), 164

Machinery, publishing practices at, 552
Macmillan, 197
Magazines, 3, 147, 549-81
  advertising in, 561, 564, 570, 575
  alumni, 577
  business, 448

Magazines (continued)
  company, 561
  design of, 3, 182, 578
  economics of, 501, 577
  editor's role in, 105, 182
  editorial page, 574
  evaluation of, 569
  industrial, 567
  literary, 501
  little, 175, 558, 579
  pulp, 482
  rationale for, 564
  subsidies of, 555
  technical business, 553
  university, 501
Mailing lists, 532, 624, 625
Male chauvinism, 209
Managers, as definers of quality, 28
Managing editors, 614
Manuals, 448, 460, 452, 582-90, 632
Manuscripts
  acceptance of, 116, 111, 467
  acquisition of, 44, 145, 174, 221, 558, 105
  common faults of, 332
  costs of, 44, 92, 180, 350
  edited and unedited compared, 363
  ethics of rewriting, 99
  evaluation of, 79, 92, 116, 169, 192, 200, 252, 262, 295, 524, 527
  legal issues of, 48, 174, 338
  literary shortcoming of, 538, 547
  loss of, 427
  marking of, 227
  medical, 426, 252
  multiple publication of, 506
  patterns of review of, 277
  preparation of, 389
  processing of, 86, 92, 168, 215, 250, 492, 495, 496

Subject Index

Manuscripts (continued)
    quality in, 92
    rejection of, 44, 48, 65, 70, 86, 105, 116, 140, 161, 480, 496, 498, 508, 516, 525, 535, 536, 537, 538, 548
    remunerated, 506
    review of, 65, 380
    revision of, 91, 217, 237, 321
    rewriting of authors' by editors, 99
    selection of, 74, 225, 499, 508
    solicited, 506
    standardization of, 146
    tracking of, 148, 303, 355, 379, 461, 475, 631
    unsolicited, 74, 558
Maps, paper selection for, 295
Marketing, 104, 152, 208, 477, 473, 621
Mathematical copy, editing of, 294, 364
Matthews Chinese Dictionary, 108
McCall's, 573
Medical journalism, 534
Medical terminology, 401
Megatrends (Naisbett), 369
Memoirs. See Autobiographies, of editors.
Memorandums, 34
Mendel, Gregor, 359
Merck Manual, The, history of, 584
Merton, 111
Metaphoric transfer, 268
Microfiche, 121
Microfilm, 543
Minimal editing, 137
Minutes, 34, 506
Modern English Usage (Fowler), 233, 277
Multiauthor works, 113

Naked Lunch, 81

Nameplates, 3, 600
National Endowment for the Arts, 550
New Directions Publishing Corporation, 111
New editions, 33
New England Journal of Medicine, 99, 264
New products, publishing information on, 551
New Yorker, The, 80, 223
Newsletters, 147, 560, 591-601,
Newspapers, 3, 506, 602-20
Nonfiction, 213, 214, 231
Novels, 188, 468, 471
Nowell, Elizabeth, 69
Numbers, 34, 260, 401, 475
Nutrition Today, 99

Oak Ridge National Laboratory, editing at, 414
Obituaries, of scientists, 527
Obscenity, 81, 168, 607
Of Time and the River (Wolfe), 164
Offset, 182, 463, 558
O'Hara, John, 39
Ohio State University Press, 93
On-line documents, 24
O'Neill, Eugene 39, 40
Ontario Review, The, 526
Opera synopses, 469
Optical character recognition, 618
Oral presentations, 78, 623, 628
Organization, 64, 200, 328
Outlines, 20, 83, 268, 279, 553, 631, 632, 633
Overediting, 233, 396
Overprints and screens, 147

Package Inserts, 621
Packagers. See Book producers.
Page charges, 449, 532
Page proofs, 435, 553, 626

Paper, 451, 452, 532, 557
Paperbacks. See Books, paperback.
Parallelism, 43, 185, 279
Partisan Review, 167
Pasteup, 594, 597
Patents, 622
Patient Care, roundtable for, 581
Peer review. See Referees and Review process.
Perkins, Maxwell, 8, 69, 128, 164, 165, 234
Permissions, 227. See also Copyright.
Peterson, Roger Tory, 23
Photocomposition, 558
Photographs, 3, 247, 552, 604
  boxing of, 554
  commissioning of, 182
  credits for, 147
  cropping of, 147, 554, 558, 592, 600, 602, 625
  editing of, 168
  evaluation of, 558
  halftones, 592
  preparation of by editor, 241
  research of, 182
  screening of, 600
Photography, 147, 168, 519
Photomechanical transfer, 592
Plagiarism, 132, 249, 408, 528. See also Ethics.
Plant Engineering, readership survey of, 563
PLATO, 483
Poetry, 71, 82, 579
Pornography, 81, 168
Porter, Katherine Anne, 501
Pound, Ezra, 42, 111
Prefaces, 478
Prelibation, 474
Prelims, 475
Presentations, 291, 623
Press proofs, 473

Press releases, 126, 295, 624-26
Printer's errors, 557
Printers, 59, 244, 532, 552
Printing, 46, 519
  process of, 182, 408
  technology of, 134
  terminology of, 134, 168, 227, 295
  types of, 558, 592, 594, 599, 600, 626
Proceedings, 460, 506, 627-29
Production
  costs of, 455
  process of, 46, 162, 182, 227, 256, 303, 428, 473
  standards, need for, 265
Production editor, 265, 350, 389
Products, advertising of, 571, 567
Promotion and tenure, 540
Proofreaders, 134, 156, 201
Proofreading, 12, 183, 290, 385, 518, 557, 558, 561, 594, 596, 599, 618
  authors' responsibility in, 94
  of captions, 148
  by editors, 241
  of figures, 134
  of graphics, 412
  of headings, 148
  hints on, 94
  marks used in, 118, 134
  methods of, 3, 53, 94, 117, 147, 201, 473, 475
  pitfalls of, 201
  by Poe's editor's, 6
  preparation for, 94
  by secretaries, 260
  time needed for, 354
  of titles, 148
Proofreading and Copyediting: A Practical Guide to Style for the 1970's (McNaughton), 134
Proofs, 33, 295, 408, 418

Proposals, 356, 377, 630-32
Public speaking, 78
Publication date, determination of, 506
Publications, evaluation of, 20
Publications, purpose of, 328, 443, 566, 569, 594, 601, 633
Publications audit, 532
Publicity, preparation of by editor, 182
Publishers
  as champions of free speech, 234
  compared to editors, 191, 348
  as employers of freelancers, 156
  names of
    Atheneum, 9
    Dustbooks, 74
    Farrar, Straus and Cudahy, 65
    Harper and Row, 9
    Houghton Mifflin Company, 23
    Jargon Society, Inc., The, 42
    Knopf, 127
    Liverwright, 39, 40
    New Directions Publishing Corporation, 111
    Random House, 40
    Riverside Press, 23
    Scribners, 144
  as promoters of new writers, 152
  as selectors of books, 42
  standards of, variation in, 34
Publishing
  adversarial decisions in, 79
  of books, 73, 75
  changing the nature of, 72
  conservatism in, 418
  control of, by white males, 176
  cooperatives, 71
  cost of, 205, 458, 554
  decline of, 35
  editors in, 57, 103

Publishing (continued)
  of fiction, 84
  fraud in, 58
  history of, 205
  management of, 12
  process of, 74, 92, 227, 518
  profit motive in, 71, 212
  publicity in, 67
  quality in, 72, 79
  schedule in, 167, 536
  in the United Kingdom, 50
  by university presses, 221
  writers in, 186
Punctuation, 12, 29, 34, 177, 207, 260, 314, 326, 383, 475, 610

Quality, 163, 262, 452, 534
  decline in, 183, 194, 458
  in editing, 157, 187
  editor's judgment of, 502
  Ladder of, 138
  literary, 550
  of publications, 579
  in publishing decisions, 161
  and time, 559
Queries, 156, 310, 439, 475. See also Letters.
Questionnaires, 409, 458, 494

Racism, 619
Rage to Live, A (O'Hara), 39
Rapid debugging, 100
Readability, 43, 147, 217, 260, 288, 319, 326, 353, 373, 398, 455, 487, 554
Readers' reports, 129, 91, 116, 129. See also Refereeing.
Readership. See Audience.
Readership surveys, 547, 556, 563, 575, 578, 594, 601
Reading protocols, 217, 238
Redactor. See Editors.
Refereeing, 408, 531, 536, 538, 629

Referees, 282, 295, 324, 343, 437, 496, 502, 512, 517, 521, 530
  acknowledgement of, 366
  anonymity of, 129
  as citing problems in authors' style, 38
  comments of, documentation of, 146
  critical competence of, 338
  criticism of, 234
  editing comments of, 140
  enlisting of, 309
  of journals, 335
  reports of, 7
  selection of, 129, 367, 495, 511, 518
  of Third World authors, 438
  unaligned, 318
Reference books, 260
Reference checking in journals, 500
Reference citations, 155, 294, 383, 475, 506, 542, 586
Religion, 67
Repackaging, 182
Reporters, 558, 602, 603, 613
Reporting vs. advertising, 567
Reports, 34, 259, 298, 384, 448, 612, 632, 633-35
Reprints, 33, 408, 476, 479, 532, 626
Reproduction rights, 463, 532
Request for Proposal, 630, 631
Research by editors, 89
Research on editing, 304, 332, 337, 530
Resumes, 630
Retractions, 245, 249
Review articles, 345, 401
Review journals, 174, 502
Review process, 309, 328, 401, 433, 480, 494, 495, 499, 509, 527, 532, 543
  and citation analysis, 319

Review process (continued)
  at FDA, Bureau of Foods, 417
  editor's legal responsibilities in, 308
  equivalent of, 410
  ethics of, 58
  guidelines for, 506
  ineffectiveness of, 245, 514
  research needed about, 504
  role of board members in, 44, 225
  for scientific papers, 340
  time per manuscript in, 518
  validity and reliability of, 504
Reviews, 295, 481
Revising, 19, 27, 67, 187, 216, 217
Rewriting, 312, 349, 374, 387, 410, 420, 478, 491, 503, 507, 525, 552, 575, 581, 625, 633
Rhetoric, 187
Rogers, Carl, 368
Roof bolts, 148
Roosevelt, Theodore, letters of, 93
Ross, Harold, 85, 222, 223
Roundtables, 581
Rule of Threes, 600

SI/metric usage, 29
Sales. See Marketing.
Scholarship, types of, 93
Scientific information services, 318
Scientific Writing for Graduate Students, 246
Scientists, 170, 289, 296
Scriblerian, The, editing at, 546
Scribner's, 128, 144, 234
Scripps Clinic and Research Foundation, editorial practices at, 520
Secondary literature, use of, 360
Semantics, 428, 446
Seminars, 430

Sensibility, gustant and salivant, 474
Sentences, 184, 297
Sequential Thematic Organization of Proposals, 631
Sexism, 12, 478, 545, 616
Shaw, Irwin, 39
Sierra Club, 595
Sifton's law, 84
Silent Spring (Carson), 23
Simon and Schuster, 196
Sizing wheel, 554
Slides, 299, 377, 448
Slush pile, 197, 477
Snow, C. P., 144, 289
Society for Technical Communication, 158, 596
Somacluster, 474
Sounding-board effect, 590
Southern Review, The, 501
Spanish, 446
Speccing, 3
Spelling, 12, 29, 34, 266, 314, 326, 475, 610, 612
Spender, Stephen, 39
Standards, 158, 388, 418, 435, 505, 508, 550, 599, 605, 635
Steinbeck, John, 68
Stereotyping, elimination of, 34
Storyboards, 623, 631
Stringers. See Freelancers.
Style books, Introduction, 29, 33, 34, 118, 134, 226, 227, 591, 609
Style guides, 13, 118, 185, 291, 293, 294, 339, 383, 390, 585, 589
  cost effectiveness of, 518
  development of, 290
  group-compiled, 107
  in-house, 447, 635
  for journals, 367
  need for, 354
  samples of, 260
  for tabular data, 302

Style sheets. See Style guides.
Style, 13, 174, 200, 227, 230, 237, 239, 295, 339, 343, 387, 394, 401, 427, 473, 475, 478, 491, 496, 500, 586, 587, 591, 594, 599, 604
  accuracy, clarity, and usefulness in, 2
  author's, 80, 195
  diversity in, 120
  elements of, 156
  of illustrations, 434
  kinds of, 120
  and legibility analysis, 319
  Lincoln's, 6
  literary, 635
  publication, 358
  questionnaire on, 304
Subheadings, 147, 207, 643
Subtitles, 20, 43
Surnames, Chinese, editing of, 108
Swanberg, Bill, 144
Swenson, May, 144
Symbols, 29, 427, 637
Symposia, 33, 405, 506
Syntax, 314, 475
Syteme International units, 475

Tables, 227, 258, 281, 292, 294, 301, 302, 314, 401, 406, 448, 475
Tabloids, 147
Tact, 388, 497
Tallahassee *Democrat,* 616
Tate, Allen, 165
Teaching English in a Two-Year College, 507
Teaching Materials, 636
Technical communication, 372, 253, 254, 255
Technical Communication, 536, 537, 538
Television, 608

Textbooks. See Books, textbooks.
Textual studies of Thomas Wolfe's novels, 69
Third World authors. See Authors, Third World.
Thomas, Dylan, 111
Thompson, Morton, 144
Time, 574
Titles, 7, 20, 43, 97, 150, 208, 268, 503
Tone, 368, 434, 515, 552, 587
Topic sentences, 20, 268
Trade names, 571
Trade paperbacks, 479
Trade publishing, 77, 477
Training Magazine, 568
Transactions, 506
Translations, 132, 391, 394, 448, 451, 637
Transliterations. See Lectures.
TriQuarterly, 550
Tropical Products Institute publications, types of, 261
Troubleshooting, editorial, 168
Tutorials, 587
Twerps, 579
Type, 134, 152, 227, 319, 455, 544, 591, 594, 596, 597, 599
Typesetters, 76, 554, 584, 591, 592
Type-styling. See Typography.
Typing corrections, material for, 148
Typographical errors, 106, 183, 202, 628
Typography, 3, 226, 266, 295, 364, 452, 519, 553, 554, 557, 558, 593, 600, 602, 612
Typos. See Typographical errors.

Underediting, 233
United States Government Printing Office Style Manual, 226
University, freedom of, 577

University of California, 423
University of California Press, 73
University of Toronto Press, 97, 98
University presses
 compared to commercial presses, 50
 editor's role in, 90, 91, 161
 editorial committee of, 160, 225
 freelance editors at, 203
 goal of, 160
 as producers of critical editions, 93
 survey of, 221
Usability testing, 204, 432
Usage, 12, 55, 296, 326, 446, 475, 582, 585, 610

Variable-speed reading technique, 553
Velikovsky, 359
Video display terminal, 618, 620. See also Computers.
Videotape packaging, 121
Visuals. See Graphics.
Volunteers, 592, 595

Warren, Robert Penn, 501
Watts, Alfred, 202
Web and the Rock, The (Wolfe) 69
Welty, Eudora, 501
White space, 455, 554, 599, 600
Williams, Tennessee, 111
Williams, William Carlos, 111
Wolfe, Thomas, 8, 69, 128, 164, 165
Women, in publishing, 494
Woollcott, Alexander, 85
Word processing, 162, 592. See also Computers.
Workshops, 430
World Health Organization, editing at, 391
Writers. See Authors.

Writing
  clarity in, 279
  compared to editing, 181, 186, 300
  evaluation of, 260, 283, 592
  process of, 401

Writing (continued)
  of scientific manuscripts, 309
  technical, 385

Yale Press, 93
Years with Ross, The (Thurber), 222, 223

About the Author

BRUCE W. SPECK is an Assistant Professor at Memphis State University where he teaches in the Professional Writing Program. He has also taught writing at the University of Nebraska-Lincoln, where he received his Ph.D. in rhetoric and composition, and Indiana-Purdue University at Fort Wayne. In addition to his interest in editing, Professor Speck writes about ethics.